PUZZLEWRIGHT GUIDE TO

Solving Sudoku

Hundreds of Puzzles

Plus Techniques to Help You Crack Them All

Peter Gordon

Puzzles by Frank Longo

An Imprint of Sterling Publishing
387 Park Avenue South
New York, NY 10016

PUZZLEWRIGHT PRESS and the distinctive Puzzlewright Press logo are registered trademarks of Sterling Publishing Co., Inc.

First Puzzlewright Press edition 2012.
This book was previously published under the title
Mensa Guide to Solving Sudoku.

ISBN 978-1-4027-9945-7

Distributed in Canada by Sterling Publishing
c/o Canadian Manda Group, 165 Dufferin Street
Toronto, Ontario, Canada M6K 3H6
Distributed in the United Kingdom by GMC Distribution Services
Castle Place, 166 High Street, Lewes, East Sussex, England BN7 1XU
Distributed in Australia by Capricorn Link (Australia) Pty. Ltd.
P.O. Box 704, Windsor, NSW 2756, Australia

For information about custom editions, special sales, and premium and corporate purchases, please contact Sterling Special Sales at 800-805-5489 or specialsales@sterlingpublishing.com.

Manufactured in the United States of America

4 6 8 10 9 7 5 3

www.puzzlewright.com

CONTENTS

INTRODUCTION / 5

1. ONE-CHOICE / 11

2. SCANNING / 17

3. ELIMINATION / 25

4. SUBSETS / 33

5. INTERACTION / 43

6. CANDIDATE-FREE SOLVING / 47

7. THE X-WING FAMILY / 51

8. GORDONIAN LOGIC / 59

9. FORCING CHAINS AND GRID COLORING / 71

10. BILOCATION AND BIVALUE GRAPHS / 81

11. GUESSING / 85

PUZZLES / 87

ANSWERS / 205

A NOTE TO READERS

In this book, solving techniques are introduced one at a time in each chapter. Within the chapter in which a technique is introduced, the technique is explained step-by-step. Any use of a technique that is from the immediately preceding chapter will also be explained in detail, but if a technique is two or more chapters old, then it will usually be assumed that readers can do those steps by themselves.

Following most chapters are 12 puzzles that require the techniques introduced in that chapter (and may use any of the previously learned techniques). Starting on page 87 are 704 puzzles that start out easy and get progressively harder.

INTRODUCTION

How can a puzzle that has instructions consisting of one sentence result in a book with more than 60 pages on how to solve? That's the beauty of sudoku. Despite its brief instructions, the puzzle can be extremely challenging to solve.

Virtually all sudoku puzzles being published today are made by computers, so books can be created literally overnight. Typically these books include a few pages on how to solve, going into only the most basic strategies. Yet the puzzles in many of these books require much more advanced strategies.

Since I've been writing and editing puzzles for decades, when friends and relatives got stuck on sudoku puzzles, I was the one they turned to. Over and over I would teach advanced strategies to whatever friend had just gotten addicted to the puzzle. My parents would save a puzzle they got stuck on, then bring it with them when they visited me. I'd teach them a new strategy to get through the puzzle, then they'd be back a few weeks later with a tougher puzzle, asking for more help. It was getting ridiculous. They were spending more time learning sudoku strategies than playing with the grandkids. Something had to be done.

That something is this book. Now if anyone asks me for help with a puzzle, I can just hand over the book and go back to the sudoku I was working on.

THE RULE

To solve a sudoku, you need to follow one rule:

Put the numbers from 1 to 9 into the grid so that all nine rows, all nine columns, and all nine 3×3 boxes contain all nine digits.

Below is an example of a puzzle and its solution.

Sample Sudoku Puzzle

	6		7	4			2	
		2	6					4
			8				7	
		6					1	9
3								6
2	1					4		
	5				3			
9					7	3		
	7			8	1		5	

Sample Sudoku Answer

1	6	5	7	4	9	8	2	3
7	8	2	6	3	5	1	9	4
4	3	9	8	1	2	6	7	5
5	4	6	3	7	8	2	1	9
3	9	7	1	2	4	5	8	6
2	1	8	9	5	6	4	3	7
8	5	4	2	9	3	7	6	1
9	2	1	5	6	7	3	4	8
6	7	3	4	8	1	9	5	2

SUDOKU HISTORY

Sudoku first appeared in the magazine *Dell Pencil Puzzles & Word Games* in the May 1979 issue, under the title "Number Place." It is believed to have been created by Howard Garns, an architect who died in the 1980s. A copy of the original set of puzzles appears on page 32.

Like many American logic puzzles, it became popular in Japanese puzzle magazines. There, the name was changed by the publisher Nikoli to "Suuji wa dokushin ni kagiru," which roughly translates to "the numbers are only single" (with the sense of "single" being "unmarried"—that is, no number has a match). The title eventually got shortened, taking the "su" of "suuji" and the "doku" of "dokushin" to make "sudoku," or "single number." Eventually, Nikoli also added two conditions to the puzzle. First, no more than 30 numbers could be given at the start, and second, the pattern of digits must be symmetric.

Below are three sudoku grids. The first is the sample puzzle from the previous page. The second is that same puzzle rotated 180°. The third is the first two placed on top of each other. Notice how the open spaces are the same in all three grids.

In 1997, a New Zealander named Wayne Gould, who had recently retired as a judge in Hong Kong, went to Japan on vacation and discovered the puzzle. Intrigued by it, Gould spent his spare time writing a computer program to generate the puzzles. In September 2004 he convinced *The Conway Daily Sun*, a New Hampshire newspaper, to run the puzzle. In a brilliant move, he gave the puzzle to the newspaper for free, in exchange for having his website, sudoku.com, appear next to the puzzle. In November 2004, Gould convinced *The Times* of London to take the puzzle. Its popularity skyrocketed. To this day, no newspaper pays Gould anything for his puzzles, but they all have to include the Web address, and it is there that his sudoku program can be downloaded (free for a trial, but not free for keeps). Gould, shown above, has become quite wealthy from the puzzle.

Donald Christensen

Wayne Gould

ADDITIONAL RULES

Why are the additional rules of limiting the givens to 30 and keeping them symmetric important? A puzzle with 80 givens and one empty space wouldn't be much of a challenge. (I've seen sudoku books for kids with 72 of the 81 numbers given at the start!) You need to draw the line somewhere, and 30 givens is what was decided. Puzzles where more than half the numbers are given aren't much fun to solve. As for symmetry, it certainly looks nicer when the givens are placed symmetrically, and there's no downside to it, since the puzzles can be made

Sample Sudoku

	6		7	4			2	
		2	6					4
			8				7	
		6					1	9
3								6
2	1					4		
	5				3			
9					7	3		
	7			8	1		5	

Sample Sudoku Flipped

	5		1	8			7	
		3	7					9
			3				5	
		4					1	2
6								3
9	1					6		
	7				8			
4					6	2		
	2			4	7		6	

Both Puzzles Combined

	6/5		7/1	4/8			2/7	
		2/3	6/7					4/9
			8/3				7/5	
		6/4					1/1	9/2
3/6								6/3
2/9	1/1					4/6		
	5/7				3/8			
9/4					7/6	3/2		
	7/2			8/4	1/7		5/6	

as difficult as desired while keeping the givens symmetric. When I asked Wayne Gould what he thought of puzzles that are unsymmetric with more than 30 givens, he said that the people responsible for them are "lazy" and "they cannot be expecting much from their solvers." "Publishers of such puzzles are underestimating their audience," he added.

There is one final rule that most solvers don't think about much, but as we will see, it is of vital importance. The rule is that a sudoku puzzle must have a unique answer; that is, there must be only one possible way to fill the spaces with the numbers to meet the requirements of the puzzle. In the Gordonian Logic chapter, this rule will be exploited to its fullest potential.

TERMINOLOGY

Over the next three pages are diagrams showing what all the terms are. Each little square that holds a number is a cell. There are 81 cells in the entire puzzle. A row consists of nine cells going across. There are nine rows, starting with row 1 at the top down to row 9 at the bottom. Not surprisingly, nine cells going down make a column. There are nine columns, starting with column 1 on the left and moving across to column 9 on the right. Each of the 3×3 squares outlined by heavy lines is called a box. There are nine boxes. The top three are, from left to right, boxes 1, 2, and 3. The ones below that are 4, 5, and 6. The bottom three are 7, 8, and 9.

In addition, there are big rows and big columns. A big row is a set of three rows that is also a set of three boxes. The top big row is big row 1, and the bottom one is big row 3. A big column is just like a big row, except vertical. The left big column is called big column 1.

Every cell has 20 other cells that are part of its row, column, or box. These are called the cell's buddies. The rule of sudoku can be restated as this: Put in the numbers 1 to 9 so that no two buddies are the same.

Next, there are the cells themselves. We can't say "the seventh cell from the left of row 6" or "the cell in row 6 and column 7." We need a quick way to refer to each cell. I've tried several different ways, and the simplest is to refer to each cell as a two-digit number. The first digit is the cell's row, the second digit is the cell's column. So the cell in row 6 and column 7 is simply cell 67. Here is a chart showing all the cell names.

The Cell Names

11	12	13	14	15	16	17	18	19
21	22	23	24	25	26	27	28	29
31	32	33	34	35	36	37	38	39
41	42	43	44	45	46	47	48	49
51	52	53	54	55	56	57	58	59
61	62	63	64	65	66	67	68	69
71	72	73	74	75	76	77	78	79
81	82	83	84	85	86	87	88	89
91	92	93	94	95	96	97	98	99

Finally, there are what are known as candidates. These are little numbers written in a cell that indicate what numbers could possibly go there. In the beginning, these will be any of the nine digits that aren't in the cell's buddies. But later we will learn strategies to remove candidates from a cell even if that number isn't among the cell's buddies.

THANKS

I simply cannot thank Frank Longo and Corey Kosak enough for all the work they've put into this book. Corey's programming ability has put Frank's sudoku program in a class by itself. And every time I came up with a new Gordonian Logic twist, Corey was up to the task. No one, and I mean no one, makes better sudoku.

Thanks also to Wayne Gould, for filling me in on the history of sudoku; David Eppstein, for allowing me to use his methods in Chapter 10; and Francis Heaney, who came up with the Franciscan Rectangles method and helped in the editing of the manuscript.

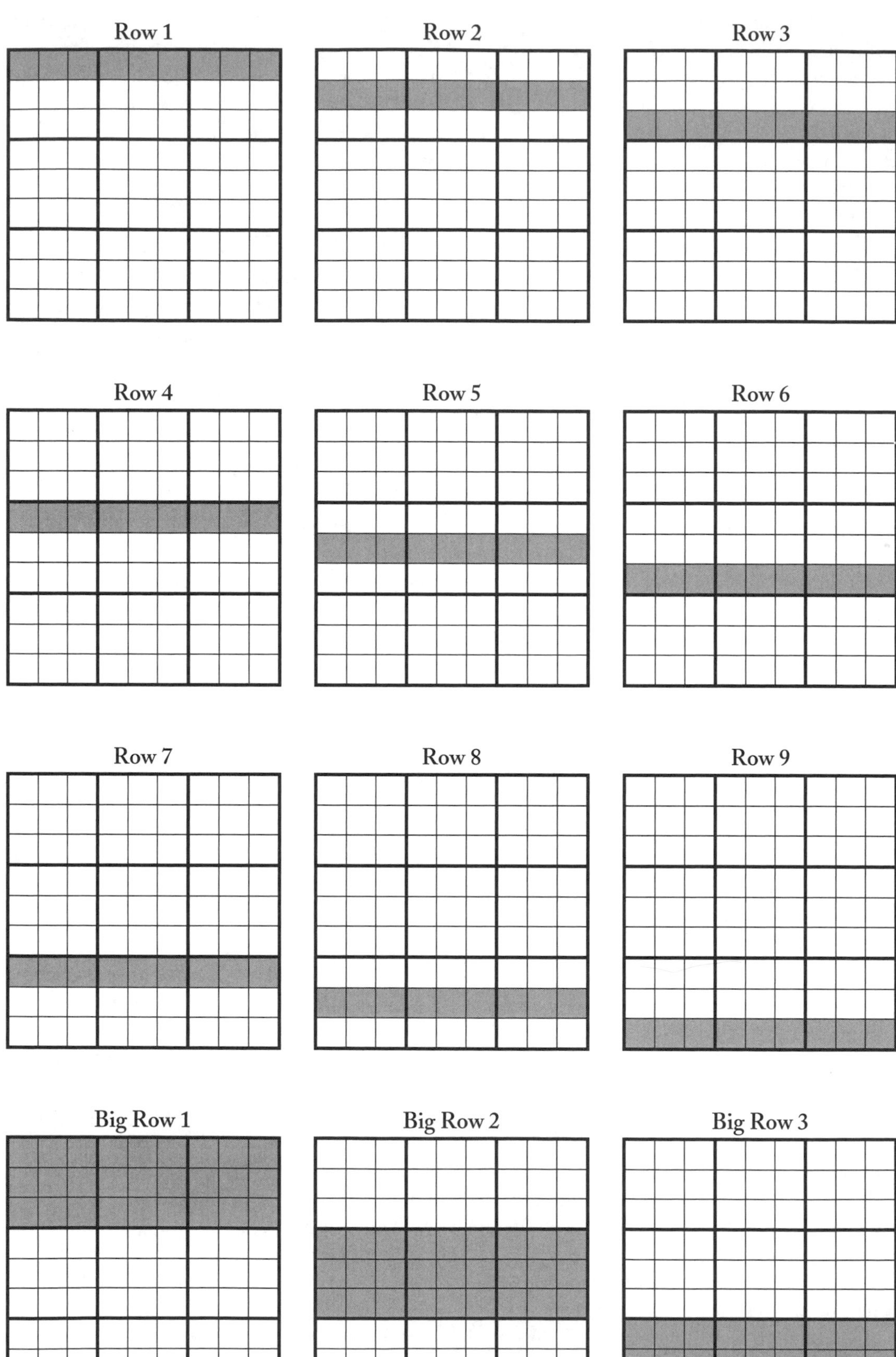
Row 1
Row 2
Row 3
Row 4
Row 5
Row 6
Row 7
Row 8
Row 9
Big Row 1
Big Row 2
Big Row 3

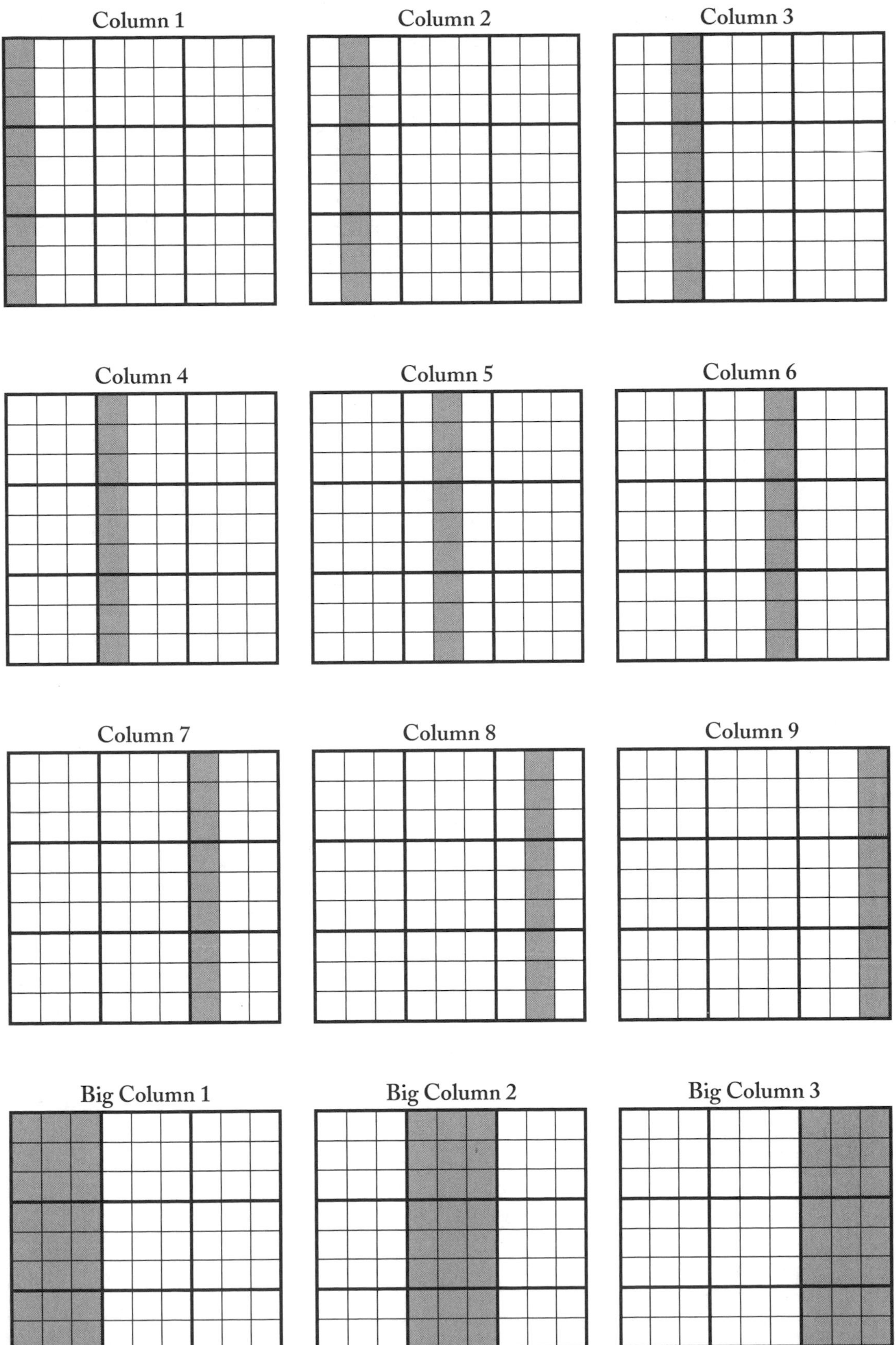
Column 1
Column 2
Column 3
Column 4
Column 5
Column 6
Column 7
Column 8
Column 9
Big Column 1
Big Column 2
Big Column 3

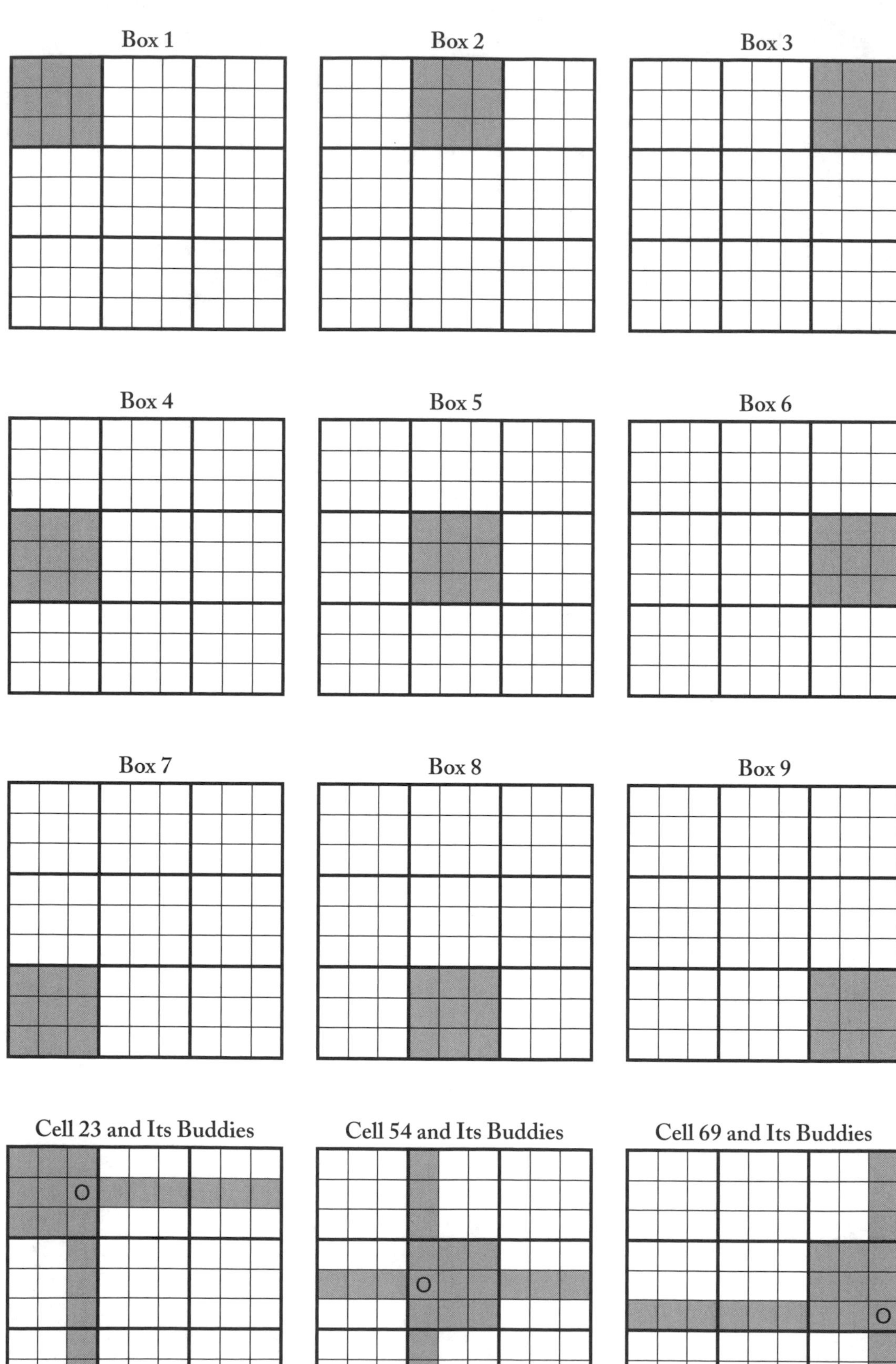
Box 1
Box 2
Box 3
Box 4
Box 5
Box 6
Box 7
Box 8
Box 9
Cell 23 and Its Buddies
O
Cell 54 and Its Buddies
O
Cell 69 and Its Buddies
O

1
ONE-CHOICE

You don't have to be Einstein to figure out what number goes in the empty cell in the sample sudoku row below.

3	7	5	2	9	1	6		8

If you can count from 1 to 9, you can figure out that the missing number is 4. My daughter in kindergarten had no trouble with this puzzle.

It's also just as easy to find the missing number when a box has eight cells filled:

2	9	8
1	5	4
	7	6

Here, every number except a 3 appears, so you can fill in the empty cell with a 3.

While it's simple to recognize that you can use this method when a row, column, or box has eight of its nine cells filled, it can also be used in other situations. Look at Example 1. What number goes in cell 25? It can't be a 1, 2, or 7, since row 2 already has those numbers. It can't be a 3, 4, or 9, since box 2 already has those numbers. And it can't be a 6 or 8, since column 5 already has those numbers. So it can't be a 1, 2, 3, 4, 6, 7, 8, or 9. It must be a 5.

This is the concept of the one-choice method. Find a cell in which there is only one possible number that can go in the cell, and put it in.

Example 1

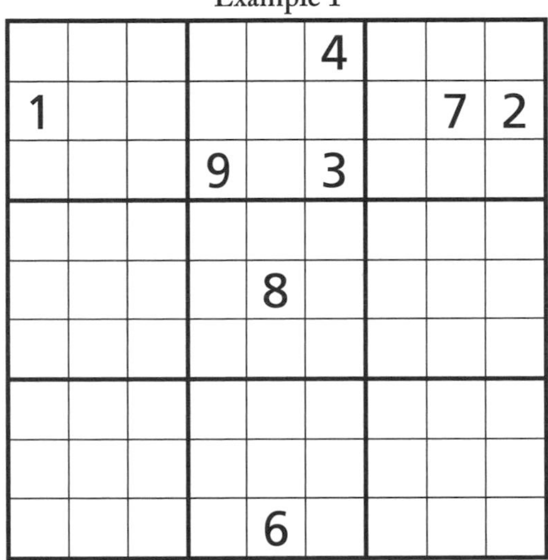

					4			
1							7	2
			9		3			
				8				
				6				

Is it possible to solve an entire puzzle using just one-choice? Sometimes. While you normally wouldn't solve a puzzle this way, let's solve one this way as an exercise.

Look at cells 13, 41, and 97 in Example 2 on the next page. Each of them can be filled with the one-choice method. Fill in an 8 at 13, a 4 at 41, and a 4 at 97. Those were the only three cells that could be filled using one-choice, but now that they are filled in, more cells can be filled in using one-choice. Cells 23, 33, 48, and 87 must be 3, 6, 6, and 1, respectively. Continuing on with those four numbers entered, we get five more numbers to fill at cells 17, 42, 77, 89, and 93. Those are filled with 5, 2, 6, 9, and 5, respectively. After those go in, we can put a 1 in cell 19, a 9 in cell 46, a

5 in cell 49, a 4 in cell 73, a 4 in cell 84, and a 3 in cell 98.

Example 2

2			3	6	4			
	7			5				6
5	4							3
		7	8			3		
	5	9				7	1	
		1			5	9		
7							2	8
6				7			5	
			6	2	1			7

We're now at this point:

Example 2-1

2		8	3	6	4	5		1
	7	3		5				6
5	4	6						3
4	2	7	8		9	3	6	5
	5	9				7	1	
		1			5	9		
7		4				6	2	8
6			4	7		1	5	9
		5	6	2	1	4	3	7

Continuing along, a 9 goes in cell 12, a 1 in cell 45, a 2 in cell 54, a 3 in cell 76, and a 2 in cell 83. After placing those five numbers in, we now know that cell 18 is a 7, cell 21 is a 1, cell 56 is a 6, cell 59 is a 4, cell 64 is a 7, cell 72 is a 1, cell 75 is a 9, cell 86 is an 8, and cell 92 is an 8. We're in the homestretch now, and the grid looks like this:

Example 2-2

2	9	8	3	6	4	5	7	1
1	7	3		5				6
5	4	6						3
4	2	7	8	1	9	3	6	5
	5	9	2		6	7	1	4
		1	7		5	9		
7	1	4		9	3	6	2	8
6		2	4	7	8	1	5	9
	8	5	6	2	1	4	3	7

Two more passes through the puzzle will finish it. Put a 9 in cell 24, a 2 in cell 26, an 8 in cell 35, a 3 in cell 55, an 8 in cell 68, a 2 in cell 69, a 5 in cell 74, a 3 in cell 82, and a 9 in cell 91. This leaves 10 open cells, and every one of them has just one choice. Cell 27 is an 8, cell 28 is a 4, cell 34 is a 1, cell 36 is a 7, cell 37 is a 2, cell 38 is a 9, cell 51 is an 8, cell 61 is a 3, cell 62 is a 6, and cell 65 is a 4. Voilà! A completed puzzle, and all we had to do was use the one-choice method.

Example 2 Answer

2	9	8	3	6	4	5	7	1
1	7	3	9	5	2	8	4	6
5	4	6	1	8	7	2	9	3
4	2	7	8	1	9	3	6	5
8	5	9	2	3	6	7	1	4
3	6	1	7	4	5	9	8	2
7	1	4	5	9	3	6	2	8
6	3	2	4	7	8	1	5	9
9	8	5	6	2	1	4	3	7

DRAWBACKS

In the above example, I told you what cell to look at in order to use one-choice. But without being told which cells to look at, using one-choice can be slow. It's easy to spot a row, column, or box with eight numbers already filled, but finding a cell that can be filled with one-choice when the other eight numbers are spread among the cell's row, column, and box takes more time. There are better methods to find cells to fill, which we will see in the next chapter. But when you get stuck on a puzzle, going through each cell to see if one-choice can be used will often give you what you need to continue.

The simplest way to determine what cells can be filled with one-choice is to write small numbers in each cell that indicate all the possible numbers that can go in that cell. These are called candidates. Any cell that has just one small number in it can be filled with one-choice. Once you fill in a number, you remove that number from the candidates of all other cells in that row, column, and box (the cell's buddies). Once you understand all the other solving methods, you'll see that this is far from the most efficient way to solve an easy puzzle, but working with candidates is critical to solving harder puzzles, so you might as well learn how to work with them now. Example 2-3 shows the same puzzle we've been working on, but with all the candidates listed.

Example 2-3

2	189	8	**3**	**6**	**4**	158	789	159
1389	**7**	38	129	**5**	289	1248	489	**6**
5	**4**	68	1279	189	2789	128	789	**3**
4	26	**7**	**8**	149	269	**3**	46	245
348	**5**	**9**	24	34	236	**7**	**1**	24
348	2368	**1**	247	34	**5**	**9**	468	24
7	139	345	459	349	39	146	**2**	**8**
6	12389	2348	49	**7**	389	14	**5**	149
3489	389	3458	**6**	**2**	**1**	4	349	**7**

Cells 13, 41, and 97 all have just one candidate in them, so they can be filled in with one-choice. Put a big 8 in cell 13, and remove the 8 candidates from cell 13's buddies. This takes away the little 8's in cells 12, 17, 18, 21, 23, 33, 83, and 93. Similarly, put big 4's in cells 41 and 97, and remove all the little 4's from the buddies of cells 41 and 97. The puzzle now looks like this:

Example 2-4

2	19	**8**	**3**	**6**	**4**	15	79	159
139	**7**	3	129	**5**	289	128	489	**6**
5	**4**	6	1279	189	2789	128	789	**3**
4	26	**7**	**8**	19	269	**3**	6	25
38	**5**	**9**	24	34	236	**7**	**1**	24
38	2368	**1**	247	34	**5**	**9**	468	24
7	139	345	459	349	39	16	**2**	**8**
6	12389	234	49	**7**	389	1	**5**	19
389	389	35	**6**	**2**	**1**	**4**	39	**7**

At each subsequent stage, if any cell has a single candidate in it, you'll replace it with a big number and remove that number from the candidates of that cell's buddies. The next seven diagrams show what the grid looks like after each pass. Follow along each of the grids. It is the same as what was filled in earlier in this chapter, but now the candidates are there, which makes it easier to see. Once you understand this, you're ready to learn the next method, which is scanning.

Example 2-5

2	19	**8**	**3**	**6**	**4**	5	79	159
19	**7**	**3**	129	**5**	289	28	489	**6**
5	**4**	**6**	1279	189	2789	28	789	**3**
4	2	**7**	**8**	19	29	**3**	**6**	25
38	**5**	**9**	24	34	236	**7**	**1**	24
38	2368	**1**	247	34	**5**	**9**	48	24
7	139	45	459	349	39	6	**2**	**8**
6	2389	24	49	**7**	389	**1**	**5**	9
389	389	5	**6**	**2**	**1**	**4**	39	**7**

Example 2-6

2	19	8	3	6	4	5	79	1
19	7	3	129	5	289	28	489	6
5	4	6	1279	189	2789	28	789	3
4	2	7	8	19	9	3	6	5
38	5	9	24	34	236	7	1	24
38	368	1	247	34	5	9	48	24
7	139	4	459	349	39	6	2	8
6	38	24	4	7	38	1	5	9
389	389	5	6	2	1	4	3	7

Example 2-7

2	9	8	3	6	4	5	79	1
19	7	3	129	5	28	28	489	6
5	4	6	1279	189	278	28	789	3
4	2	7	8	1	9	3	6	5
38	5	9	2	34	236	7	1	24
38	368	1	27	34	5	9	48	24
7	139	4	59	39	3	6	2	8
6	38	2	4	7	38	1	5	9
89	89	5	6	2	1	4	3	7

Example 2-8

2	9	8	3	6	4	5	7	1
1	7	3	19	5	28	28	489	6
5	4	6	179	89	278	28	789	3
4	2	7	8	1	9	3	6	5
38	5	9	2	34	6	7	1	4
38	368	1	7	34	5	9	48	24
7	1	4	59	9	3	6	2	8
6	38	2	4	7	8	1	5	9
89	8	5	6	2	1	4	3	7

Example 2-9

2	9	8	3	6	4	5	7	1
1	7	3	9	5	2	28	489	6
5	4	6	19	8	27	28	89	3
4	2	7	8	1	9	3	6	5
38	5	9	2	3	6	7	1	4
38	36	1	7	34	5	9	8	2
7	1	4	5	9	3	6	2	8
6	3	2	4	7	8	1	5	9
9	8	5	6	2	1	4	3	7

Example 2-10

2	9	8	3	6	4	5	7	1
1	7	3	9	5	2	8	4	6
5	4	6	1	8	7	2	9	3
4	2	7	8	1	9	3	6	5
8	5	9	2	3	6	7	1	4
3	6	1	7	4	5	9	8	2
7	1	4	5	9	3	6	2	8
6	3	2	4	7	8	1	5	9
9	8	5	6	2	1	4	3	7

Example 2 Answer

2	9	8	3	6	4	5	7	1
1	7	3	9	5	2	8	4	6
5	4	6	1	8	7	2	9	3
4	2	7	8	1	9	3	6	5
8	5	9	2	3	6	7	1	4
3	6	1	7	4	5	9	8	2
7	1	4	5	9	3	6	2	8
6	3	2	4	7	8	1	5	9
9	8	5	6	2	1	4	3	7

1

	7			5		4		
3		5		4	6			1
4	2	6						
				1		3		
		9	7		8	2		
		2		9				
						8	3	6
1			4	8		5		7
		8		6			9	

2

4	8					7		
3	9							
		6	1	5	9		8	
				7	2		3	1
		9				6		
2	5		4	6				
	1		5	2	8	3		
							5	9
		2					1	4

3

8					1		5	9
		7					6	
		5	7	8			1	4
	8		9					1
		9				6		
7					6		9	
3	6			1	9	2		
	1					9		
9	7		2					8

4

	2			9		1		
	4			3	7			9
5			6		2	7		
	7		8					
1			7		6			4
					4		8	
		9	4		5			3
3			9	8			2	
		5		7			6	

5

2				1	9			
			3		8		5	2
3			7					
	4	2				5	7	
	1		6		3		8	
	8	3				4	6	
					7			8
8	5		9		2			
			1	8				5

6

6	8		4	9				
		4			7			8
		7				6		2
			7		1		6	
	7			2			1	
	2		9		5			
3		2				9		
7			1			5		
				5	8		7	6

7

		1		8			6	3
	4	9			3			
		7	6				1	
				1			3	9
1			8		9			5
9	7			5				
	9				2	8		
			9			3	5	
5	3			6		7		

8

3		1					5	
		5			1			8
	9			8		3		
			4	9			7	1
	2		7		5		6	
8	1			6	2			
		6		5			9	
4			1			6		
	3					7		5

9

6				9		1		
			7		8	3		
	5		6	4			9	
5	6							2
8		4				7		6
9							8	1
	1			3	9		5	
		6	8		5			
		5		2				9

10

		5	1	6				
	9				7	1	8	
	8		4			7		
		1	7	8				2
8				5	9	6		
		7			4		3	
	2	4	8				6	
				7	6	2		

11

	9			6				1
			1	8			2	
2			9			8		
3	2					6		9
		9		1		5		
7		6					3	4
		4			8			3
	8			7	9			
5				3			9	

12

	6	1	8					
5		9	2	4		1	8	
4								
						9	1	7
				6				
1	8	4						
								3
	1	5		7	3	4		9
					5	7	6	

2 SCANNING

Every row in a sudoku puzzle contains every number from 1 to 9. So it follows that every big row, which contains three rows, will have every number from 1 to 9 three times. If you can find a big row that has a given number twice, then you can narrow down the cells that contain the third instance of the number. This is known as scanning. Here's an example:

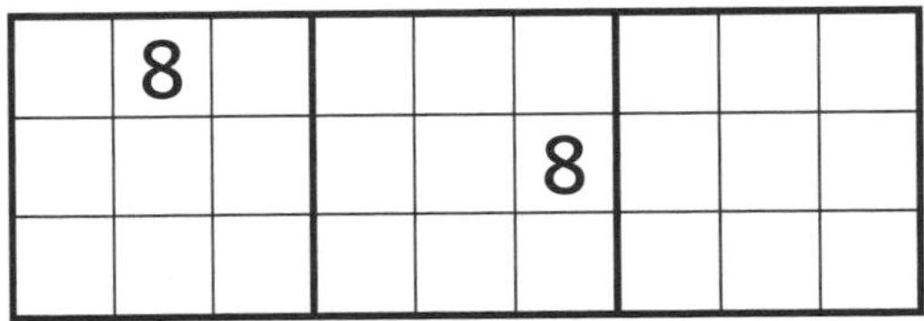

There are two 8's in this big row. Where can the third 8 go? It can't go in the top row, since there's already an 8 in it. It can't go in the second row, since there's already an 8 in it. So it must go in the third row. But where in the third row? It can't go in the left box, since that already has an 8. Similarly, the middle box is not possible, since that has an 8 in it already. So we can narrow down the location of the 8 to three cells: The cells that are in the right box and in the third row. The last 8 of this big row must appear in one of the three cells in the circled area:

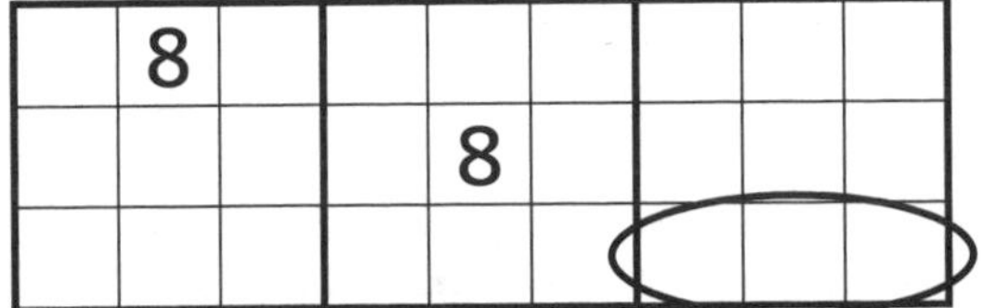

When you can find a big row with two of the same number in it, you can narrow down the possible places for the third occurrence of the number to three cells. The number has to be in the row that doesn't already contain one of the two numbers as well as in the box that doesn't already contain one of the two numbers. This intersection of a row and a box is always three cells. Here are some examples, with the possible locations of the third number circled:

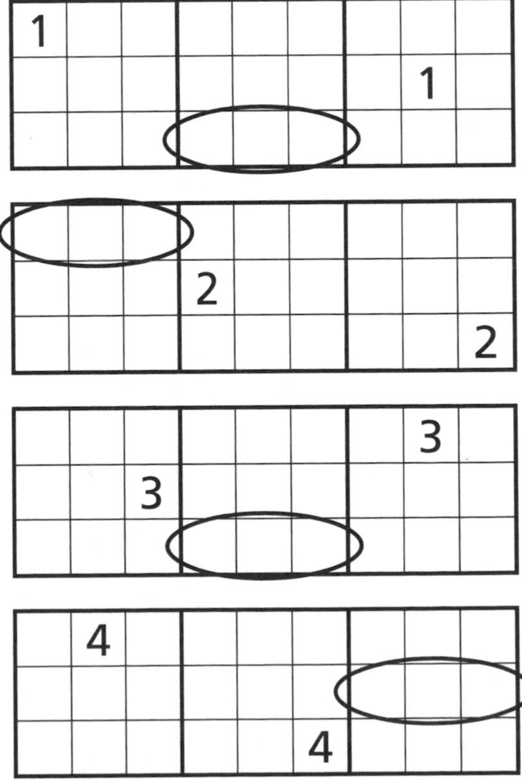

Now watch what happens when we add a few other numbers. Let's say you have this big row:

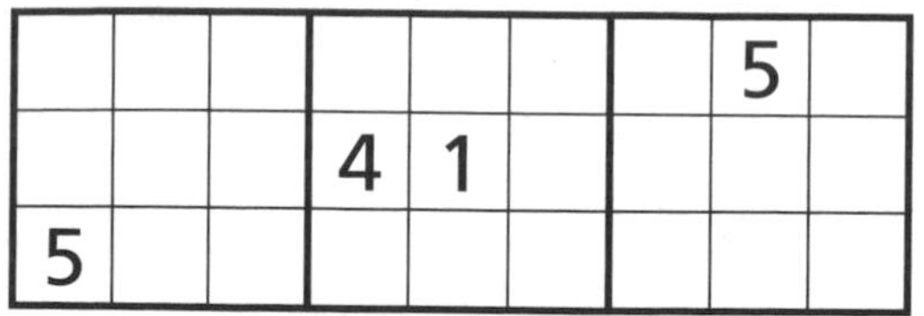

We can narrow down that the third five has to go in the middle row and in the middle box, like so:

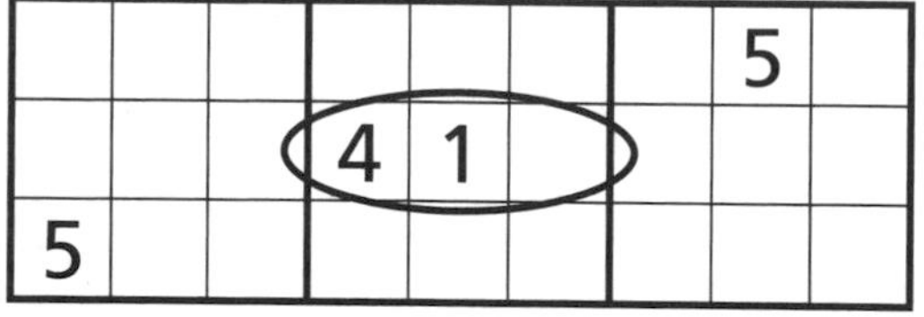

But two of those three cells are already filled with other numbers, so there's only one place the 5 can go: in the sixth cell of the second row.

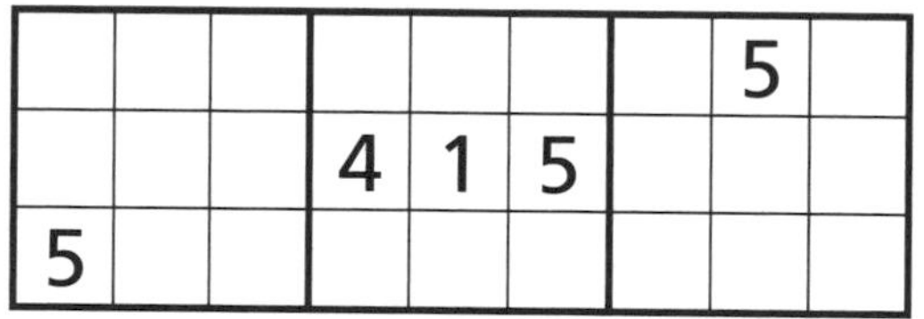

SOLVING USING SCANNING

Let's take a look at an example.

Example 3

				5		1	2	
		9			2	6	7	8
3		2		1				
		8					3	1
	1						5	
2	3					8		
				6		4		9
9	6	7	4			5		
	2	1		8				

Quickly now, what three cells can you fill in using one-choice? It takes a long time to see that cell 24 must be a 3, cell 37 must be a 9, and cell 98 must be a 6, so let's imagine you didn't notice them. Instead, look for a big row or big column that has any number exactly two times. (In all the examples above, we used big rows, but the exact same conclusions can be made about big columns with two occurrences of a given number.)

Check out big column 1. It has two 3's in it, at cell 31 and cell 62. The last 3 in that big column must go in column 3, somewhere in box 7—in other words, in one of the three cells 73, 83, and 93. But cells 83 and 93 already have numbers in them, so the 3 must go in cell 73.

Now look at big column 3. It has two 1's in it. The third 1 must go in either cell 78, 88, or 98. Can we tell which? All three of those cells are empty, but if we look across those rows, we see that row 9 already has a 1 in it. That eliminates 98 as a possibility, leaving 78 and 88 as the only possibilities. Unfortunately, there's no way at this point to narrow it down any further. So what do you do? Should you guess? The answer to that is an emphatic no. You should never guess in a sudoku puzzle. If you're not certain where a number goes, don't put it in. Just continue looking around for another number to place. Let's keep looking at big column 3. There are two 5's in it, so the last one needs to go in either cell 19, 29, or 39. Cell 29 already has an 8 in it, so that's out as a possibility. That leaves cells 19 and 39. Looking across rows 1 and 3 shows us that a 5 is in row 1 at cell 15. That means that a 5 can't also go in cell 19, so it must go in cell 39.

It is even possible to use scanning when you have just one number in a big row or big column. Look at the 3 in cell 31. Scanning across row 3, we see that a 3 cannot go in cell 37, 38, or 39 (we've already put a 5 in cell 39, but even if we hadn't, the 3 still couldn't have gone there). Since cells 17, 18, 27, 28, and 29 are all already filled with numbers, the 3 in cell 31 is enough to determine that cell 19 is also a 3.

Whenever I put in a number using horizontal scanning, I like to immediately look vertically to see if that gave me enough information to make a conclusion based on vertical scanning.

Example 3-1

				5		1	2	3
		9			2	6	7	8
3		2		1				5
		8					3	1
	1						5	
2	3					8		
		3		6		4		9
9	6	7	4			5		
	2	1		8				

The 3 added to cell 19 means that big column 3 now has two 3's in it. Using scanning, the last 3 must go in cell 97. Since we used vertical scanning to get that 3, now scan horizontally from cell 97 to see if that gave you enough information to place another 3. Big row 3 has two 3's in it (at cells 73 and 97), but all this tells us is that the last 3 must go in either cell 85 or 86. Since we don't know for sure, we don't write anything in. Instead, we look for other scanning possibilities.

The simplest way to make sure you don't miss a scanning opportunity is to start with the 1's and work your way up to the 9's. There are two 1's in big row 1. The third 1 has to go in cell 21, since cell 23 is occupied and cell 22 is not possible with a 1 already in cell 52. Put in the 1. No further 1's can be placed, so move on to the 2's.

Scanning the 2's gives us information about box 9. The 2 in cell 92 eliminates cells 98 and 99 from being 2's (cell 97 already has a 3). And the 2 in cell 18 eliminates cells 78, 88, and 98 from being 2's. Those two 2's mean that the only place in box 9 to place a 2 is in cell 89. Put a 2 there. Now that there's a 2 in cell 89, we can scan across big row 3 and conclude that the last 2 in that big row must be in cell 74; it can't go in cell 76 because there's already a 2 in that column at cell 26. There are only two more boxes that need 2's in them (boxes 5 and 6), but we can't conclude yet where the 2's go. The puzzle now looks like this:

Example 3-2

				5		1	2	3
1		9			2	6	7	8
3		2		1				5
		8					3	1
	1						5	
2	3					8		
		3	2	6		4		9
9	6	7	4			5		2
	2	1		8		3		

Moving on to the 3's gets us nowhere, so we continue on to the 4's.

There are only two 4's in the puzzle (at cells 77 and 84), but those two are enough to tell us where two more 4's go. Scanning big row 3 tells us that the third 4 must go in cell 91, and scanning big column 3 eliminates the 4 from cell 37, meaning that cell 38 must be a 4. Here's where we stand:

Example 3-3

				5		1	2	3
1		9			2	6	7	8
3		2		1			4	5
		8					3	1
	1						5	
2	3					8		
		3	2	6		4		9
9	6	7	4			5		2
4	2	1		8		3		

Now just because we're doing lots of scanning, it doesn't mean that one-choice should be forgotten. We have eight numbers in box 3 filled in, so the empty cell must be a 9.

Back to scanning, we're up to 5's. In big row 1, the 5's in cells 15 and 39 mean that cell 22 must be a 5. Since we used horizontal scanning to get that 5, now look vertically from the just-placed 5 to see if that gives you any more information. Indeed, it does. Scanning down from the 5 in cell 22 eliminates the 5 from being in cell 72, so it has to be in cell 71. Put it in. Now box 7 has all but one number in it, so the last cell (cell 72) must be an 8. When we added the 5 to cell 71, we placed the second 5 in big column 1, and that's enough to tell us, using scanning, that cell 63 is a 5, since the 5 in cell 58 prevents a 5 from going in cell 53. That's it for the 5's. The puzzle now looks like this:

Example 3-4

				5		1	2	3
1	5	9			2	6	7	8
3		2		1		9	4	5
		8					3	1
	1						5	
2	3	5				8		
5	8	3	2	6		4		9
9	6	7	4			5		2
4	2	1		8		3		

Scanning 6's doesn't help at all, so we move on to 7's. The 7 in cell 28 eliminates 7's from the cells in column 8 of box 9. That leaves just cell 99 for the 7. Put it in. Now scan across big row 3 and we can conclude that cell 76 is a 7. That 7 is the eighth number in its row, so use one-choice to conclude that cell 78 is a 1. Since we've added a 1, let's see if scanning with it helps. Looking at big row 3, we see that a 1 must go in cell 86. This is the eighth 1 that has been placed in the puzzle. That means there are eight rows with 1's in them, eight columns with 1's in them, and eight boxes with 1's in them. Whenever you have eight of a number already placed, simply find the row and column that are missing the number, and put it in. It will obviously be in the box that's missing the number. In this case it's cell 64 that has to have the last 1. Now that all nine 1's have been placed, we never have to think about 1's again in this puzzle. I like to write the numbers 1 to 9 above the puzzle grid, and as I get the last occurrence of a number, I cross it out to make sure I don't waste any time thinking about a number that is already fully taken care of. Here's where we stand:

Example 3-5

				5		1	2	3
1	5	9			2	6	7	8
3		2		1		9	4	5
		8					3	1
	1						5	
2	3	5	1			8		
5	8	3	2	6	7	4	1	9
9	6	7	4		1	5		2
4	2	1		8		3		7

Back to scanning. We're up to 8's. In big row 3, the last 8 has to go in cell 88. This leaves one number missing from box 9. It's a 6. Put a 6 in cell 98. Now column 8 is missing just one number, so put the missing 9 in cell 68. The 8 in cell 88 also made row 8 almost complete. Only the 3 is missing, so put it in cell 85. Continuing to scan 8's gives us an 8 in cell 11 after scanning big column 1. That's all we can do with 8's, so we move on to 9's. Scanning big column 1 puts a 9 in cell 42.

We've hit 9, and we can't conclude anything more. So are we done with scanning? Hardly. All those numbers we've added mean that plenty of scanning opportunities exist for some of the numbers that didn't work before. You can glance around and try whatever number catches your eye, or you can methodically go through the numbers again. I like to do it in order, and since it's my book, that's how we'll do it! Write your own book if you don't like it. Back to number 2. What happened to number 1, I hear you ask? Did you forget that we've already placed all the 1's in the puzzle, so we never have to think about 1 again until we start a new puzzle? Spending any time on number 1 is a waste. Go straight to 2. The grid so far:

Example 3-6

8				5		1	2	3
1	5	9			2	6	7	8
3		2		1		9	4	5
	9	8					3	1
	1						5	
2	3	5	1			8	9	
5	8	3	2	6	7	4	1	9
9	6	7	4	3	1	5	8	2
4	2	1		8		3	6	7

There are two 2's missing from the grid, in boxes 5 and 6. But we can't conclude where they go using scanning, so we move along to 3's. Scanning big row 1 puts a 3 in cell 24, and that's the eighth 3 in the puzzle. The last 3 has to go in cell 56. Cross 3 off the list, since we'll never have to think about them again. The 3 in cell 24 was the eighth number in that row. The ninth number must be what's missing, so put a 4 in cell 25. Scanning 4's in big column 1, we see only one 4. But that 4, in cell 91, means that no 4 can go in cells 41 and 51, so the only cell left in box 4 for a 4 is cell 53. Now we have two 4's in big column 1, and the third 4 must go in cell 12. Scanning 4's in two directions at once, using the 4's in cells 53 and 77, we see that in box 6, the only empty cell that can hold a 4 is cell 69. With eight 4's placed, the last one has to go in cell 46. Cross 4 off the list of numbers to think about, since they're all placed. We're almost ready to move on to 5's, but first put a 7 in cell 32, since that's the only number missing from column 2, and put a 6 in cell 13, since that's what's missing from column 3. And in column 9, put a 6 in the only remaining hole. In big row 2, there are two 5's, and the last 5 must go in cell 44. This leaves just one more 5 to place, and the only spot left is cell 96. Cross 5 off the list. Now row 9 and box 8 are missing just one number, so we use one-choice and put in a 9 in cell 94. The puzzle is almost done. This is what it looks like:

Example 3-7

8	4	6		5		1	2	3
1	5	9	3	4	2	6	7	8
3	7	2		1		9	4	5
	9	8	5		4		3	1
	1	4			3		5	6
2	3	5	1			8	9	4
5	8	3	2	6	7	4	1	9
9	6	7	4	3	1	5	8	2
4	2	1	9	8	5	3	6	7

We're up to the 6's a second time. Scanning big row 2 puts a 6 in cell 41. Now with the 6 in cell 41, scanning big row 2 again forces a 6 into cell 66, which means the ninth 6 in the puzzle

COUNTING CAREFULLY

Back on page 11, how did you figure out what number was missing from that initial sudoku row? Did you say to yourself, "There's the 1, there's the 2, there's the 3, there's no four—it's a four!" and stop right there? While that works almost all the time, it's worth the extra second or two to continue on to make sure 5, 6, 7, 8, and 9 really are in the row. Every once in a while you'll discover one of those missing, and realize that the 4 really was in the row, and you just missed it. A few seconds spent being extra careful can save you from filling in the wrong number, and never making a mistake will save you time in the long run. So count carefully.

has to be in cell 34. Rows 3 and 6 and column 1 have all but one number filled in, so put a 7 in cell 51, a 7 in cell 65, and an 8 in cell 36. Putting those in leaves one hole in column 6, so cell 16 is a 9, which leaves a 7 left for cell 14. That 7 leaves just one number left for column 4, so cell 54 is an 8. All that's left to fill are cells 45, 47, 55, and 57, as shown below.

Example 3-8

8	4	6	7	5	9	1	2	3
1	5	9	3	4	2	6	7	8
3	7	2	6	1	8	9	4	5
6	9	8	5		4		3	1
7	1	4	8		3		5	6
2	3	5	1	7	6	8	9	4
5	8	3	2	6	7	4	1	9
9	6	7	4	3	1	5	8	2
4	2	1	9	8	5	3	6	7

We're up to 7, and there's only one missing. Eight rows, eight columns, and eight boxes have 7's in them. Cell 47 is where it has to go. That leaves 2's for cells 45 and 57, and one empty cell. Row 5, column 5, and box 5 are all missing a 9, so in it goes. Finished.

Example 3 Answer

8	4	6	7	5	9	1	2	3
1	5	9	3	4	2	6	7	8
3	7	2	6	1	8	9	4	5
6	9	8	5	2	4	7	3	1
7	1	4	8	9	3	2	5	6
2	3	5	1	7	6	8	9	4
5	8	3	2	6	7	4	1	9
9	6	7	4	3	1	5	8	2
4	2	1	9	8	5	3	6	7

13

4						9		
	1			3	9			
	9			4			7	8
8		1	3			6		
			2		4			
		4			8	1		3
6	8			2			9	
			8	9			3	
		3						5

14

	9	2						3
		3	4					
				3		1	4	8
	6		2	5		3	8	
				8				
	3	5		6	4		9	
5	2	1		9				
					7	9		
9						5	3	

15

	1	8	3			2		
5		6	1					
2				9			8	
7			9		5			
	9			6			5	
			8		4			2
	7			3				9
					2	8		7
		1			9	3	6	

16

				9	4			1
	1	5				3		9
8	3	9						
		6	9				3	
			8	4	6			
	7				1	6		
						7	4	8
3		4				2	9	
5			4	8				

17

	1		5				6	
		6		7		3		9
			8		6			4
		9	3	8				
	3						4	
				9	7	6		
8			4		3			
3		4		5		1		
	9				1		3	

18

		2	6		4	1		
1				8				6
	8	7	2					4
						6	5	
	6		3		5		7	
	2	1						
9					8	5	6	
2				3				8
		8	1		7	2		

19

	3		5					
6				1	2		4	9
		9			4		8	
		4						3
5			1	2	3			4
3						5		
	4		3			9		
1	5		4	7				2
					8		1	

20

6		1		3	9	7		
3		5		1				
					4			5
7					5			
	6						7	
			7					6
4			1					
				7		5		8
		7	8	9		1		3

21

3							4	
6	1		3					7
	9		8			1		
			2				5	
		3	4		7	2		
	2				6			
		4			2		8	
5					4		7	2
	3							6

22

		1	9		5			
	3	5	6					2
		9		2				
8	2	3						
1			2	5	7			6
						4	2	1
				8		1		
5					2	9	3	
			4		3	2		

23

		1					5	
6				5	1			
		7			4	1	3	
					7		8	
5		8		6		7		3
	1		3					
	4	6	2			3		
			4	3				9
	9					4		

24

		8	9	2			7	4
9								1
			1				5	
	9			5		4		
		5				8		
		4		6			1	
	7				9			
4								8
5	6			4	7	3		

3
ELIMINATION

We now have under our belts two of the three basic strategies for solving sudoku puzzles: one-choice and scanning. It's time to learn the third basic strategy: elimination.

Let's look at a puzzle.

Example 4

			1			2		
	4	8			2			
			8	3	9			5
9		6				8		
4								6
		7				5		1
6			9	5	4			
			3			7	5	
		2			1			

We start to solve this by using scanning:

- Scanning 2's in big row 3 and big column 2 forces cell 85 to be a 2.
- Scanning 4's in big column 1 and big row 3 puts a 4 in cell 83.
- Scanning 4's in big row 1 and big column 2 forces cell 15 to be a 4.

At this point, scanning doesn't help, so we must resort to one-choice. Only one cell can be found using one-choice.

- Cell 33 can be only a 1.

Once that 1 is in cell 33, there is another one-choice.

- Cell 73 can be only a 3.

Again, adding that number gives two more one-choice cells.

- Cell 53 can be only a 5.
- Cell 77 can be only a 1.
- Cell 13 can be only a 9.
- Scanning 1's in big row 1 puts a 1 in cell 28.

Now what? If you go through every cell, you will not find any that can be solved using one-choice. And no matter how you try scanning, you will not be able to place any other numbers. What you need to finish this puzzle is what's known as elimination. Here is the grid as it stands now:

Example 4-1

		9	1	4		2		
	4	8			2		1	
		1	8	3	9			5
9		6				8		
4		5						6
		7				5		1
6		3	9	5	4	1		
		4	3	2		7	5	
		2			1			

While it's not necessary to put in all the possible candidates, we'll do so for clarity. This is shown in the grid below.

Example 4-2

357	3567	9	1	4	567	2	3678	378
357	4	8	567	67	2	369	1	379
27	267	1	8	3	9	46	467	5
9	123	6	2457	17	357	8	2347	2347
4	1238	5	27	1789	378	39	2379	6
238	238	7	246	689	368	5	2349	1
6	78	3	9	5	4	1	28	28
18	189	4	3	2	68	7	5	89
578	5789	2	67	678	1	3469	34689	3489

Take a look at row 7. A 7 has to go somewhere in that row. The only open cells are 72, 78, and 79. But a 7 can't go in 78 or 79, so it must go in 72. We have eliminated all the possible cells in a particular row except one, and thus concluded that the number must go in that cell. This is the principle of elimination. Find a row (or a column) in which a certain number can go in only one of the cells in that row (or column), and you can confidently fill it in. (Scanning is simply elimination in a box.)

In row 8, only one of the four remaining open cells can have a 6 in it, so the 6 must go in cell 86. In column 1, only one of the remaining six open cells can have a 1 in it, so the 1 must go in cell 81.

Now the puzzle looks like Example 4-3, and we can go back to scanning and one-choice to progress further.

- Cell 94 can be only a 7.
- Once that 7 is in, cell 54 can be only a 2.
- The 7 at cell 94 also forces cell 95 to be an 8.
- The 8 in cell 95 forces cell 91 to be a 5.
- That 5 forces cell 92 to be a 9.
- That 9 forces cell 82 to be an 8.
- That 8 forces cell 89 to be a 9.

By using elimination, we were able to fill in three cells that allowed us to then use one-choice to fill in several more cells. The elimination got us this far:

Example 4-3

357	356	9	1	4	57	2	3678	378
357	4	8	567	67	2	369	1	379
27	26	1	8	3	9	46	467	5
9	123	6	2457	17	357	8	2347	2347
4	1238	5	27	1789	378	39	2379	6
238	238	7	246	689	38	5	2349	1
6	7	3	9	5	4	1	28	28
1	89	4	3	2	6	7	5	89
58	589	2	7	78	1	3469	34689	3489

After the one-choice cells are filled in, the puzzle looks like this:

Example 4-4

37	356	9	1	4	57	2	3678	378
37	4	8	56	67	2	369	1	37
27	26	1	8	3	9	46	467	5
9	123	6	45	17	357	8	2347	2347
4	13	5	2	179	378	39	379	6
238	23	7	46	69	38	5	2349	1
6	7	3	9	5	4	1	28	28
1	8	4	3	2	6	7	5	9
5	9	2	7	8	1	346	346	34

No further progress can be made using one-choice, but scanning lets us continue:

- Scanning 5's in big column 1 puts a 5 in cell 12.
- Once that 5 is in place, scanning 5's in big row 1 puts a 5 in cell 24.
- Now 5's can be scanned in big column 2 to conclude that cell 46 is a 5, finishing off the 5's.

- Scanning 6's in big column 1 puts a 6 in cell 32.
- Scanning the 6 in big column 2 puts a 6 in cell 25.
- Once those two 6's are in place, we can scan 6's in big row 1 to put a 6 in cell 18.
- That 6 allows big column 3 to be scanned, and a 6 has to go in cell 97.
- With eight of the 6's in place, the last one has to go in cell 64.

The puzzle now looks like so:

Example 4-5

37	5	9	1	4	7	2	6	378
37	4	8	5	6	2	39	1	37
27	6	1	8	3	9	4	47	5
9	123	6	4	17	5	8	2347	2347
4	13	5	2	179	378	39	379	6
238	23	7	6	9	38	5	2349	1
6	7	3	9	5	4	1	28	28
1	8	4	3	2	6	7	5	9
5	9	2	7	8	1	6	34	34

The puzzle can now be finished by using one-choice.

- Cell 16 can be only a 7.
- Cell 37 can be only a 4.
- Cell 44 can be only a 4.
- Cell 65 can be only a 9.

Put those in, then continue with one-choice.

- Cell 11 can be only a 3.
- Cell 38 can be only a 7.

Once those are in we know some more.

- Cell 19 can be only an 8.
- Cell 21 can be only a 7.
- Cell 29 can be only a 3.
- Cell 31 can be only a 2.

With those four numbers in place, one-choice gives us four more cells.

- Cell 27 can be only a 9.
- Cell 61 can be only an 8.
- Cell 79 can be only a 2.
- Cell 99 can be only a 4.

Almost finished. Five more cells can now be determined with one-choice.

- Cell 49 can be only a 7.
- Cell 57 can be only a 3.
- Cell 66 can be only a 3.
- Cell 78 can be only an 8.
- Cell 98 can be only a 3.

Two steps left to go. Six more cells can be determined with one-choice.

- Cell 45 can be only a 1.
- Cell 48 can be only a 2.
- Cell 52 can be only a 1.
- Cell 56 can be only an 8.
- Cell 58 can be only a 9.
- Cell 62 can be only a 2.

That leaves three cells to fill. All of them are one-choice.

- Cell 42 can be only a 3.
- Cell 55 can be only a 7.
- Cell 68 can be only a 4.

Example 4 Answer

3	5	9	1	4	7	2	6	8
7	4	8	5	6	2	9	1	3
2	6	1	8	3	9	4	7	5
9	3	6	4	1	5	8	2	7
4	1	5	2	7	8	3	9	6
8	2	7	6	9	3	5	4	1
6	7	3	9	5	4	1	8	2
1	8	4	3	2	6	7	5	9
5	9	2	7	8	1	6	3	4

You now know all you need to know to solve basic sudoku puzzles. Scanning, one-choice, and elimination should get you through any puzzle that's labeled as "easy." I'll take you through one more puzzle step-by-step. After that, I'll skip the basic steps, letting you figure them out on your own. Here we go.

Example 5

7		2					3	4
			3			2	9	8
		3			4			
9	4			7	6			
8								6
			8	2			4	7
			4			6		
6	7	4			2			
5	3					4		2

The cool thing about this puzzle is that while it has no 1's anywhere in it, you can immediately place a 1 in cell 31, since no other number can go there. And if you put that 1 in, then you can scan big row 1 and conclude that cell 17 is also a 1. So with zero 1's in the starting grid, we can immediately put two in.

But it's not typical to start a puzzle with one-choice, since they're not too easy to spot in the beginning, so let's ignore that information for now (but do remember it, since it will come in handy later), and start with scanning, which is typical.

- Scan big row 1 for 2's and put a 2 in cell 34.
- Scan big row 2 and big column 1 and put a 2 in cell 52.
- Scan big column 1 again and put a 2 in cell 71.
- Scan big row 2 and finish off the 2's with a 2 in cell 48.
- Scan big column 1 for 3's and put a 3 in cell 61.
- Scan big column 1 for 4's and put a 4 in cell 21.
- Scan big column 2 and put the last 4 in cell 55.
- Now the one-choice in cell 31 is obvious, since column 1 has eight numbers in it. Put a 1 in cell 31.
- Since we just put in that 1, we might as well scan 1's in big row 1. That gives us a 1 in cell 17.
- Scanning 6's in big column 3 provides us with a 6 in cell 38.
- In big row 2, scanning 7's puts a 7 in cell 53.
- Continuing with 7's, the single 7 in cell 69 is enough to scan big column 3 and put a 7 in cell 37.
- Box 3 has eight numbers filled, so use one-choice and put a 5 in cell 39.
- Scanning big row 1 for 7's will start us on our way to finishing off the 7's. We can conclude that cell 26 is a 7.
- Once we have that, scanning big column 2 puts a 7 in cell 94.
- With eight 7's in place, a quick scan puts the last 7 in cell 78.
- The 8's in big row 2 can be scanned to put an 8 in cell 47.
- Starting back at 1 again, big row 1 has two 1's in it, and scanning them puts a 1 in cell 25.
- Scanning horizontally from the 3 in cell 61 and vertically from the 3 in cell 24 tells us that box 5 has a 3 in cell 56.
- Once the 3 is in cell 56, scanning big row 2 lets us conclude that cell 49 must be a 3.
- That 3, along with the one in cell 18, can be scanned to put a 3 in cell 87.
- One 3 remains to be placed. The only row without a 3 is row 7, and the only column without a 3 is column 5, so cell 75 is a 3.

At this point, the puzzle looks like the grid at the top of the next page. It can be finished using just scanning and one-choice, but I want to throw in some elimination as a review. Often, you'll have more than one way to finish a puzzle, and deciding which one to use is arbitrary. As long as you can validly conclude that a cell has to be a certain number, you should put it in. It doesn't matter if you figure it out using scanning, one-choice, or elimination, as long as you know for sure that it's correct. Never put in a number that you're not sure about.

Example 5-1

7		2				1	3	4
4			3	1	7	2	9	8
1		3	2		4	7	6	5
9	4			7	6	8	2	3
8	2	7		4	3			6
3			8	2			4	7
2			4	3		6	7	
6	7	4			2	3		
5	3		7			4		2

You can now determine the contents of cell 95 by scanning 6's in big row 3. But you can also figure it out using elimination in row 9. Where can the 6 in row 9 go? It can't go in cell 93 since box 7 already has a 6 in it at cell 81. It can't go in cell 96 since column 6 has a 6 in it already at cell 46. And it can't go in cell 98 due to the 6 in cell 38. So there's only one cell that's left for the 6. It must go in cell 95.

Let's do elimination in box 6. Where can the 1 go? Cells 57 and 67 are out because column 7 has a 1 in it at cell 17. So the only cell left in box 6 is 58. It must contain the 1. As you can see, elimination in a box is the same as scanning. You could have scanned down big column 3 with the 1 in cell 17 to come to the same conclusion about cell 58 being a 1.

Now look at column 8. There are two empty cells left, and they must contain the missing 5 and 8. Which goes where? Look across rows 8 and 9 to see if either one contains a 5 or 8. Cell 91 is a 5, so we know that the 5 can't go in cell 98, and must instead go in cell 88, putting the 8 in cell 98. This is equivalent to doing one-choice on cell 98. It can't be a 1, 2, 3, 4, 6, 7, or 9 from column 8, and it can't be a 5 from cell 91, so it must be an 8.

Even though cell 85 has two possibilities (8 and 9), and even though scanning 8's is inconclusive, we can use elimination to determine that cell 85 is an 8. We do this by looking at row 8. The two other open cells in row 8 (84 and 89) already have 8's in their columns, so the only place in row 8 that can have an 8 is cell 85. Put it in.

One-choice finishes off the puzzle:

- Cell 35 has to be a 9.
- Cell 15 has to be a 5.
- Cell 16 has to be an 8.
- Cell 14 has to be a 6.
- Cell 12 has to be a 9.
- Cell 32 has to be an 8.
- Cell 72 has to be a 1.
- Cell 79 has to be a 9.
- Cell 89 has to be a 1.
- Cell 84 has to be a 9.
- Cell 96 has to be a 1.
- Cell 93 has to be a 9.
- Cell 73 has to be an 8.
- Cell 76 has to be a 5.
- Cell 66 has to be a 9.
- Cell 67 has to be a 5.
- Cell 57 has to be a 9.
- Cell 54 has to be a 5.
- Cell 44 has to be a 1.
- Cell 43 has to be a 5.
- Cell 23 has to be a 6.
- Cell 22 has to be a 5.
- Cell 62 has to be a 6.
- Cell 63 has to be a 1.

Example 5 Answer

7	9	2	6	5	8	1	3	4
4	5	6	3	1	7	2	9	8
1	8	3	2	9	4	7	6	5
9	4	5	1	7	6	8	2	3
8	2	7	5	4	3	9	1	6
3	6	1	8	2	9	5	4	7
2	1	8	4	3	5	6	7	9
6	7	4	9	8	2	3	5	1
5	3	9	7	6	1	4	8	2

Throughout the book, I will explain in depth any new method or any method from the previous chapter. But methods that are more than a chapter old will often be skipped.

25

			2	7			6	
	2			9	6			8
	9				4			
1	4		7					5
		2				1		
7					5		9	6
			4				5	
6			9	3			2	
	7			5	2			

26

				3	2	4		
9		5					6	
6					4			
	1		9					
	2	9		8		1	5	
					5		8	
			8					3
	5					6		9
		1	2	5				

27

	2							4
1			2		8			
				3	1		2	
5		2						9
	9	3				4	7	
4						1		5
	6		7	4				
			3		2			7
3							4	

28

	9							
		3	5		1		8	
5			6	9		4		
3	1	6				5		2
				2				
2		8				1	9	7
		1		6	3			8
	6		8		2	3		
							2	

29

			5	2	3	7	1	
2		3			7	9		
						5		
	4			5	9	8		
		9	3	8			5	
		4						
		5	9			1		2
	6	7	2	1	5			

30

4				2			6	
	1			3		8		9
					7		5	
	7		6			1		
			9		2			
		8			4		9	
	4		7					
7		6		5			1	
	5			9				4

31

		8				5	4	
		5	2		4			8
9				5	6			
	4				1			2
7								6
8			7				5	
			4	1				3
4			6		2	8		
	1	2				6		

32

7								
9					3	6	5	
		4	9	1	2	8		
2					9			
	9	1		3		2	4	
			2					5
		7	1	2	8	3		
	8	9	4					1
								7

33

8	9		4			6		2
		7	2			9	3	
				3				4
				2		3		
7								5
		4		7				
9				8				
	7	8			9	4		
6		2			5		9	7

34

						6	9	
			9	1		8		
				6		2		4
3					1		2	
		5	3		7	9		
	1		6					3
1		3		7				
		6		2	4			
	2	8						

35

8				4	1			
	4	6		3		8		
2			5				7	
3	2				4			
		8	3		7	6		
			1				8	3
	5				3			8
		7		5		2	1	
			6	1				7

36

7	3		1		5			
		4		3				2
8								
			9			3		
		7	5	1	4	6		
		6			7			
								7
9				7		8		
			8		2		3	9

THE ORIGINAL NUMBER PLACE PUZZLES

Here is a reprint from the May 1979 issue of *Dell Pencil Puzzles & Word Games*: the first sudoku-type puzzles ever printed. Note that the "Solutions are on page 62" is from the original magazine. In this book, you need to look on page 39.

NUMBER PLACE

In this puzzle, your job is to place a number into every empty box so that each row across, each column down, and each small 9-box square within the large square (there are 9 of these) will contain each number from 1 through 9. Remember that no number may appear more than once in any row across, any column down, or within any small 9-box square; this will help you solve the puzzle. The numbers in circles below the diagram will give you a head start—each of these four numbers goes into one of the circle boxes in the diagram (not necessarily in the order given).

Solutions are on page 62.

1

○	2	3			1	7		
		8	4	6			1	
9				5			4	8
5		4	3				2	○
	9		8	7		1		
1			○		4	9		5
	7				6	8		2
8		1	7		2			
	6			3	○		7	1

④ ⑥ START ⑦ ⑧

2

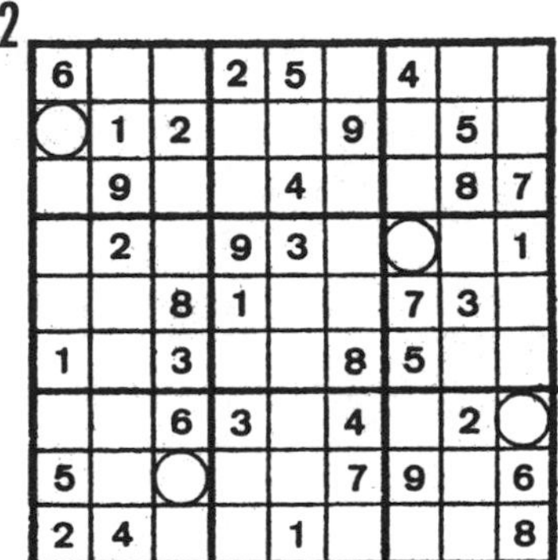

6			2	5		4		
○	1	2			9		5	
	9			4			8	7
	2		9	3		○		1
		8	1			7	3	
1		3			8	5		
		6	3		4		2	○
5		○			7	9		6
2	4			1				8

① ④ START ⑤ ⑧

4

SUBSETS

Now that you understand one-choice, scanning, and elimination, you're ready for more complicated solving tips. Let's start with a sample puzzle.

PAIRS

Example 6

		4		8			1	
8	6			5				
			4		1		6	5
6	5						3	
3								2
	4						8	9
9	3		8		7			
				1			2	7
	1			6		5		

We can get pretty far using the methods we know up to this point, but eventually we get stuck. In order to proceed further, we'll need to put in all the possible candidates for what can go in each cell. Here is the grid when no more basic strategy works, with the candidates indicated.

Example 6-1

5	279	4	2679	8	269	29	1	3
8	6	1	29	5	3	29	7	4
27	279	3	4	79	1	8	6	5
6	5	2789	279	479	289	47	3	1
3	79	789	1	479	689	467	5	2
1	4	27	2567	3	256	67	8	9
9	3	5	8	2	7	1	4	6
4	8	6	59	1	59	3	2	7
27	1	27	3	6	4	5	9	8

Now look at cells 63 and 93. Both of them contain either a 2 or a 7. We don't know which is the 2 and which is the 7, but we know that one of them is a 2, and the other is a 7. Since both of these cells are in column 3, no other cells in column 3 can contain a 2 or 7. We can eliminate 2 and 7 from the candidate lists of cells 43 and 53. Another way of looking at this is that if cell 43 were a 2, then both cells 63 and 93 would have to be 7's, which is not possible, So cell 43 cannot be a 2. Similarly, cell 43 cannot be a 7, and cell 53 cannot be a 7. So we eliminate the 2's and 7's from cells 43 and 53 and take a new look at the grid.

Example 6-2

5	279	4	2679	8	269	29	1	3
8	6	1	29	5	3	29	7	4
27	279	3	4	79	1	8	6	5
6	5	89	279	479	289	47	3	1
3	79	89	1	479	689	467	5	2
1	4	27	2567	3	256	67	8	9
9	3	5	8	2	7	1	4	6
4	8	6	59	1	59	3	2	7
27	1	27	3	6	4	5	9	8

Now take a look at box 4. Using elimination, there's only one cell that can contain a 2, so a 2 must go in cell 63. After that 2 is in place, the puzzle is solvable using the basic strategies.

Example 6 Answer

5	9	4	7	8	6	2	1	3
8	6	1	2	5	3	9	7	4
7	2	3	4	9	1	8	6	5
6	5	8	9	7	2	4	3	1
3	7	9	1	4	8	6	5	2
1	4	2	6	3	5	7	8	9
9	3	5	8	2	7	1	4	6
4	8	6	5	1	9	3	2	7
2	1	7	3	6	4	5	9	8

TRIPLETS

What worked above for a subset of two numbers also works for three. Here's an example:

Example 7

4				8		3	2	
7	9	8		3				
		3	5				9	
			2				3	
		2				5		
	7				6			
	8				3	1		
				2		8	5	4
	5	7		1				3

Using scanning and one-choice, we can get this far:

Example 7-1

4		5		8		3	2	
7	9	8		3				5
		3	5				9	8
			2		5		3	
		2				5		
5	7				6			
	8	4		5	3	1	7	
				2		8	5	4
	5	7		1			6	3

We can use elimination to go further. Look at column 2. Where can a 2 go? There is only one spot: cell 32. Once that 2 is in place, scanning big row 1 puts another 2 in cell 26. Then elimination is needed again. In column 5, there's just one place that a 6 can go, so put it in cell 35. Continue with one-choice and scanning to get to this point:

Example 7-2

4	6	5		8		3	2	
7	9	8		3	2	6		5
1	2	3	5	6			9	8
			2		5		3	
		2				5		
5	7				6			
	8	4		5	3	1	7	
				2		8	5	4
	5	7		1			6	3

Three more eliminations, and we get to a sticking point, so we need to put in candidates. First, there's just one place for a 3 in row 6, in cell 64. Once that 3 is in place, there's only one cell in row 6 that can hold an 8. So it goes in cell 68. Finally, in row 4, the only place for an 8 is in cell 41.

Example 7-3

4	6	5	179	8	179	3	2	17
7	9	8	14	3	2	6	14	5
1	2	3	5	6	47	47	9	8
8	14	169	2	479	5	479	3	1679
369	134	2	14789	479	14789	5	14	1679
5	7	19	3	49	6	249	8	129
269	8	4	69	5	3	1	7	29
369	13	169	679	2	79	8	5	4
29	5	7	489	1	489	29	6	3

Now look at cells 45, 55, and 65. All three contain just the numbers 4, 7, and 9. That means that those three numbers will be in those three cells in some order, which means that 4, 7, and 9 can't appear in any other cells in box 5. So we can eliminate 4, 7, and 9 as possibilities from cells 54 and 56. Watch what happens when we do that.

Example 7-4

4	6	5	179	8	179	3	2	17
7	9	8	14	3	2	6	14	5
1	2	3	5	6	47	47	9	8
8	14	169	2	479	5	479	3	1679
369	134	2	18	479	18	5	14	1679
5	7	19	3	49	6	249	8	129
269	8	4	69	5	3	1	7	29
369	13	169	679	2	79	8	5	4
29	5	7	489	1	489	29	6	3

Now look at row 5. We're back to the pairs we just learned about. Cells 54 and 56 contain 1 and 8 in some order, so cell 58 cannot contain a 1 (otherwise both cells 54 and 56 would have to be 8's). Since cell 58 can't be a 1, it has to be a 4. Bingo! Once you know cell 58 is a 4, the rest is just scanning and one-choice.

Example 7 Answer

4	6	5	9	8	1	3	2	7
7	9	8	4	3	2	6	1	5
1	2	3	5	6	7	4	9	8
8	4	1	2	9	5	7	3	6
6	3	2	1	7	8	5	4	9
5	7	9	3	4	6	2	8	1
9	8	4	6	5	3	1	7	2
3	1	6	7	2	9	8	5	4
2	5	7	8	1	4	9	6	3

For triplets, note that the possible candidate arrangements often include cases where each individual cell has only two candidates. Thus (assuming X, Y, and Z represent the three digits), in addition to easy-to-spot arrangements like XYZ-XYZ-XYZ, XYZ-XYZ-XY, and XYZ-XY-YZ, those taking the form of XY-YZ-XZ are just as valid, and occur frequently.

QUADRUPLETS

What works for pairs and triplets also works for quadruplets. Here's a puzzle:

Example 8

					4		1	7
5		4		9				2
	1			3		4		
	3	1	4					
		7		8		5		
					2	6	3	
		6		4			7	
7				1		2		5
8	4		3					

Scanning and one-choice get us to this point:

Example 8-1

3					4	9	1	7
5	7	4		9		3		2
	1			3		4	5	
	3	1	4			7		
		7		8	3	5		
					2	6	3	
1		6		4		8	7	3
7	9	3		1		2	4	5
8	4		3			1		

With elimination, we can add one more cell, but then we need candidates. In column 6, the 1 can go in just one cell, 26. Adding that and the candidates gives this:

Example 8-2

3	268	28	2568	256	4	9	1	7
5	7	4	68	9	1	3	68	2
269	1	289	2678	3	678	4	5	68
269	3	1	4	56	569	7	289	89
2469	26	7	169	8	3	5	29	149
49	58	589	1579	57	2	6	3	1489
1	25	6	259	4	59	8	7	3
7	9	3	68	1	68	2	4	5
8	4	25	3	2567	5679	1	69	69

What you're looking for here are two cells in the same row, column, or box with the same two numbers in them; three cells in the same row, column, or box with the same three numbers shared among them; four cells in the same row, column, or box with the same four numbers shared among them; etc. Cells 98 and 99 fit the bill. Two cells, both with just two numbers (6 and 9) in them. We can eliminate 6 and 9 from the other cells in that row. But doing that doesn't give us much help. If we look at box 4, though, progress can be made. Cells 41, 51, 52, and 61 contain the numbers 2, 4, 6, and 9 only. So those four cells will have those four numbers in some order, and no other cells in box 4 can contain a 2, 4, 6, or 9.

Example 8-3

3	268	28	2568	256	4	9	1	7
5	7	4	68	9	1	3	68	2
269	1	289	2678	3	678	4	5	68
269	3	1	4	56	569	7	289	89
2469	26	7	169	8	3	5	29	149
49	58	58	1579	57	2	6	3	1489
1	25	6	259	4	59	8	7	3
7	9	3	68	1	68	2	4	5
8	4	25	3	257	57	1	69	69

This removes the 9 candidate from cell 63, which allows us to use elimination to figure out that the only cell in column 3 that can now contain a 9 is cell 33. That's not much help, but removing the 9 from cell 63 also created a pair: cells 62 and 63 must both be either a 5 or 8. That means the 5's and 8's from row 6 can be removed from the other cells, resulting in cell 65 being a 7.

Example 8-4

3	268	28	2568	256	4	9	1	7
5	7	4	68	9	1	3	68	2
26	1	9	2678	3	678	4	5	68
269	3	1	4	56	569	7	289	89
2469	26	7	169	8	3	5	29	149
49	58	58	19	7	2	6	3	149
1	25	6	259	4	59	8	7	3
7	9	3	68	1	68	2	4	5
8	4	25	3	25	57	1	69	69

Back to elimination to finish it off. There's only one spot in column 4 for a 7: cell 34. Once that 7 is in place, the only cell in row 3 that can hold a 2 is cell 31. After that's in place, the puzzle can be finished off with scanning and one-choice.

Example 8 Answer

3	6	8	5	2	4	9	1	7
5	7	4	6	9	1	3	8	2
2	1	9	7	3	8	4	5	6
9	3	1	4	6	5	7	2	8
6	2	7	1	8	3	5	9	4
4	8	5	9	7	2	6	3	1
1	5	6	2	4	9	8	7	3
7	9	3	8	1	6	2	4	5
8	4	2	3	5	7	1	6	9

QUINTUPLETS

After quadruplets comes, not surprisingly, quintuplets. Here's the puzzle:

Example 9

					4			5
	9	6		7		8		
						2	7	
1			6					3
			5	1	2			
6					3			8
	5	8						
		2		6		5	3	
9			4					

Using basic strategies, we get this far:

Example 9-1

					4	3	6	5
	9	6		7		8		
					6	2	7	9
1			6					3
			5	1	2			
6					3			8
	5	8						
		2		6		5	3	
9	6		4				8	

In box 3, the two empty cells must contain a 1 and a 4. That means that cell 26 cannot be a 1, so all that's left is a 5. Scanning big column 2 places a 5 at cell 95. Then we can conclude that the 2 in row 9 must be in cell 99 and the 5 in column 1 must be in cell 31 (using elimination).

With cells 95 and 99 filled, we can put a 3 in cell 93 using elimination. Then scanning big column 1 puts a 1 in cell 82.

That brings us to this point:

Example 9-2

278	278	17	1289	289	4	3	6	5
23	9	6	23	7	5	8	14	14
5	348	14	138	38	6	2	7	9
1	2478	4579	6	489	789	479	2459	3
3478	3478	479	5	1	2	4679	49	467
6	247	4579	79	49	3	1479	12459	8
47	5	8	12379	239	179	14679	149	1467
47	1	2	789	6	789	5	3	47
9	6	3	4	5	17	17	8	2

Looking at all the candidates in row 7, we find a quintuplet: the five candidates 1, 4, 6, 7, and 9 occupy the five cells 71, 76, 77, 78, and 79. So we can eliminate any of these numbers from the remaining cells in that row, leaving candidates 2 and 3 in cells 74 and 75. But another way to approach this is to look at row 7's candidates and realize that the candidates 2 and 3 appear only in the two cells 74 and 75. Since this is true, we can call these a hidden pair. We can eliminate all the other candidates from those two cells, leaving only the 2 and 3. Either way you look at it, the end result is the same. This dichotomy can be extended further to hidden triplets, hidden quadruplets, etc., but any of these higher than pairs are very difficult to spot, and using the regular subsets technique is much easier.

Example 9-3

278	278	17	1289	289	4	3	6	5
23	9	6	23	7	5	8	14	14
5	348	14	138	38	6	2	7	9
1	2478	4579	6	489	789	479	2459	3
3478	3478	479	5	1	2	4679	49	467
6	247	4579	79	49	3	1479	12459	8
47	5	8	23	23	179	14679	149	1467
47	1	2	789	6	789	5	3	47
9	6	3	4	5	17	17	8	2

At this point, we have a few more subsets. Cells 71 and 81 both contain 4 and 7, so that's a pair. All the 4's and 7's can be eliminated from the remaining cells in column 1. Cell 81 also forms a pair with cell 89. The 7's in cells 84 and 86 can be eliminated. And thanks to our noticing the hidden pair in row 7, we now have cell 74 limited to a 2 or 3, which forms a pair with cell 24. The 2's and 3's in the other cells in column 4 can be removed.

Example 9-4

28	278	17	189	289	4	3	6	5
23	9	6	23	7	5	8	14	14
5	348	14	18	38	6	2	7	9
1	2478	4579	6	489	789	479	2459	3
38	3478	479	5	1	2	4679	49	467
6	247	4579	79	49	3	1479	12459	8
47	5	8	23	23	179	14679	149	1467
47	1	2	89	6	89	5	3	47
9	6	3	4	5	17	17	8	2

Now elimination can be used to determine that the only cell in column 4 that can contain a 7 is cell 64. We can also find one more subset, a triplet, which finally allows us to break through. Cells 28, 58, and 78 are all made up of 1's, 4's, and 9's, so cells 48 and 68 can have their 1, 4, and 9 candidates removed. This gives the grid below, where cell 67 is the only cell in row 6 that can be a 1. After that, the puzzle can be finished with scanning and one-choice.

Example 9-5

28	278	17	189	289	4	3	6	5
23	9	6	23	7	5	8	14	14
5	348	14	18	38	6	2	7	9
1	2478	4579	6	489	89	479	25	3
38	3478	479	5	1	2	4679	49	467
6	24	459	7	49	3	149	25	8
47	5	8	23	23	179	14679	149	1467
47	1	2	89	6	89	5	3	47
9	6	3	4	5	17	17	8	2

Example 9 Answer

2	8	7	1	9	4	3	6	5
3	9	6	2	7	5	8	4	1
5	4	1	8	3	6	2	7	9
1	7	5	6	8	9	4	2	3
8	3	4	5	1	2	6	9	7
6	2	9	7	4	3	1	5	8
4	5	8	3	2	7	9	1	6
7	1	2	9	6	8	5	3	4
9	6	3	4	5	1	7	8	2

The subsets rule can be succinctly summed up as follows: When a certain number of different candidate digits in a row, column, or box are shared among the same number of cells (two digits occupy two cells, three digits occupy three cells, etc.), any of those digits can be removed as candidates from anywhere else they appear in that row, box, or column.

ANSWERS TO PUZZLES FROM PAGE 32

NUMBER PLACE

1

4	2	3	9	8	1	7	5	6
7	5	8	4	6	3	2	1	9
9	1	6	2	5	7	3	4	8
5	8	4	3	1	9	6	2	7
6	9	2	8	7	5	1	3	4
1	3	7	6	2	4	9	8	5
3	7	5	1	4	6	8	9	2
8	4	1	7	9	2	5	6	3
2	6	9	5	3	8	4	7	1

2

6	8	7	2	5	3	4	1	9
4	1	2	7	8	9	6	5	3
3	9	5	6	4	1	2	8	7
7	2	4	9	3	5	8	6	1
9	5	8	1	6	2	7	3	4
1	6	3	4	7	8	5	9	2
8	7	6	3	9	4	1	2	5
5	3	1	8	2	7	9	4	6
2	4	9	5	1	6	3	7	8

37

		5			7	6		
					1	7		
		3		6			5	4
2	3							
	6	8	4		3	1	2	
							3	6
1	4			5		9		
		6	1					
		9	6			5		

38

				8				6
		1					3	4
			6		5			8
			8			9	5	
5	7						6	3
	6	3			9			
3			7		1			
7	1					6		
9				2				

39

6				8	9			
3						9	1	8
1		8						
7			8		2			
		2				4		
			7		1			6
						3		9
2	7	6						5
			5	7				4

40

	6		9				1	7
		5	7		6	4		
				1				3
2					1	8		4
3		8	6					1
5				6				
		3	8		2	9		
8	2				7		3	

41

8	1		2					6
	5		1					
	3			9				
				8	5	9		
3		8				2		5
		4	7	6				
				3			4	
					8		1	
6					1		3	9

42

		3		6	9			
	9			4	2	6		
6	2							
4	5						6	
		2	6		1	4		
	6						7	3
							3	8
		1	5	9			4	
			1	3		9		

43

3	1				9			
	2			8	4		1	
5			7					
		7					8	2
	6						5	
2	3					4		
					8			5
	8		1	4			3	
			6				7	1

44

				6	9			
		3				9		
1	9		5		8			3
3		6			5	2		
	4						9	
		1	2			5		4
8			1		3		5	7
		5				1		
			9	5				

45

		6		9	3			
				2		4	9	
	1		7			6		3
			8			3		
	5			6			8	
		7			5			
3		9			6		4	
	8	2		7				
			9	3		5		

46

		9				2		3
2					6			5
			3	2	4			
		4	2		9			
7								1
			8		7	9		
			6	4	8			
5			9					7
6		3				8		

47

5	1			9				7
						2		
7	9	4				5		
				5	4		8	9
			8	3	9			
9	3		1	7				
		9				6	5	8
		3						
8				2			1	3

48

			9				5	
7	9	4						
				3	6			1
			6					5
	4	3				8	7	
8					4			
9			3	5				
						1	8	3
	2				7			

SUDOKU VARIETIES: THE SPICE OF PUZZLING LIFE

Are you getting bored with 9×9 grids made up of 3×3 boxes to be filled with the digits 1 to 9? There are dozens of sudoku variants to keep your solving experience fresh. Here are a few:

In wordoku, the digits are replaced with letters. Underneath the grid, the nine letters needed are given in an easy-to-remember order. The solving experience is the same, but when you're done, a row, column, or diagonal spells a word. You don't need to find the word to logically get through the puzzle, but spotting it early can certainly help.

In samurai sudoku you get five sudoku grids that overlap at the corner boxes. No individual puzzle has enough information to solve it, but together they all interact to allow you to logically reach the answer.

Sudoku puzzles don't need to be 9×9. You can find 10×10 puzzles (which include the digit 0), 12×12 puzzles, or even 16×16 puzzles. Just make sure the cells are big enough to allow you enough room to write candidates. Smaller puzzles (usually 6×6) are widely available in books for kids.

In the 6×6, 10×10, and 12×12 puzzles, the boxes are typically rectangles, but those regions can be any shape at all. You can also find 9×9 puzzles where instead of 3×3 squares, the shapes vary.

There are also puzzles that have added restrictions given, such as nine shaded cells that must all be different, or diagonals whose digits are all different, or both. Others require that shaded cells be odd (or even).

The fun part of these is figuring out new strategies that you can't normally use in regular sudoku. I like to try these every now and then, but being a traditionalist, I always end up going back to standard sudoku. If you're into Diet Black Cherry Vanilla Coke, then maybe these are for you. I'll stick with the classic.

5
INTERACTION

At this point, it is assumed you can do scanning, one-choice, and elimination on your own. We won't show the details to them anymore.

Example 10

			1	8				
	3		4		6			
	8	1				4		
2	6				5	7		
	4			7			6	
		8	9				4	2
		4				6	1	
			8		4		7	
				9	3			

After the basics, we have this grid:

Example 10-1

4	257	2567	1	8	279	259	3	5679
579	3	257	4	25	6	1	259	8
5679	8	1	57	3	279	4	259	5679
2	6	9	3	4	5	7	8	1
1	4	35	2	7	8	359	6	59
357	57	8	9	6	1	35	4	2
8	9	4	57	25	27	6	1	3
356	25	2356	8	1	4	259	7	59
57	1	257	6	9	3	8	25	4

In row 2, the 7 can only appear in 21 or 23. Because these two cells also happen to lie in box 1, we can eliminate candidate 7's anywhere else they appear in box 1. I call this "interaction," because the two cells 21 and 23 interact with the other cells in the box to change their candidates.

At this same point in the solving process, another interaction can be found: In column 8, the 9 can only appear in cell 28 or 38. Both of these cells also lie in box 3, so eliminate any other candidate 9's from box 3.

Example 10-2

4	25	256	1	8	279	25	3	567
579	3	257	4	25	6	1	259	8
569	8	1	57	3	279	4	259	567
2	6	9	3	4	5	7	8	1
1	4	35	2	7	8	359	6	59
357	57	8	9	6	1	35	4	2
8	9	4	57	25	27	6	1	3
356	25	2356	8	1	4	259	7	59
57	1	257	6	9	3	8	25	4

This creates a pair in cells 12 and 17. The 2 and 5 candidates can be removed from cell 13, making that a 6, and then the puzzle can be solved with basic strategies.

Example 10 Answer

4	5	6	1	8	9	2	3	7
7	3	2	4	5	6	1	9	8
9	8	1	7	3	2	4	5	6
2	6	9	3	4	5	7	8	1
1	4	5	2	7	8	3	6	9
3	7	8	9	6	1	5	4	2
8	9	4	5	2	7	6	1	3
6	2	3	8	1	4	9	7	5
5	1	7	6	9	3	8	2	4

In summary, interaction occurs when a certain number can appear in a row or column only in cells that also happen to lie entirely within a box. Then that digit can be removed as candidates from anywhere else in that box. Similarly, if the only places for a number in a box lie in one row (or one column), then that number can be eliminated from the the candidates in that row (or column) outside the box.

ADD SOME COLOR TO YOUR SUDOKU SOLVING

Sudoku is an unforgiving puzzle. If you make a careless mistake and write in the wrong number somewhere, you might not notice the error until several moves later when you reach some sort of contradiction, like two 6's in the same row. Once you realize you've made a mistake, there's no way to go back and figure out where the mistake was made, so you usually have to start over from scratch.

If you find this happening more often than you'd like to admit, there is a trick to help: Solve with colored pencils. Start with red, then after you have filled in 10 numbers or so, switch to orange for the next 10. Continue on through the rainbow (skipping yellow, since it doesn't show up well on white). If you find you have an error, erase the most recent color, and try again. If you get the same error, go back two colors and try again. Continue removing one color at a time until you no longer get the error. Then berate yourself for not being careful about only putting in numbers you are certain of.

One more solving tip: Don't walk and solve. I learned this the hard way. After breaking through a puzzle that had an X-wing and a swordfish (see page 51), my train arrived at the station. I was so close to finishing that I continued to solve while walking home. Glancing up occasionally to make sure I didn't walk into any trees, I wasn't concentrating enough, and I filled in a wrong number. Since I was working in pen and I had no idea which numbers I had just added, the puzzle was wrecked.

49

4								
		2			5	7		
			6	9			3	8
		9	5					1
8		1				9		5
6					4	8		
1	8			4	6			
		6	7			2		
								6

50

	8		2		3	6		5
						3		
		7		9				1
		9		6				4
	5	1		7		9	2	
4				5		8		
1				8		4		
		2						
6		8	4		1		9	

51

	6				2			4
		5	6					
1	2			3				
		8	7				3	1
		4				8		
9	1				8	4		
				9			6	8
					6	3		
5			4				2	

52

2	4			5				6
					3		5	1
	1							
		8			9	4		5
			6	3	5			
6		2	4			9		
							8	
9	6		3					
8				1			9	7

53

3			2					6
							7	
	1			8	6	4		9
		3		1	8			4
8								2
9			3	2		7		
2		8	1	5			4	
	5							
6					4			5

54

		8			1	3		
	7	3					6	
				5		9		4
				9				6
		4	5		6	8		
6				7				
3		9		2				
	4					2	5	
		6	9			1		

55

	3							4
			6			1		
6	4			5			2	
		7		4				
	9	4		1		6	8	
				8		9		
	6			9			5	8
		8			2			
2							9	

56

					9	2		
1	7			8	3			
4		5						
	8		9	7				
9								7
				2	5		9	
						9		1
			1	4			5	8
		6	3					

57

					9		1	
5		1	3					2
	7	2						
		4	5	8				
	5						9	
				4	1	2		
						3	2	
7					3	4		8
	2		7					

58

			1				4	
7	8				2			
				8		2	3	
						6	2	9
	6						1	
1	3	5						
	5	6		9				
			4				9	8
	4				3			

59

					2	1		4
		2	9		6			7
		7		5			3	
	8							9
			6		5			
9							2	
	1			6		4		
5			2		4	6		
4		8	1					

60

						1		
			8			3		5
	1		2		6	8		
4				8	2	7		
3								4
		9	6	4				3
		4	9		3		5	
6		3			7			
		2						

6
CANDIDATE-FREE SOLVING

I solved my first sudoku puzzle in 2000 while editing a book called *Mensa Math & Logic Puzzles* by Dave Tuller and Michael Rios. Four pages in the book are devoted to "Number Place" puzzles of various sizes, and nine of the puzzles are shaped like standard sudoku puzzles (though they don't follow the symmetry rule). So I had to develop my own solving methods years before the puzzle became so popular that it launched countless online forums on solving tips.

In doing this, I developed a technique that doesn't involve writing candidates. It is much simpler to comprehend, so I am including it here. The problem with it, though, is that when you encounter a puzzle that requires some of the more advanced solving techniques that you will learn in the chapters to follow, this technique doesn't work too well, and at some point you'll have to write in candidates. That can get quite ugly when you already have lots of other little numbers written all over the grid, which is what this technique tells you to do.

Here's an example:

Example 11

	7			2	3	9		
	8			6				
		1	5		4			
	4					6		5
2								1
5		6					3	
			9		1	8		
				3			6	
		3	6	4			1	

You start the puzzle just like you normally would, by scanning. A 1 goes in cell 27, then a 1 in cell 14. A 3 goes in cell 79, which puts a 3 in cell 37, which puts a 3 in cell 21, which puts a 3 in cell 52, which allows the 3's to be finished off with a 3 in cell 44. A 6 goes in cell 56, which allows us to place a 5 in cell 55. The 8 in cell 22 prevents an 8 from going in cells 24 and 26, so the only cell left in box 2 for an 8 is cell 35. Now a 9 can be placed in cell 26 and box 2 can be finished off with a 7 in cell 24. Using one-choice, a 7 can be put in cell 75, but then we're stuck with this setup:

Example 11-1

7		1	2	3	9			
	7		1	2	3	9		
3	8		7	6	9	1		
		1	5	8	4	3		
	4		3			6		5
2	3			5	6			1
5		6					3	
			9	7	1	8		3
				3			6	
		3	6	4			1	

But we're not really stuck at all. Check out the 5's. Using scanning, we can determine that in box 1, the 5 has to go in either cell 13 or 23. So write a little 5 on the line separating those cells. In box 3, the 5 must be in either cell 18 or 28. Again, put a small 5 on the line between those cells. Ditto for a little 5 between cells 86 and 96. It now looks something like this (your version probably doesn't use gray numbers, though):

Example 11-2

	7		1	2	3	9		
3	8		7	6	9	1		
		1	5	8	4	3		
	4		3			6		5
2	3			5	6			1
5		6					3	
			9	7	1	8		3
				3			6	
		3	6	4			1	

Now look at box 9. We know from scanning that a 5 can't go in cells 89 or 99. But that little 5 that we just added to the line between cells 18 and 28 also tells us that the 5 can't go in cell 78. We don't yet know whether the 5 in column 8 will go in cell 18 or 28, but it doesn't matter. Either way, a 5 can't go in cell 78. So now in box 9, we've narrowed down the placement of the 5 to two cells. Put it on the line between those cells.

Example 11-3

	7		1	2	3	9		
3	8		7	6	9	1		
		1	5	8	4	3		
	4		3			6		5
2	3			5	6			1
5		6					3	
			9	7	1	8		3
				3			6	
		3	6	4			1	

Now comes the fun part. See those two little 5's in boxes 8 and 9? We don't know where they're going to go, but it's either in cells 86 and 97 or in cells 87 and 96. In either case, rows 8 and 9 have their 5's accounted for by those two little guys. So we scan over to box 7, and with the 5 in cell 61, we can narrow down the 5's placement to cells 72 and 73. But wait! The little 5 in box 1 is going in either cell 13 or 23, so there can't be a 5 in cell 73. Thus, we know for sure that cell 72 is a 5. Once cell 72 has a 5 in it, by elimination we know that cell 71 is a 6. From there it's easy, but I'll go through a few more steps to show what to do when you get to a 5. After placing the 6 in cell 71, cells 11 and 31 can be filled (using one-choice) with 4 and 9, respectively. That leaves 5 as the only possibility for cell 13, so put it in and remove the 5 from the line. Now that you have a 5 in cell 13, that "pushes down" the 5 from the line separating cells 18 and 28 into cell 28 for certain. From there, you're on your own.

Note how these numbers are different from candidates. They are not simply possibilities. They are definite. It's just that their exact placement is not certain.

Example 11 Answer

4	7	5	1	2	3	9	8	6
3	8	2	7	6	9	1	5	4
9	6	1	5	8	4	3	7	2
8	4	7	3	1	2	6	9	5
2	3	9	8	5	6	7	4	1
5	1	6	4	9	7	2	3	8
6	5	4	9	7	1	8	2	3
1	9	8	2	3	5	4	6	7
7	2	3	6	4	8	5	1	9

Here's one more to show this method.

Example 12

		8				5		7
		1		6	8	9		
			1				8	
					2			5
	9		4		7		2	
4			9					
	5				6			
		3	5	4		1		
1		9				8		

Using one-choice, scanning, and elimination, you get to this point:

Example 12-1

		8			4	5	1	7
5		1		6	8	9		
			1		5		8	
	1	7	6		2	4	9	5
	9		4		7		2	1
4			9		1			8
	5		8	1	6			9
	8	3	5	4	9	1		
1		9			3	8	5	

Continuing with little numbers, we get this:

Example 12-2

		8			4	5	1	7
5		1		6	8	9		
			1		5		8	
	1	7	6		2	4	9	5
	9		4		7		2	1
4			9		1			8
	5		8	1	6			9
	8	3	5	4	9	1		
1		9			3	8	5	

The little 6 in box 1 was determined using elimination in row 1. The diagonal 7 in box 2 means that a 7 goes in cell 24 or 35. Likewise, the little 6 in box 7 belongs in either cell 81 or 92. Once all those little numbers have been written in, we can put in some more. The little 7 in row 9 means that a 7 can't go in cell 92, so the 7 in box 7 is limited to cells 71 and 81. And once a 7 is put on the line between cells 71 and 81, then in box 1 we can determine that a 7 must be in either cell 22 or 32. Also, now that we have that little 6 in box 1, we know a 6 can't go in cell 33, so the 6 in column 3 is now limited to cells 53 and 63. Finally, with the 3 limited to cells 29 and 39 in box 3, there is only one possibility left for cell 28, a 4. So now the grid looks like this:

Example 12-3

		8			4	5	1	7
5		1		6	8	9	4	
			1		5		8	
	1	7	6		2	4	9	5
	9		4		7		2	1
4			9		1			8
	5		8	1	6			9
	8	3	5	4	9	1		
1		9			3	8	5	

A 4 can now go in cell 99 from scanning. Once that's in place, the only thing left for cell 92 is a 6, since the 2 and 7 are already in that row in cells 94 and 95. That 6 in cell 92 bumps the little 6 in box 1 into cell 11. The 4 at cell 99 also allows us to scan big row 3 and put a 4 in cell 73. That 4 forces the last 4 into cell 32, which bumps that little 7 in box 1 into cell 22, which in turn bumps the little 7 in box 2 into cell 35. Also, in cells 53 and 63 there are a 5 and a 6 to put in, so there's no room for the little 2 in cell 63. It must go in cell 62. The puzzle now looks like Example 12-4, and at this point you could erase all the little numbers and solve it using just one-choice, so I'll leave the rest to you.

Example 12-4

6		8			4	5	1	7
5	7	1		6	8	9	4	
	4		1	7	5		8	
	1	7	6		2	4	9	5
	9		4		7		2	1
4	2		9		1			8
	5	4	8	1	6			9
	8	3	5	4	9	1		
1	6	9			3	8	5	4

Example 12 Answer

6	3	8	2	9	4	5	1	7
5	7	1	3	6	8	9	4	2
9	4	2	1	7	5	6	8	3
3	1	7	6	8	2	4	9	5
8	9	6	4	5	7	3	2	1
4	2	5	9	3	1	7	6	8
7	5	4	8	1	6	2	3	9
2	8	3	5	4	9	1	7	6
1	6	9	7	2	3	8	5	4

LITTLE NUMBERS ARE NOT JUST FOR NEIGHBORS

The little numbers that I've drawn in this chapter are not limited to adjacent cells (or even diagonally adjacent cells, as I've shown). In diagram 12-2, for example, we know a 4 goes in either cell 73 or 92 in box 7. So write a 4 somewhere between them and draw lines from it pointing to those two cells. If a number is limited to three or more cells, you still can indicate it somehow. It's certainly not pretty, and when you're done the entire grid can be a huge mess, especially if you have to start writing in candidates, but there's nothing quite like filling in the last number of a puzzle that has cross-outs galore in nearly every cell. Plus, the looks you get from the people seated next to you who have never solved a sudoku are priceless.

7
THE X-WING FAMILY

The X-wing, and its sister solving methods (swordfish, jellyfish, and squirmbag), are found in some of the hardest sudoku puzzles.

X-WING

Here is a puzzle that uses an X-wing:

Example 13

9			3					7
5			9			2		
				2	4	3		
					8		6	
4	6			9			1	3
	9		4					
		3	5	7				
		1			9			2
7					2			5

Using basic strategies, we get stuck at this point:

Example 13-1

9	12	246	3	158	156	16	48	7
5	3	467	9	18	167	2	48	16
8	17	67	167	2	4	3	5	9
3	27	257	17	15	8	9	6	4
4	6	8	2	9	57	57	1	3
1	9	57	4	6	3	57	2	8
2	4	3	5	7	16	8	9	16
6	5	1	8	3	9	4	7	2
7	8	9	16	4	2	16	3	5

In columns 2 and 4, the only cells with 7 candidates are 32, 42, 34, and 44. Because these four cells lie in only two different rows (3 and 4), we know that 32 and 44 will contain 7's, or 34 and 42 will contain 7's. In either case, the 7's in rows 3 and 4 will appear in columns 2 and 4. In other words, if cell 33 contained a 7, then neither cell 32 or 34 could contain a 7, so then cells 42 and 44 would both have to be 7's, but that's impossible, since they're in the same row. This grouping is known as an X-wing, and gets its name from the shape formed by connecting cells 34 to 42 and cells 32 to 44, which forms an X. Because of the X-wing, we can eliminate all the 7 candidates wherever else they appear in rows 3 and 4. That means that cell 33 has to be a 6.

Example 13-2

9	12	24	3	158	156	16	48	7
5	3	47	9	18	167	2	48	16
8	17	6	17	2	4	3	5	9
3	27	25	17	15	8	9	6	4
4	6	8	2	9	57	57	1	3
1	9	57	4	6	3	57	2	8
2	4	3	5	7	16	8	9	16
6	5	1	8	3	9	4	7	2
7	8	9	16	4	2	16	3	5

After the 6 is in place at cell 33, another 6 can be placed in cell 94 with elimination (a 6 can't go anywhere else in column 4), and it's smooth sailing from there using basic strategies.

Example 13 Answer

9	2	4	3	1	5	6	8	7
5	3	7	9	8	6	2	4	1
8	1	6	7	2	4	3	5	9
3	7	2	1	5	8	9	6	4
4	6	8	2	9	7	5	1	3
1	9	5	4	6	3	7	2	8
2	4	3	5	7	1	8	9	6
6	5	1	8	3	9	4	7	2
7	8	9	6	4	2	1	3	5

SWORDFISH

Swordfish is similar to X-wing, except it involves three rows (or columns) at once, instead of two. The origins of the names of this and higher-level X-wings are a mystery. Here's a puzzle using swordfish:

Example 14

	3							
			9		3	2		1
6	7			2			3	
9			8		7			
		7				5		
			3		6			7
	8			9			1	6
1		2	5		8			
							2	

We get this far with the basics:

Example 14-1

2	3	14589	1467	145678	145	4679	456789	489
458	45	458	9	45678	3	2	45678	1
6	7	14589	14	2	145	49	3	489
9	1456	13456	8	145	7	1346	46	2
348	146	7	2	14	9	5	468	348
458	2	1458	3	145	6	149	489	7
3457	8	345	47	9	2	347	1	6
1	469	2	5	3467	8	3479	479	349
347	469	3469	1467	13467	14	8	2	5

Now we need to use interaction. The 1 in column 2 will be in either cell 42 or 52, so we can remove the 1 candidates from the other cells in box 4. Similarly, the 9 in column 2 will be in cell 82 or 92, so the 9 can be removed from the candidate list in cell 93. The 9 candidate in cell 82 can be removed because a 9 has to be in row 8 of box 9. The 1, 4, and 5 form a triplet in cells 45, 55, and 65, so 1, 4, and 5 can be removed from the rest of that column.

Example 14-2

2	3	14589	1467	678	145	4679	456789	489
458	45	458	9	678	3	2	45678	1
6	7	14589	14	2	145	49	3	489
9	1456	3456	8	145	7	1346	46	2
348	146	7	2	14	9	5	468	348
458	2	458	3	145	6	149	489	7
3457	8	345	47	9	2	347	1	6
1	46	2	5	367	8	3479	479	349
347	469	346	1467	367	14	8	2	5

Now column 2 has just one 9 in it, so make cell 92 a 9. Cells 21, 22, and 23 form a triplet with 4, 5, and 8. All the 4's, 5's, and 8's can be removed from cells 13, 33, 25, and 28.

Example 14-3

2	3	19	1467	678	145	4679	456789	489
458	45	458	9	67	3	2	67	1
6	7	19	14	2	145	49	3	489
9	1456	3456	8	145	7	1346	46	2
348	146	7	2	14	9	5	468	348
458	2	458	3	145	6	149	489	7
3457	8	345	47	9	2	347	1	6
1	46	2	5	367	8	3479	479	349
347	9	346	1467	367	14	8	2	5

Using previously learned methods, we get to the grid in the next column (in row 1 a triplet allowed us to eliminate candidates 1, 4, and 9 in cells 14 and 17).

Example 14-4

2	3	19	67	8	14	67	5	49
458	45	458	9	67	3	2	67	1
6	7	19	14	2	5	49	3	8
9	1456	3456	8	145	7	1346	46	2
348	146	7	2	14	9	5	468	34
458	2	458	3	145	6	149	489	7
3457	8	345	47	9	2	347	1	6
1	46	2	5	367	8	3479	479	349
347	9	346	1467	367	14	8	2	5

Now we have a swordfish. In rows 2, 5, and 8, the only cells with 6's as candidates are 25, 28, 52, 58, 82, and 85. Because these cells lie in exactly three different columns (2, 5, and 8), we can eliminate the 6 candidates wherever else they appear in columns 2, 5, and 8.

Example 14 Swordfish

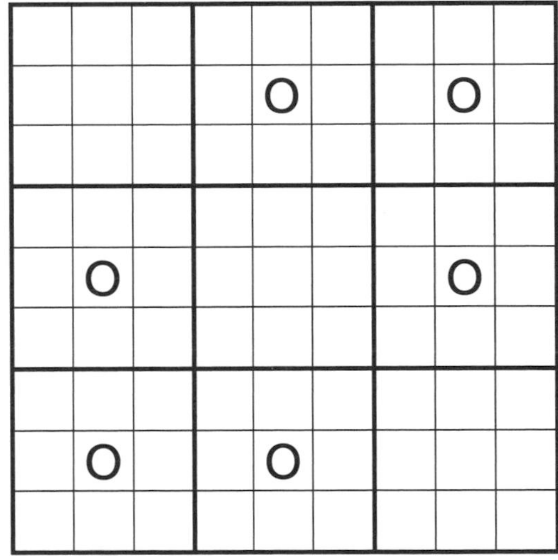

In the diagram above, the circles show where the 6's can go in rows 2, 5, and 8. There are two possible arrangements. One is with 6's in cells 25, 58, and 82. The other is with 6's in cells 28, 52, and 85. But in either case, a 6 will be in one of cells 52 and 82, one of cells 25 and 85, and one of cells 28 and 58. Therefore, the 6's are accounted for in columns 2, 5, and 8, and can be removed from the candidates in those columns outside of rows 2, 5, and 8.

It is important to note that a swordfish doesn't have to have just two possible places for the 6 in each row. If cell 22 also had a 6 candidate, or cell 55, or cell 88 (or any combination of these), it would still be a swordfish. We'd know that the 6's in columns 2, 5, and 8 had to go somewhere in rows 2, 5, and 8, and could be eliminated from the other cells in those columns.

Removing the 6's, we get this:

Example 14-5

2	3	19	1467	8	14	4679	5	489
458	45	458	9	67	3	2	67	1
6	7	19	14	2	5	49	3	8
9	145	3456	8	145	7	1346	4	2
348	146	7	2	14	9	5	468	34
458	2	458	3	145	6	149	489	7
3457	8	345	47	9	2	347	1	6
1	46	2	5	367	8	3479	479	349
347	9	346	1467	37	14	8	2	5

By removing the 6 from cell 48 with the swordfish, we now know it has to be a 4, and the rest can be solved using basic strategies.

Example 14 Answer

2	3	9	6	8	1	7	5	4
8	5	4	9	7	3	2	6	1
6	7	1	4	2	5	9	3	8
9	1	3	8	5	7	6	4	2
4	6	7	2	1	9	5	8	3
5	2	8	3	4	6	1	9	7
3	8	5	7	9	2	4	1	6
1	4	2	5	6	8	3	7	9
7	9	6	1	3	4	8	2	5

JELLYFISH

Just as we went from pairs to triplets to quadruplets in the subsets section, here we move from X-wing to swordfish to jellyfish:

Example 15

	2			1	8			4
	5				6		3	2
7				5		8		9
			4		7			
6		2		9				5
2	9		3				4	
3			6	8			9	

We get stuck after using basic strategies at this point:

Example 15-1

9	2	3	7	1	8	6	5	4
148	1467	14678	25	3	25	9	18	178
18	5	178	9	4	6	17	3	2
7	134	14	12	5	123	8	6	9
5	8	9	4	6	7	13	2	13
6	13	2	8	9	13	4	7	5
2	9	168	3	7	15	15	4	168
148	1467	14678	15	2	9	1357	18	13678
3	17	5	6	8	4	2	9	17

Using interaction, we can eliminate some candidates. The 8's in cells 21 and 23 can be removed since we know that the 8 in row 3 will be in cell 31 or 33. Cells 76 and 77 form a pair and allow us to eliminate 1's in cells 73 and 79.

Example 15-2

9	2	3	7	1	8	6	5	4
14	1467	1467	25	3	25	9	18	178
18	5	178	9	4	6	17	3	2
7	134	14	12	5	123	8	6	9
5	8	9	4	6	7	13	2	13
6	13	2	8	9	13	4	7	5
2	9	68	3	7	15	15	4	68
148	1467	14678	15	2	9	1357	18	13678
3	17	5	6	8	4	2	9	17

At this point we must use jellyfish to continue. In rows 5, 6, 7, and 9, the only cells with 1 candidates are 57, 59, 62, 66, 76, 77, 92, and 99. Because these eight cells lie in exactly four different columns (2, 6, 7, and 9), we can eliminate candidate 1's wherever else they appear in columns 2, 6, 7, and 9. This removes 1's from the cells 22, 42, 82, 46, 37, 87, 29, and 89.

Example 15 Jellyfish

						O		O
	O				O			
					O	O		
	O							O

This is just like the swordfish, but involving four rows instead of three. Note again that it doesn't have to be exactly two occurrences of each number in the rows for this to work. As long as they all fall in four columns, it doesn't matter if the rows have 2, 3, or 4 possible places for 1's to go.

Example 15-3

9	2	3	7	1	8	6	5	4
14	467	1467	25	3	25	9	18	78
18	5	178	9	4	6	7	3	2
7	34	14	12	5	23	8	6	9
5	8	9	4	6	7	13	2	13
6	13	2	8	9	13	4	7	5
2	9	68	3	7	15	15	4	68
148	467	14678	15	2	9	357	18	3678
3	17	5	6	8	4	2	9	17

With the 1 removed from cell 37, that becomes a 7. And putting a 7 in cell 37 makes cell 29 an 8, since the jellyfish also removed the 1 candidate from cell 29. Then we're home free with basic strategies.

Example 15 Answer

9	2	3	7	1	8	6	5	4
4	6	7	2	3	5	9	1	8
8	5	1	9	4	6	7	3	2
7	3	4	1	5	2	8	6	9
5	8	9	4	6	7	1	2	3
6	1	2	8	9	3	4	7	5
2	9	8	3	7	1	5	4	6
1	4	6	5	2	9	3	8	7
3	7	5	6	8	4	2	9	1

SQUIRMBAG

On to the squirmbag, which is just like a jellyfish except with one more level.

Example 16

1					8		4	
		4		3				9
	2		4		6		8	
		5	9	7		2		
		2		4	1	5		
	8		1		9		5	
5				8		7		
	4		3					1

You won't likely ever find a puzzle that requires you to use a squirmbag. They're extremely rare (even the jellyfish is quite rare). In this puzzle, it's not needed for solving, but we'll use it anyway, just to demonstrate the concept. Suppose you get to this point and you don't see any more obvious moves:

Example 16-1

1	3579	379	257	259	8	6	4	257
8	567	4	257	3	257	1	27	9
79	2	79	4	1	6	3	8	57
4	16	5	9	7	3	2	16	8
367	1367	8	256	256	25	9	1367	3467
3679	3679	2	8	4	1	5	367	367
2367	8	367	1	26	9	4	5	236
5	369	1	26	8	24	7	2369	236
2679	4	679	3	256	257	8	269	1

In columns 1, 3, 4, 5, and 9, the cells with 6's among the candidates are 51, 61, 71, 91, 73, 93, 54, 84, 55, 75, 95, 59, 69, 79, and 89. Because these cells lie in exactly five different rows (5, 6, 7, 8, and 9), we can eliminate the 6's wherever else they appear in rows 5, 6, 7, 8, and 9.

Here's a diagram of the cells with the 6's that form the squirmbag:

Example 16 Squirmbag

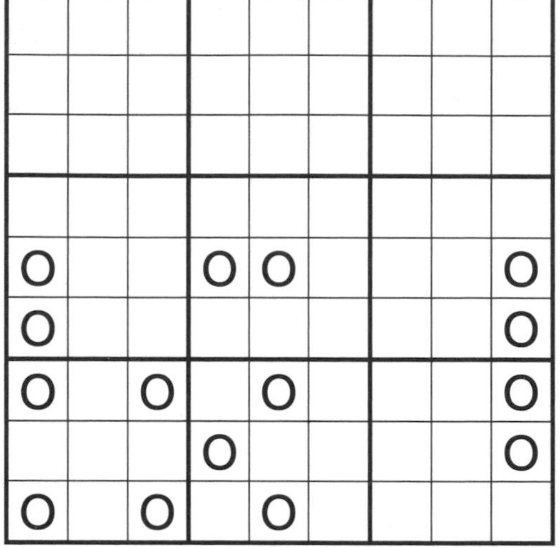

The cells that have their 6's eliminated are 52, 62, 82, 58, 68, 88, and 98. That leaves just one 6 in column 8, at cell 48. That 6 forces cell 42 to be a 1, and then column 2 has just one 6, at cell 22. From there the puzzle can be solved using scanning, one-choice, and elimination.

Example 16 Answer

1	5	3	7	9	8	6	4	2
8	6	4	5	3	2	1	7	9
7	2	9	4	1	6	3	8	5
4	1	5	9	7	3	2	6	8
3	7	8	6	2	5	9	1	4
6	9	2	8	4	1	5	3	7
2	8	7	1	6	9	4	5	3
5	3	1	2	8	4	7	9	6
9	4	6	3	5	7	8	2	1

61

			9					2
				4		1	9	
			1	5		7	4	6
		6		2		5		
5				1				4
		1		3		2		
9	5	3		6	2			
	6	7		9				
2					5			

62

	6	5		2				9
			4					
7	2				5		3	
		9				3	8	
2								7
	5	8				2		
	1		7				9	6
					6			
6				9		8	5	

63

	5	9	3		6			
7					1			
	2			7		3		
			6		5		4	
1				8				2
	9		1		7			
		2		3			8	
			8					9
			5		9	1	2	

64

	3	8	2				7	
6	7		9				2	
			1					
7						8		
		4		7		2		
		5						4
					3			
	9				1		5	7
	8				4	9	6	

65

	4				2	1	7	
6		1						
		5	7			4		
5	3			2				
			4		9			
				7			4	8
		8			5	2		
						6		4
	2	6	1				3	

66

1		4				6		2
			9	2				4
				5	4			
6		1				7		5
	8			3			1	
4		5				2		8
			2	1				
9				6	7			
7		2				8		1

67

4		1					9	
					7	3		
	7		4				6	
	4		6	3	1			7
6								3
3			5	9	2		4	
	3				6		7	
		2	7					
	9					1		2

68

		5			7	1		
		7		1		5		4
					8			9
					6			1
		8				7		
6			9					
5			8					
4		2		7		8		
		1	5			2		

69

	6		8		5	7		
				7				5
			6			1	3	
3								6
	1		4		9		5	
9								1
	9	1			4			
8				2				
		5	7		3		9	

70

	3			1		5		
					5		6	
		8	4		7		2	3
			1					2
	2	1				6	4	
4					9			
3	6		5		1	8		
	8		7					
		5		2			1	

71

			4				6	
		1		6		3		8
	6				3		5	
6				8		1		
	3		2		4		9	
		4		3				2
	8		7				3	
2		6		9		8		
	4				8			

72

8						6		1
		4	1			9	7	
		7	8					
		1	2				5	9
				9				
5	8				6	2		
					5	3		
	4	8			3	1		
9		5						4

8
GORDONIAN LOGIC

If you ask a casual sudoku solver what the rules to the puzzle are, chances are that the answer you get will explain that every row, column, and 3×3 box must contain the numbers 1 to 9, and that will be it. As noted earlier, there are a few other rules. One states that you can have no more than 30 given numbers at the start. Another says that the cells that are occupied with numbers at the start need to be symmetric (so if the upper left cell has a number in it, the lower right cell must have one, too). Another rule (not followed by everyone) is that you should be able to reach the solution through logical means. And the final rule is that the puzzle can have only one possible answer. That rule is the key to Gordonian Logic.

GORDONIAN RECTANGLES

Early on in the sudoku craze, Frank Longo, who wrote all the examples and puzzles in this book, sent me a puzzle that he claimed was not solvable without guessing. I love a challenge, so I gave it a shot. The starting grid is shown, labeled Example 17. I was breezing through the puzzle, thinking to myself that the puzzle was for beginners, until I got to the point shown in Example 17-1.

Example 17

		8	4	1	3	5		
	2	5						3
			3	7			2	9
8	6			2	1			
5						1	6	
		9	6	5	8	7		

Example 17-1

6	9	8	4	1	3	5	7	2
37	34	47	257	69	2579	69	8	1
1	2	5	78	689	79	69	4	3
4	5	1	3	7	6	8	2	9
9	7	2	58	48	45	3	1	6
8	6	3	9	2	1	4	5	7
5	34	47	27	349	2479	1	6	8
37	8	6	1	34	47	2	9	5
2	1	9	6	5	8	7	3	4

I wasn't stumped yet, though. The cells 24 and 26 are the only ones in row 2 that have 2's and 5's as candidates, so they form a hidden pair. The other possibilities can be removed from those cells. And in row 8, the 4 has to be in either cell 85 or 86, so the 4's can be removed from the candidate lists of cells 75 and 76. That leaves this grid:

Example 17-2

6	9	8	4	1	3	5	7	2
37	34	47	25	69	25	69	8	1
1	2	5	78	689	79	69	4	3
4	5	1	3	7	6	8	2	9
9	7	2	58	48	45	3	1	6
8	6	3	9	2	1	4	5	7
5	34	47	27	39	279	1	6	8
37	8	6	1	34	47	2	9	5
2	1	9	6	5	8	7	3	4

I then stared at this grid for a long, long time. Finally I had a breakthrough that revolutionized my sudoku solving. It was a method that turned hard-to-solve puzzles into mere pushovers. I dubbed it Gordonian Rectangles. Here's how it works. Suppose that cell 35 isn't an 8. You'd then have this as part of the grid:

Example 17 With No 8 at Cell 35

				69		69		
				69		69		

With no 8 at cell 35, how would you finish this puzzle? No matter what other numbers you put in, you'd never have anything to tell you where the 6's and 9's went in cells 25, 27, 35, and 37. Rows 2 and 3, columns 5 and 7, and boxes 2 and 3 each have pairs with the numbers 6 and 9 in those four cells, so nothing will determine if the 6's go in 27 and 35 and the 9's in 25 and 37, or vice versa. In other words, without the 8 in cell 35, there would be two valid answers. But since the puzzle was tested by Frank's computer, I knew that it had to have just one valid solution, so I reasoned that if the 8 weren't in cell 35, the rest of the numbers would necessarily form an impossibility. They had to, or else the two possible ways to place the 6's and 9's shown below and on the next page would create two valid answers. So, if not having an 8 in cell 35 meant there would be an impossible situation somewhere in the puzzle eventually, then an 8 necessarily had to go in cell 35. I confidently filled in the 8. The diagram is shown in Example 17-3, with the 8's removed from cell 35's buddies.

Example 17 With No 8 at Cell 35 Answer 1

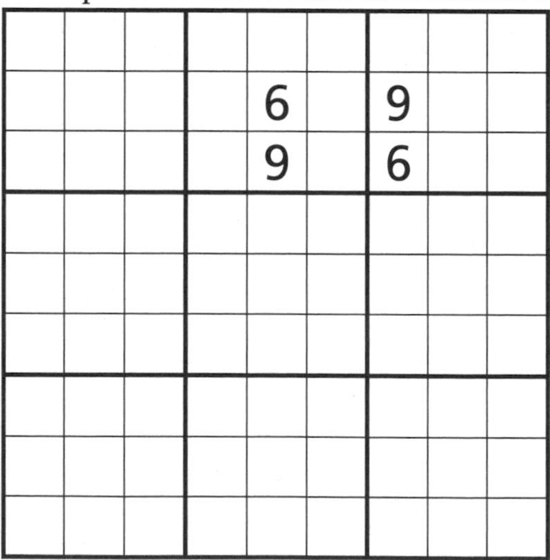

Example 17 With No 8 at Cell 35 Answer 2

				9		6		
				6		9		

Example 17-3

6	9	8	4	1	3	5	7	2
37	34	47	25	69	25	69	8	1
1	2	5	7	8	79	69	4	3
4	5	1	3	7	6	8	2	9
9	7	2	58	4	45	3	1	6
8	6	3	9	2	1	4	5	7
5	34	47	27	39	279	1	6	8
37	8	6	1	34	47	2	9	5
2	1	9	6	5	8	7	3	4

Once that 8 is placed, the puzzle can be solved on autopilot.

Example 17 Answer

6	9	8	4	1	3	5	7	2
3	4	7	5	6	2	9	8	1
1	2	5	7	8	9	6	4	3
4	5	1	3	7	6	8	2	9
9	7	2	8	4	5	3	1	6
8	6	3	9	2	1	4	5	7
5	3	4	2	9	7	1	6	8
7	8	6	1	3	4	2	9	5
2	1	9	6	5	8	7	3	4

Let's look at another:

Example 18

	3	4			5			8
						4	9	1
				2			6	
	1		5					7
		2	1	7	4	6		
5					3		1	
	6			4				
3	8	1						
4			7			5	3	

After using the methods we know, this is where we get stuck:

Example 18-1

19	3	4	69	169	5	27	27	8
2	5	6	8	3	7	4	9	1
19	7	8	4	2	19	3	6	5
6	1	3	5	89	289	289	4	7
8	9	2	1	7	4	6	5	3
5	4	7	269	689	3	289	1	29
7	6	5	3	4	29	1	8	29
3	8	1	29	5	6	279	27	4
4	2	9	7	18	18	5	3	6

Can you spot where the Gordonian Rectangle is? Unlike X-wing and its cousins, Gordonian Rectangles are simple to see. Within one box, you need to have two cells that have the same pair of numbers in either the same row or the same column. Then you need to look to see if you can form a rectangle with one corner having the same pair, and another with that pair plus a third number. In this diagram, cells 11 and 31 form the start of a Gordonian Rectangle, and cell 36 has the same pair, but cell 16 would have to have three candidates including 1 and 9 for this to qualify, but instead it's already known to be a 5. Cells 95 and 96 start off a potential Gordonian Rectangle, but there is no other cell with the pair of 1 and 8 as possibilities in column 5 or 6. The only potential one left is with the cells at 17 and 18, and sure enough, cell 88 has the same two candidates, while cell 87 has those two plus one more. If cell 87 were not a 9, we'd have two solutions if the rest of the puzzle worked, and we know that can't be, so we know that cell 87 must be a 9. Once that 9 is placed, the rest of the numbers fall into place.

Example 18 Answer

1	3	4	9	6	5	7	2	8
2	5	6	8	3	7	4	9	1
9	7	8	4	2	1	3	6	5
6	1	3	5	9	2	8	4	7
8	9	2	1	7	4	6	5	3
5	4	7	6	8	3	2	1	9
7	6	5	3	4	9	1	8	2
3	8	1	2	5	6	9	7	4
4	2	9	7	1	8	5	3	6

GORDONIAN RECTANGLES PLUS

It didn't take long to realize that if the corner of the rectangle with the third candidate also had additional candidates, you could still get somewhere using Gordonian Rectangles. My sudoku buddy and coauthor Frank Longo dubbed this Gordonian Rectangles Plus. Here's an example:

Example 19

			3		4	1		
3			2	9				6
7						3		
	6				3	2		
			7		5			
		7	1				4	
		2						5
6				1	9			8
		5	6		7			

After doing all the stuff we've already learned, this is what you have:

Example 19-1

89	59	6	3	7	4	1	58	2
3	45	48	2	9	1	578	578	6
7	2	1	8	5	6	3	9	4
15	6	48	9	48	3	2	15	7
2	14	9	7	468	5	68	1368	13
58	3	7	1	68	2	568	4	9
19	19	2	4	3	8	67	67	5
6	7	3	5	1	9	4	2	8
4	8	5	6	2	7	9	13	13

The Gordonian Rectangle Plus is in cells 58, 59, 98, and 99. We can't tell if cell 58 is a 6 or an 8, but we know for certain that it can't be 1 or 3, since that would mean two valid answers. Once we eliminate 1 and 3 from cell 58's candidates, we have a pair. Both cell 57 and 58 have 6 and 8 as their only candidates, so one must be 6 and the other must be 8. That means that cell 55 can't have a 6 or 8 in it, so it must be a 4. Putting that 4 in reduces the puzzle to a gimme.

Example 19 Answer

9	5	6	3	7	4	1	8	2
3	4	8	2	9	1	7	5	6
7	2	1	8	5	6	3	9	4
5	6	4	9	8	3	2	1	7
2	1	9	7	4	5	8	6	3
8	3	7	1	6	2	5	4	9
1	9	2	4	3	8	6	7	5
6	7	3	5	1	9	4	2	8
4	8	5	6	2	7	9	3	1

SOME WARNINGS

You need to be careful when you're looking for Gordonian Rectangles to remember that the four corners must fall in only two boxes. Here is a setup that is *not* a Gordonian Rectangle:

Not a Gordonian Rectangle

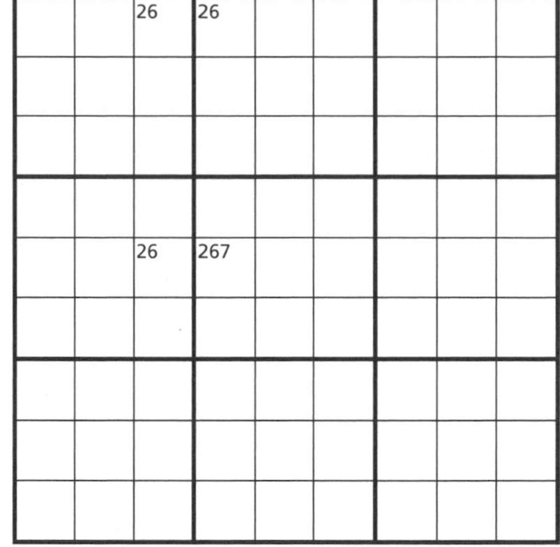

This is not a Gordonian Rectangle because the four corners of the rectangle are in four different boxes. Cell 54 doesn't necessarily need to be a 7. It *could* be a 7, but it could just as easily be a 2 or 6. When the rest of the cells are filled in, it's not possible to swap the contents of the rectangle's corners and still keep the solution valid.

Another concern is that the solution may not be unique. How do you know when sitting down with a puzzle that there is only one answer? Well, technically, you don't. But you also don't know that the puzzle will work at all. The fact that it's in a newspaper and that only one answer will appear the next day, or it's in a magazine or book with a single answer in the answer section tells you that it's presumably been checked to make sure there is just one possible answer. What's interesting is that the programmers can't use Gordonian Rectangles when testing their puzzle unless they have first checked some other way to see if the puzzle has a unique solution. Online sites that automatically solve puzzles, like sudokusolver.co.uk, never *assume* that a puzzle has a unique solution, since they are used by sudoku writers to make sure their hand-generated puzzles are unique, so they often can't solve puzzles involving Gordonian Rectangles (the three puzzles above couldn't be solved by the online solver) unless you allow it to guess and then check the solution.

ONE-SIDED GORDONIAN RECTANGLES

Once I got started on Gordonian Rectangles, the ideas just kept coming. Here's another one:

Example 20

					3		2	
			6	4				
	3	5		7		8		1
	9				7			2
3		2				1		9
1			2				7	
2		4		9		3	6	
				3	4			
	8		7					

Without Gordonian Logic, you stop here:

Example 20-1

478	14	179	158	58	3	79	2	6
78	2	179	6	4	18	79	3	5
6	3	5	9	7	2	8	4	1
45	9	68	3	1	7	46	58	2
3	7	2	4	6	58	1	58	9
1	45	68	2	58	9	46	7	3
2	15	4	158	9	158	3	6	7
57	6	17	15	3	4	2	9	8
9	8	3	7	2	6	5	1	4

A One-Sided Gordonian Rectangle occurs when you have four cells in two different boxes where two adjacent sides have the same two candidates and the other two sides have those two candidates plus the same third candidate. Cells 13, 23, 17, and 27 form one. If we assume that cells 13 and 23 both do not contain a 1, that would result in two valid solutions, since we could have either 7's in cells 13 and 27 and 9's in cells 23 and 17, or 9's in cells 13 and 27 and 7's in cells 23 and 17. Since we know that there is one solution only, we know that either cell 13 or 23 has to have a 1 in it. And that tells us that cell 83 cannot contain a 1, so it must be a 7. Once you place that 7, the rest of the puzzle is a walk in the park.

Example 20 Answer

7	4	1	8	5	3	9	2	6
8	2	9	6	4	1	7	3	5
6	3	5	9	7	2	8	4	1
4	9	8	3	1	7	6	5	2
3	7	2	4	6	5	1	8	9
1	5	6	2	8	9	4	7	3
2	1	4	5	9	8	3	6	7
5	6	7	1	3	4	2	9	8
9	8	3	7	2	6	5	1	4

GORDONIAN POLYGONS

What works for rectangles also works for figures of more than four sides. The idea for these came to me while walking home from work after spending too much time on sudoku books.

Example 21

		8						
	6		8		4	9	3	
4					2	1		
2	9	3				4	5	
				4				
	4	1				3	6	9
		6	2					3
	8	4	5		9		2	
						8		

Using all of our standard methods gets us to this point:

Example 21-1

35	2	8	136	9	16	56	7	4
1	6	57	8	57	4	9	3	2
4	357	9	36	57	2	1	8	56
2	9	3	16	168	168	4	5	7
6	57	57	9	4	3	2	1	8
8	4	1	7	2	5	3	6	9
9	15	6	2	18	178	57	4	3
37	8	4	5	136	9	67	2	16
357	135	2	4	136	167	8	9	156

Check out the contents of cells 23, 25, 32, 35, 52, and 53. Each cell contains just the candidates 5 and 7, except for cell 32, which has 3 as an additional candidate. These cells form a polygon as shown below in which the vertices are in pairs in each row, column, and box. There are exactly two vertices in rows 2, 3, and 5, exactly two vertices in columns 2, 3, and 5, and exactly two vertices in boxes 1, 2, and 4. If cell 32 weren't a 3, there would be no way to ever determine whether those six cells are (going clockwise from cell 32) 5-7-5-7-5-7 or 7-5-7-5-7-5. So cell 32 must be a 3.

Example 21 Gordonian Polygon

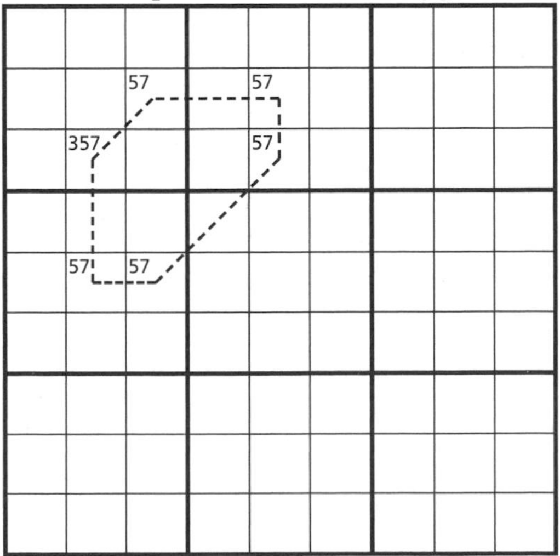

With the 3 in cell 32, finishing up is a snap.

Example 21 Answer

5	2	8	3	9	1	6	7	4
1	6	7	8	5	4	9	3	2
4	3	9	6	7	2	1	8	5
2	9	3	1	6	8	4	5	7
6	7	5	9	4	3	2	1	8
8	4	1	7	2	5	3	6	9
9	1	6	2	8	7	5	4	3
3	8	4	5	1	9	7	2	6
7	5	2	4	3	6	8	9	1

GORDONIAN POLYGONS PLUS

Just as Gordonian Rectangles led to Gordonian Rectangles Plus, Gordonian Polygons leads to Gordonian Polygons Plus. In these you have a polygon where all but one vertex has two candidates, and the last vertex has those same two candidates plus two or more others. You can narrow down the possibilities of the last vertex to the candidates that aren't shared with the other vertices. As always, an example helps.

Example 22

	2							
4					9			5
	8		3		5			2
9				8		1		
5	3		7		1		6	8
		6		5				9
6			9		4		8	
3			1					7
							4	

Things appear to be stuck at this point:

Example 22-1

17	2	5	8	1467	67	3469	39	346
4	6	3	2	17	9	8	17	5
17	8	9	3	46	5	46	17	2
9	47	247	6	8	23	1	5	34
5	3	24	7	9	1	24	6	8
8	1	6	4	5	23	7	23	9
6	57	17	9	237	4	235	8	13
3	459	48	1	26	68	2569	29	7
2	79	178	5	367	678	369	4	136

To find the Gordonian Polygon, look for a pair of candidates that appears several times. If you can connect them with one cell that has those two candidates plus at least one other, and the vertices are in pairs in all the rows, columns, and boxes, then you've got it. Here, all those cells with candidates 1 and 7 stand out like a sore thumb. Connecting cells 11, 31, 38, 28, and 25 with the key cell, 15, creates a Gordonian Polygon Plus, since cell 15 has more than three candidates. We can eliminate candidates 1 and 7 from cell 15, leaving 4 and 6 as candidates, which form a pair with cell 35. Because of that pair, the 6 in column 5 will be in cell 15 or 35, so a 6 can't be in cell 85, which means cell 85 has to be a 2. Put the 2 in and the rest is duck soup.

Example 22 Answer

1	2	5	8	6	7	9	3	4
4	6	3	2	1	9	8	7	5
7	8	9	3	4	5	6	1	2
9	7	4	6	8	2	1	5	3
5	3	2	7	9	1	4	6	8
8	1	6	4	5	3	7	2	9
6	5	7	9	3	4	2	8	1
3	4	8	1	2	6	5	9	7
2	9	1	5	7	8	3	4	6

ONE-SIDED GORDONIAN POLYGONS

You had to know it was coming.

Example 23

	6			8				
		9	4	5			2	
	1		7			4	3	
		6						2
		7		2		6		
8						7		
	9	2			5		6	
	7			6	4	8		
				7			4	

Here's the point at which Gordonian Logic is needed to continue:

Example 23-1

23	6	4	13	8	123	59	7	59
7	38	9	4	5	36	1	2	68
25	1	58	7	9	26	4	3	68
1359	345	6	159	34	7	59	8	2
1359	345	7	159	2	8	6	159	34
8	2	15	6	34	19	7	159	34
4	9	2	8	1	5	3	6	7
15	7	3	2	6	4	8	59	159
6	58	158	39	7	39	2	4	15

The One-Sided Gordonian Polygon is at cells 42, 45, 52, 59, 65, and 69. It's just like a Gordonian Polygon except that two adjacent vertices have three candidates. In this case, they're cells 42 and 52. One of those two must be a 5, so we know that cell 92 cannot be a 5, and thus must be an 8. That gives you a green light to speed ahead to the finish.

Example 23 Answer

2	6	4	3	8	1	5	7	9
7	3	9	4	5	6	1	2	8
5	1	8	7	9	2	4	3	6
3	5	6	1	4	7	9	8	2
9	4	7	5	2	8	6	1	3
8	2	1	6	3	9	7	5	4
4	9	2	8	1	5	3	6	7
1	7	3	2	6	4	8	9	5
6	8	5	9	7	3	2	4	1

STILL MORE GORDONIAN SHAPES

Once you understand the concept of Gordonian Logic, you can use it whenever you encounter a situation where there is a potential for two solutions. Since you know there can't be two solutions, you can choose the candidate that prevents it. Here are two examples.

EXTENDED GORDONIAN RECTANGLES

This variant on the Gordonian Rectangle was discovered by Francis Heaney, and is sometimes called a Franciscan Rectangle. Here's the situation in a nutshell:

Extended Gordonian Rectangle

		23			12			13
		23			12			134

Here we know that the cell with three candidates must be a 4. If it weren't a 4, there would be two valid solutions, as shown in the next column, and we know there is one solution only, so we know a 1 or 3 in the "134" cell must lead to an impossibility.

Extended Gordonian Rectangle Possibilities

		3			2			1
		2			1			3

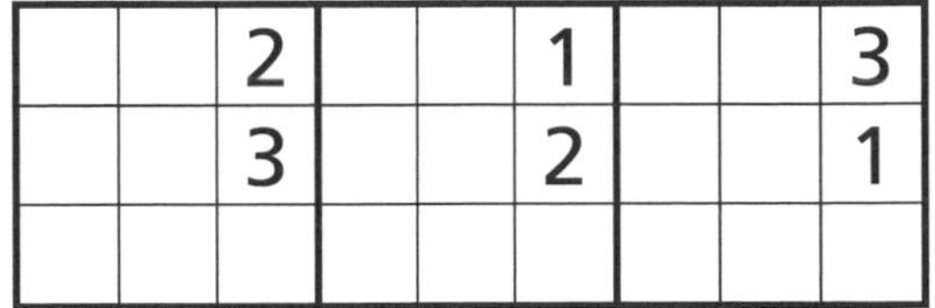

		2			1			3
		3			2			1

Of course, this type of Gordonian Rectangle can be one-sided, as well. If the cell with candidates 1 and 3 instead had the candidates 1, 3, and 4, we'd know that the 4 had to be somewhere in one of the two cells with 1, 3, and 4, and we could eliminate 4 as a candidate from other cells in that column.

Below is an example of a puzzle that requires the use of an Extended Gordonian Rectangle.

Example 24

3						4		
	1	4		6	7			
		9			2		1	6
	3				8	9	4	
				5				
	9	2	6				7	
6	2		9			7		
			2	7		6	8	
		8						2

We get halted in our tracks at this point:

Example 24-1

3	6	5	8	9	1	4	2	7
2	1	4	35	6	7	8	35	9
78	78	9	345	34	2	35	1	6
1	3	6	7	2	8	9	4	5
48	48	7	1	5	9	2	6	3
5	9	2	6	34	34	1	7	8
6	2	13	9	8	345	7	35	14
9	45	13	2	7	345	6	8	14
47	457	8	34	1	6	35	9	2

Looking at cells 31, 32, 51, 52, 91, and 92, we know that if cell 92 were not a 5, then there would be two valid ways to arrange the numbers 4, 7, and 8 in those six cells, so we can conclude that cell 92 must be a 5. Once you have that 5, it's a cinch to finish. (In this same diagram is an unhelpful One-Sided Extended Gordonian Rectangle, in cells 73, 83, 76, 86, 79, and 89. We know that either cell 76 or 86 is a 5, but that gets us nowhere.)

Example 24 Answer

3	6	5	8	9	1	4	2	7
2	1	4	5	6	7	8	3	9
8	7	9	3	4	2	5	1	6
1	3	6	7	2	8	9	4	5
4	8	7	1	5	9	2	6	3
5	9	2	6	3	4	1	7	8
6	2	1	9	8	3	7	5	4
9	4	3	2	7	5	6	8	1
7	5	8	4	1	6	3	9	2

GORDONIAN RECTANGLE WING

This is sort of a combination between a Gordonian Rectangle and an XY-wing, which you will learn about in Chapter 9. Suppose you come to a situation like this:

Gordonian Rectangle Wing

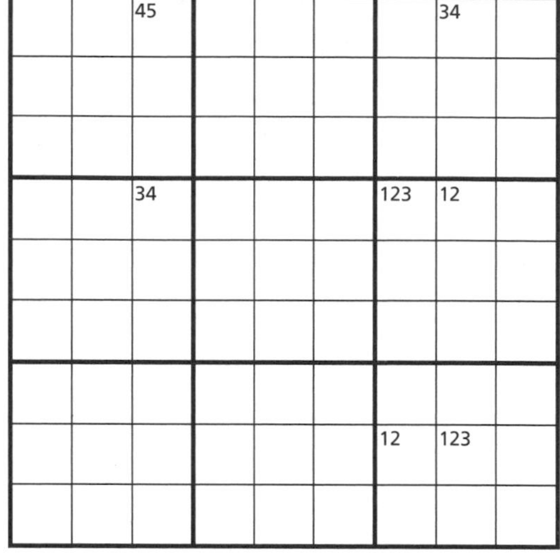

Cells 47, 48, 87, and 88 form a kind of Gordonian Rectangle. We know for certain that a 3 has to be in either cell 47 or cell 88. If cell 47 is a 3, then cell 43 would have to be a 4, which means that cell 13 would be a 5. And if cell 88 is a 3, then cell 18 would have to be a 4, and again that means that cell 13 would be a 5. So while we don't know if it's cell 47 or 88 that is the 3, we know that one of them has to be a 3, and no matter which of them is a 3, the result is the same: Cell 13 is a 5.

Naturally, the same kind of situation can arise with Gordonian Polygons. The possibilities are almost endless. For example, in the above diagram, if cell 58, 68, 77, or 97 had 3's in its candidate list, the 3 could be removed, since having a 3 in any of those cells would create two solutions in cells 47, 48, 87, and 88.

73

7			1				2	
		5		7				
8			2		4			
6		1			8	3		
5								2
		7	9			4		5
			6		1			4
				8		2		
	9				2			6

74

4			6					
	8		9	1		3		
	9		5		8			
	3	6						
		7		4		5		
						2	3	
			4		6		9	
		4		5	2		6	
					1			8

75

3						7	6	
	5							
	1	7	9		2			
9		6		4	5			
		4				5		
			3	1		9		4
			2		7	1	8	
							3	
	7	1						2

76

8							4	
	6				9	7	2	
		2		7		8		
3			6				9	
6			2		8			5
	1				5			4
		4		5		3		
	8	6	7				1	
	3							6

77

	3	6			5			
					8		7	5
						2		
7			8		9			
8	1						9	7
			1		3			4
		9						
2	6		3					
			6			4	5	

78

			7		5			
		5		2		8		
	9		8		1		7	
9		2				3		5
	5						8	
3		1				6		4
	1		5		8		4	
		4		1		7		
			4		3			

79

					2			6
		6	4	7		3		
1		9						
9	4						8	
7		2		8		5		9
	5						1	7
						9		3
		8		6	7	1		
4			5					

80

		2	5					
	3			7				
	5			6		3	9	2
		1	4			5		
		3				9		
		4			1	6		
6	7	9		1			5	
				9			8	
					7	1		

81

		5	7			3		
3		2	8		6			
8				4				7
5						1		
	8		9		1		4	
		1						5
6				9				4
			2		4	8		3
		4			5	9		

82

9						3		8
	2		9	7		5		
		3					2	
				5	9			
1		2		6		7		3
			2	1				
	7					8		
		4		3	5		1	
5		8						2

83

						7	8	
			5	8				
8		3		4			9	
				7	5	9		3
3		4	1	2				
	1			9		2		8
				6	7			
	9	6						

84

				4	8	3	7	
3	2	6	7					
	8				6			
1				2		6		
	4						3	
		2		8				5
			6				5	
					4	1	8	2
	7	1	8	9				

9
FORCING CHAINS AND GRID COLORING

On rare occasions in really hard puzzles you will still be stuck even if you try all of the previous methods. For those puzzles, you need to bring out the heavy artillery.

FORCING CHAINS

In a forcing chain, you examine all the possibilities of a situation and hope they all lead to one result. If they do, you know that result is true.

XY-WING

An XY-wing occurs when you have a situation like this:

XY-Wing

O	XY	O		XZ				
YZ			O	O	O			

We don't know whether cell 12 is an X or a Y, but we know it has to be one of those two. Let's try both possibilities, and see what happens to the cells with the circles in them.

XY-Wing With Cell 12 = X

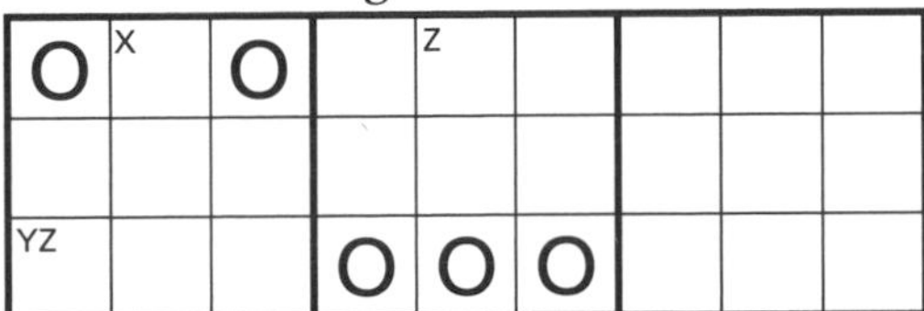

XY-Wing With Cell 12 = Y

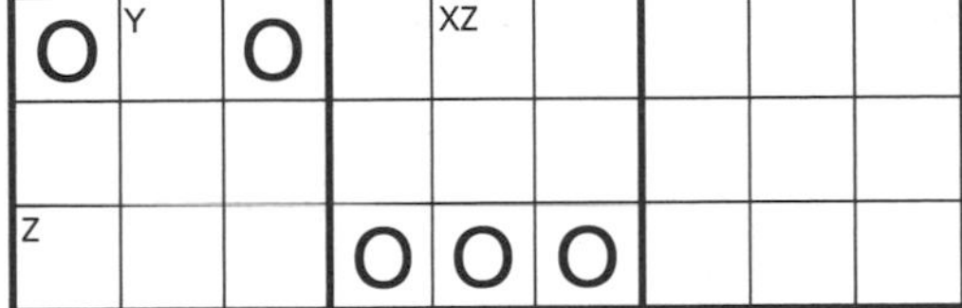

In the case where cell 12 is X, cell 15 becomes a Z, which eliminates the Z candidates from the circled cells. In the case where cell 12 is a Y, cell 31 becomes a Z, and also eliminates the Z candidates from the circled cells. So no matter what the contents of cell 12, we can eliminate the Z candidates from the circled cells. That's an XY-wing.

Here's a puzzle that requires XY-wing:

Example 25

				2	7	8		
		3	5					2
5	2							4
							6	8
		8		4		7		
1	5							
6							3	1
2					5	4		
		7	3	9				

Using what we know up to this point, we arrive at this grid:

Example 25-1

49	1469	1469	169	2	7	8	5	3
78	78	3	5	16	4	169	19	2
5	2	169	1689	1368	13689	16	7	4
3479	479	249	129	5	139	123	6	8
39	69	8	1269	4	1369	7	12	5
1	5	26	7	368	368	23	4	9
6	89	5	4	7	28	29	3	1
2	3	19	168	168	5	4	89	7
48	148	7	3	9	128	5	28	6

At this point there are three different examples of XY-wings found.

1) Cells 72, 77, and 98 form an XY-wing. The candidates in these cells are 8 and 9, 2 and 9, and 2 and 8, respectively. Whether you choose the 2 or the 9 for cell 77, neither cell 91 nor 92 can be 8. If cell 77 is a 2, then cell 98 has to be an 8, which would eliminate 8's from the candidates for cells 91 and 92. If cell 77 is a 9 instead, then cell 72 has to be an 8, which again eliminates the 8's from the candidates for cells 91 and 92. No matter what cell 77 is, be it a 2 or a 9, we know that cells 91 and 92 cannot contain 8's. Once we remove those 8's, we know cell 91 is a 4.

2) Cells 76, 77, and 88 form an XY-wing. The candidates in these cells are 2 and 8, 2 and 9, and 8 and 9, respectively. Whether you choose the 2 or the 9 for cell 77, neither cell 84 nor 85 can be 8, so we can eliminate candidate 8 from cells 84 and 85. That leaves only one cell (88) in row 8 that can contain an 8.

3) Cells 11, 91, and 72 form an XY-wing. The candidates in these cells are 4 and 9, 4 and 8, and 8 and 9, respectively. Whether you choose the 4 or the 8 for cell 91, cell 12 can't be 9, so we can eliminate the 9 candidate from cell 12.

Doing the second XY-wing above is all you need to reach the solution using basic methods.

Example 25 Answer

9	6	4	1	2	7	8	5	3
8	7	3	5	6	4	1	9	2
5	2	1	8	3	9	6	7	4
7	4	2	9	5	1	3	6	8
3	9	8	2	4	6	7	1	5
1	5	6	7	8	3	2	4	9
6	8	5	4	7	2	9	3	1
2	3	9	6	1	5	4	8	7
4	1	7	3	9	8	5	2	6

XYZ-WING

To explain the XYZ-wing, it is easiest to use the term "buddy," so first I'll refresh your memory on what that is. A buddy is a cell that shares a row, column, or box with another cell. So the buddies of cell 43 are 13, 23, 33, 41, 42, 44, 45, 46, 47, 48, 49, 51, 52, 53, 61, 62, 63, 73, 83, and 93. Every cell has 20 buddies.

In an XYZ-wing, you're looking for a cell that has the candidates XYZ and that also has buddies that contain the candidates XZ and YZ. Any cell that's buddies to all three of the XYZ, XZ, and YZ cells cannot contain a Z.

Example 26

7								5
2	1	6		5			7	
				9			6	
1		8	2					
9		3				4		1
					4	3		9
	6			4				
	7			6		5	3	4
3								8

The XYZ-wing comes into play here:

Example 26-1

7	38	9	136	12	26	18	4	5
2	1	6	4	5	8	9	7	3
4	38	5	13	9	7	18	6	2
1	4	8	2	3	9	7	5	6
9	25	3	567	78	56	4	28	1
6	25	7	15	18	4	3	28	9
5	6	1	8	4	3	2	9	7
8	7	2	9	6	1	5	3	4
3	9	4	57	27	25	6	1	8

This is very similar to XY-wing except the three relevant cells contain candidates in the form XYZ, XZ, YZ rather than XY, XZ, YZ. Cells 54, 56, and 94 form an XYZ-wing. Whether cell 54 is a 5, 6, or 7, cell 64 can't be 5, so we can eliminate candidate 5 from cell 64.

Example 26 Answer

7	3	9	6	1	2	8	4	5
2	1	6	4	5	8	9	7	3
4	8	5	3	9	7	1	6	2
1	4	8	2	3	9	7	5	6
9	2	3	5	7	6	4	8	1
6	5	7	1	8	4	3	2	9
5	6	1	8	4	3	2	9	7
8	7	2	9	6	1	5	3	4
3	9	4	7	2	5	6	1	8

LONGER CHAINS

Sometimes you can find situations more complex than XY-wing or XYZ-wing where there are two possibilities, either of which leads to the same result. Here's an example:

Example 27

	5	1		6				9
				1				
			5			7	8	
		5					9	
	2		6	4	8		1	
	1					2		
	4	7			2			
				5				
9				3		8	4	

This leads to the following sticking point:

Example 27-1

8	5	1	7	6	34	34	2	9
2	7	34	8	1	9	6	5	34
34	9	6	5	2	34	7	8	1
6	38	5	2	7	1	34	9	348
37	2	9	6	4	8	5	1	37
47	1	48	3	9	5	2	6	78
5	4	7	9	8	2	1	3	6
1	38	38	4	5	6	9	7	2
9	6	2	1	3	7	8	4	5

At cell 51, if you choose the 3, it forces a 4 at cell 31, which forces a 3 at cell 23, which forces a 4 at 29. Back to cell 51. If instead you choose the 7, it forces a 3 at cell 59, which forces a 4 at 29. So in either case, cell 29 has to be 4. Knowing that gives you enough to finish off the puzzle.

Example 27 Answer

8	5	1	7	6	4	3	2	9
2	7	3	8	1	9	6	5	4
4	9	6	5	2	3	7	8	1
6	8	5	2	7	1	4	9	3
3	2	9	6	4	8	5	1	7
7	1	4	3	9	5	2	6	8
5	4	7	9	8	2	1	3	6
1	3	8	4	5	6	9	7	2
9	6	2	1	3	7	8	4	5

In other chains, you can reach a point where a cell has no possibilities.

Example 28

	7			6	8			
6					9	7		
			7				3	
5		2	4					
4			8		3			2
					5	9		8
	4				1			
		5	6					4
			3	2			9	

We get very close to the end before we stall.

Example 28-1

13	7	13	5	6	8	4	2	9
6	2	4	1	3	9	7	8	5
89	5	89	7	4	2	1	3	6
5	8	2	4	9	6	3	7	1
4	19	19	8	7	3	6	5	2
7	36	36	2	1	5	9	4	8
2	4	7	9	5	1	8	6	3
39	39	5	6	8	7	2	1	4
18	16	168	3	2	4	5	9	7

If you choose 1 at cell 13, it forces a 3 at cell 11. It also forces 9 at cell 53, which forces 8 at cell 33, which forces a 9 at 31. This is an impasse because now cell 81 has no possibilities. So we can exclude the 1 from cell 13, put in a 3 there, and zoom to the finish line.

Example 28 Answer

1	7	3	5	6	8	4	2	9
6	2	4	1	3	9	7	8	5
9	5	8	7	4	2	1	3	6
5	8	2	4	9	6	3	7	1
4	1	9	8	7	3	6	5	2
7	3	6	2	1	5	9	4	8
2	4	7	9	5	1	8	6	3
3	9	5	6	8	7	2	1	4
8	6	1	3	2	4	5	9	7

In still other chains, you can reach a point where there's no place for a certain number.

Example 29

	2		6			9		1
	6				9			7
					8		6	3
			8				3	
4								5
	5				2			
5	3		1					
7			2				1	
1		4			6		9	

This is how far you can get:

Example 29-1

38	2	5	6	34	7	9	48	1
38	6	1	34	2	9	48	5	7
9	4	7	5	1	8	2	6	3
2	17	9	8	45	15	47	3	6
4	17	38	9	6	13	78	2	5
6	5	38	347	347	2	1	48	9
5	3	2	1	9	4	6	7	8
7	9	6	2	8	35	35	1	4
1	8	4	37	357	6	35	9	2

If you choose 4 at cell 27, it forces an 8 at cell 18, which forces a 3 at cell 11, which forces a 4 at cell 15. This is an impasse because now there is no place for a 4 anywhere in row 4. So we can exclude the 4 from cell 27, making it an 8. From unfinishable to solved in one easy logical chain.

Example 29 Answer

8	2	5	6	3	7	9	4	1
3	6	1	4	2	9	8	5	7
9	4	7	5	1	8	2	6	3
2	7	9	8	5	1	4	3	6
4	1	8	9	6	3	7	2	5
6	5	3	7	4	2	1	8	9
5	3	2	1	9	4	6	7	8
7	9	6	2	8	5	3	1	4
1	8	4	3	7	6	5	9	2

GRID COLORING

In grid coloring, you pick a number and follow it around the grid to see what happens. It can be thought of as a "true-false test." Choose a candidate number from a cell and suppose that number is correct for that cell, and call that cell true. Then anywhere else that number appears within the cell's buddies, those cells are false. This in turn causes other appearances of that number to become true or false. If doing this leads to some contradiction or impossibility, then you can safely remove that candidate as a possibility from your starting cell. The reason that this technique is usually referred to as grid coloring is that this can be easily visualized using colors. For example, all the "true" cells might be colored blue, while the "false" cells are colored red. And in very advanced grid coloring techniques, a third color might even be used to indicate that the number might or might not appear in a certain cell (that is, it could be true *or* false).

TURBOT FISH

One basic grid coloring technique is known as turbot fish. It requires five cells that are arranged so that two pairs of cells are in the same rows, two pairs are in the same columns, and two cells are in the same box. If three or four of the pairs are the only places where a particular number can go, you have a turbot fish. If there are only two such pairs, then it still works, as long as those two pairs don't share a cell.

Example 30

	1	3	5		8	9		
					9			
2		8		4				
	6					4		5
		4				3		
1		5					8	
				1		8		6
			2					
		2	8		4	7	9	

We get to the turbot fish at this point:

Example 30-1

47	1	3	5	267	8	9	467	247
457	457	6	137	237	9	12	347	8
2	9	8	1367	4	1367	16	5	37
3789	6	79	1379	3789	2	4	17	5
789	278	4	1679	56789	1567	3	167	279
1	237	5	4	3679	367	26	8	279
34579	3457	79	379	1	357	8	2	6
6789	78	1	2	679	67	5	34	34
356	35	2	8	356	4	7	9	1

There are two turbot fish situations here:

1) Cells 34, 37, 54, 58, and 67 form a turbot fish. (If you draw a line connecting cell 54 to 34 to 37 to 67 to 58 and back to 54 you get something resembling a fish swimming up and to the left, which is where the name comes from.) The pairs of cells in this turbot fish are 34 and 37, 37 and 67, 67 and 58, 58 and 54, and 54 and 34. The pairs 37 and 67, 67 and 58, and 54 and 34 are the only cells in their column or box that can have a 6, so we've found a turbot fish. If cell 37 *is* a 6, then cell 34 *is not* a 6, cell 67 *is not* a 6, cell 58 *is* a 6, and cell 54 *is not* a 6. This is an impossibility, because now there is no place for a 6 anywhere in column 4. So we can exclude the 6 from cell 37, which means that cell 67 must be a 6.

2) Cells 18, 34, 37, 54, and 58 form another turbot fish. (This one looks nothing like a fish.) Only the pairs in the rows have other places where the 6 can go, so we have three sides with the necessary trait, enough for it to work. If cell 58 *is* a 6, then cell 54 *is not* a 6, cell 18 *is not* a 6, cell 37 *is* a 6, and cell 34 *is not* a 6. This is an impossibility, because now there is no place for a 6 anywhere in column 4. So we can exclude the 6 from cell 58, making cell 18 a 6.

Either one of these two conclusions that can be made using turbot fish allows you to reach the answer swimmingly.

Example 30 Answer

7	1	3	5	2	8	9	6	4
5	4	6	1	7	9	2	3	8
2	9	8	3	4	6	1	5	7
3	6	9	7	8	2	4	1	5
8	2	4	6	5	1	3	7	9
1	7	5	4	9	3	6	8	2
4	3	7	9	1	5	8	2	6
9	8	1	2	6	7	5	4	3
6	5	2	8	3	4	7	9	1

OTHER GRID COLORING

In this grid, we'll eventually take a close look at the 8's.

Example 31

		9					4	
	7	2		5	3			
		6		4			3	7
				9	6			1
			1		4			
1			5	7				
7	2			1		4		
			6	3		7	8	
	6					9		

We hit the wall at this point:

Example 31-1

358	38	9	7	6	1	2	4	58
4	7	2	8	5	3	1	69	69
58	1	6	2	4	9	58	3	7
2	58	4	3	9	6	58	7	1
6	589	7	1	28	4	3	259	589
1	389	38	5	7	28	6	29	4
7	2	358	9	1	58	4	56	356
9	4	1	6	3	25	7	8	25
38	6	358	4	28	7	9	1	235

If cell 12 *is* an 8, cell 19 *is not* an 8, cell 63 *is* an 8, cell 66 *is not* an 8, cell 55 *is* an 8, and cell 59 *is not* an 8. This is an impossibility, because now there is no place for an 8 anywhere in column 9. So we can exclude the 8 from cell 12, which means cell 12 has to be a 3. After that 3 is placed, the puzzle is a piece of cake.

Example 31 Answer

5	3	9	7	6	1	2	4	8
4	7	2	8	5	3	1	9	6
8	1	6	2	4	9	5	3	7
2	5	4	3	9	6	8	7	1
6	8	7	1	2	4	3	5	9
1	9	3	5	7	8	6	2	4
7	2	8	9	1	5	4	6	3
9	4	1	6	3	2	7	8	5
3	6	5	4	8	7	9	1	2

The puzzles on the next two pages require the techniques of XY-wing, XYZ-wing, and/or turbot fish, except for the final puzzle (#96), which uses a short grid coloring that isn't a turbot fish.

85

		7	6				2	
5					4			
4		9	8				7	
6	4							
		8				9		
							5	8
	1				9	8		2
			4					1
	2				3	4		

86

	4		9			2		
	6	7						
				3	6			
	5	3	2			4		7
8		4			9	1	6	
			4	8				
						3	5	
		1			5		9	

87

4					8			7
	8							
3			1	9	5			
	2	5		1		8		
		1		3		5	6	
			8	4	9			2
							5	
2			7					3

88

5		1		2				
			9	6		3		
	3		4			2		
2		3					1	
6		4				8		7
	7					6		2
		6			5		2	
		2		4	9			
				3		7		9

89

		1	5	9		6		
5		6		1				
	4						1	
	9					2	7	
6				2				1
	8	3					5	
	6						8	
				5		7		2
		2		7	4	3		

90

				9				2
7	1	9						
			5		7			
9	8		1	2			3	
	3						5	
	4			8	3		2	1
			6		4			
						7	8	6
2				3				

91

4					9	5	3	7
8	5					4		
		7						2
7				2		6		
			6	4	7			
		2		1				9
9						2		
		3					7	8
2	7	8	5					6

92

2	7			9				
8			2				9	
	6		3			4		
					5			3
	8	3				7	5	
1			4					
		2			9		6	
	4				8			2
				2			3	5

93

	1			8			7	9
3	9							
6			9	7		1		
		1			7			
4				6				7
			3			5		
		6		9	4			8
							5	2
8	5			3			9	

94

		7			9			6
	5				8			
					3	4	7	
1					6	8	4	5
4	8	2	9					1
	7	4	6					
			3				2	
5			8			9		

95

		3			4	2	9	
				7	9	3		
			8	3				1
	4		6	9				
3	9						8	2
				8	2		4	
7				5	1			
		1	3	6				
	3	6	9			1		

96

					7			
			5				2	9
4				3		7		6
	9				4		3	5
	2		6		3		9	
3	1		7				4	
2		6		7				8
7	4				5			
			2					

WHERE IN THE WORLD WIDE WEB?

Sudoku is everywhere on the Web. As of this writing, "sudoku" gets over 100 million hits on Google. Here are some sites that are of interest.

waynegouldpuzzles.com is the site of Wayne Gould, who brought worldwide attention to the puzzle. You can download his sudoku program here (PC only).

websudoku.com has billions of free puzzles in four difficulty levels: easy, medium, hard, and evil. You can solve online or print out the puzzles to take them with you.

kossky.sitesled.com/games/sudoku/solver/en/solver.html can help you along on a puzzle if you get stuck. Simply type in the grid, and it will solve it, showing step-by-step reasoning on how it progressed. On harder puzzles (such as ones using Gordonian Logic) you'll have to click the "allow guess-and-check" option or else it won't be able to finish, and on those the descriptions of the steps are less helpful.

arxiv.org/abs/cs.DS/0507053 is the site of Professor David Eppstein's paper on the solving methods discussed in Chapter 10.

en.wikipedia.org/wiki/Sudoku is the Wikipedia entry on sudoku, which has fun sudoku facts aplenty.

worldpuzzle.org/championships/wsc/2011-eger-hungary is the site for the sixth World Sudoku Championship, which took place in November 2011 in Eger, Hungary. Thomas Snyder, an American bioengineering researcher, won the event for his third time. Kota Morinishi of Japan was second, and Tiit Vunk of Estonia finished third. If you're a really fast solver, check the site for upcoming tournaments.

sudoku.org.uk is a very extensive site that's home to all things British that have to do with sudoku. (Sudoku was wildly popular in England before the craze spread to the U.S.) Tough sudoku varieties, blank worksheets, articles, competitions, and an active discussion forum can all be found here.

angusj.com/sudoku has a free downloadable program (Simple Sudoku) that has puzzles as well as a solving aid that keeps track of candidates for you.

10

BILOCATION AND BIVALUE GRAPHS

I am indebted to David Eppstein, a computer science professor at the University of California, Irvine, for allowing me to spread the word on the techniques in this chapter, which he developed.

BILOCATION GRAPHS

In a bilocation graph, you make a diagram of cells that contain candidates that appear in no other possible places in that particular row, column, or box.

NONREPETITIVE BILOCATION CYCLE

To find a nonrepetitive bilocation cycle you start at any cell, then move to another cell in the same row, column, or box so that the cell you are moving from and the cell that you are moving to are the only two cells in that particular row, column, or box that can have a particular number. Then from the new cell, pick a different number, and find a new cell that is in its row, column, or box (making sure that there are no other places for that new number in that particular row, column, or box). Continue like this until you get back to the starting cell, and you've found a nonrepetitive bilocation cycle. Here's an example and the sticking point:

Example 32

			7		1			4
1		4	2			5		3
				3		6		
		8			9	7	6	
	9	5	1			8		
		1		2				
3		6			5	4		9
8			4		3			

Example 32-1

56	3568	39	7	569	1	2	89	4
1	67	4	2	69	8	5	79	3
579	58	2	59	3	4	6	1	78
2	134	8	35	45	9	7	6	15
67	136	37	356	8	2	9	4	15
46	9	5	1	47	67	8	3	2
4579	45	1	69	2	67	3	58	78
3	27	6	8	1	5	4	27	9
8	25	79	4	79	3	1	25	6

Example 32 Nonrepetitive Bilocation Cycle

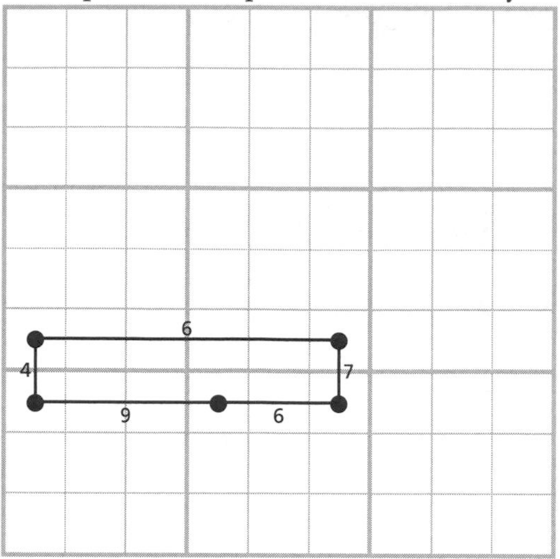

Example 32 Answer

6	3	9	7	5	1	2	8	4
1	7	4	2	6	8	5	9	3
5	8	2	9	3	4	6	1	7
2	1	8	3	4	9	7	6	5
7	6	3	5	8	2	9	4	1
4	9	5	1	7	6	8	3	2
9	4	1	6	2	7	3	5	8
3	2	6	8	1	5	4	7	9
8	5	7	4	9	3	1	2	6

This diagram shows cells 61 and 66 connected by a 6, since a 6 has to appear in one of those two cells; cells 66 and 76 connected by a 7, since a 7 has to appear in one of those two cells; cells 76 and 74 connected by a 6, since a 6 has to appear in one of those two cells; cells 74 and 71 connected by a 9, since a 9 has to appear in one of those two cells; and cells 71 and 61 connected by a 4, since a 4 has to appear in one of those two cells. It makes a complete cycle, and the numbers along the edges don't repeat along any two sections that share a node.

So we know that in the cells with the five node points, the numbers starting at the upper left and going around clockwise will either be 4-6-7-6-9 or 6-7-6-9-4. What this means is that cell 71 has to be either a 4 or a 9, so we can remove the 5 and 7 from its candidate list. That means that the 5 in column 1 must appear in either cell 11 or cell 31, which in turn means, via interaction, that cell 32 cannot be a 5. Removing the 5 candidate from cell 32 is the magic moment. It forces that cell to be an 8, and lets us coast to the finish line.

REPETITIVE BILOCATION CYCLE

A repetitive bilocation cycle is the same thing, except that there is exactly one case where the numbers coming out of two consecutive nodes in the cycle are the same.

Example 33

8				1			6	9
	4				3			
	6	1	5			8		
3	1	6		4				
				9		1	7	3
		7			6	4	1	
			3				8	
6	8			7				2

Eventually you get to this grid:

Example 33-1

8	25	3	47	1	47	25	6	9
59	4	29	8	6	3	7	25	1
7	6	1	5	2	9	8	3	4
3	1	6	27	4	57	9	25	8
59	7	89	12	3	158	25	4	6
4	25	28	6	9	58	1	7	3
2	3	7	9	8	6	4	1	5
1	9	4	3	5	2	6	8	7
6	8	5	14	7	14	3	9	2

Example 33 Answer

8	2	3	7	1	4	5	6	9
5	4	9	8	6	3	7	2	1
7	6	1	5	2	9	8	3	4
3	1	6	2	4	7	9	5	8
9	7	8	1	3	5	2	4	6
4	5	2	6	9	8	1	7	3
2	3	7	9	8	6	4	1	5
1	9	4	3	5	2	6	8	7
6	8	5	4	7	1	3	9	2

Here is one bilocation graph you can form:

Example 33 Repetitive Bilocation Graph

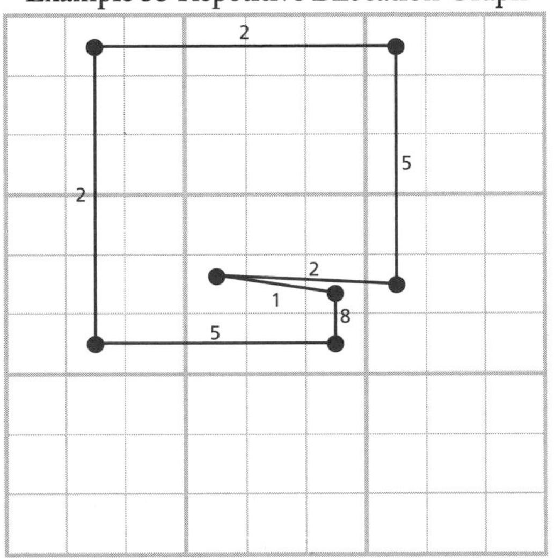

The graph shows a complete cycle. Between any two nodes, the number on the line must go in one of the two nodes. So, for example, the 8 must go in either cell 56 or 66. Now examine the upper left node. It has a 2 coming out of both sides. If cell 12 were not a 2, that would force cells 17 and 62 to be 2's, which wouldn't leave enough room for all the other numbers in the cycle to fit in. The 5's would be forced into cells 57 and 66, which would force a 2 in cell 54 and an 8 in cell 56, leaving no place for the 1 that is limited to cells 54 and 56. So cell 12 must be a 2. From there it's a cakewalk.

BIVALUE GRAPHS

Bivalue graphs are much easier to find. They are cycles of buddy cells that each have just two candidates in them. They must be nonrepetitive to be helpful. Here's an example:

Example 34

5							3	
	9	8		6			7	
				2	3	1		
	1		9					
		7				3		
					5		8	
		2	4	9				
	7			5		4	6	
	6							2

We get this far using the standard methods:

Example 34-1

5	2	1	78	478	9	68	3	468
3	9	8	15	6	14	2	7	45
7	4	6	58	2	3	1	59	589
2468	1	45	9	3	2478	56	24	67
24689	58	7	1268	148	1248	3	24	1569
2469	3	49	1267	147	5	69	8	1679
18	58	2	4	9	6	7	15	3
19	7	39	1238	5	128	4	6	89
149	6	3459	1378	178	178	589	19	2

Cells 43, 47, 67, and 63 form a nonrepetitive bivalue graph, as shown below.

Example 34 Nonrepetitive Bivalue Cycle

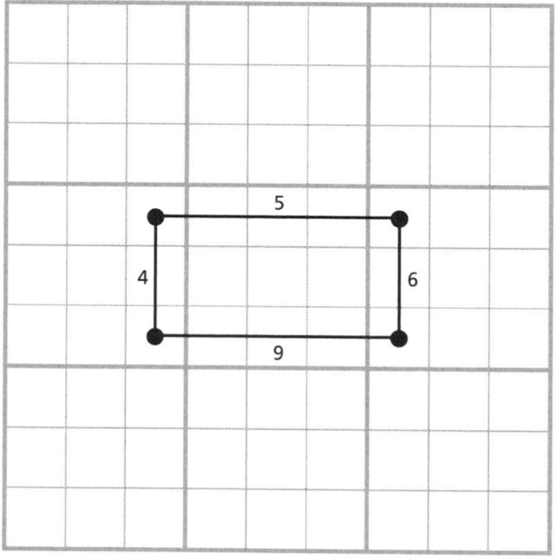

In the cyclic sequence of cells 43, 47, 67, 63, and back to 43, each cell has two candidates, each of which can also be placed at one of the cell's two neighbors in the sequence. Starting in the upper left of the cycle and going around clockwise, the cells will be either 5-6-9-4 or 4-5-6-9. In either case, a 4 must go in either 43 or 63, so we can eliminate the 4 candidates from cells 41, 51, 61, and 93. Also, a 6 must go in either 47 or 67, allowing us to eliminate the 6 candidates from 49, 59, 69, and 17. Finally, a 9 must go in either 63 or 67, so we can eliminate the 9 candidate from 61 and 69. The most helpful of these results is the elimination of the 6 candidate from cell 17, which forces it to be an 8, allowing us to finish off the puzzle posthaste.

Example 34 Answer

5	2	1	7	4	9	8	3	6
3	9	8	5	6	1	2	7	4
7	4	6	8	2	3	1	5	9
2	1	5	9	3	8	6	4	7
9	8	7	6	1	4	3	2	5
6	3	4	2	7	5	9	8	1
8	5	2	4	9	6	7	1	3
1	7	9	3	5	2	4	6	8
4	6	3	1	8	7	5	9	2

Lots more information about these methods can be found in the paper "Nonrepetitive Paths and Cycles in Graphs With Application to Sudoku" by Professor Eppstein, on the Web at arxiv.org/abs/cs.DS/0507053.

11
GUESSING

You now know all that you need to know to solve all the puzzles in the puzzle section of this book. What do you do if, when solving puzzles from another source, you get to a point where none of the methods in this book can finish off the puzzle? My first recommendation would be to no longer solve puzzles from that source. Any sudoku author who requires you to guess is not making quality puzzles. If even single-iteration chains and grid colorings result in nothing definitive, the only thing left is bifurcation, or flat-out guessing, where you simply choose a candidate for a cell as if it were the right one and solve from that point to see where it leads. If it's the incorrect choice it will ultimately lead to some kind of contradiction, and you'll then go back to your bifurcation point and choose a different candidate and go through the process again. You'll want to choose as a bifurcation point a cell with as few candidates as possible, preferably two. However, it's possible that even this will not be enough to solve the puzzle, as it may require multilayered bifurcation in order to crack it. This guess-and-check method is also known by its Japanese name, "nishio."

It's also very helpful to guess correctly, since then you'll stumble onto the answer and not have to go back to try the other possibilities. Peeking at the answer grid for the contents of the key cell is an *excellent* way to keep your guessing batting average close to perfect (just make sure nobody sees you doing it).

Here is a puzzle, and the point where we reach a screeching halt:

Example 35

		2			8	3		
			4	7				6
4			2				1	
		4					9	
1		6				4		7
	9					2		
	2				7			3
7				1	4			
		3	9			7		

Example 35-1

569	156	2	156	569	8	3	7	4
3569	1358	589	4	7	1359	58	2	6
4	35678	578	2	356	356	58	1	9
2	3578	4	5678	3568	356	1	9	58
1	58	6	58	29	29	4	3	7
358	9	578	1578	4	135	2	6	58
5689	2	1	568	568	7	69	4	3
7	568	589	3	1	4	69	58	2
568	4	3	9	2568	256	7	58	1

The candidates at cell 77 are 6 and 9. If you choose a 6, it almost works, and you can get down to having just two uncommitted cells left (cells 26 and 35), but it can't be finished.

If you choose a 9 instead, you can solve it all the way to the end. You of course noticed the Gordonian Rectangle at cells 23, 33, 27, and 37 that allowed you to put a 7 in cell 33, right?

Example 35 Answer

5	6	2	1	9	8	3	7	4
9	1	8	4	7	3	5	2	6
4	3	7	2	6	5	8	1	9
2	7	4	8	3	6	1	9	5
1	8	6	5	2	9	4	3	7
3	9	5	7	4	1	2	6	8
8	2	1	6	5	7	9	4	3
7	5	9	3	1	4	6	8	2
6	4	3	9	8	2	7	5	1

No other puzzles in this book require you to guess like this.

TO GUESS OR NOT TO GUESS

Back on page 18 I wrote, "Should you guess? The answer to that is an emphatic no." So why am I saying you should guess here? The simple answer is that I lied on page 18. Please forgive me, but there was a reason. The only time you'll need to guess is when you are doing a ridiculously hard puzzle written by someone who thinks guessing should be allowed. Good sudoku writers don't allow that, so if you're doing puzzles from a good source (anything by Frank Longo is sure to be good), then you'll never have to guess.

Also, if I had said it was okay to guess, you would have been guessing left and right instead of learning all the strategies you need to avoid guessing. So now that you know everything, try all the other strategies, and if they all fail, then I still emphatically say you shouldn't guess. You should instead throw away the puzzle and get a new puzzle from a source that doesn't require guessing. If you can't stand the idea of throwing away an uncompleted puzzle, then be sure to switch pencil colors so you know what to erase if you come to a dead end (see the sidebar on page 44 for more on that).

PUZZLES

97

				1	2	5		
3	2		9					
		1			7		3	
		2		3			7	6
9		6				2		5
1	7			5		9		
	5		6			8		
					5		6	9
		9	1	4				

98

7		4	5					
		6			8			
8	2		6	3			9	
6	8			9			7	
	4						8	
	3			1			2	6
	6			8	5		3	9
			2			6		
					3	2		4

99

	1		7	2				
7	3							
9	4	8	5					1
1			8	4		3		
		3				2		
		9		6	7			4
6					1	4	9	3
							7	5
				9	5		1	

100

			5		4		6	9
		9		6			5	
		1		8		7		
7			4				8	2
	6						3	
5	8				6			7
		8		3		5		
	9			4		8		
4	2		8		7			

101

9					4	7		
		5		9			1	
7					5		9	8
5		2	1					
	1			6			8	
					3	1		9
8	5		2					4
	6			8		9		
		7	6					2

102

		2			7	8	3	4
	6			4	8	5		
4			1	3				
	2	4						
			9		3			
						6	1	
				6	2			8
		6	8	9			7	
3	9	8	5			2		

103

	2	5	4	7				
6					3		7	
		3			6			1
	5						3	6
		2	9		7	1		
9	6						8	
3			6			2		
	4		1					7
				9	4	3	5	

104

7		1				4		
9					4		6	1
		4		1	5			
3			6		1			
	8			9			3	
			5		7			6
			2	4		7		
4	1		9					3
		7				9		4

105

2	9	1				5		
8				4			3	
				2	1		6	
		6	4		2		8	
1								4
	7		5		6	2		
	2		7	9				
	4			5				6
		3				4	7	9

106

	9		4	7				
6	2						7	
		3			8	6	9	5
		4			7			
	5	7				9	4	
			3			1		
2	1	6	7			8		
	8						2	9
				8	4		1	

107

				9	5	7		
	9		7	4				
2	7	3						4
		2			6			
8		5				1		6
			2			9		
6						8	7	9
				6	8		1	
		8	5	7				

108

4		7			1			
				4	2		7	6
6	1		7		5			
		3			7		8	
		1				6		
	4		8			2		
			5		3		4	8
7	8		2	6				
			1			5		2

109

		1		8			6	3
8		9	6					
7			4				5	
4			2	6		3		
	9						1	
		2		3	4			6
	1				6			8
					7	6		1
6	7			9		5		

110

1		4		3			2	
	2		9			8	3	
	9		1					
		7			9		1	2
2								4
3	4		6			7		
					4		8	
	8	2			5		7	
	5			1		4		3

111

8		4			9	7		2
					8		1	3
1				7			5	
				8	2		3	
		2				6		
	1		7	5				
	3			6				4
9	7		8					
2		6	3			5		7

112

	2				1		6	
8		4			5			
5		6			3	9	1	
			1	2				
2				3				6
				8	9			
	9	2	3			5		4
			4			6		3
	8		7				2	

113

		6			9		3	4
5			6		4			
4	2	7		3				
1				7		2		
	7						4	
		5		4				1
				5		4	1	9
			4		6			2
3	4		1			7		

114

1	2				8			
	8		2				4	
		4		7		3		
3				1		4		
2		9				5		3
		6		8				1
		1		5		8		
	3				9		1	
			4				6	5

115

	5	8		4	3	2		
2				6		8		
1	3		2					
					7	4		
7	2						6	5
		6	1					
					5		8	9
		9		2				4
		1	8	9		6	3	

116

				6	4	7		3
5			1	9				
	6	7						1
	2			4		1		
	9		7		8		6	
		8		2			7	
2						8	1	
				7	9			5
4		3	5	8				

117

8				6	3			
		9		8	5			4
	7	6	1					
	5	8						6
3	9						8	5
6						4	9	
					8	6	7	
1			6	7		9		
			5	2				8

118

7	6			2			3	
	5			9	4	2		
4					8	1		
		3	2	6				
2								3
				1	3	5		
		6	9					1
		4	1	5			7	
	8			3			6	5

119

		4	5			2		8
			3			4	7	
2	6						9	
	2			3	5			
3				2				9
			6	9			4	
	7						6	4
	5	6			8			
8		1			6	5		

120

	1			4			8	
9		4					5	
	2	8	9	6				
	7	6		2	3			
2								7
			4	7		3	6	
				1	8	6	9	
	3					1		8
	5			9			3	

121

3	1							
	2			1	7			
	4	6	9			2		
			5		2	1		4
2								5
9		1	8		6			
		3			8	5	7	
			6	5			9	
							1	3

122

	2		9		4		6	7
	9		5					8
		6		2				
		5		7			4	3
		9				7		
1	7			6		5		
				5		3		
6					7		5	
7	5		6		8		2	

123

		2	5	6				
9	6							5
	5		8		9	7		
		3					2	1
	4			9			6	
1	8					5		
		1	9		7		4	
4							7	9
				3	1	8		

124

9			2	4			3	
6					9		7	
2						5	1	
		1			5			8
		9		2		7		
7			6			4		
	7	4						5
	9		4					3
	3			1	6			7

125

			7	4		5		
			9		5			4
					8	3	6	
	4	3				1	9	
7				8				3
	8	2				6	7	
	6	1	8					
3			1		6			
		5		2	7			

126

4			8	1				6
5					7	8	4	
		6		4			3	
	4					2	5	
			9		4			
	6	3					7	
	5			8		3		
	2	8	6					5
7				9	3			2

127

			4	1				6
	1		5			4	8	
		9					5	2
	5			6	4			
9		2				8		4
			8	7			1	
8	3					6		
	9	1			5		7	
2				8	7			

128

8	6					2		
			6			7		3
	1	5	7					
		2		6	1		7	
1								2
	7		8	2		5		
					8	3	5	
2		6			4			
		9					2	8

129

2			4	9				
9						4	7	
4	3	1						
			6		9	8	4	
5				2				6
	8	9	5		3			
						3	8	1
	9	2						7
				8	6			4

130

7	5	4			6			
		1				6		
	9		5	2			7	
2				4	7			
8			9		2			6
			8	6				1
	3			9	8		5	
		5				8		
			7			9	1	2

131

			8	3			2	9
	8	2			1			
					9	8	6	
	1				5			6
	6			8			9	
8			2				5	
	5	9	4					
			1			9	7	
1	3			5	8			

132

		9	6				5	4
		1			9		3	
3								7
				4	7	8	2	9
				9				
9	7	3	5	8				
5								8
	1		9			5		
8	9				4	6		

133

7	1				2			
		9	7			5		
				1	5		3	
6				7			5	
4		7	5		6	9		1
	2			8				7
	7		6	5				
		3			8	6		
			3				2	9

134

	7			1		3		
5	1				6	7		
3			9	4				
		1	8					
4	5						7	2
					3	5		
				6	4			7
		8	1				2	4
		9		8			5	

135

		4		5				3
					2		4	7
			1		3	9	2	
7		1	9					
4	9						3	8
					6	4		1
	4	5	8		9			
3	1		4					
6				3		1		

136

5	6					1		
	7	2		6				
	3				5		7	2
		8	5	4	9			
1								6
			6	1	3	5		
7	8		3				4	
				8		2	6	
		9					1	3

137

4	6		7					5
1		7			8			
		3		5				6
			9			5	4	
7	8						9	3
	9	4			1			
9				8		3		
			6			7		9
6					4		8	1

138

4				2	7			
	6		3					2
2					5	1	8	9
1					6		9	
		8				3		
	7		8					4
8	1	4	5					7
6					1		4	
			4	8				6

139

		5			7	6		
4				6			7	
		8	9					5
1				8		5		2
	2			4			9	
5		4		7				1
8					2	9		
	6			1				4
		3	6			7		

140

7	8					6		
		5		8	3	2	9	
				5	7		8	
	7		4					3
3								1
9					5		7	
	5		9	6				
	3	2	7	4		8		
		9					4	6

141

		1	5					6
8		5			2			
	3			8		7		
		6		7				1
	4	3	6		8	9	7	
5				3		8		
		4		2			3	
			9			6		8
1					7	2		

142

6		2	4		5			
	5	1			9			
				6			5	8
4		3		7				
	2			9			8	
				2		4		1
7	8			5				
			6			8	3	
			9		8	2		4

143

		9	4	6			5	3
8		6						2
	1		9	7				
		4			5			
	9			2			1	
			7			9		
				1	7		3	
6						2		5
9	2			5	6	8		

144

		6		8				3
			7		4			6
	7	8	5					1
				5	1		3	
	3	5				8	1	
	1		8	9				
3					8	7	5	
9			4		2			
2				6		1		

145

		1	9			3		
2			1					8
	8	7			5	2		
	2			3				1
	6			9			5	
1				5			8	
		3	8			6	4	
7					3			9
		2			4	1		

146

9	1		4		6			
4			2	9				
7		8					6	
	8	5				1		
	9			2			4	
		2				9	8	
	6					3		5
				5	4			7
			3		9		2	4

147

	8	5					1	
3				5			9	
2						5		3
	5	4	7					2
			8	4	1			
7					2	8	3	
5		2						6
	4			7				1
	6					4	2	

148

4	7				5			
9	1							4
	8	2	9					
	6	3		7		8		
			3	1	2			
		7		9		5	1	
					1	9	8	
6							3	2
			8				4	7

149

8	4			2				
9		5	6					3
	6				1			7
		9	3				7	
		7	2		6	5		
	8				9	3		
2			4				3	
6					7	2		9
				9			8	4

150

	1	4			8	6		
	3	5			7		4	
6					1			8
			6	4				
4				1				9
				9	3			
7			1					3
	9		3			5	2	
		3	5			7	6	

151

		7	9				6	
4		9		6			2	
	1			5	8			4
9					2			7
		4				8		
3			8					9
6			5	7			8	
	7			4		3		2
	4				9	5		

152

		5		8		4	1	
8				5		7		
	9		2		7			
5	3		1					
	6	8				9	4	
					8		6	3
			3		4		5	
		9		1				4
	1	7		9		3		

153

9	1							5
			1			8	2	9
8		4		6	5			
	9			8	3			
		2				6		
			4	5			9	
			5	1		3		7
3	7	1			6			
5							1	6

154

8	1		4	6			2	
		6			3		7	
3	5			9				
	6	4						
		5	7		9	3		
						4	5	
				1			8	9
	9		2			1		
	7			3	8		6	2

155

5					4		1	
6	3							
9	8			3	5		4	
	6	8	2			5		
			3		6			
		2			7	8	3	
	9		6	7			8	5
							7	3
	7		8					4

156

		4			9	6		
	2			8	4		5	
8		9					1	
			6		1		8	
2				3				4
	6		4		8			
	7					1		2
	9		1	6			4	
		5	8			3		

157

6	1							3
			6	3		5		
	2	8	9		1		7	
						3		7
		1		6		8		
5		9						
	9		1		5	6	3	
		6		8	9			
1							9	8

158

4		9	6					
	5	6		1		4		
1				5				2
			7			8	3	
	9			3			5	
	4	5			1			
6				2				8
		2		8		5	4	
					6	3		9

159

	2	1	6				9	
3			4				6	
8			9					2
	3			2		8		
1	4						5	3
		8		5			2	
6					3			4
	7				1			6
	8				7	1	3	

160

2			6	7				
		4	1		5			
6						9	3	
	9			6			1	4
3		7				6		9
1	8			9			7	
	1	3						5
			4		2	7		
				5	3			6

161

	3		2			9		
				5		2		8
	7		9		6		4	
5		8				3	2	
				6				
	6	4				8		7
	1		6		4		5	
7		9		2				
		6			9		8	

162

		4	1			5		
			6	9				3
3							7	1
	5	2			7		9	
		7		2		4		
	1		3			7	6	
5	4							7
8				3	4			
		6			2	1		

163

7			9	4	8			
		8		2				
3	2		1				4	
	5					3		9
	3	9				7	8	
2		7					1	
	1				6		3	4
				8		1		
			2	1	5			6

164

					4		2	9
9		8		7			1	
2	5					4		
			6	3				8
		4	9		1	6		
7				5	8			
		3					8	2
	8			4		5		1
1	2		3					

165

	7	2		1	5			
	4		2	3				
6			8					9
				7			8	6
2		6				7		5
9	3			5				
5					4			8
				2	3		5	
			5	8		2	4	

166

			5	6	4	9		8
	1		8			5		
8	5	6						
3		5						
	7		9		8		2	
						1		7
						8	3	1
		4			2		5	
9		3	1	7	5			

167

				9		7		
	4		5		3	1		
						5	8	6
5	7		3				9	
4				7				5
	3				6		4	7
3	2	4						
		8	7		1		6	
		7		3				

168

	3			6				7
	7	6			1			
1		5		3				
		1	6				7	
3			2		9			5
	5				3	6		
				9		4		2
			7			3	9	
6				5			1	

169

		5					6	
1			2	7			9	
2				9	5		4	
		8	5				2	3
		6				9		
5	7				3	1		
	9		6	4				2
	5			3	8			9
	3					6		

170

	4		7			6	3	
8		5	4					
	3				6		8	5
		2		4				1
			8		1			
6				5		8		
9	7		1				5	
					4	9		8
	5	3			8		2	

171

7		5					6	
		8	2	1				
			9		7			1
			7	2		8	1	
9	8						3	5
	2	4		5	3			
3			4		6			
				9	2	4		
	4					6		9

172

			3	6			2	
1	3		4					
4	9	2				1		
				5		4	6	1
			7		9			
2	1	3		4				
		8				6	1	7
					7		5	9
	5			2	6			

173

			4	3				9
3	4			5				1
		9	7		2			
9	3	6						7
	1						6	
4						3	9	5
			2		5	4		
8				7			2	6
5				1	6			

174

		9	5				4	
	8		6			5		2
2				7			1	
				4		3		9
9			8		7			1
1		4		5				
	4			9				6
6		7			4		3	
	5				8	1		

175

6	1			9				
				6		8	1	3
2					3			5
		8	2			7		
9			3		6			8
		7			1	2		
5			8					6
8	3	9		4				
				3			8	7

176

	1					2	3	
	2	6	5					9
			7	3				6
5			2					4
		8		9		5		
6					7			3
7				1	8			
8					6	3	4	
	4	9					7	

177

	6		5			4		
1					2		8	
4			8			7		
				3	9	6		1
	5			8			2	
3		6	1	4				
		7			8			9
	1		3					8
		2			1		4	

178

	8		6			5		
			4				6	7
	6	2	1					8
7	9			6				
		5		3		7		
				5			4	1
8					6	9	1	
9	2				8			
		4			7		3	

179

		9	3			8		4
				4			3	1
	4			6			5	
9					3	2		
2	6						8	5
		4	2					6
	8			3			9	
4	3			5				
1		6			8	5		

180

		1		6	5		2	
5	4							1
			4	7		5		
3	1					6		
		9	6		8	4		
		6					3	9
		5		9	4			
2							9	5
	8		1	5		2		

181

7			1	3				
		4		6			8	1
	9	1			8			
6		8	5	1				
	1						6	
				2	3	8		9
			4			7	9	
1	6			9		5		
				5	6			2

182

			6		1			2
2				5	9			
	1	5	4			7	6	
	6			9			7	
		9				3		
	2			6			1	
	7	3			5	8	2	
			2	8				7
8			9		3			

183

8	4					3		7
		3	5					
			3			2	6	
9	5		6	3				
7				1				6
				9	8		7	4
	1	6			3			
					2	1		
2		9					4	8

184

2	8				9	4		
3		7	1					
	9		7			2		
	3		5	1				
5			2		3			4
				7	4		6	
		2			7		1	
					1	8		7
		9	4				5	2

185

7			3		1	5		
					8	6		3
8	3		9					
	8			1	9			
	9			2			5	
			5	3			2	
					2		4	5
4		2	7					
		7	6		3			8

186

		8		7	9			
	5		2		4			
9					5	8	7	6
4		3			6			
	7						3	
			4			5		7
3	4	7	5					8
			3		1		5	
			8	4		6		

187

8			5	4				
	2					4	8	3
4		9			6			
9		2		7			3	
			3		5			
	7			8		1		4
			6			9		8
7	9	1					2	
				1	3			7

188

9	6			5	1			
	5				4		1	
8		2		3				
		7						2
	9	8	7		2	3	4	
4						9		
				4		5		1
	4		3				2	
			5	7			9	3

189

2			7	3		4		
1	6		8					
	4	3					9	5
			3	4				
6		1				7		9
				1	7			
8	2					9	6	
					5		7	1
		7		9	2			3

190

6			9			7		
	5			8				1
9		3			6	2		
	7				9			3
	2	4				6	1	
1			5				2	
		5	2			1		6
4				7			9	
		2			5			8

191

			4			1		7
1		9	8		7			
				1	6		4	
					3	4	9	
2	1						3	5
	5	3	6					
	8		7	3				
			5		1	3		6
5		1			9			

192

8					4		6	
		5		7				3
2					9	5	8	
6	7				2			4
				4				
4			6				2	8
	2	1	5					9
3				2		8		
	4		1					2

193

5		6	7					
7	1			2				6
		8			1	3		
9	2			7				
	6		5		9		3	
				6			5	7
		9	2			4		
3				1			9	8
					7	1		5

194

	8			6	5		1	
	7		9	3				
		3		7	8			
7		1						3
3		8				1		5
4						8		2
			6	4		9		
				2	1		6	
	6		3	5			2	

195

8				9		5		
4			8				6	
		7	4		3		2	
3			2	7				
	2	9				8	3	
				3	9			4
	3		6		5	4		
	7				2			1
		1		4				5

196

3		1					5	
4	7		1			6	2	
			3	7				8
	2	3						4
			9		7			
6						9	1	
7				3	5			
	4	6			1		8	7
	3					2		5

197

7			2				4	
5	9		3		4			
		8		1			7	
2		6					5	
		7	6		2	8		
	5					6		2
	3			8		5		
			5		1		6	4
	7				6			8

198

		2			8	1		
	7				1	4		
1	3			6				
	1				9			2
2				7				6
8			2				5	
				5			8	9
		7	6				2	
		1	3			6		

199

	4			6			7	
	6		9			8		5
		2			8			4
			2	5				
3		7				9		8
				8	3			
4			3			2		
5		9			1		6	
	3			4			8	

200

7							6	8
9			7					4
			9	3				5
				8		3		2
	3	8				5	4	
5		9		4				
4				2	6			
3					7			1
2	5							3

201

5		1		4	6			
	3		7			4		
2					5			1
	5			8		3		
	7		9		4		2	
		2		7			4	
6			3					4
		3			7		1	
			6	9		5		8

202

	2		1					9
			3			2		4
9	5		6					
		6		1	9	3		
	4			3			9	
		7	4	5		8		
					8		2	6
8		2			1			
1					3		7	

203

9	3			4	6			
	2							
4		8	2		9	5		
8	5			7				3
		2				9		
3				1			7	2
		5	3		4	1		9
							3	
			6	9			2	5

204

				1			8	7
7					5	4		2
			4			3	6	
5			1		3			
	8			2			5	
			6		9			8
	9	5			7			
4		3	5					6
8	2			4				

205

				4				5
	4		6	7			1	9
		5	8			3		
					2	1		
1	8						3	7
		6	1					
		7			9	8		
8	3			2	6		4	
2				8				

206

		6	7				9	
	9			4		5		
4	8					3		7
3		5	6					
			3		4			
					7	4		9
5		9					4	2
		8		7			5	
	3				2	6		

207

8		5		9				
7	9							5
	2	3	1					
	4			7	3		2	
		7	8		1	9		
	3		9	6			7	
					6	4	5	
2							3	9
				1		2		7

208

		5	9					1
	6			4			7	
4	8				6	5		2
							6	7
		3		5		4		
8	7							
3		2	5				1	4
	4			1			9	
6					4	3		

209

		5			4	2	9	
4		2	3				1	
		1		2			4	
7					1			
			4		8			
			9					7
	8			4		9		
	4				2	6		8
	5	9	6			3		

210

	9		3					1
2		6		4				
		5				7	6	4
		4			8		3	
			4	5	3			
	2		9			4		
3	5	2				8		
				7		6		3
9					4		5	

211

				1			7	4
7			5		9	8		
		8						5
	4			5	8		2	
8	7						3	6
	6		3	7			4	
5						2		
		6	2		5			1
2	8			9				

212

			9			5	1	
	7				1	6		
			4		3		7	9
1	3					9	5	
				1				
	5	2					3	4
6	4		5		9			
		8	6				2	
	2	5			7			

213

3	9	6				8		
				4		3		2
	8				5			9
1			6				9	
5								1
	7				9			4
8			5				1	
6		3		1				
		1				2	5	3

214

9	8						1	
		2	6		1			
1		4						7
				2	3		5	
6		9		5		4		3
	2		9	4				
2						5		1
			5		7	6		
	5						8	9

215

		3				8	9	
8				7			6	
			3	8				
6					3		1	2
	4		6		1		7	
9	3		7					5
				4	7			
	2			6				8
	5	4				1		

216

			5		3			7
			2			9	8	3
	6		9		1			
		9				2		4
		7		2		1		
2		4				7		
			6		9		7	
7	9	3			2			
5			4		7			

217

5		2			8	7		
	8	7				3		
			1	7	6			
9						5		7
	4			9			3	
6		1						2
			9	5	7			
		5				9	6	
		9	8			1		5

218

	3	1	7					2
	8			9		4	3	
2			5					
		3		5		6		
	7		2		3		5	
		9		4		7		
					9			1
	6	7		8			4	
8					5	3	6	

219

8	1				4			
6	2					4		
					5			7
		9		5	6		2	
4			9	8	3			5
	5		7	2		9		
2			8					
		4					9	8
			6				7	4

220

	4		1			2	6	
	5			3		1		
1			8					4
	3				5		8	
9				7				3
	8		3				2	
7					3			9
		6		4			3	
	9	8			1		7	

221

		6		2		5		
4	9						8	
3	5				4			
					6	3		9
	3		9	8	1		6	
9		7	5					
			4				1	8
	7						3	4
		1		6		7		

222

		7				4		
4			9		7	5	1	6
				3				9
	3	2	4			6		
	4						2	
		1			6	8	3	
2				5				
3	6	5	7		8			2
		4				3		

223

7	3		5					
	1	4		7			8	
		2				7		9
	2	9	1	6				
			8		7			
				9	5	1	2	
8		5				2		
	7			4		3	5	
					2		6	4

224

5		3	1					
	9			6			5	8
4		6	3	8				
					6	1		
6	3						4	2
		2	9					
				5	1	7		6
3	4			7			2	
					3	4		5

225

	4		8				1	2
		1		7	6			
	8		3	1			9	
4		6			3			
2								3
			6			2		5
	1			5	8		3	
			2	3		5		
5	9				4		2	

226

4		2				5		
7			4		1			
	1	9		2	8		4	
2						1		
	4	3				7	2	
		7						3
	2		1	7		8	3	
			5		2			7
		5				6		2

227

2			6		5	8	7	
	6			2				9
		5	8			4		
			1			3		
	3			8			6	
		2			9			
		8			6	1		
1				7			9	
	9	4	5		3			7

228

2		3				1		
	9	7	2					
		4	9	3				
6	2				1	8	4	
	3						2	
	1	5	4				3	6
				2	9	3		
					4	6	5	
		1				2		8

229

6		1					7	
	4	7					5	9
				2		8		
			7				9	
7			4	8	2			5
	3				5			
		2		4				
5	9					3	6	
	1					5		2

230

5				9	6	7		
3	9		1					
	7	8						4
2				4	7			
		9				8		
			8	3				9
9						1	8	
					1		9	2
		7	5	2				6

231

	7	8		5				
2	3		8					6
4		6		9	2			
					5	7	2	
5								3
	2	3	7					
			5	1		3		7
3					9		1	8
				8		6	9	

232

		9	5				1	
			2	9				5
	2	4				6	8	
		8					7	2
	7	1				5	9	
9	5					8		
	8	5				3	2	
2				5	7			
	6				8	9		

233

	1		8					4
			3		6		1	
6	8			5				
8	5						3	
		6		2		4		
	4						6	9
				3			9	2
	6		5		9			
1					2		8	

234

1						3	8	
			2		9		1	
9		4						
		1		3		8		
2	3	8		7		1	4	5
		5		4		7		
						2		3
	5		3		7			
	6	2						8

235

6								
8			4					
	3	2	6			9	8	
	1		7	9			2	
7	9		3		2		6	1
	6			4	8		3	
	5	6			7	2	4	
					9			6
								7

236

	6							9
2		3		5		8		
1						7	4	
			5			9		3
			8		4			
9		1			7			
	2	8						5
		4		7		6		1
3							7	

237

	1				7			6
9					6			
	5		3	4		1		
		1		7	2	4		
	6	9				2	5	
		5	4	6		3		
		4		2	5		7	
			7					5
5			6				3	

238

		4	1		6			
	6			4	2		1	8
1	5							
		3		1			8	
			5		8			
	9			6		4		
							7	2
2	7		4	3			9	
			7		5	8		

239

6		3	9			8		
5	4			7				
			5			7		4
	3						7	9
			1	4	9			
1	9						5	
3		9			2			
				3			2	7
		2			5	6		1

240

		3		4				
			2				9	
7		8	1		6			5
	6					1	4	
1		2	6		4	5		9
	5	4					2	
5			4		1	2		3
	8				3			
				7		9		

241

				4	5		2	
					1	4	9	
9				7				5
6	5		4		3	2		
		3				1		
		1	6		7		3	4
3				9				6
	2	6	7					
	7		3	6				

242

8			3	1	5			
	7	5						
		9	7					4
		4	6				2	
9	6						4	5
	8				3	1		
2					8	4		
						6	1	
			4	5	9			7

243

		5				1	3	6
		8	3		6		7	
	3			9				
8	9				1			
5				6				4
			2				5	7
				5			2	
	6		9		2	4		
4	5	2				7		

244

	4				7		6	
	6		4					9
1			3	6				
		3	7		2	1		4
		1				8		
4		8	1		3	9		
				7	6			3
5					1		2	
	1		5				9	

245

2			3				7	
9	3	7		2				8
						2	3	
	8	4						6
		6	5		4	9		
1						4	8	
	7	2						
8				7		6	2	1
	9				2			5

246

	4		3	6				
		6					5	
	9	7	8		4			6
			6			1		
3				1				2
		4			7			
5			4		3	7	1	
	2					5		
				7	9		6	

247

4		1						3
	9	7	3					5
		2						7
	1		9	7			6	
9			2		3			8
	5			8	4		7	
1						7		
7					6	2	8	
8						5		1

248

		1				7		4
		6					8	2
8	7				9			
				8			4	5
9			5		4			3
5	2			3				
			2				5	1
7	1					9		
2		5				3		

249

	9			1		7		
3								9
	6		7	9			3	
		6						8
		7	4	3	9	2		
5						9		
	5			7	2		8	
4								6
		3		4			9	

250

	7			3	4			
		5	7					1
8				2		7		3
		9	3				2	
	6			4			3	
	3				9	1		
5		2		9				7
9					2	6		
			5	8			4	

251

					4	7	8	
9			6		8			3
1				3	5			
		6			1	3		
5								7
		8	3			4		
			8	4				2
7			9		3			8
	3	2	1					

252

9			4			8		3
		4		1		9		
7					6			
					1		9	4
		9	8		2	7		
4	3		7					
			6					5
		7		3		2		
1		6			8			7

253

	4		2		6	8		
6			8	5				
	1	8				9		
1						5		
	2		6	3	1		4	
		3						6
		4				3	7	
				2	3			4
		9	7		4		8	

254

				5	7	6		1
4			9		1			
	8			3		9		
8	5	7						
	9			6			1	
						7	3	5
		3		2			7	
			3		6			8
2		8	5	9				

255

1				7				
					1			6
	2	6				1	8	
	5	7	3		9			
	8						4	
			7		6	5	3	
	3	8				4	7	
5			9					
				2				3

256

6	2	4				8		1
9	8							
1			4	8			2	
5			6	2				
			1		7			
				5	4			6
	1			9	2			4
							9	3
3		8				6	1	2

257

		6	2			7		
					3	9	4	8
				7			5	6
1		7	4					9
	4						1	
8					9	4		7
7	1			9				
3	2	9	8					
		4			2	3		

258

	5		2	3		4	7	
4								
	2	8		5	1		9	
3							5	
			8	7	2			
	7							8
	3		7	8		5	6	
								7
	4	7		9	5		3	

259

1							6	9
	5	4	3					
3	9			8				
	1	7					2	
		9	1		8	4		
	4					1	9	
				1			4	8
					2	9	1	
5	6							2

260

	7		6		1			
4	1				5			3
			3	4				
2	6					3		
1	9						6	7
		7					4	1
				3	4			
8			5				3	4
			9		6		7	

261

	5				1			
3				7				
2	4		3	6		7		
		2			4		1	
		9	8		7	3		
	8		2			4		
		7		5	6		4	2
				4				1
			9				8	

262

	6						4	8
				8	9			7
9	8			3		5		
8		9				4		
			2		5			
		7				1		6
		4		5			1	3
5			8	2				
1	9						5	

263

	5	7	4		9			
1							4	7
					7	5	8	2
			6	7	1			
7								1
			3	4	2			
4	6	9	5					
3	2							4
			2		4	6	9	

264

8		5			6			
6	3				7			
				8		5	2	6
7				4				5
	2		3		5		4	
9				1				2
3	4	9		6				
			7				8	9
			9			6		1

265

6			1	3	2	4		
5	2							7
			9				8	
4						7	9	
			8	5	1			
	8	2						6
	9				3			
8							7	1
		1	7	6	8			3

266

			6				9	5
4		6		8			7	2
				1		4		
	6		9			3		
			7		2			
		5			1		2	
		3		7				
9	7			2		5		4
1	5				6			

267

		8	2					3
				1		4	5	
5	1		3				9	
4			9			8		
			6		5			
		5			7			9
	7				1		2	4
	3	4		9				
2					8	1		

268

9	1					8		
5			7					
6	8	3			1		5	
		2		4	3			
4				7				3
			9	5		7		
	7		5			6	3	9
					6			5
		6					8	1

269

9						6		
6					2			3
		7	5	6	3		4	
		5	8				7	
			3	7	9			
	3				4	2		
	4		7	3	6	8		
3			4					2
		8						7

270

	4	7						1
9					3			
	2	6		7		9	4	
7		4	3					
	9						8	
					8	2		3
	1	8		6		3	7	
			1					4
4						1	5	

271

2				6			5	
	9			8	1			
1		4			7	6		
				1		5		3
	2						4	
3		6		2				
		7	5			4		8
			1	4			7	
	3			9				5

272

	5			4				7
3			9				8	2
		8			3			
	7		6		8		5	3
		2				8		
8	9		5		4		7	
			3			7		
2	6				5			8
1				8			3	

273

6					1			2
				6	5		8	
1	5		3					
			2	3		4		
3		2				9		5
		8		9	4			
					3		9	1
	9		6	5				
2			4					7

274

6			8				3	7
			7	9			5	
4					5			
3		6			8	2		
		1	4		7	9		
		9	2			4		6
			3					8
	3			2	9			
1	5				4			9

275

2	4			8			7	
		5			1			3
1		6	3					
4	6				3			
		8		5		2		
			2				1	8
					8	6		7
6			5			9		
	7			4			3	1

276

	8		4		9		7	
4		6						3
9				8				4
		9			5		2	
		1		7		5		
	6		1			9		
6				2				7
1						4		2
	3		5		4		8	

277

	7		1		8	4		
9	4		3					
		8		4		1		9
		4	2				7	
5								1
	3				4	5		
7		2		8		6		
					2		5	8
		9	6		5		1	

278

2			3		7			
	9						5	
	5		8		4			3
5		9					3	1
		2		6		4		
3	7					6		9
7			6		2		9	
	4						1	
			1		9			4

279

					9	3		
9	5		8		1	7	2	
				3				8
	4		6		7			
7								5
			5		2		6	
6				5				
	7	9	4		8		1	6
		2	9					

280

5		4		6				
			5				6	1
	3				9			7
		5	9					
9	8						4	5
					5	1		
3			2				5	
2	7				8			
				9		8		6

281

6						8	9	
		3	6		8			1
	1		4			5		7
	3		5	8				
			7		3			
				1	2		3	
3		1			6		5	
2			8		5	3		
	9	7						8

282

5		9	6				3	
			9	8				4
6			7				5	8
					1	2		
	5						6	
		8	2					
2	4				7			3
8				9	3			
	3				8	4		5

283

					3	4	6	
	6		4	8				
3								7
8				5	1	9	4	
		9	2		6	7		
	5	3	9	4				2
2								6
				6	2		8	
	3	8	1					

284

1			2	3				
	3	5			8	6		
8	7					5		
		2	4					6
	5						1	
9					3	4		
		4					8	5
		8	7			1	2	
				8	1			4

285

	7	4						1
			7	4	5			9
8	9		6					
2		8					4	
		5		8		6		
	6					2		8
					7		8	3
7			4	1	2			
4						7	1	

286

		5	4	8	6		7	
				2				
2	7		9					6
8	2					5		
		3	2		1	8		
		9					1	2
9					8		6	5
				5				
	8		6	7	9	1		

287

			5			9		6
9				4				5
			2		9		4	
	5					7		
	1	3	4		5	2	9	
		2					1	
	6		3		8			
1				5				2
7		5			2			

288

	1							8
3					2	5		
					4	1	3	7
7	3		4	8		6		
6								3
		9		6	3		5	4
2	7	3	6					
		6	9					5
1							8	

289

4	3							6
5			3	6		9		
	6	1		4			5	
			7		8	2		
7								8
		9	5		6			
	7			8		3	6	
		8		1	5			4
2							8	1

290

	9	1						
3			9	5				8
	8				6	5		1
					8			2
6	5		2		9		7	3
1			4					
7		3	6				8	
9				3	7			6
						3	4	

291

	2			3		7		
4		9					3	
8			2				5	6
				4	1		6	
		2	7		9	3		
	6		3	8				
2	9				4			3
	3					5		4
		1		5			2	

292

				3	8			5
		5	6				7	
8					5		6	1
	9					7		
	8	1				9	5	
		3					4	
6	5		1					4
	4				3	6		
9			8	4				

293

8	4		7					
9	1					4		
		2	8		9			
2		5		3				
		7	5		8	6		
				9		7		3
			9		4	3		
		4					8	9
					2		1	4

294

	8				9		6	
		1	5		8			9
			6	7				2
		5		8				
1	7						3	8
				6		9		
9				5	6			
8			4		1	2		
	4		8				7	

295

	7				3			1
9		4			7			2
1				9			7	
	4	9			6			
		1		4		9		
			9			1	3	
	1			2				3
6			7			8		5
8			6				1	

296

9			3		5			
		1		6				
5	2		7		9	4		
				3	8	6		
8	9						4	1
		2	9	5				
		8	5		3		9	4
				9		2		
			1		4			6

297

8		3		6				5
5			3	1		9		
1	4						6	
			5		2			
	2						7	
			1		8			
	9						8	7
		1		8	6			9
4				5		1		2

298

4		5		1				
	2	6	4		8			
		8			2		5	
5			9			2		6
			1		3			
2		3			5			7
	4		2			3		
			8		1	7	2	
				9		6		1

299

	8	5	3		6		1	
				1			2	
1					2		6	
		6			5			
			6	9	8			
			1			5		
	1		7					8
	3			4				
	2		8		9	1	5	

300

				4	5		8	
						5		3
	7				3	4		2
6				7	4			
2								8
			6	3				4
8		9	3				1	
3		1						
	6		8	1				

301

		1	5	3				
						9	3	
2			4	9		5		
9					1			
7	4						5	8
			6					3
		5		6	8			2
	6	2						
				1	3	6		

302

		8		3			6	
			2		4		7	
					5			1
		6		4		9		
7		1		5		6		4
		9		8		5		
8			4					
	9		7		8			
	4			9		8		

303

2			4		6			7
		8		3			6	
	5			7				4
	4	1						
8								1
						5	8	
7				2			9	
	1			8		2		
5			7		9			6

304

					5			7
9					7		5	
	2		9	8			4	
7					3		1	9
			8		6			
8	3		7					4
	4			9	8		7	
	8		5					6
2			6					

305

	9		6		7		3	
		1	5	8			9	
						6		
		9	2					4
			9		1			
4					6	8		
		8						
	2			7	4	5		
	3		1		9		7	

306

9				4	1		6	
4				8	3		9	
						3		
1		2	3					8
				1				
3					5	1		2
		7						
	5		4	3				6
	1		9	2				4

307

		4	9		7			
	1		8	5				
6		7	3					9
8						1	6	
2				4				7
	3	1						2
1					9	2		3
				3	6		9	
			4		1	6		

308

					9			
6			8		1		7	
5	1	4		7				
		6		8				4
1								5
4				6		1		
				3		5	9	7
	3		4		5			6
			9					

309

		9		2	4	1		
					1		7	4
6				5		9		
						2	6	5
2								1
1	9	6						
		8		3				7
9	2		4					
		4	2	7		5		

310

	2		1				3	
		3		8	9			
1					7	2		6
9	6						4	
				9				
	8						9	7
4		9	8					1
			7	5		9		
	7				1		8	

311

5	6				9		4	
		7	6				8	3
4	8							
		8		6				9
			1		8			
6				9		8		
							1	5
8	9				4	6		
	2		3				7	8

312

7	1			4	5			
	4	9				2		
								6
		2		9				8
6			8		2			9
4				5		7		
3								
		7				3	8	
			6	8			7	5

313

	2				9			
	9	6				7		
5	1				2		6	
1			7			8		
	4		5		3		9	
		9			8			3
	8		4				7	1
		5				6	8	
			9				2	

314

	9							
			4		2			9
		1	3	9			8	
6			7				5	1
		8		1		9		
2	1				6			7
	6			7	8	5		
1			6		9			
							2	

315

8	5	7			9			2
3			2					
				3				
	7			4	2	6		
		4	3		5	1		
		8	1	7			3	
				2				
					7			3
9			6			7	5	4

316

			6			4	7	
2					7	1	9	
			2		3	6		5
					1			
	8	2		6		9	3	
			3					
8		1	7		4			
	6	3	1					9
	5	9			6			

317

	6	8						
7						4		3
		1			7		8	
	2				1	9		6
	9		5		2		4	
5		7	8				3	
	7		6			5		
6		4						9
						6	1	

318

	4					9	3	6
2					3	7		4
			4					
		5		8	4	2		
			1		7			
		7	2	6		3		
					1			
8		6	7					5
7	2	9					6	

319

		8	9	7			4	
			8				9	2
	6			4	2			8
		7	1	5				
	1						3	
				6	8	7		
8			6	3			1	
1	9				4			
	5			9	1	2		

320

		4	1			9		
	1		6					
				9	3			8
	7				4	2		9
	9		7		2		1	
8		3	9				7	
5			4	1				
					9		8	
		9			8	7		

321

9					5			
	2	7			4	5		
						6		2
	9					2	7	4
				1				
6	7	2					8	
8		3						
		6	9			7	1	
			8					5

322

	9		1	6		8		
5				7				1
		8				6		
3	5							
	2	1	3		5	7	4	
							3	2
		7				2		
2				9				6
		6		5	1		9	

323

	8		7					1
					1		9	
	4	1					6	
	1		5	6				
5		8		7		4		3
				3	4		5	
	2					9	1	
	9		4					
6					8		7	

324

1			5	3				4
					4			
5	8	4		1			6	
	3			2	1			
		2		7		6		
			9	6			5	
	5			9		3	4	7
			2					
9				4	8			2

325

7		8	5	6				
	3							
	4				2		9	7
					1			9
4	1						2	6
9			8					
3	9		4				7	
							6	
				1	7	4		5

326

	8							
		7		5		9		
3		2	7			5	8	6
6						8	9	
			5	1	8			
	4	8						3
7	1	6			4	2		5
		5		2		6		
							1	

327

1	4							
7		2		5		9		
	3	6			1			8
		7	2					1
	5						9	
9					4	8		
3			6			7	2	
		4		7		1		5
							8	3

328

		7	6	3				1
	4				1			3
		9			2		7	
			4	9				
	3		5		7		4	
				2	6			
	6		9			1		
2			1				5	
5				8	4	7		

329

		7			8		4	
						9		
6	1	4		3				
	6				2	7		5
7			3		6			4
5		2	1				6	
				7		1	8	6
		5						
	2		8			3		

330

		7	8					
		8	1			3		
	2			3	9			
	3			6	5		4	
		2		4		5		
	6		7	1			3	
			5	8			6	
		4			1	7		
					7	2		

331

	7	4	1					
6		2		4			7	3
1								
		3		2			5	
		7	5		6	4		
	5			8		7		
								4
7	4			1		9		8
					9	5	1	

332

	9	8				6		
		6			7			
2			5				8	
7		3		8	5		2	
	8						3	
	2		9	7		5		8
	7				1			9
			3			7		
		2				4	5	

333

				5	3	4		8
8				2		5		
1					9		2	
3	9							
		4				1		
							6	4
	8		6					2
		2		8				9
6		1	4	9				

334

				5		7	2	
		5		2		6		4
3	2		7				9	
	3	6			2			
9								2
			1			9	3	
	1				9		6	5
5		8		7		2		
	4	2		1				

335

3		5	9	8			4	
			5			7		3
						8		
				5	1			
7		4	3		9	5		6
			8	4				
		3						
4		1			7			
	6			1	8	3		5

336

	6					8	7	
	1		2					
	8			7	3			
		8			4			1
		7	5		1	3		
9			3			2		
			8	1			5	
					6		4	
	7	5					2	

337

					6		1	9
	9		8					
		6		5		7		3
6	1		4					
	2			1			6	
					3		9	8
4		2		9		6		
					5		8	
7	8		3					

338

2		5	9					
7			5					9
	3	9	2			7		
		2		1				3
	5						8	
8				4		5		
		6			2	9	4	
1					6			5
					7	8		1

339

3	7	8			9			6
2			6	3				
								5
	8					4		
		3	2	4	7	5		
		7					9	
8								
				5	1			4
4			9			6	1	3

340

		4	7				3	
			8	2		7	4	
2		1						6
		6					1	
			4		7			
	8					3		
4						5		1
	1	2		6	8			
	9				5	8		

341

3			9					
		4				8	1	
		9		8	5			
						6	2	
	6			2			8	
	5	3						
			1	7		4		
	9	6				5		
					9			2

342

5			2	8				9
				5	7	8		
						4	1	
	6	2	7					
					6	3	9	
	2	8						
		4	6	2				
6				4	9			3

343

		5	8	3				
	1						3	
7				5	2			4
		6		7				8
		1	5		6	4		
9				8		2		
4			7	6				1
	9						6	
				9	8	3		

344

8			3			9		
	4						1	3
		6				8	2	
		9		3	2			
			9	7	8			
			5	1		3		
	6	8				7		
4	7						5	
		1			6			2

345

	4				2	5		
		6	1	5			3	4
2						8		9
7			9		5			
	9						4	
			6		1			5
6		7						3
3	2			6	4	7		
		4	2				9	

346

	3					6	1	
5	1							
7		9	6			2		
2				8	6			9
1				2				6
9			7	1				2
		8			4	5		1
							8	4
	9	1					2	

347

7								3
2		3	8			4		
			3			9	8	7
5	1			6			4	
			2		1			
	3			7			1	2
3	4	5			6			
		6			5	8		4
8								5

348

6		1	3					7
2	3		8				5	
9				1				
	6			8				5
			5	7	3			
5				2			8	
				3				4
	4				5		1	6
1					8	2		9

349

				3			6	
				2	4			5
	3	5	1					
8			2	9		5	7	
		3				4		
	2	7		4	5			3
					1	7	9	
1			7	5				
	9			6				

350

					9		6	7
				3	1			2
						5		
	7	8		6		2	9	
		2		5		8		
	9	3		2		4	5	
		4						
2			6	1				
6	1		3					

351

				3	5		6	
7	5				2	9		4
2								
				6		4		1
				4				
9		8		2				
								2
4		5	2				3	7
	3		8	7				

352

		9		4	8	3		
			2					5
6	5				9		8	
		7					3	
1		5		7		4		6
	3					7		
	7		4				9	3
9					5			
		4	6	9		1		

353

		9		8	1		3	2
8								
	4	1			7		8	
		8			2			5
4				9				8
3			8			7		
	2		3			9	4	
								6
5	8		6	7		2		

354

	3	6		7				
	9		8					
1	2			3				5
		8			7	4		
4								3
		3	4			1		
6				1			3	2
					3		7	
				2		6	8	

355

		8		9	6			7
4	9			7		3		
	6	3	8				9	
			7			1		
		7			9			
	7				1	8	2	
		6		5			3	4
2			6	4		7		

356

	3	9						
	5	7	3					
			1			4		9
				6			8	3
9		5				6		1
6	8			9				
5		2			4			
					8	1	4	
						3	2	

357

		5			6			
4	7		8	9		6		2
		6				3		1
					9		4	
9			3		5			6
	6		4					
1		8				7		
6		2		4	8		1	9
			6			8		

358

	7				9			
5			1					8
		6	2			4		7
		2	6				3	9
		1				8		
3	6				8	7		
2		5			6	9		
9					7			2
			9				8	

359

			2	1			6	
						9		
2	5		7				3	
	1	3				5		6
	4			5			9	
5		6				3	8	
	6				7		4	8
		5						
	2			4	1			

360

9					6			2
					5		1	
5		1	3	2		7		
		4				9	7	
7								1
	9	6				4		
		7		3	1	8		6
	4		8					
8			6					5

361

	2	4			8			
				3				8
				2			1	4
	6	1	8		2			
		3		9		7		
			7		3	1	5	
3	4			8				
6				1				
			9			2	4	

362

3	9		2			8		
4								
6				7				5
		9		4	2			
		5	1		3	6		
			6	8		7		
1				6				3
								9
		2			7		1	6

363

8		4	1	3	2		9	
	1				9		3	
						6	8	9
		2		9		7		
9	8	6						
	6		3				1	
	3		5	4	7	9		2

364

2	8							
		6			2			1
			6	3	7	2		4
	6				1			
4			2		6			9
			4				6	
1		5	9	2	4			
6			3			1		
							9	5

365

1	8		2				4	
	4			8		7	9	
								5
			7			2	6	
			6		2			
	3	6			5			
3								
	9	8		7			5	
	5				4		3	8

366

	1		4	2				
						8	4	2
2				5	9			7
		6					8	
		5	7	1	6	9		
	3					7		
3			9	4				8
4	2	9						
				7	5		9	

367

	5					3		
3		6	9		1			
			7	8		4		
6		5		1				8
			8		4			
8				7		1		2
		2		3	8			
			2		9	6		1
		3					8	

368

		9	1	5			2	4
	4				3			1
	2				4			
			3			6		
			8	4	6			
		6			9			
			6				9	
1			9				8	
9	6			3	2	7		

369

			7					6
2		7				9	8	
6		1					4	7
			6				1	
		3	1	8	2	5		
	5				3			
5	1					8		3
	8	6				4		9
4					5			

370

	4	1					3	2
				1				8
			4	9	8	5		
					1		6	
6								7
	5		2					
		3	1	8	4			
2				3				
9	7					8	1	

371

		5	8	3				
			4	6	2	8		
4					5			6
		9					7	
7			5		3			2
	6					5		
9			2					4
		4	6	8	7			
				9	4	2		

372

	6		2	9				
			8		1			7
		9					8	
		6				3		
	4	1		3		7	9	
		8				1		
	7					8		
3			6		9			
				1	8		7	

373

		8	9				4	7
				1	3			9
4			7			6		
			3					6
		4	6		7	9		
8					2			
		1			6			8
6			5	3				
3	9				1	7		

374

6	4						9	
9	3		4	7			2	
		5	3	2				
2						6		
			8		1			
		9						1
				9	5	3		
	2			1	3		4	9
	9						5	7

375

		8		7			2	
3	6						7	
						6	3	
		3	4					5
	7	4	5	8	9	3	6	
9					6	2		
	3	9						
	2						1	6
	4			5		9		

376

		2	8		4			6
	4	7						3
				6			9	
			5				6	
		9	4		3	1		
	2				7			
	8			7				
1						7	3	
2			9		6	8		

377

	8				1	9		
4		9		8		1	2	7
				9				6
	5					2		
			7	1	3			
		3					8	
9				3				
5	3	4		6		7		8
		1	8				5	

378

			2					
	6	2		1	8			
	8			4		5		3
		4	8				6	
	9						5	
	2				1	9		
6		8		3			4	
			4	9		1	8	
					7			

379

6			9		4			
4		8	5			6		9
	2	5			8	3	6	
	3						7	
	4	7	3			1	8	
5		4			7	8		1
			8		2			7

380

		2		6	3		1	
			5					3
					9	4		
1		6		5				9
	4						5	
3				7		2		4
		8	7					
9					8			
	2		1	4		7		

381

			2					
5					7			8
7		3		9	4		2	
	8							2
		2		7		6		
1							4	
	5		4	6		2		7
6			1					5
					8			

382

	8		2					
				5			2	7
2	1						8	
		2	7			8	3	
			5		4			
	4	9			2	7		
	3						7	5
8	9			4				
					9		6	

383

				3	4			
5		1						4
		6			5	8	1	
	1				6	9		8
	7			5			4	
9		3	4				7	
	5	8	3			4		
1						3		9
			5	1				

384

	4							9
9	6				4	5	8	
2			9	8		3		
			2	9		8		
		2		7	6			
		9		4	7			3
	3	1	5				4	7
5							9	

385

9								6
		6	7	5			3	
	8	7			4		5	
6							8	
			8		6			
	2							7
	4		1			6	7	
	6			8	5	9		
8								2

386

6						9		1
9		1			7			5
	4			8	1	6		
				2	9			
		8				2		
			4	5				
		6	3	7			9	
1			2			7		8
7		2						6

387

				9	7			
		6	2					
5			3		1	8		
1			9			5		
	9	7	5		2	3	8	
		5			8			9
		8	7		4			5
					3	1		
			1	8				

388

1	2					9		
		8					1	
	6		4			7		5
		6	9		1		7	
		3		5		2		
	7		3		8	1		
5		1			4		3	
	8					5		
		7					9	8

389

5			7			1	8	
						4		3
1			4					
			1	6		8		9
		9		8		6		
8		4		2	7			
					3			8
9		1						
	2	6			9			4

390

	5	9	3	4			2	
							7	6
				6	1			
5						4		
	6	8		3		7	5	
		4						1
			1	7				
8	9							
	2			8	5	3	4	

391

	5							
4		8			2		6	
			1			8	3	
		7	5	3				
	4		6		9		5	
				7	8	2		
	2	9			6			
	1		2			4		5
							7	

392

		5						
	4		3			2		1
1		8			4			
			5			3		7
	8	4		6		9	2	
9		3			7			
			9			1		2
4		7			2		6	
						7		

393

								3
9	6	5			8	7		
						6	1	5
				8		9		
		6	3		9	5		
		1		6				
4	2	3						
		9	2			3	5	8
8								

394

7			6			2		4
3					1			
6		1		5				
8	6			4		3		
		2				7		
		7		2			9	6
				1		8		7
			8					1
1		6			4			9

395

6	9		7			1		
			8		5		9	
							7	6
9					6	4		
	4						1	
		5	9					8
3	2							
	6		1		3			
		9			7		8	1

396

				1	7	3		
5					3			8
		7		2				
		2			8			7
	8	6				9	5	
3			5			1		
				8		5		
6			4					1
		1	7	5				

397

		7						8
	3			9	8			6
					2	1		9
				3				
5	2	6		1		7	4	3
				7				
8		5	9					
7			6	5			3	
6						5		

398

		3		7				9
	4			6			8	
	9		4		2			
			3			1		8
		2		4		9		
3		4			7			
			8		6		5	
	2			5			9	
5				1		3		

399

		5			6			9
		1				8		
9	4				3			
4			3		5			
	9			7			1	
			4		1			7
			8				4	1
		8				7		
5			9			3		

400

		3		9	5			
		8		3			6	
7	1							9
				4	9	8		
		4		7		1		
		9	6	1				
2							8	1
	7			5		2		
			3	2		6		

401

4	9		3		2			6
8		6						3
	7		1			8		
				9			3	
3								5
	4			2				
		4			9		8	
2						5		4
6			5		4		9	2

402

				1	6			7
6	1				2	5		8
			5					
	7							6
		8	2		9	3		
2							4	
					5			
1		6	9				3	5
3			1	8				

403

8	4				3		7	
	6		8	9				
		3						9
3				8				4
		8		6		1		
9				3				2
1						5		
				1	5		4	
	3		7				9	1

404

8	7						1	
2				4				
3			9					
4		5	1				9	2
				7				
7	8				2	6		4
					8			3
				2				1
	2						4	9

405

	3		9			1	6	8
		2	7					
				6				
4			6	7			1	
9				4				6
	6			8	5			3
				9				
					7	3		
8	1	9			4		7	

406

5		7		3				
3			8		6	5	2	
			1					8
	2	6						1
		4				2		
1						4	3	
6					8			
	4	9	7		5			3
				4		9		2

407

		5	3					9
4			6					
				2		4	8	5
							2	4
		6		4		7		
2	9							
6	5	2		7				
					1			8
3					6	9		

408

	7					2		
								7
2	5	6			1		8	
	1	4	9				2	
		9	5		4	8		
	3				8	7	9	
	8		4			3	5	1
6								
		5					7	

409

			9			8		
9				1		7	4	
	2	6					9	
1							7	
		3	8		6	9		
	6							3
	4					5	3	
	1	9		3				4
		5			2			

410

	8				9	4		2
5		9	1				7	
		6		5				9
			9	4				
		4	5		8	9		
				3	1			
6				1		7		
	9				6	1		5
1		8	3				6	

411

3				5		4		
			8					3
	4		3					8
	9	6	7				8	1
	2						7	
7	3				1	6	4	
1					8		2	
6					5			
		4		3				6

412

			2			5	1	
	1	8						
					9	7	6	8
3			1	6				2
4				9	7			3
8	6	3	7					
						8	2	
	4	5			6			

413

		4	1					
	7					4		6
1	9			5				
5	2				3			4
		9				1		
4			9				6	7
				3			8	1
8		6					3	
					5	7		

414

8		4	1					
					3		7	9
				7				8
	2	8			7			
4	3						1	5
			9			8	6	
5				8				
2	6		3					
					2	3		6

415

					4		3	9
	6		7		9	5		2
			3		2	1		
			2			7		
	4						9	
		3			5			
		1	4		7			
4		2	5		3		1	
6	9		8					

416

			1		9		3	
		4		5	2			
1	7							
	9	6		8		3		
	5	2				6	9	
		8		6		5	7	
							4	3
			5	1		7		
	8		4		3			

417

		5						6
	6		7			1	3	
	3	2						
			4	7		3		5
4				5				1
2		3		6	9			
						4	1	
	9	1			6		7	
3						2		

418

	9		7			1		8
	6	4	2					
7				3	4			
8					9	5		
				5				
		3	8					1
			5	2				7
					3	8	9	
4		6			7		1	

419

		2				9		7
6						1	8	4
9				8			3	
			7	9		5		
				4				
		1		2	6			
	6			1				5
8	3	9						1
1		4				3		

420

	2	5	8					
		8			5	9		
9			7			3		
				5	7	2		
5								1
		3	6	1				
		4			8			3
		9	1			8		
					4	6	7	

421

3						5		
9	6	8		7				
	7		8			3		
	5				8			
	9	7				4	2	
			6				8	
		3			2		9	
				4		2	5	1
		9						4

422

	8			4	3		1	
						6		
	6	7			9			
	1			5		7	4	
		4		2		3		
	3	5		6			2	
			7			1	6	
		3						
	4		2	8			7	

423

					9	6	3	
		3			6		2	
6	2		5		3			1
8		2				5		4
4		5				1		3
2			9		4		1	6
	4		1			8		
	9	7	3					

424

	6		8	3		5		1
				1		7	6	
9			6					4
5								
1		4				9		7
								5
2					1			9
	1	3		2				
8		7		6	5		1	

425

7					5		2	
				1	2		6	
5								8
	5		8	2		9		
3				9				2
		9		5	6		7	
6								4
	4		5	7				
	7		9					5

426

			9	6	1		5	4
3					2		9	1
			3				2	
		5						2
			1	2	6			
4						9		
	4				7			
7	8		2					6
9	6		8	3	4			

427

1			9					4
	8			5	6		1	
		5			8			
	7	3	5	9				
	5						4	
				3	2	8	7	
			4			2		
	4		7	6			5	
5					1			7

428

				4		2	1	
	4					5		
	2		5	8				9
	5		9			8		
				7				
		7			3		4	
2				6	7		8	
		1					2	
	3	5		1				

429

			5		9	6	4	3
								8
	9				2			
7			4			5	2	
		6				4		
	2	4			8			7
			8				5	
2								
9	5	8	7		1			

430

	1		8	6			9	
		3						7
7	6		5		9			
				8		7		
8	3	5				9	4	1
		7		4				
			4		1		3	6
2						4		
	4			5	8		1	

431

	3		6			8		
				2			6	
		1	3		8		2	
	6		7			4		5
	7						1	
1		4			5		7	
	1		5		4	7		
	4			1				
		3			6		4	

432

					6		5	
6			9		3			
		3	8	4				
						1	6	
1			5		2			3
	9	8						
				7	9	4		
			4		1			2
	8		6					

433

	9			5	7		6	8
	7				3			
1		4				8	2	
	8	7				6	5	
	3	6				1		7
			2				8	
7	4		1	8			9	

434

	2	9						
				4	8		7	
5			6					
2		1	4					
3	7		5		9		8	4
					7	9		2
					1			9
	4		8	9				
						7	6	

435

		1	8				9	
				2	9	7		
9		8				1		2
2	6		5					
8		7				4		6
					6		7	5
1		2				3		7
		6	7	4				
	7				1	5		

436

					2	5		
	8		1		4		2	
						4		1
	6		9			8		3
		1	4		3	2		
3		9			1		5	
5		6						
	9		2		7		8	
		8	6					

437

9			5		7			
8			1				9	
2	6							
					4		6	
		7	9	1	2	3		
	2		7					
							4	7
	5				1			3
			2		5			6

438

				2		7		5
	6	2						
1			9			2		
	8	1	2	9				
	2						9	
				5	6	3	2	
		8			1			2
						1	8	
7		5		4				

439

			7			4		1
			9			5	6	
					1	7	8	
	2		1	3				
		9	2		7	8		
				6	8		3	
	5	2	6					
	9	8			2			
4		3			5			

440

8		7	9					
		6		2				4
			8		7		5	
4	8						6	
		9				4		
	3						9	5
	4		7		1			
9				4		1		
					5	3		6

441

	1	5						
7		9			3			6
		6	5			2		
		3	6					
	5	2	3		1	9	6	
					4	3		
		7			8	4		
8			2			6		9
						1	2	

442

		9				1	5	
	8			5			4	
5			9					
		5		7	8	2		
9				2				4
		3	4	9		6		
					6			1
	1			4			8	
	9	6				7		

443

	5		1			8		6
	9						2	
6	1	7						4
2			5	6				9
			9		3			
5				4	2			3
1						9	5	8
	2						4	
8		4			5		6	

444

	5	4	8				2	3
		7			3			8
		6	1				9	
			4					5
	2						7	
9					6			
	6				1	7		
8			9			2		
7	1				4	8	6	

445

		4		3		9		
					1			
3	1		8	2			4	6
		2			7			
	5			9			1	
			1			6		
8	3			1	6		7	4
			7					
		6		8		1		

446

	2	9					6	
			1			7		9
8		6				2		
2					7	6		3
			8		9			
1		4	6					8
		7				3		6
9		1			3			
	8					4	1	

447

		9			4	6	2	
6	1						4	
		4	6					8
1		8		7				
		3		9		8		
				6		1		3
9					3	2		
	7						3	1
	8	1	2			4		

448

		6	5			4		
		1		9			8	
			4					5
8		3	6					1
			7		3			
4					1	3		9
9					7			
	1			2		5		
		4			5	2		

449

1		9						
						2		9
		2	8		1		5	
3			9			8		
	4		1		7		9	
		8			5			2
	9		5		4	7		
6		4						
						6		4

450

		2	6					
		7		4		6		2
4					5	7	1	
	4						3	
7								1
	8						9	
	7	8	2					3
5		9		1		2		
					7	9		

451

		7	4	5				3
						9	8	
					9		5	
7		2			8			5
		8		1		3		
6			7			8		2
	4		3					
	9	1						
8				9	1	4		

452

								7
1	8			7		6		
	6	7	8			4	5	
			9	3		5		
	1						6	
		5		6	4			
	5	9			7	3	2	
		6		2			9	5
8								

453

		9	1			2	5	
1			8			9		
	7				2	1	4	
2	1	5						
				8				
						5	1	7
	4	1	2				9	
		6			8			4
	9	2			4	8		

454

							7	
					6			3
			3		7	4	8	
3		6			8			1
		4	6		9	5		
1			7			9		6
	8	9	4		2			
5			9					
	2							

455

8				6		3		
		1	8					9
6					1	7		2
					2	5		7
	1			5			3	
3		5	4					
7		9	1					8
1					8	2		
		6		2				3

456

	2						7	3
9				2				
			3	8			2	6
1	5	6			2			
	3						9	
			6			4	5	1
4	7			6	1			
				3				7
3	9						6	

457

					6			8
		6		1		7		
2					7	5	9	
	8				2	3		
1				3				5
		3	6				8	
	9	4	7					2
		2		6		8		
6			1					

458

					5	6		
8		7		9			1	
						8	5	3
4		2			7			
	6			5			7	
			6			9		2
2	8	3						
	1			6		7		8
		6	2					

459

						5		9
7	8	2				1		
9			6				8	
			8		2		5	
2								6
	6		4		5			
	2				6			4
		1				7	9	5
4		9						

460

				5	1	6		
1				3		4		
	5				6		7	
	3					8		6
5	2						9	7
8		4					1	
	1		9				2	
		2		7				4
		7	1	4				

461

			5		9		7	
1	3		7					
7		9				8		
8	7							2
			2	3	4			
2							9	1
		2				6		9
					2		5	8
	5		4		6			

462

		8						
1			2		7	8		9
6	7		3					
					9			6
7		6		2		1		5
4			6					
					8		2	3
2		5	4		3			8
						7		

463

		5	1		3		4	
4	2				5		1	
		7				5		
				8				
8		2	5		7	4		6
				1				
		8				3		
	5		7				2	9
	9		8		2	7		

464

			1			2		
	3		7	5				4
1		6					3	
			3			4		1
4			2		6			3
8		3			1			
	7					3		6
3				9	7		2	
		9			5			

465

				9	1			
3			2	8				
	7		3			2	1	
8		9				4		
	3			5			7	
		2				6		9
	6	3			9		2	
				3	2			7
			6	1				

466

			3					4
		8	7	1				
	5				8			7
	1		8				2	9
	6			7			1	
9	8				1		7	
4			2				8	
				4	7	3		
1					6			

467

3			1					
	4				9	5	3	
	2			5			1	8
	1		4		7	9		
		4	9		1		5	
2	6			1			9	
	3	1	7				6	
					6			5

468

3		4		6	5		7	
5			8		4			6
		8						
	8	2						
		7	9		6	5		
						1	6	
						7		
4			3		7			1
	9		4	1		6		2

469

					2		9	
2					7		8	5
			5	9		3	4	
	3							7
6		8				2		9
1							3	
	6	4		7	9			
9	7		6					3
	2		4					

470

1					9			
		7	3			5	4	
				6	8	3		
5					3	1		
	1			8			5	
		2	9					6
		1	8	2				
	9	4			5	8		
			6					3

471

9	5			1			7	
		1	5					8
6	3						4	
5	9							
			4		2			
							3	6
	8						6	2
7					3	5		
	4			5			9	7

472

					6			
		8	7	1			2	
	5	4				7		
3		6		5				7
	8		3		2		1	
5				7		6		3
		2				9	5	
	6			2	1	3		
			5					

473

	4				6	3		
		8	3	9			7	
	5							2
				3		7		
	7		9	8	5		4	
		4		6				
5							6	
	9			2	8	1		
		3	6				8	

474

					4	1		
					3		9	
	9		1			3	5	
5	4				2			
	3	7		6		9	2	
			7				3	4
	1	3			5		6	
	6		8					
		2	9					

475

		5			3		8	
			8				3	6
				6		5	4	
1		2		4				
3		6		5		2		4
				2		3		8
	6	4		3				
7	1				6			
	2		7			9		

476

	4				1			
	7				6	2	1	
2		1			9	7		
5			3	2				
	2						8	
				1	7			3
		9	1			8		2
	3	6	7				5	
			5				3	

477

		4			3			1
	8					3		6
6	2			8				
	6			1	8			
		5	9		6	7		
			3	4			1	
				5			8	7
5		6					3	
2			4			9		

478

			9					8
	9			8	6			3
2		6			7	9		
1		8		7			3	
		9				7		
	2			3		8		6
		3	5			6		2
4			2	9			8	
8					4			

479

5		1			7			
8			9		4			
	2	7					9	
		9			5			1
	1	6				2	5	
2			3			9		
	7					5	1	
			7		1			6
			5			7		8

480

		2	6					1
	7	4			5	3		
				8				
	8			4				9
4	9						7	3
3				6			1	
				3				
		8	7			9	5	
7					4	1		

481

	6	3		4		9		
9			6					
							3	1
8			7					4
		7	1		8	5		
2					9			8
5	8							
					6			2
		6		5		1	7	

482

9				4	6			7
6	8		2				3	
			8					9
	7		6					
			7	3	1			
					4		8	
3					5			
	5				9		4	2
7			3	6				1

483

		2			3	4	6	
			2				9	
3				6			8	2
						1	3	
	6		8		4		2	
	7	4						
4	2			9				3
	5				1			
	3	6	7			5		

484

				4		5	9	
1		5	9					
					7	6		4
		6	7					5
	1			9			6	
8					4	1		
6		9	3					
					5	9		2
	7	8		2				

485

9	1		3					
	5			8				3
		8		4		6		
		1	7				5	9
				9				
2	7				6	3		
		4		2		7		
3				6			9	
					3		4	6

486

9								
					4		8	9
	1			9		4		2
5	2			7				4
	7		8		9		2	
1				6			3	7
4		3		5			6	
6	5		9					
								3

487

	2		7		5	4		
8			3				7	
						3	5	
					8		1	7
	7	3				8	4	
4	8		6					
	6	5						
	3				2			4
		8	9		7		6	

488

	4		2	6				
	1	3	9					4
		5			1			
	3		7			8		
		7				3		
		8			2		7	
			8			4		
2					7	5	8	
				1	4		2	

489

1						4		
4		6	7					
7	5						3	
6				3	7	1		2
			9		4			
9		5	1	2				4
	7						2	3
					2	7		1
		1						8

490

		6		4		2		
5			1					
	8		5				9	
							3	2
		9	3	7	1	8		
4	6							
	9				5		6	
					8			4
		4		6		5		

491

9			2	3				7
	6			1				
		4	7			1		
		2					5	
	9		5		8		3	
	7					6		
		6			2	4		
				9			1	
1				4	3			5

492

		3		8	1	6		
	1		5	2				7
		9			7			5
								2
2	7						4	6
3								
5			8			9		
4				9	5		6	
		1	7	3		2		

493

		6					5	7
7	9		1					
	8					9		
	5		6	4		8		
			7		5			
		2		9	1		4	
		1					7	
					2		8	9
2	7					5		

494

					4			
2	7				1			4
			7	5		9		1
						3	5	8
6	8						2	7
5	1	2						
7		9		4	3			
1			2				6	3
			6					

495

	6		4	3			9	7
						2		6
					8		5	
8					7	4		
	2						3	
		4	8					5
	8		1					
5		3						
1	4			9	3		2	

496

6				7	8		5	9
7				4				6
							2	
	7				9	6		5
9								3
5		1	8				9	
	5							
4				8				7
2	3		6	9				1

497

5					7	2		
			2			3	8	
6		3						
			5	2				1
			8		6			
9				7	4			
						6		3
	8	5			1			
		4	9					5

498

2			8				5	
		6						8
	3			1	6	2		
			4	3				9
5								4
8				2	9			
		1	3	5			4	
3						7		
	8				4			2

499

		9		7	3			2
	6		9			7		
			4				8	
		5				6	4	
		7		3		8		
	8	4				5		
	9				7			
		2			1		7	
5			2	9		4		

500

	2			3	4			
1	5							
		4			1	7		
5					2		1	
		7				6		
	6		3					9
		2	8			9		
							7	4
			6	9			2	

501

				9			2	
9	3						6	1
			6		7			
	9	4	5				7	
		7		2		6		
	5				1	4	9	
			2		9			
1	2						3	6
	4			3				

502

8								
2				4			6	1
		3		6	1	5		
	3	4					8	
		8	3		9	2		
	2					7	1	
		2	1	5		4		
6	8			7				5
								2

503

	9	3	5		1			
8		4					5	
		7		9				
		1	6	5				
	8		7		3		1	
				8	9	5		
				7		8		
	3					2		6
			8		5	1	9	

504

	4							3
9	1				6	4		2
				1		8		
					9			
7	5		1		2		6	4
			5					
		6		7				
4		5	8				7	6
8							2	

505

	1	6			3			
			7	2			3	
	9					8		
9					4		2	
5								6
	6		9					7
		4					8	
	8			1	7			
			3			2	5	

506

	4			6	3			
3		6		5				
5	2	7						
1		2						6
			6	8	9			
9						5		3
						7	5	8
				3		6		4
			1	7			3	

507

7		6					1	9
				4	5		3	
4	9			7		8		
6				9				3
		8		1			6	2
	6		2	8				
2	1					6		7

508

	5					3		
	2				5	1		
1			9		8		7	2
					9			
	7	6		3		4	9	
			5					
2	3		7		4			6
		5	8				3	
		4					1	

509

3								
6			1		4	3		
		4	5	3			8	
	9					4	5	
7				4				3
	8	5					7	
	7			2	9	8		
		9	4		7			5
								7

510

6			3			5	9	8
		9						4
5							1	
		5	8	4	6			
				2				
			5	1	7	2		
	3							2
1						9		
8	2	4			5			3

511

	7	5		8			4	
		1	2					
8			5					
7				2			1	
	1	3	7		5	2	9	
	5			4				6
					9			1
					2	9		
	6			7		8	5	

512

7	6							
		2		3	1			
		4	6			7		
				8		9	1	
		7	4		5	8		
	3	1		2				
		8			9	1		
			1	4		6		
							9	7

513

2			6				3	5
8	6	3		2		4		7
5			3	4				
			1		8			
				7	6			1
6		8		1		3	2	4
3	1				5			8

514

6		8					4	
1				2	5			3
		2	3				8	4
		1		5		9		
3	9				4	2		
9			2	4				1
	4					3		5

515

1			2					
				9		8		7
		7	3		6			9
				7		1		
7	5						4	8
		6		3				
2			4		3	7		
3		8		6				
					9			6

516

			5		3		2	8
	3			4		5		
						1	4	
6	5			8				
9			6		1			2
				2			5	6
	1	7						
		5		7			3	
2	6		8		9			

517

				6				
5		1	8	3			7	
3	9							
		3			4	7	2	
4			6		7			8
	5	7	1			9		
							8	5
	3			7	8	6		9
				4				

518

	2						6	1
					6			9
			7	5			8	
				2		1	7	3
		9				2		
1	7	2		3				
	4			7	9			
6			8					
5	3						9	

519

8	6							
5					8		9	
1		7	4					
3			9		2		1	
	1		6		3		2	
	7		5		4			3
					7	9		4
	9		3					1
							6	2

520

	6	1	3					8
					6			3
		2	4	1				
		7				3		4
2								9
9		5				2		
				9	2	5		
6			1					
8					7	4	1	

521

2							1	
4			6					
	7			4				
			1		5	6	8	
1								7
	5	6	2		3			
				8			7	
					1			3
	9							5

522

	9	7					5	4
		5	9				6	
					2	3		
			4			1	2	
9				3				5
	2	8			5			
		9	7					
	3				4	5		
6	5					4	9	

523

8		3	6					
	4	5					1	
			2					5
1					4			
4	2			3			9	6
			7					8
7					9			
	1					5	8	
					8	3		9

524

	7		1				6	
	9	8						2
		1			6	9	5	
7	8				2			
			4	6	5			
			3				2	9
	6	7	2			4		
1						5	9	
	5				1		8	

525

		9			7		2	
4	3						1	
5					3		9	4
					4	3		
			9		2			
		7	5					
3	6		7					8
	2						5	6
	1		8			2		

526

	1			4		2		
			8			1	9	
						6		4
1	4				9	8		2
		5				4		
2		3	4				1	7
6		8						
	3	1			8			
		7		5			4	

527

		7	6	4				
9			8					
5		8			1			6
	9	3						2
				6				
1						4	7	
4			1			2		3
					8			1
				5	6	7		

528

	1	6		7				
			1		8	6		
	2	7			4			
							1	9
5	9	1				3	4	6
3	8							
			8			1	6	
		3	2		1			
				4		2	5	

529

	1	3						
2		7	3				9	
		4		5	1			
1	2				3			
			9	2	5			
			1				3	6
			7	1		4		
	9				8	7		3
						5	1	

530

				7	6	8		
			2				4	3
							5	9
	7		9	6			1	
9								7
	5			1	3		8	
4	8							
2	3				4			
		9	5	2				

531

6	4	2			5			
	5	1	2					
			1	8				
				2	7	3	5	
		3				4		
	7	5	3	9				
				1	3			
					2	6	9	
			8			5	3	4

532

		8		1				6
	5							
	7				3	5		
					9		8	7
2			4		7			5
5	8		1					
		3	5				9	
							2	
1				2		4		

533

	4			2		1		
							4	
			8		6	3		
4	1							6
		2	4		7	8		
5							7	3
		4	7		2			
	8							
		5		9			2	

534

			7					
1						4	5	
	7		1	5			8	
			9	2				8
2		3				1		9
5				8	1			
	9			3	6		2	
	3	7						6
					7			

535

			7	4				
4		8		3	5	7	2	
	3	7	2					
	4	6						
8	9						4	6
						8	5	
					2	3	8	
	8	3	5	9		6		4
				8	3			

536

2				6			8	
	9	5		7	8	1		
		6						4
8					5	9		
	3		6		9		1	
		9	3					8
1						8		
		3	8	2		5	7	
	5			3				2

537

	7			2		8		
					8			7
8	6			4			2	3
			2			5		
		3	7		9	6		
		6			4			
7	1			3			6	9
9			4					
		4		9			7	

538

4				3			1	
	1		9		7			
		7		1		4		
		6						3
3	9			2			6	8
2						9		
		5		8		6		
			1		5		3	
	8			9				2

539

		7	6		1			8
			4				6	5
							7	
			5	2	6	9		
		2		9		6		
		6	1	4	7			
	3							
1	6				8			
8			9		4	3		

540

		4		7		5	6	
6				4	2			
		9			5			4
4						2	1	5
3								6
5	1	8						3
9			7			6		
			4	1				2
	8	3		9		4		

541

	3			4	2		7	
8								2
1		5				4		
9			6	8			5	
				2				
	8			5	3			6
		1				5		3
3								8
	6		5	3			1	

542

		4	7		8			
	2	7				5	1	
1			3					7
	7			6				8
	1						6	
5				2			3	
2					1			4
	4	1				3	2	
			2		9	1		

543

							8	9
				3		4		
			1		7	3		
6				8		1	9	2
	2						4	
1	3	9		2				5
		7	9		2			
		2		5				
4	9							

544

				1	9	5	2	
9	1						6	
2								9
		4		9	1			
			6	2	4			
			8	7		9		
6								7
	7						1	8
	8	5	2	4				

545

	4	2	5		6	3	8	
	3							
9		5				7		
	9				4			
6			8		3			5
			2				1	
		1				8		7
							5	
	7	8	6		2	1	9	

546

1	8		5					4
4				1				
5	3	9						
			6		2		3	
	2		1	5	3		8	
	1		7		9			
						8	6	2
				6				3
6					5		1	7

547

			9				2	8
				8				9
6				2			5	
	4				7			5
		7				1		
2			3				9	
	3			6				7
7				5				
1	6				8			

548

	7				4			
			3					9
8		4		1	5		7	
6							1	
1		7				4		8
	4							6
	8		4	9		6		5
5					2			
			1				9	

549

	5		2		1	6		
				7				
3		7		9				
	6		3				4	1
	8						6	
5	4				9		2	
				8		1		4
				3				
		8	6		4		3	

550

	9			3			5	
	4		5					
1						4		9
9		3		1				2
8				4				6
4				6		1		8
3		9						4
					6		3	
	7			8			2	

551

			7	6		5		
			3				4	8
		9			5		6	
2					6		7	1
7	4		8					5
	5		1			2		
9	7				8			
		1		9	7			

552

	1						9	
3						7	8	
			2	8		4		
			6	9		5		
		7	4		5	3		
		4		2	3			
		1		3	8			
	8	3						9
	6						4	

553

			4				9	7
			9			2		5
			7		3			
		3				6	5	
7								8
	6	4				3		
			6		5			
8		6			2			
2	5				7			

554

		7	5			3		8
5		2		4				
	1		6					
	3	5		9				
	7						8	
				3		5	6	
					9		3	
				5		8		6
3		9			1	2		

555

				3		2	4	
	4		5					1
		7						8
1	2			4				
			3	7	2			
				9			8	2
8						7		
3					6		9	
	7	9		2				

556

				8				7
	5	9						
7					5	9	6	
2		4			1	7		
1			8		7			4
		5	4			1		3
	1	3	9					5
						8	2	
5				7				

557

	1	8	6			2		3
					7			
			3				9	1
			9		2	7	5	
		9				6		
	7	6	8		3			
6	5				9			
			7					
9		4			1	3	6	

558

		5		2				
2			7			1	4	3
	4						5	
9						5		7
			5		1			
7		8						1
	6						1	
8	7	4			5			9
				3		7		

559

			6		2			
		6		7		8		
7						1	9	
	3	8		2				4
		7				5		
6				4		9	3	
	7	3						1
		2		1		3		
			4		7			

560

			6	4		5		
	2				5			
						2	4	3
4	8		1					6
9				3				8
7					6		9	2
6	7	9						
			5				3	
		3		6	1			

561

	9					8		
	5				1		2	
8				7		5		4
2			9					3
			3	6	2			
9					7			8
6		4		3				2
	2		4				7	
		9					6	

562

			4	5		2		
5			8	3				9
	7	3			9			4
3	9	8						2
6						7	3	1
8			2			1	9	
4				9	6			8
		9		8	5			

563

5				7	9			
		4						7
7	6			8		9		
9					5	6		
	5						8	
		6	2					3
		5		3			2	1
8						3		
			6	1				8

564

2	6				1			
		9					3	2
	4			8				7
8			9					
9	3	1	7		8	2	5	6
					3			8
3				9			8	
7	9					3		
			6				2	9

565

6			9			5	2	
2		3				7		
					1			
				3				9
	8	4	5		9	6	3	
9				4				
			3					
		2				3		7
	9	5			8			6

566

			5			6		
3				7			8	
1			6		9	5		
2	6						3	
		7				8		
	3						7	4
		5	4		3			6
	2			6				8
		4			2			

567

4	2		8			6		
				5				7
6			1		4			
9	4					1		5
	5						9	
1		8					6	4
			7		8			9
2				4				
		4			3		8	6

568

	7	8	9			1		
	9				5			
			7	1		6		
9		5			1	7		6
	3						1	
7		1	8			9		3
		3		4	7			
			1				6	
		7			3	2	4	

569

					4			7
	5	6				1		
		1	6				9	
	8	4			7			2
			2		3			
1			4			7	3	
	1				9	3		
		5				6	4	
4			3					

570

9			8		3			
							4	8
				4	2			6
	9	8			6	5		
1		5				6		7
		2	5			9	8	
6			3	7				
8	1							
			6		8			1

571

		9		5			8	
		6	1			4		9
	5		6					1
		2	4	1				
	1						6	
				3	5	1		
6					1		4	
5		4			3	9		
	2			7		5		

572

5							1	6
	3	1			4		9	
					2			
3		5	9		6		2	
				7				
	6		1		5	9		3
			8					
	7		2			8	6	
9	8							7

573

			9					
4	7				2	6		
2				4	3			
	3	2					1	4
		8				3		
9	1					5	6	
			4	2				8
		9	1				4	3
					5			

574

		7				1	5	4
				1	3			
			2					8
	2				9		8	
3		5		2		6		7
	9		5				4	
1					4			
			3	6				
6	5	9				4		

575

	8	7	5					
			3				5	
	3			8		7		
4							1	
5				3				9
	6							5
		1		6			7	
	4				1			
					2	3	6	

576

7		4		2	9			
	9	5	1	8				
8		3						
1					4			5
	3						4	
5			6					1
						3		9
				7	5	2	1	
			9	4		5		8

577

	8	9	2					
7				4				
			5		1		8	
8		3						7
2	4		9	6	7		3	8
1						5		6
	7		4		5			
				1				3
					9	2	5	

578

	8			3		1		
4	1							5
			1		4		9	
		1			8			
8	3		7		1		6	2
			6			7		
	5		3		2			
1							8	3
		3		8			2	

579

6					3			
		5		4				3
		8			9	1		7
1				8		4		2
		2				6		
7		3		2				5
3		4	1			5		
5				9		3		
			4					9

580

3			6				1	4
		2			3	9		5
1		9	4					
	9			8				3
4				3			5	
					5	7		1
5		6	7			3		
7	1				4			2

581

	1	5			3			
			4				9	
9			8			1		5
		9		4	6			1
		4				7		
1			5	3		4		
6		7			8			4
	2				4			
			2			6	8	

582

	4	2	6					
				1			2	9
				8	2			
1		8					6	
7				3				5
	5					3		1
			8	6				
3	2			5				
					7	4	9	

583

4								5
3			2				6	
5				9		8	2	
	1		3		9			
		4				7		
			7		6		1	
	5	2		7				9
	6				8			2
8								7

584

			7	5		6		2
					9	3		
			3				1	8
		7				1		6
			2	4	1			
4		1				5		
7	4				2			
		2	1					
3		9		6	5			

585

2			9		1	4		
	7		8					2
						9		
	2		3	6				
8	3			4			1	9
				9	8		2	
		8						
1					6		5	
		3	2		9			8

586

9			3					
				7		8		
4	1		8				5	9
					7	6	9	
	6			4			2	
	9	8	1					
1	3				8		4	6
		5		3				
					1			5

587

			4		7		1	5
				2				
			1		9	7	6	
	7	6					2	1
		3				6		
4	9					5	3	
	8	9	5		1			
				6				
2	5		8		4			

588

3				4		6	2	
9			2					
		2		1	3			5
	3					1		7
2		6				9		4
1		8					6	
5			8	6		2		
					1			6
	2	3		7				1

589

			4			8	1	
6	1					4		
	9			7				3
	5				2			
			5	3	1			
			7				8	
2				9			7	
		6					5	9
	7	9			5			

590

							2	9
	6	4	8	2				
				5				3
9			4			5		
1				7				6
		6			3			7
6				8				
				6	5	3	7	
2	5							

591

	7	9			4		2	
	4							1
				8		3		
5					3			6
			2		9			
2			7					3
		1		9				
3							1	
	2		1			7	8	

592

						8		
4		9	2	8	5		7	
8								4
		3			8	5	6	
				7				
	5	6	3			2		
1								8
	8		7	3	1	9		6
		7						

593

8	2							
		1			3			6
9		3			5			
					8		9	
	9	5	2		7	1	4	
	4		9					
			6			5		4
1			5			3		
							2	7

594

9			7			3		
3					4			
	4	6	8	1				
2						7		
4		7		3		5		1
		8						4
				5	9	4	7	
			1					9
		3			6			5

595

		9					6	3
1				6	3			9
			1	4			8	
		1					3	
5			6		2			1
	2					7		
	6			9	1			
8			3	7				5
9	3					6		

596

7	1	2	4					
		9		2				
8					5		6	
	5	3						
4			5		7			1
						5	4	
	7		6					3
				4		2		
					1	6	8	7

597

7			1	3			2	
			6					
	4		7			6	8	3
		3				9	7	6
6	9	5				8		
8	1	2			7		3	
					2			
	3			5	1			7

598

	7							5
5		1			2			9
			3					4
		5		7	3		9	
	8			5			4	
	2		6	8		3		
4					6			
6			9			4		3
8							2	

599

	4				2	6		
		3				5	4	
				6	1		3	
			9			4		
4	8						9	3
		7			4			
	5		2	8				
	2	4				7		
		9	1				8	

600

			5	7	3	1		
					6		2	3
6						7	8	
9						5		
			1	6	4			
		3						6
	5	9						8
3	4		6					
		6	4	5	9			

601

		1			5			
		2		4			6	
6			2				9	
1			3			7		
3				5				6
		7			4			3
	9				1			4
	3			2		6		
			6			5		

602

			8	7	6	9		
								7
	8			2		4	3	
5						6	4	
	6	8				1	7	
	7	1						5
	5	2		4			1	
3								
		7	2	1	8			

603

		8	6		2			3
5		6			8			
	9						1	
	5	7					8	4
6	2					5	3	
	4						7	
			3			8		9
7			1		5	3		

604

			5	6		8	1	7
			4					
							4	6
	2			9				4
	1	8				3	7	
4				3			5	
7	3							
					9			
6	9	2		7	4			

605

4			3		2			
	9		8				4	
			1			8	9	
6							1	
	2	7				9	5	
	4							8
	6	5			4			
	7				8		3	
			7		3			2

606

								5
3					4		2	
4			5		7	9	8	3
7	2				6			
				5				
			8				1	6
1	5	2	4		3			8
	3		9					2
8								

607

	5				1			3
2			9					
7		3			8	2		9
	7					6		
			6	9	3			
		4					2	
3		7	5			4		1
					4			2
5			1				9	

608

		4		9		7		
					5	1	6	9
	1							8
			6				3	
4			9	8	2			1
	2				7			
2							8	
9	4	6	3					
		5		1		3		

609

7	5	8			2			
				3				
3	1			7			8	
8	6				5		2	
		7				4		
	9		4				7	8
	8			2			4	9
				5				
			8			7	6	1

610

					1		6	
				9	2	1		
4		1	3					9
		3		5			9	
7	9						3	6
	4			7		5		
8					7	6		5
		4	6	3				
	2		4					

611

	9	3	5	1	4		7	2
	4		9	7				5
			2					
	7	1					5	
	6					8	9	
					5			
7				4	2		6	
9	2		1	6	8	5	3	

612

			7			9	4	
9	3				6			
		6	8					1
8				3				
	7	9		6		3	1	
				7				5
4					7	6		
			5				2	9
	8	5			9			

613

		5						
	7	8	2		9			
3	6			4				9
5						2	8	
			9		8			
	8	1						4
1				7			6	3
			4		5	9	2	
						4		

614

	7					9	4	8
		2	9					
				5	6		1	2
					9	7	5	
9				7				6
	6	5	3					
1	5		2	6				
					4	5		
6	8	3					2	

615

1	3			6				5
					8			
	7				5		1	
		2				6		3
			4		1			
9		8				1		
	9		8				2	
			7					
7				9			8	4

616

		3		2	1	5		
				5			6	7
			4					
	2					6	1	
6	1		2	9	5		4	3
	5	7					9	
					7			
1	4			3				
		5	1	6		3		

617

		3				2		
	9			1			5	
			2			7	1	
			5			3		4
			8		4			
5		2			1			
	6	4			2			
	8			7			6	
		9				1		

618

	2		3		6	4		
				2				7
							1	3
8		9			5			
		6		8		5		
			4			9		8
5	9							
2				1				
		7	9		8		5	

619

7	6					3	9	
1		2	4					
	4	5	8				7	
4								
8			6	1	4			7
								8
	1				8	7	6	
					6	4		2
	5	4					1	9

620

		2			8		1	
5	7				2			4
8		3				5		
					3			1
7	3			8			4	9
9			7					
		5				1		6
2			9				3	5
	6		3			8		

621

		3			8		1	7
						8		
5					9		3	4
4					3	6		
6			9	7	4			5
		2	6					1
8	4		7					3
		5						
2	3		8			7		

622

		9		5		3		7
2				7	6	5	1	
7			1					2
	8							
		4		1		9		
							8	
4					1			8
	2	8	7	3				5
9		1		8		4		

623

		7				9		1
			2		1	7		
	1				8			2
8					3	2		
	4						7	
		1	6					8
5			8				6	
		6	5		4			
2		3				4		

624

1	2	3						8
	7	8	1			9	2	
6	4			3				7
			6		7			
9				4			3	2
	3	1			9	2	6	
2						4	8	1

625

5	3				9	7		
				5				6
2		9						
	5		2					1
	4		5	8	3		9	
9					1		3	
						1		5
8				6				
		5	1				4	3

626

6							1	8
		7		9	1			
8	2				3			
5	3					1		
				4				
		4					5	2
			9				8	5
			4	5		2		
4	9							7

627

1	7				2			9
	8			9				
	9		6				2	5
						8	7	
			8	1	7			
	6	8						
6	3				9		1	
				4			3	
9			2				6	7

628

			3		4			9
2		7						1
				1		4	6	
		9	2					
	6	1				8	2	
					6	7		
	5	3		2				
9						3		6
1			6		7			

629

	2	6					9	
					9	7	5	
3					8			
6					2		4	9
	8		5		4		6	
1	4		3					8
			9					2
	7	8	2					
	3					9	8	

630

		1						4
7			8	3				
4				2	9		7	8
						5		
5	1			6			9	7
		4						
9	2		5	1				6
				7	3			5
1						7		

631

1					5			
	2	8	9		7			
	4		3		2			1
	7					5		4
8		2					6	
9			4		3		8	
			6		9	3	4	
			1					2

632

			8				7	
		8					5	
			1		9	3	2	
	3	7		6			1	
6								3
	1			4		7	9	
	8	2	3		7			
	6					1		
	5				2			

633

			1					2
	9			4	5		8	
5		1		3				4
							7	9
		9	8		4	3		
8	7							
1				8		9		3
	4		7	6			5	
2					9			

634

		7						2
9		5						
8				1	9	5		
		2	9	8				3
	8		2		4		1	
3				7	5	2		
		3	4	6				8
						7		4
6						3		

635

								2
	9			6	8			
3			4		7	1		8
9	1				4			
4		3				8		7
			7				1	9
7		2	3		5			1
			6	7			4	
1								

636

		4		9			1	
6		2	4					
1								8
			2			7		
4		9	5		6	3		2
		6			3			
9								5
					4	1		7
	1			6		9		

637

		8	6		5			7
		5		4		9		8
			1			6	5	
1		4					9	
			5		3			
	3					1		5
	7	9			6			
6		3		5		2		
4			3		8	5		

638

			8		3		5	
4						9	3	
				9		7	2	
			3	5			7	
5		7				2		3
	4			8	7			
	9	4		6				
	7	6						5
	8		1		9			

639

6			9		5		2	3
					7		6	9
	4	3					9	8
5		9		8		7		1
8	2					6	3	
9	7		6					
2	5		3		1			6

640

9			4		2			
						5		
				9	1		6	2
	3	9				8		
7	4		1		3		5	9
		1				3	7	
4	1		7	5				
		3						
			8		4			7

641

8			2					6
	2				5	1	4	
		1					3	
	3			7				4
		4				9		
2				9			7	
	8					4		
	4	6	7				8	
7					4			1

642

		4						1
1	6	8	4				9	
	3			6				
		6			1		2	3
		1				7		
2	4		8			1		
				8			6	
	8				4	5	7	2
5						8		

643

		7	4		1			
	5		3			7		
3								4
			1	5			6	
4		5		8		9		3
	6			4	3			
9								7
		3			9		2	
			6		8	3		

644

9					1	6		
			5			4	8	
		8		3				1
8	4						7	
		9				2		
	1						4	5
5				9		8		
	9	6			4			
		1	3					2

645

							1	
			6	9				4
			8	3	4		7	
	8	1			2	7	9	
	2			7			8	
	7	3	9			2	6	
	9		3	4	8			
7				2	6			
	6							

646

		9	6	2				
	3					4		
			9		5			7
				7		6	4	
			5	8	6			
	2	1		4				
9			7		8			
		4					1	
				5	1	8		

647

		1	7			5		
							7	9
4			9	2				
1	4			5			8	
6				8				2
	8			7			6	3
				9	4			5
5	6							
		9			6	7		

648

8				1	6	9		
1			7		9			
	9		4					8
9		5						3
7	2						8	1
3						5		9
6					1		2	
			9		3			6
		1	2	6				5

649

			5	3	1		6	
		3			2	4	8	
								5
	6	7	8			3		1
1		4			7	9	5	
8								
	3	1	2			5		
	5		7	8	9			

650

	9			3				
		5	1		7			
	8	2	5		9			
	3		9					2
9		4	2		8	7		3
2					3		6	
			8		5	9	7	
			7		4	3		
				9			8	

651

					6			5
		4		2			7	
8	5		7					6
	9				3			
1		3	6		2	5		9
			5				8	
5					9		3	7
	6			1		8		
2			3					

652

	9	4		8			3	
			4					
					7			1
		5			4	1		7
6			9		5			2
7		2	3			8		
5			6					
					9			
	6			4		9	7	

653

9	3		6			4		
		2	7					
8				4		3		1
5								
6			8		4			3
								9
3		7		5				2
					6	9		
		4			2		5	6

654

			6	8		4	5	
						2		
				4	9		7	3
		1	3			7	4	
8								1
	7	4			1	5		
5	4		1	6				
		6						
	8	9		2	7			

655

9		8				5		
		3	9				4	
1		7			4			3
7	3			9	2			
			8	3			9	2
3			6			2		4
	5				3	8		
		4				1		7

656

1		2					7	3
7				1		8	9	
3					5	1		
			7		6			
5				4				8
			3		8			
		9	4					5
	5	1		3				9
2	7					6		4

657

					7			2
	6	9			8		1	
	3		9			7	6	
		1					2	
			1	8	4			
	9					4		
	2	7			9		8	
	8		2			5	4	
4			8					

658

1				6				
		4			7	6		
5			9				4	8
2		7			9			
	5			7			3	
			8			9		2
9	4				1			7
		3	6			8		
				4				3

659

		2		1		7	8	
9			7			4		
5	7				8			
	4				1			
		3	6	5	9	1		
			3				2	
			1				3	7
		9			7			8
	1	7		6		2		

660

	4						9	
			4	5		1		
9	1				6		2	
		2			1	7		
			6	4	2			
		3	7			6		
	8		1				6	7
		4		9	3			
	2						3	

661

	6	9	1					
8		1		7	4			
4			8			3		
		8		6				
5	7						9	6
				4		1		
		5			6			7
			4	9		6		3
					5	9	8	

662

		9		3				5
	5				7	2		4
	2		4				1	
		2			6		5	8
5	3		1			4		
	7				9		8	
2		5	6				7	
8				7		9		

663

		4	7		9			
						4		1
6	3			8				
			9	7			2	6
		6		3		7		
9	2			5	4			
				9			4	7
8		5						
			3		7	1		

664

				8	2	5		4
		7	5					
	8				1			
9				6		3	1	
		1		9		4		
	7	3		5				8
			7				9	
					6	1		
3		4	9	1				

665

	2					4		
					8		1	6
		5	1	6		2	9	
	8				3			4
			6	8	2			
2			7				5	
	6	2		9	1	8		
9	7		3					
		4					6	

666

					5			8
			4			6		2
3	6			2	8		4	5
4			3				6	
		8				1		
	2				6			4
8	7		6	3			5	1
5		4			7			
2			8					

667

5	9							
	7	1		3				
4		8	6			9		
8					3		5	
		6				1		
	1		9					3
		3			6	2		8
				2		6	4	
							7	1

668

4					5	2	8	
7	6			2				
		3	7	4			6	
6						8	7	
	7	1						2
	9			6	7	1		
				1			3	8
	3	6	8					4

669

								3
9		1	4		3		7	
	2		7					
4			2			8		7
	6						3	
5		2			6			4
					4		8	
	3		9		2	6		1
2								

670

			4			2	6	
		1			7		5	
				5				
1	8			9		5	3	
3								2
	5	6		1			4	9
				4				
	7		8			4		
	3	5			6			

671

3	9			8			2	
6			3					
	1		2			4		6
				5			9	
2								1
	6			1				
5		1			7		8	
					5			3
	3			2			4	5

672

4		2		9				
	9				1			6
5						2		
						7	3	
2			3		7			1
	7	5						
		8						2
7			5				8	
				6		3		4

673

	9	7		1		6		
	4	8		5	3	2		
					9			
					1			2
	8						3	
3			2					
			8					
		3	1	7		4	6	
		4		9		3	8	

674

				3			4	
		3			5	8		
	7	9						3
	3			4			5	
5			3		2			4
	2			7			9	
4						9	3	
		5	7			1		
	8			6				

675

				3			5	
			8		5	4	2	
4	3			9		1		
		7	9		3			
5								1
			5		2	6		
		3		5			1	8
	5	8	6		1			
	1			2				

676

9							1	2
	1	8			9	3		
	2	4	1					
8				6	3		2	
				1				
	4		7	2				9
					4	2	6	
		2	6			8	7	
5	7							4

677

		8				2	4	
					5			
4	9			8		1	7	
	6			7	9	5		
				6				
		2	3	4			9	
	7	3		5			1	4
			1					
	1	5				3		

678

	2				5	3		
				4		1		
3				9	8			4
	1					4	6	
	5						3	
	4	2					5	
4			3	8				5
		9		1				
		7	4				1	

679

	4			8		2		
8			9				3	
1			5		6	8		
						4		7
	1						2	
2		3						
		6	7		4			5
	9				8			6
		5		3			9	

680

		7			9		2	
4				1		8		
	5		3					
	9				3			6
	3		2		8		7	
2			1				8	
					1		5	
		5		4				8
	1		5			6		

681

4	2	9	5					
5	3				6			9
		1	3					
						6	1	
1		2		6		4		8
	4	3						
					8	2		
3			2				5	6
					4	1	9	7

682

4								8
	5		1			3	4	2
	8		9					
	4	7	3		6		1	
	3		5		4	6	8	
					7		5	
6	2	4			5		3	
1								6

683

	1	4					5	
9	6	8	2					
			4					
	5	1	7					2
		7		3		8		
8					5	3	1	
					6			
					7	5	2	1
	8					4	3	

684

5	1	2			8			
8			1	4			9	
		6		5				8
2	6							5
		8				1		
1							7	3
7				2		8		
	8			3	7			9
			8			4	6	7

685

			1	3			5	8
			9			2	6	
						4		
	2	3	6			9		
	4						7	
		6			8	1	2	
		8						
	6	2			5			
5	3			4	2			

686

		9	4				1	
				8				3
	1	7	9			6		5
		3			6			
2				1				6
			8			9		
4		2			8	3	6	
1				7				
	5				3	7		

687

	2				6	9		8
	8			2				4
		1				7	2	
7					1			
			2	4	8			
			6					9
	7	8				4		
9				1			7	
6		3	4				5	

688

3				8	1	2		9
								6
	7		2	4				
	8	3	5					
				9				
					4	5	8	
				5	3		9	
2								
8		1	7	6				5

689

7			5				9	
		6				7		3
				1			8	
					3	6	7	
			9		1			
	7	5	2					
	3			6				
6		7				4		
	8				5			1

690

			7		6		3	
	3		4	2				1
2		9	5					
4	9					6		
		6	2		9	7		
		2					5	9
					2	5		6
9				6	5		4	
	7		8		4			

691

			5			9		
		9						6
		6	3		9		7	4
		2		4		8		
8				1				9
		1		5		6		
9	3		8		5	7		
2						5		
		7			1			

692

					8	7		9
1		9	5				2	
3				9				6
8				6		2		3
			8		3			
5		3		4				1
4				5				7
	3				4	6		2
7		8	3					

693

		7		5		6	4	
	8					7		
	3		7	2				9
9		1			5			
			6			4		3
6				9	1		7	
		4					8	
	9	8		4		1		

694

	5	4					9	
9					4			
						2	5	4
		1	8		3		4	
		9		5		7		
	4		1		6	8		
6	3	2						
			2					8
	9					4	7	

695

		5					4	3
	7	1					9	
3				9				
				5				2
5	9		4	3	6		7	1
6				1				
				6				9
	5					7	2	
1	4					3		

696

1	8					3		
	6			3		5		
	5			4				
2		6			5			
7			9		3			2
			8			4		7
				9			2	
		1		6			3	
		9					1	4

697

	6		8					
		2	7					4
			2	1		6	8	7
1	3							
		8	5		1	3		
							5	1
7	4	1		2	6			
9					8	4		
					9		1	

698

		6		8	2		5	1
	2			1			4	6
					6	8		
	6					4		3
1		3					9	
		7	9					
5	9			6			8	
4	1		2	7		5		

699

	7		4		8			6
		8		9				
5						8		
		1			3	6	9	
7	4						8	1
	3	5	1			2		
		7						2
				2		1		
6			8		1		3	

700

						2		
	9	2	3					8
6			1	8		9	7	
	3		4					
2		9		3		5		1
					6		9	
	2	6		4	1			7
8					5	6	1	
		1						

701

		1						
2	5				4			
		7			2		9	1
	6			1				
5			2		6			8
				7			3	
1	9		6			4		
			3				6	5
						9		

702

8				9			2	3
3			6				7	9
						6	8	
					2		1	
		6		3		2		
	8		1					
	1	4						
2	5				9			7
6	7			8				2

703

		4						2
	6				9	3		
1	8		2					
	7			4	1			
4		5	6		3	1		8
			9	5			3	
					2		5	9
		8	7				6	
2						8		

704

			3				6	
	6		1	4				
		9						1
3	2				8	5		
4				3				9
		6	4				8	2
2						7		
				7	6		5	
	9				4			

705

	5		7			1	6	
				8	3	9		4
				2	6	8		
	7						8	6
4	6						1	
		9	4	7				
5		2	3	6				
	4	7			8		5	

706

					4	6		
			7	1			4	3
	4						1	
4	8			6	9			
	7	1				2	5	
			5	7			8	4
	1						3	
6	3			8	7			
		8	3					

707

	4	5	3					9
					2			3
			4	9				5
4	3		7			8		
		6				9		
		2			3		4	1
2				3	5			
5			9					
9					6	2	5	

708

				7				
	3		5			4		
5						1	7	8
			4		5		8	6
6								4
3	2		1		6			
7	6	8						1
		2			7		3	
				2				

709

		9				1		8
	1	8			9	5	2	
2							9	6
			1				7	
8				2				5
	6				8			
4	9							1
	8	3	7			9	6	
7		6				3		

710

	8		6		1			5
					5		1	
				8				7
	3	1						4
			1	3	2			
5						1	2	
3				2				
	9		5					
8			9		6		4	

711

4		2		5		7		3
					3			
			8				9	5
3		6					4	
	5		7		4		6	
	2					9		8
8	4				7			
			3					
5		3		6		8		1

712

		7	9		2		3	6
	8		6					
	3				1			
		2	7					3
	7	5		4		6	2	
3					9	7		
			1				6	
					6		9	
4	9		3		7	2		

713

	7		5			3		
8					3	9		
				8				7
	5	2	8					
	1		7		5		8	
					9	6	1	
4				2				
		8	6					4
		6			7		9	

714

				1		6	5	
			7		6	1		
	1						8	
2			3	7				
		9	2		1	4		
				5	4			3
	7						4	
		6	9		3			
	3	5		4				

715

4				5		8		
5			1		6			4
				6	1		5	
	7	9				3	4	
	1		7	3				
3			2		5			7
		1		8				6

716

	7		6		4			9
5			2			4		
		3						1
		9	4	5				
8								4
				9	8	5		
7						9		
		1			6			8
9			1		5		7	

717

		3						
	1	2					9	6
	5			2	7			3
6			7					
		8	1		5	9		
					9			1
9			3	5			8	
3	8					7	1	
						3		

718

5			1	7		9		
			4					8
					2	1		
1	4							
7	6						4	5
							8	1
		9	5					
6					3			
		2		6	8			7

719

				1	6		8	
						3		
8					2		6	
		5	7		9	2	4	
		7		5		9		
	9	6	3		4	8		
	7		2					3
		9						
	2		5	9				

720

	4				5			
			4		8	7		3
			2	3				
	5					3		8
8	1						2	7
3		2					9	
				8	4			
4		1	7		6			
			9				8	

721

	8			6			5	4
1							9	
3			8					
			7	2		1		
	1						6	
		8		9	1			
					2			1
	4							9
5	6			4			8	

722

		2	9					8
			5		6			3
	7	6		8				
				2			8	
	9	1				4	3	
	4			5				
				1		3	2	
9			7		2			
1					5	7		

723

9							4	
		3	5			1		
			1		7	6		
8	6		7	1				
				3	4		5	8
		8	9		1			
		7			5	2		
	9							7

724

				6		9		
3							2	
8		4			2			3
7	9			8	6			
5				3				9
			2	7			5	6
9			8			3		7
	1							5
		8		5				

725

5	9		1			3	2	
8			5					6
						4		
					6		7	
		6	8		7	1		
	3		2					
		8						
1					2			9
	4	2			1		6	3

726

	8		7		2	5		
								6
	5					3		1
		4		9				
	1		2		7		5	
				5		9		
3		2					9	
4								
		8	5		4		7	

727

2						4		
	8		4			5		2
			1				3	
				9		3		
1		4				7		5
		9		5				
	7				8			
5		1			6		4	
		2						9

728

6		8		1	3			
5				8	2			
9						6		
	4					1		9
		9		4		8		
7		1					2	
		5						6
			7	2				8
			1	6		2		4

729

6		5						
			6	1	5			
	3	7				6		
					7	5	2	
1				9				7
	2	8	1					
		4				2	3	
			3	2	9			
						1		8

730

5	2	1			7			
6	9		3	5	1			
				2				
7						9	2	
8				6				3
	5	3						1
				7				
			4	8	6		7	2
			5			6	9	8

731

				1	2		5	3
		3						8
			9			7		
4				5				
	5		4		6		2	
				7				1
		6			1			
9						8		
2	4		7	8				

732

					2		1	
4				3	7	9		
	9	2					4	
3		9						
	1			2			5	
						8		7
	3					6	7	
		5	1	6				2
	4		3					

733

		7					5	4
1						7	3	
				9	5	2		
			3			4	1	7
8	4	1			2			
		3	9	2				
	1	5						6
2	8					1		

734

	2				3		6	1
		9			2			
		1		8				9
				6		8	9	
			2		1			
	9	7		4				
8				3		5		
			8			3		
2	7		5				4	

735

		5					8	
	3				8		6	
			5		6	3		
				4		1		
	5	4	6		3	9	2	
		9		2				
		7	2		1			
	1		7				5	
	2					8		

736

4		8	7					5
	2							
			9	8	4			6
	5	4						1
		3				5		
1						6	8	
8			3	9	5			
							1	
3					6	2		8

737

			2	6		1		
4	2				1			
6			3			7		
	3							
1	5		8		9		3	4
							8	
		3			6			9
			9				5	1
		8		4	2			

738

9		1		4				
			1		3			
	7	4	5		6			1
	5				2	4		
6				1				3
		9	6				1	
5			3		1	8	9	
			2		8			
				7		5		2

739

7								
	5		3			9		
				6	8	5	3	
4						6	2	
	6						5	
	2	1						4
	4	2	8	1				
		3			9		8	
								7

740

5	8		2			9	1	
3			1	8				
7	1			2			5	
			5		9			
	9			3			7	6
				1	8			3
	2	3			7		6	5

741

8	9							3
				3	1	6		
	3		2			1		
			3		5			4
		8		4		2		
1			7		2			
		7			3		5	
		5	6	9				
3							7	2

742

5								3
9	4	1						
3			9		5			
	8	2		3				
	9			4			7	
				8		3	1	
			6		1			8
						5	9	6
8								1

743

4	3				1			
5							3	
9	6		2			8		
								4
	1	8	9		4	6	7	
2								
		4			7		8	6
	9							3
			6				2	7

744

	6			3				7
	2	4	7		8			5
	1					5		8
		2	9		3	6		
8		3					4	
4			1		6	9	5	
1				4			8	

745

			5				6	
		5	1	3			9	
					9			5
		9	6			4		8
		2				7		
7		6			1	9		
4			2					
	2			4	7	5		
	1				8			

746

	5		7		6		8	
		3					4	
7				8				3
	3	1			2			
		6				2		
			9			5	1	
9				6				1
	1					4		
	7		8		4		2	

747

	1		9		7		5	
	6				4			9
				5				4
					1	2		
		8	3		2	1		
		7	6					
3				1				
2			5				6	
	5		2		3		9	

748

	2			8				
1			9			3		7
			7	5				1
6	7					9		
	1						6	
		8					4	2
8				2	5			
2		6			8			3
				9			2	

749

	3	6	8	1		5		
			6	4				1
	1				2	9		
						2	9	
5								4
	6	1						
		9	2				5	
6				7	3			
		4		5	1	7	8	

750

9	8	6			1			
	1							7
		3					8	
		9	1	8				
	5		3		2		7	
				4	5	6		
	3					7		
8							5	
			8			9	2	4

751

	8		5		2		1	
	3					4		
					1	8	7	5
	5					9		1
				5				
3		6					4	
6	1	5	8					
		8					9	
	9		1		6		5	

752

4				8	2	5		
	8		3				7	
7								8
8			4		5			
		1				7		
			9		1			2
2								9
	6				3		8	
		9	2	4				7

753

	6			5				
2		1	6					
	3		9				4	5
					2	8		
	9						3	
		2	7					
5	8				4		9	
					9	4		3
				1			6	

754

			4		9			3
		5		1		9		
3		8			6			
				3				7
7			9		1			5
2				7				
			5			1		9
		2		9		6		
1			2		3			

755

7	5		2		3			9
4	2				1		3	
	4		6				2	1
		5				9		
1	6				7		8	
	7		1				6	2
3			7		4		9	5

756

		9						6
8	4		9			1	2	
5	1					9		
3				1				
			4	9	7			
				2				1
		5					6	2
	3	2			6		9	5
9						7		

757

		3			6	7		
5			2					
7					3			5
4	7		1				9	
	8						5	
	2				5		8	4
8			5					2
					1			8
		1	7			3		

758

2		8	5					7
4								
7				3			1	
				8				5
5	6	2		7		3	8	9
8				2				
	9			5				6
								1
6					7	4		2

759

			9					
7			6				5	4
6				7		1		2
9	3				4			
		5		2		8		
			8				3	7
8		9		3				5
5	1				7			6
					9			

760

					9			
4			8				9	
		2	5	7			3	
3					8	5		
7				9				1
		4	1					6
	8			1	7	6		
	4				6			8
			3					

761

	6				8	1	5	3
	3			5			8	2
			2					
9						7	4	
			5		9			
	4	2						5
					6			
1	9			2			6	
8	5	6	9				7	

762

						2	5	
	1			7	2			3
5			6					1
	8	3			4			
				1				
			3			8	9	
6					1			5
1			4	2			6	
	2	9						

763

	2		4					6
4	8		7				3	
					9			1
	4		9			5	6	
	5	7			3		4	
7			3					
	6				1		8	7
3					7		5	

764

	4			8			9	
2	5		4					
		7	2					
5			1				6	3
				3				
6	8				2			1
					5	9		
					4		1	2
	3			7			8	

765

4			1					9
	9	3	7		2	6		
							8	
1					6		9	
8				4				7
	5		2					1
	4							
		8	4		3	1	7	
2					8			6

766

		5	4	8		2		
8	4	3		7				
6		4			9		3	
	7						4	
	1		7			5		2
				4		8	7	1
		1		2	8	6		

767

		4						
7							6	8
	8		5		7			2
9			8		3			
5	4			6			2	1
			1		4			7
2			9		8		1	
1	5							4
						2		

768

					7	6		
	1			2	8	9		
	5		3	9			8	
		1					2	
3								8
	7					5		
	6			4	2		1	
		3	8	7			9	
		4	1					

769

				2		4		6
			1	4	5		3	
					8		5	
		2		3		6	4	
9								3
	3	4		9		1		
	9		7					
	5		9	8	3			
3		1		5				

770

9		1				2		
6	8			3	4	1		5
	4		2					
				4		3		
	3			2			5	
		9		5				
					1		2	
2		6	8	7			1	9
		7				6		8

771

	8		4	3				9
			9				7	8
9			7		6			
	9	2						
	3		2		1		8	
						2	3	
			1		9			7
6	2				4			
4				5	3		2	

772

	1		3			7		
	2						1	
	6				2	3		9
4			6	8				
2				1				5
				2	5			7
6		2	8				7	
	4						8	
		5			9		4	

773

3	7							8
		1					7	
			2		3		4	
		8		5				2
	3		4		8		6	
9				2		7		
	5		6		4			
	2					9		
8							1	4

774

	5	8	1			7		
2								
		1	4	5	6	2		
							5	6
				2				
4	9							
		9	8	1	7	4		
								7
		2			4	5	1	

775

	4		3					1
			6	8			3	
8					5		6	
2						4		
1				9				2
		7						9
	8		7					6
	3			5	6			
7					8		2	

776

		3	1			4		
	5				2			
4	1						2	
7				3				
9		2		4		8		6
				9				3
	9						3	5
			5				6	
		4			9	1		

777

				2		8	1	
3								
6	9		3	8				
4	1						5	7
		3		5		1		
5	6						2	9
				1	7		9	8
								2
	5	6		9				

778

3	8		5				2	
4	9		2				3	
6			8					
9				4	1	2		
		4	6	2				3
					6			2
	1				2		6	4
	2				5		7	1

779

		7			5	4	1	
				6			5	3
3						2		8
		8			4		3	
			8	1	2			
	9		6			8		
5		2						9
9	7			2				
	4	1	7			3		

780

				7			5	9
			8			6		
	1	9			6		7	
	7		4		2			
	3						9	
			9		8		1	
	4		7			3	6	
		1			4			
7	9			8				

781

			4			8		
5	4				9		6	
		7		6				9
2					3			
1	9						4	7
			9					2
4				7		9		
	6		8				1	4
		1			5			

782

		7					4	
				6			1	8
	3		5	9				
1		6	3					
	2						7	
					6	4		3
				5	7		9	
2	1			4				
	8					1		

783

	8		5				4	9
				8	2	5		
						8	1	
1			4					
9	7			3			2	6
					5			1
	6	9						
		2	7	4				
8	5				3		9	

784

		2			4			
		4		3			6	
5			2			8		4
7		9			6			1
		3		4		5		
8			1			3		9
4		8			2			5
	2			5		6		
			6			2		

785

	3	4			8		7	
						8		
2		8	7					
				6		2		8
	6	7		9		1	3	
9		2		1				
					2	6		5
		1						
	2		5			7	1	

786

	7			5				2
				3			6	9
1			9		2		4	
	9				6	2		
2			3		9			4
		1	2				9	
	8		4		3			7
7	3			2				
4				6			2	

787

								2
			3	1	2			5
	1		8	5			7	
1	6		9					7
	5						4	
2					1		3	9
	3			7	5		6	
5			1	9	6			
7								

788

			9					
9			1			3		
7		1	8				5	
1				6	2			
6	2						8	1
			7	1				2
	3				7	8		9
		6			1			4
					4			

789

	2			6	4	9		1
1		8		3		5		
	7			8				
7			3				5	
	3				6			2
				5			6	
		5		1		3		8
3		6	4	2			9	

790

					2			
2	4			5			3	
6				9		1	5	
4			9			3		1
	8						6	
9		1			8			5
	2	3		4				6
	6			3			1	4
			8					

791

	8				3	6		2
3			9			4		8
				8			9	
		4	5	9				
6			2		4			7
				3	8	5		
	1			2				
2		5			7			9
7		6	8				2	

792

		3			2			
		1	3					7
	2	4	1					
4	6				9	7	3	
	3	2	8				4	6
					5	3	8	
8					4	9		
			7			6		

793

8				9			4	
	6	1			2			
					6			1
5			3				6	
	1						5	
	8				1			4
7			5					
			4			9	7	
	2			1				3

794

2			6					1
	4					8	3	
			3					
		5	9	7		3		
		9				1		
		7		1	3	9		
					4			
	7	1					6	
3					8			7

795

	4					3		
	7		1	6		8		
		9		5			6	
	5			2	7			
	2	7				5	4	
			4	1			2	
	6			8		2		
		8		7	2		3	
		5					1	

796

		2		5		9		
				6			2	
	6	4			7			5
	3						9	8
		7				2		
4	5						7	
8			5			4	3	
	9			1				
		3		2		5		

797

2		5			3			
7		3				4		
	6		5	2				
					2		6	
9		2		5		8		1
	5		4					
				9	7		1	
		1				7		6
			1			3		8

798

7					2		4	
				8		9	2	
			1			5		
9			3		4		5	
		7				1		
	4		6		5			3
		2			1			
	1	4		2				
	3		8					2

799

9				6		5		
		3		5				2
		7	9		8			
3	5					2		8
	1			3			5	
2		4					1	7
			8		3	6		
6				9		7		
		5		7				9

800

		8				5	7	
					9			1
1	7			5	6	3		
	5			7		2		
			2		3			
		3		9			8	
		9	6	1			5	4
8			9					
	6	4				9		

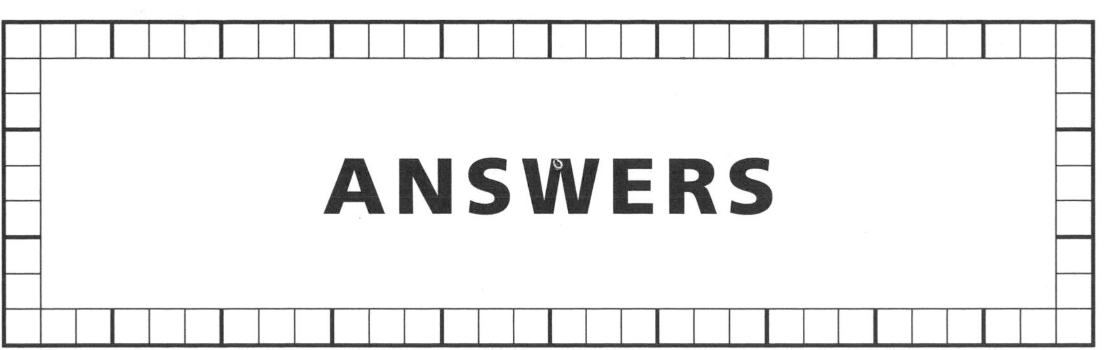

1

8	7	1	9	5	3	4	6	2
3	9	5	2	4	6	7	8	1
4	2	6	8	7	1	9	5	3
5	8	4	6	1	2	3	7	9
6	1	9	7	3	8	2	4	5
7	3	2	5	9	4	6	1	8
9	4	7	1	2	5	8	3	6
1	6	3	4	8	9	5	2	7
2	5	8	3	6	7	1	9	4

2

4	8	1	2	3	6	7	9	5
3	9	5	8	4	7	1	2	6
7	2	6	1	5	9	4	8	3
6	4	8	9	7	2	5	3	1
1	7	9	3	8	5	6	4	2
2	5	3	4	6	1	9	7	8
9	1	4	5	2	8	3	6	7
8	3	7	6	1	4	2	5	9
5	6	2	7	9	3	8	1	4

3

8	2	3	6	4	1	7	5	9
1	4	7	5	9	3	8	6	2
6	9	5	7	8	2	3	1	4
4	8	6	9	3	7	5	2	1
2	3	9	1	5	4	6	8	7
7	5	1	8	2	6	4	9	3
3	6	8	4	1	9	2	7	5
5	1	2	3	7	8	9	4	6
9	7	4	2	6	5	1	3	8

4

7	2	3	5	9	8	1	4	6
8	4	6	1	3	7	2	5	9
5	9	1	6	4	2	7	3	8
6	7	4	8	5	9	3	1	2
1	3	8	7	2	6	5	9	4
9	5	2	3	1	4	6	8	7
2	1	9	4	6	5	8	7	3
3	6	7	9	8	1	4	2	5
4	8	5	2	7	3	9	6	1

5

2	6	8	5	1	9	7	3	4
4	7	1	3	6	8	9	5	2
3	9	5	7	2	4	8	1	6
6	4	2	8	9	1	5	7	3
5	1	7	6	4	3	2	8	9
9	8	3	2	7	5	4	6	1
1	3	9	4	5	7	6	2	8
8	5	6	9	3	2	1	4	7
7	2	4	1	8	6	3	9	5

6

6	8	1	4	9	2	7	5	3
2	3	4	5	6	7	1	9	8
5	9	7	8	1	3	6	4	2
9	4	3	7	8	1	2	6	5
8	7	5	3	2	6	4	1	9
1	2	6	9	4	5	8	3	7
3	5	2	6	7	4	9	8	1
7	6	8	1	3	9	5	2	4
4	1	9	2	5	8	3	7	6

7

2	5	1	7	8	4	9	6	3
6	4	9	1	2	3	5	8	7
3	8	7	6	9	5	2	1	4
8	6	5	2	1	7	4	3	9
1	2	3	8	4	9	6	7	5
9	7	4	3	5	6	1	2	8
7	9	6	5	3	2	8	4	1
4	1	2	9	7	8	3	5	6
5	3	8	4	6	1	7	9	2

8

3	8	1	9	2	7	4	5	6
7	4	5	6	3	1	9	2	8
6	9	2	5	8	4	3	1	7
5	6	3	4	9	8	2	7	1
9	2	4	7	1	5	8	6	3
8	1	7	3	6	2	5	4	9
2	7	6	8	5	3	1	9	4
4	5	8	1	7	9	6	3	2
1	3	9	2	4	6	7	8	5

9

6	7	8	5	9	3	1	2	4
2	4	9	7	1	8	3	6	5
1	5	3	6	4	2	8	9	7
5	6	1	3	8	7	9	4	2
8	2	4	9	5	1	7	3	6
9	3	7	2	6	4	5	8	1
7	1	2	4	3	9	6	5	8
4	9	6	8	7	5	2	1	3
3	8	5	1	2	6	4	7	9

10

7	3	5	1	6	8	4	2	9
4	9	2	5	3	7	1	8	6
1	8	6	4	9	2	7	5	3
6	4	1	7	8	3	5	9	2
2	5	9	6	4	1	3	7	8
8	7	3	2	5	9	6	1	4
5	6	7	9	2	4	8	3	1
3	2	4	8	1	5	9	6	7
9	1	8	3	7	6	2	4	5

11

4	9	8	2	6	7	3	5	1
6	3	5	1	8	4	9	2	7
2	1	7	9	5	3	8	4	6
3	2	1	7	4	5	6	8	9
8	4	9	3	1	6	5	7	2
7	5	6	8	9	2	1	3	4
9	6	4	5	2	8	7	1	3
1	8	3	4	7	9	2	6	5
5	7	2	6	3	1	4	9	8

12

2	6	1	8	3	9	5	7	4
5	3	9	2	4	7	1	8	6
4	7	8	5	1	6	3	9	2
6	2	3	4	5	8	9	1	7
9	5	7	3	6	1	2	4	8
1	8	4	7	9	2	6	3	5
7	9	6	1	2	4	8	5	3
8	1	5	6	7	3	4	2	9
3	4	2	9	8	5	7	6	1

13

4	3	7	5	8	6	9	1	2
2	1	8	7	3	9	5	6	4
5	9	6	1	4	2	3	7	8
8	2	1	3	5	7	6	4	9
3	6	9	2	1	4	8	5	7
7	5	4	9	6	8	1	2	3
6	8	5	4	2	3	7	9	1
1	7	2	8	9	5	4	3	6
9	4	3	6	7	1	2	8	5

14

4	9	2	6	1	8	7	5	3
1	8	3	4	7	5	6	2	9
6	5	7	9	3	2	1	4	8
7	6	4	2	5	9	3	8	1
2	1	9	7	8	3	4	6	5
8	3	5	1	6	4	2	9	7
5	2	1	3	9	6	8	7	4
3	4	8	5	2	7	9	1	6
9	7	6	8	4	1	5	3	2

15

9	1	8	3	5	7	2	4	6
5	4	6	1	2	8	9	7	3
2	3	7	4	9	6	5	8	1
7	8	2	9	1	5	6	3	4
1	9	4	2	6	3	7	5	8
6	5	3	8	7	4	1	9	2
8	7	5	6	3	1	4	2	9
3	6	9	5	4	2	8	1	7
4	2	1	7	8	9	3	6	5

16

7	6	2	3	9	4	5	8	1
4	1	5	7	6	8	3	2	9
8	3	9	1	5	2	4	7	6
1	4	6	9	7	5	8	3	2
2	5	3	8	4	6	9	1	7
9	7	8	2	3	1	6	5	4
6	9	1	5	2	3	7	4	8
3	8	4	6	1	7	2	9	5
5	2	7	4	8	9	1	6	3

17

2	1	3	5	4	9	8	6	7
4	8	6	1	7	2	3	5	9
9	5	7	8	3	6	2	1	4
6	2	9	3	8	4	5	7	1
7	3	8	6	1	5	9	4	2
1	4	5	2	9	7	6	8	3
8	6	1	4	2	3	7	9	5
3	7	4	9	5	8	1	2	6
5	9	2	7	6	1	4	3	8

18

3	9	2	6	7	4	1	8	5
1	4	5	9	8	3	7	2	6
6	8	7	2	5	1	3	9	4
7	3	9	8	4	2	6	5	1
8	6	4	3	1	5	9	7	2
5	2	1	7	9	6	8	4	3
9	1	3	4	2	8	5	6	7
2	7	6	5	3	9	4	1	8
4	5	8	1	6	7	2	3	9

19

4	3	8	5	9	7	2	6	1
6	7	5	8	1	2	3	4	9
2	1	9	6	3	4	7	8	5
9	6	4	7	8	5	1	2	3
5	8	7	1	2	3	6	9	4
3	2	1	9	4	6	5	7	8
8	4	2	3	6	1	9	5	7
1	5	6	4	7	9	8	3	2
7	9	3	2	5	8	4	1	6

20

6	8	1	5	3	9	7	2	4
3	4	5	2	1	7	6	8	9
9	7	2	6	8	4	3	1	5
7	1	4	9	6	5	8	3	2
5	6	9	3	2	8	4	7	1
8	2	3	7	4	1	9	5	6
4	9	8	1	5	3	2	6	7
1	3	6	4	7	2	5	9	8
2	5	7	8	9	6	1	4	3

21

3	5	2	7	6	1	8	4	9
6	1	8	3	4	9	5	2	7
4	9	7	8	2	5	1	6	3
7	4	1	2	9	3	6	5	8
8	6	3	4	5	7	2	9	1
9	2	5	1	8	6	7	3	4
1	7	4	6	3	2	9	8	5
5	8	6	9	1	4	3	7	2
2	3	9	5	7	8	4	1	6

22

2	8	1	9	3	5	6	4	7
4	3	5	6	7	1	8	9	2
7	6	9	8	2	4	5	1	3
8	2	3	1	4	6	7	5	9
1	9	4	2	5	7	3	8	6
6	5	7	3	9	8	4	2	1
3	7	2	5	8	9	1	6	4
5	4	6	7	1	2	9	3	8
9	1	8	4	6	3	2	7	5

23

4	8	1	9	7	3	6	5	2
6	3	2	8	5	1	9	7	4
9	5	7	6	2	4	1	3	8
3	6	9	5	4	7	2	8	1
5	2	8	1	6	9	7	4	3
7	1	4	3	8	2	5	9	6
8	4	6	2	9	5	3	1	7
1	7	5	4	3	6	8	2	9
2	9	3	7	1	8	4	6	5

24

3	1	8	9	2	5	6	7	4
9	5	6	3	7	4	2	8	1
2	4	7	1	8	6	9	5	3
1	9	3	7	5	8	4	2	6
6	2	5	4	9	1	8	3	7
7	8	4	2	6	3	5	1	9
8	7	2	6	3	9	1	4	5
4	3	9	5	1	2	7	6	8
5	6	1	8	4	7	3	9	2

25

3	1	5	2	7	8	9	6	4
4	2	7	3	9	6	5	1	8
8	9	6	5	1	4	7	3	2
1	4	9	7	6	3	2	8	5
5	6	2	8	4	9	1	7	3
7	8	3	1	2	5	4	9	6
2	3	1	4	8	7	6	5	9
6	5	4	9	3	1	8	2	7
9	7	8	6	5	2	3	4	1

26

1	8	7	6	3	2	4	9	5
9	4	5	7	1	8	3	6	2
6	3	2	5	9	4	8	7	1
5	1	8	9	6	7	2	3	4
7	2	9	4	8	3	1	5	6
4	6	3	1	2	5	9	8	7
2	7	6	8	4	9	5	1	3
8	5	4	3	7	1	6	2	9
3	9	1	2	5	6	7	4	8

27

9	2	8	5	6	7	3	1	4
1	3	4	2	9	8	7	5	6
7	5	6	4	3	1	9	2	8
5	1	2	6	7	4	8	3	9
6	9	3	1	8	5	4	7	2
4	8	7	9	2	3	1	6	5
2	6	1	7	4	9	5	8	3
8	4	5	3	1	2	6	9	7
3	7	9	8	5	6	2	4	1

28

1	9	4	2	3	8	6	7	5
6	7	3	5	4	1	2	8	9
5	8	2	6	9	7	4	3	1
3	1	6	7	8	9	5	4	2
7	5	9	1	2	4	8	6	3
2	4	8	3	5	6	1	9	7
4	2	1	9	6	3	7	5	8
9	6	5	8	7	2	3	1	4
8	3	7	4	1	5	9	2	6

29

8	9	6	5	2	3	7	1	4
2	5	3	1	4	7	9	8	6
4	7	1	8	9	6	5	2	3
7	4	2	6	5	9	8	3	1
5	3	8	4	7	1	2	6	9
6	1	9	3	8	2	4	5	7
1	2	4	7	3	8	6	9	5
3	8	5	9	6	4	1	7	2
9	6	7	2	1	5	3	4	8

30

4	3	5	8	2	9	7	6	1
2	1	7	5	3	6	8	4	9
6	8	9	1	4	7	3	5	2
9	7	4	6	8	5	1	2	3
5	6	3	9	1	2	4	8	7
1	2	8	3	7	4	5	9	6
8	4	2	7	6	1	9	3	5
7	9	6	4	5	3	2	1	8
3	5	1	2	9	8	6	7	4

31

2	6	8	1	3	7	5	4	9
1	7	5	2	9	4	3	6	8
9	3	4	8	5	6	1	2	7
3	4	9	5	6	1	7	8	2
7	5	1	9	2	8	4	3	6
8	2	6	7	4	3	9	5	1
6	8	7	4	1	5	2	9	3
4	9	3	6	7	2	8	1	5
5	1	2	3	8	9	6	7	4

32

7	3	8	6	5	4	9	1	2
9	1	2	7	8	3	6	5	4
5	6	4	9	1	2	8	7	3
2	7	5	8	4	9	1	3	6
6	9	1	5	3	7	2	4	8
8	4	3	2	6	1	7	9	5
4	5	7	1	2	8	3	6	9
3	8	9	4	7	6	5	2	1
1	2	6	3	9	5	4	8	7

33

8	9	3	4	1	7	6	5	2
4	1	7	2	5	6	9	3	8
2	6	5	9	3	8	7	1	4
1	8	9	5	2	4	3	7	6
7	2	6	8	9	3	1	4	5
3	5	4	6	7	1	2	8	9
9	4	1	7	8	2	5	6	3
5	7	8	3	6	9	4	2	1
6	3	2	1	4	5	8	9	7

34

8	7	1	2	4	3	6	9	5
6	4	2	9	1	5	8	3	7
5	3	9	7	6	8	2	1	4
3	8	7	4	9	1	5	2	6
2	6	5	3	8	7	9	4	1
9	1	4	6	5	2	7	8	3
1	5	3	8	7	9	4	6	2
7	9	6	1	2	4	3	5	8
4	2	8	5	3	6	1	7	9

35

8	7	5	9	4	1	3	2	6
1	4	6	7	3	2	8	9	5
2	9	3	5	8	6	1	7	4
3	2	9	8	6	4	7	5	1
5	1	8	3	9	7	6	4	2
7	6	4	1	2	5	9	8	3
9	5	1	2	7	3	4	6	8
6	3	7	4	5	8	2	1	9
4	8	2	6	1	9	5	3	7

36

7	3	2	1	8	5	9	4	6
5	6	4	7	3	9	1	8	2
8	1	9	2	4	6	7	5	3
2	4	5	9	6	8	3	7	1
3	9	7	5	1	4	6	2	8
1	8	6	3	2	7	5	9	4
4	5	8	6	9	3	2	1	7
9	2	3	4	7	1	8	6	5
6	7	1	8	5	2	4	3	9

37

4	8	5	2	3	7	6	1	9
6	9	2	5	4	1	7	8	3
7	1	3	9	6	8	2	5	4
2	3	4	7	1	6	8	9	5
5	6	8	4	9	3	1	2	7
9	7	1	8	2	5	4	3	6
1	4	7	3	5	2	9	6	8
8	5	6	1	7	9	3	4	2
3	2	9	6	8	4	5	7	1

38

2	9	5	3	8	4	7	1	6
6	8	1	2	9	7	5	3	4
4	3	7	6	1	5	2	9	8
1	4	2	8	6	3	9	5	7
5	7	9	1	4	2	8	6	3
8	6	3	5	7	9	1	4	2
3	2	6	7	5	1	4	8	9
7	1	4	9	3	8	6	2	5
9	5	8	4	2	6	3	7	1

39

6	2	4	1	8	9	7	5	3
3	5	7	6	2	4	9	1	8
1	9	8	3	5	7	6	4	2
7	6	3	8	4	2	5	9	1
8	1	2	9	6	5	4	3	7
5	4	9	7	3	1	8	2	6
4	8	5	2	1	6	3	7	9
2	7	6	4	9	3	1	8	5
9	3	1	5	7	8	2	6	4

40

4	6	2	9	3	8	5	1	7
1	3	5	7	2	6	4	9	8
9	8	7	5	1	4	6	2	3
2	5	9	3	7	1	8	6	4
6	4	1	2	8	5	3	7	9
3	7	8	6	4	9	2	5	1
5	9	4	1	6	3	7	8	2
7	1	3	8	5	2	9	4	6
8	2	6	4	9	7	1	3	5

41

8	1	7	2	5	3	4	9	6
4	5	9	1	7	6	3	2	8
2	3	6	8	9	4	7	5	1
7	2	1	3	8	5	9	6	4
3	6	8	4	1	9	2	7	5
5	9	4	7	6	2	1	8	3
1	8	5	9	3	7	6	4	2
9	4	3	6	2	8	5	1	7
6	7	2	5	4	1	8	3	9

42

7	1	3	8	6	9	5	2	4
5	9	8	3	4	2	6	1	7
6	2	4	7	1	5	3	8	9
4	5	7	9	8	3	2	6	1
3	8	2	6	7	1	4	9	5
1	6	9	2	5	4	8	7	3
9	7	5	4	2	6	1	3	8
2	3	1	5	9	8	7	4	6
8	4	6	1	3	7	9	5	2

43

3	1	8	5	6	9	7	2	4
7	2	9	3	8	4	5	1	6
5	4	6	7	1	2	3	9	8
9	5	7	4	3	6	1	8	2
8	6	4	2	7	1	9	5	3
2	3	1	8	9	5	4	6	7
1	7	3	9	2	8	6	4	5
6	8	5	1	4	7	2	3	9
4	9	2	6	5	3	8	7	1

44

4	5	8	3	6	9	7	2	1
2	6	3	7	1	4	9	8	5
1	9	7	5	2	8	4	6	3
3	7	6	4	9	5	2	1	8
5	4	2	8	7	1	3	9	6
9	8	1	2	3	6	5	7	4
8	2	9	1	4	3	6	5	7
7	3	5	6	8	2	1	4	9
6	1	4	9	5	7	8	3	2

45

4	2	6	1	9	3	8	5	7
7	3	5	6	2	8	4	9	1
9	1	8	7	5	4	6	2	3
2	9	4	8	1	7	3	6	5
1	5	3	2	6	9	7	8	4
8	6	7	3	4	5	2	1	9
3	7	9	5	8	6	1	4	2
5	8	2	4	7	1	9	3	6
6	4	1	9	3	2	5	7	8

46

4	6	9	1	8	5	2	7	3
2	3	1	7	9	6	4	8	5
8	7	5	3	2	4	1	9	6
3	5	4	2	1	9	7	6	8
7	9	8	4	6	3	5	2	1
1	2	6	8	5	7	9	3	4
9	1	7	6	4	8	3	5	2
5	8	2	9	3	1	6	4	7
6	4	3	5	7	2	8	1	9

47

5	1	2	3	9	6	8	4	7
3	8	6	5	4	7	2	9	1
7	9	4	2	8	1	5	3	6
2	7	1	6	5	4	3	8	9
6	4	5	8	3	9	1	7	2
9	3	8	1	7	2	4	6	5
4	2	9	7	1	3	6	5	8
1	5	3	9	6	8	7	2	4
8	6	7	4	2	5	9	1	3

48

1	3	6	9	7	8	2	5	4
7	9	4	5	1	2	6	3	8
5	8	2	4	3	6	7	9	1
2	1	7	6	8	3	9	4	5
6	4	3	1	9	5	8	7	2
8	5	9	7	2	4	3	1	6
9	6	8	3	5	1	4	2	7
4	7	5	2	6	9	1	8	3
3	2	1	8	4	7	5	6	9

49

4	9	8	1	7	3	6	5	2
3	6	2	4	8	5	7	1	9
7	1	5	6	9	2	4	3	8
2	7	9	5	6	8	3	4	1
8	4	1	3	2	7	9	6	5
6	5	3	9	1	4	8	2	7
1	8	7	2	4	6	5	9	3
9	3	6	7	5	1	2	8	4
5	2	4	8	3	9	1	7	6

50

9	8	4	2	1	3	6	7	5
2	1	5	6	4	7	3	8	9
3	6	7	5	9	8	2	4	1
7	3	9	8	6	2	1	5	4
8	5	1	3	7	4	9	2	6
4	2	6	1	5	9	8	3	7
1	9	3	7	8	5	4	6	2
5	4	2	9	3	6	7	1	8
6	7	8	4	2	1	5	9	3

51

3	6	9	8	5	2	7	1	4
4	8	5	6	1	7	2	9	3
1	2	7	9	3	4	5	8	6
2	5	8	7	4	9	6	3	1
6	7	4	1	2	3	8	5	9
9	1	3	5	6	8	4	7	2
7	4	2	3	9	5	1	6	8
8	9	1	2	7	6	3	4	5
5	3	6	4	8	1	9	2	7

52

2	4	9	1	5	7	8	3	6
7	8	6	9	4	3	2	5	1
3	1	5	8	6	2	7	4	9
1	3	8	7	2	9	4	6	5
4	9	7	6	3	5	1	2	8
6	5	2	4	8	1	9	7	3
5	7	1	2	9	6	3	8	4
9	6	4	3	7	8	5	1	2
8	2	3	5	1	4	6	9	7

53

3	8	9	2	4	7	5	1	6
4	6	5	9	3	1	2	7	8
7	1	2	5	8	6	4	3	9
5	2	3	7	1	8	9	6	4
8	7	1	4	6	9	3	5	2
9	4	6	3	2	5	7	8	1
2	9	8	1	5	3	6	4	7
1	5	4	6	7	2	8	9	3
6	3	7	8	9	4	1	2	5

54

9	5	8	4	6	1	3	2	7
4	7	3	2	8	9	5	6	1
1	6	2	3	5	7	9	8	4
2	8	5	1	9	4	7	3	6
7	9	4	5	3	6	8	1	2
6	3	1	8	7	2	4	9	5
3	1	9	7	2	5	6	4	8
8	4	7	6	1	3	2	5	9
5	2	6	9	4	8	1	7	3

55

5	3	2	1	7	9	8	6	4
7	8	9	6	2	4	1	3	5
6	4	1	8	5	3	7	2	9
8	2	7	9	4	6	5	1	3
3	9	4	2	1	5	6	8	7
1	5	6	3	8	7	9	4	2
4	6	3	7	9	1	2	5	8
9	1	8	5	3	2	4	7	6
2	7	5	4	6	8	3	9	1

56

6	3	8	4	1	9	2	7	5
1	7	2	5	8	3	4	6	9
4	9	5	7	6	2	1	8	3
2	8	3	9	7	4	5	1	6
9	5	4	6	3	1	8	2	7
7	6	1	8	2	5	3	9	4
8	4	7	2	5	6	9	3	1
3	2	9	1	4	7	6	5	8
5	1	6	3	9	8	7	4	2

57

8	4	6	2	7	9	5	1	3
5	9	1	3	6	4	8	7	2
3	7	2	8	1	5	6	4	9
9	1	4	5	8	2	7	3	6
2	5	8	6	3	7	1	9	4
6	3	7	9	4	1	2	8	5
1	8	5	4	9	6	3	2	7
7	6	9	1	2	3	4	5	8
4	2	3	7	5	8	9	6	1

58

5	2	3	1	7	9	8	4	6
7	8	4	6	3	2	9	5	1
6	9	1	5	8	4	2	3	7
4	7	8	3	1	5	6	2	9
2	6	9	7	4	8	3	1	5
1	3	5	9	2	6	7	8	4
8	5	6	2	9	1	4	7	3
3	1	2	4	6	7	5	9	8
9	4	7	8	5	3	1	6	2

59

8	9	5	3	7	2	1	6	4
1	3	2	9	4	6	8	5	7
6	4	7	8	5	1	9	3	2
7	8	6	4	2	3	5	1	9
3	2	1	6	9	5	7	4	8
9	5	4	7	1	8	3	2	6
2	1	9	5	6	7	4	8	3
5	7	3	2	8	4	6	9	1
4	6	8	1	3	9	2	7	5

60

9	3	8	5	7	4	1	6	2
2	4	6	8	1	9	3	7	5
5	1	7	2	3	6	8	4	9
4	6	5	3	8	2	7	9	1
3	2	1	7	9	5	6	8	4
8	7	9	6	4	1	5	2	3
1	8	4	9	6	3	2	5	7
6	5	3	4	2	7	9	1	8
7	9	2	1	5	8	4	3	6

61

1	4	8	9	7	6	3	5	2
6	7	5	2	4	3	1	9	8
3	2	9	1	5	8	7	4	6
7	9	6	8	2	4	5	1	3
5	3	2	6	1	7	9	8	4
4	8	1	5	3	9	2	6	7
9	5	3	4	6	2	8	7	1
8	6	7	3	9	1	4	2	5
2	1	4	7	8	5	6	3	9

62

8	6	5	1	2	3	7	4	9
3	9	1	4	6	7	5	2	8
7	2	4	9	8	5	6	3	1
4	7	9	6	1	2	3	8	5
2	3	6	8	5	4	9	1	7
1	5	8	3	7	9	2	6	4
5	1	2	7	3	8	4	9	6
9	8	3	5	4	6	1	7	2
6	4	7	2	9	1	8	5	3

63

8	5	9	3	4	6	2	1	7
7	4	3	2	5	1	9	6	8
6	2	1	9	7	8	3	5	4
2	3	8	6	9	5	7	4	1
1	7	6	4	8	3	5	9	2
5	9	4	1	2	7	8	3	6
9	1	2	7	3	4	6	8	5
3	6	5	8	1	2	4	7	9
4	8	7	5	6	9	1	2	3

64

9	3	8	2	4	6	5	7	1
6	7	1	9	8	5	4	2	3
5	4	2	1	3	7	6	8	9
7	6	9	4	1	2	8	3	5
3	1	4	5	7	8	2	9	6
8	2	5	3	6	9	7	1	4
2	5	7	6	9	3	1	4	8
4	9	6	8	2	1	3	5	7
1	8	3	7	5	4	9	6	2

65

3	4	9	5	8	2	1	7	6
6	7	1	9	3	4	8	5	2
2	8	5	7	1	6	4	9	3
5	3	4	8	2	1	7	6	9
8	6	7	4	5	9	3	2	1
9	1	2	6	7	3	5	4	8
4	9	8	3	6	5	2	1	7
1	5	3	2	9	7	6	8	4
7	2	6	1	4	8	9	3	5

66

1	5	4	7	8	3	6	9	2
8	7	6	9	2	1	3	5	4
3	2	9	6	5	4	1	8	7
6	9	1	8	4	2	7	3	5
2	8	7	5	3	6	4	1	9
4	3	5	1	7	9	2	6	8
5	4	3	2	1	8	9	7	6
9	1	8	4	6	7	5	2	3
7	6	2	3	9	5	8	4	1

67

4	6	1	2	5	3	7	9	8
5	2	8	9	6	7	3	1	4
9	7	3	4	1	8	2	6	5
2	4	9	6	3	1	8	5	7
6	1	5	8	7	4	9	2	3
3	8	7	5	9	2	6	4	1
8	3	4	1	2	6	5	7	9
1	5	2	7	8	9	4	3	6
7	9	6	3	4	5	1	8	2

68

3	4	5	6	9	7	1	2	8
8	9	7	3	1	2	5	6	4
1	2	6	4	5	8	3	7	9
2	5	4	7	3	6	9	8	1
9	1	8	2	4	5	7	3	6
6	7	3	9	8	1	4	5	2
5	3	9	8	2	4	6	1	7
4	6	2	1	7	3	8	9	5
7	8	1	5	6	9	2	4	3

69

1	6	3	8	9	5	7	4	2
4	2	9	3	7	1	6	8	5
5	7	8	6	4	2	1	3	9
3	8	4	1	5	7	9	2	6
7	1	2	4	6	9	8	5	3
9	5	6	2	3	8	4	7	1
2	9	1	5	8	4	3	6	7
8	3	7	9	2	6	5	1	4
6	4	5	7	1	3	2	9	8

70

6	3	4	9	1	2	5	8	7
2	9	7	3	8	5	4	6	1
5	1	8	4	6	7	9	2	3
8	5	3	1	4	6	7	9	2
9	2	1	8	7	3	6	4	5
4	7	6	2	5	9	1	3	8
3	6	2	5	9	1	8	7	4
1	8	9	7	3	4	2	5	6
7	4	5	6	2	8	3	1	9

71

8	5	3	4	1	2	7	6	9
4	7	1	5	6	9	3	2	8
9	6	2	8	7	3	4	5	1
6	2	5	9	8	7	1	4	3
1	3	8	2	5	4	6	9	7
7	9	4	1	3	6	5	8	2
5	8	9	7	4	1	2	3	6
2	1	6	3	9	5	8	7	4
3	4	7	6	2	8	9	1	5

72

8	5	2	3	7	9	6	4	1
3	6	4	1	5	2	9	7	8
1	9	7	8	6	4	5	3	2
6	7	1	2	3	8	4	5	9
4	2	3	5	9	1	7	8	6
5	8	9	7	4	6	2	1	3
2	1	6	4	8	5	3	9	7
7	4	8	9	2	3	1	6	5
9	3	5	6	1	7	8	2	4

73

7	6	4	1	3	5	9	2	8
9	2	5	8	7	6	1	4	3
8	1	3	2	9	4	5	6	7
6	4	1	5	2	8	3	7	9
5	3	9	4	1	7	6	8	2
2	8	7	9	6	3	4	1	5
3	7	2	6	5	1	8	9	4
4	5	6	7	8	9	2	3	1
1	9	8	3	4	2	7	5	6

74

4	7	5	6	2	3	8	1	9
6	8	2	9	1	4	3	7	5
3	9	1	5	7	8	6	2	4
5	3	6	2	8	7	9	4	1
1	2	7	3	4	9	5	8	6
8	4	9	1	6	5	2	3	7
7	5	8	4	3	6	1	9	2
9	1	4	8	5	2	7	6	3
2	6	3	7	9	1	4	5	8

75

3	9	2	5	8	4	7	6	1
4	5	8	6	7	1	2	9	3
6	1	7	9	3	2	8	4	5
9	2	6	7	4	5	3	1	8
1	3	4	8	2	9	5	7	6
7	8	5	3	1	6	9	2	4
5	4	3	2	6	7	1	8	9
2	6	9	1	5	8	4	3	7
8	7	1	4	9	3	6	5	2

76

8	7	3	1	6	2	5	4	9
4	6	1	5	8	9	7	2	3
9	5	2	4	7	3	8	6	1
3	4	5	6	1	7	2	9	8
6	9	7	2	4	8	1	3	5
2	1	8	3	9	5	6	7	4
1	2	4	9	5	6	3	8	7
5	8	6	7	3	4	9	1	2
7	3	9	8	2	1	4	5	6

77

9	3	6	7	2	5	1	4	8
1	4	2	9	3	8	6	7	5
5	7	8	4	1	6	2	3	9
7	2	3	8	4	9	5	1	6
8	1	4	5	6	2	3	9	7
6	9	5	1	7	3	8	2	4
4	5	9	2	8	1	7	6	3
2	6	7	3	5	4	9	8	1
3	8	1	6	9	7	4	5	2

78

1	6	8	7	9	5	4	3	2
7	4	5	3	2	6	8	9	1
2	9	3	8	4	1	5	7	6
9	7	2	6	8	4	3	1	5
4	5	6	1	3	2	9	8	7
3	8	1	9	5	7	6	2	4
6	1	9	5	7	8	2	4	3
5	3	4	2	1	9	7	6	8
8	2	7	4	6	3	1	5	9

79

5	7	4	3	1	2	8	9	6
2	8	6	4	7	9	3	5	1
1	3	9	6	5	8	7	2	4
9	4	1	7	3	5	6	8	2
7	6	2	1	8	4	5	3	9
8	5	3	9	2	6	4	1	7
6	2	5	8	4	1	9	7	3
3	9	8	2	6	7	1	4	5
4	1	7	5	9	3	2	6	8

80

9	1	2	5	4	3	8	7	6
8	3	6	9	7	2	4	1	5
4	5	7	1	6	8	3	9	2
2	6	1	4	8	9	5	3	7
7	8	3	6	2	5	9	4	1
5	9	4	7	3	1	6	2	8
6	7	9	8	1	4	2	5	3
1	2	5	3	9	6	7	8	4
3	4	8	2	5	7	1	6	9

81

4	6	5	7	2	9	3	8	1
3	7	2	8	1	6	4	5	9
8	1	9	5	4	3	2	6	7
5	9	6	4	7	2	1	3	8
7	8	3	9	5	1	6	4	2
2	4	1	6	3	8	7	9	5
6	3	8	1	9	7	5	2	4
9	5	7	2	6	4	8	1	3
1	2	4	3	8	5	9	7	6

82

9	4	5	6	2	1	3	7	8
8	2	1	9	7	3	5	4	6
7	6	3	5	8	4	1	2	9
4	8	7	3	5	9	2	6	1
1	5	2	4	6	8	7	9	3
6	3	9	2	1	7	4	8	5
3	7	6	1	9	2	8	5	4
2	9	4	8	3	5	6	1	7
5	1	8	7	4	6	9	3	2

83

6	4	5	9	1	3	7	8	2
9	7	1	5	8	2	4	3	6
8	2	3	7	4	6	1	9	5
1	8	2	6	7	5	9	4	3
7	5	9	4	3	8	6	2	1
3	6	4	1	2	9	8	5	7
5	1	7	3	9	4	2	6	8
4	3	8	2	6	7	5	1	9
2	9	6	8	5	1	3	7	4

84

9	1	5	2	4	8	3	7	6
3	2	6	7	5	1	8	9	4
4	8	7	9	3	6	5	2	1
1	9	3	5	2	7	6	4	8
5	4	8	1	6	9	2	3	7
7	6	2	4	8	3	9	1	5
8	3	4	6	1	2	7	5	9
6	5	9	3	7	4	1	8	2
2	7	1	8	9	5	4	6	3

85

1	8	7	6	9	5	3	2	4
5	6	2	3	7	4	1	8	9
4	3	9	8	2	1	5	7	6
6	4	5	9	3	8	2	1	7
2	7	8	1	5	6	9	4	3
3	9	1	2	4	7	6	5	8
7	1	4	5	6	9	8	3	2
9	5	3	4	8	2	7	6	1
8	2	6	7	1	3	4	9	5

86

3	4	5	9	1	8	2	7	6
1	6	7	5	4	2	8	3	9
2	9	8	7	3	6	5	4	1
9	5	3	2	6	1	4	8	7
7	1	6	8	5	4	9	2	3
8	2	4	3	7	9	1	6	5
5	7	9	4	8	3	6	1	2
6	8	2	1	9	7	3	5	4
4	3	1	6	2	5	7	9	8

87

4	5	9	3	6	8	1	2	7
1	8	6	4	7	2	3	9	5
3	7	2	1	9	5	4	8	6
7	2	5	9	1	6	8	3	4
6	9	3	5	8	4	2	7	1
8	4	1	2	3	7	5	6	9
5	3	7	8	4	9	6	1	2
9	1	4	6	2	3	7	5	8
2	6	8	7	5	1	9	4	3

88

5	6	1	3	2	7	9	4	8
4	2	7	9	6	8	3	5	1
9	3	8	4	5	1	2	7	6
2	8	3	7	9	6	4	1	5
6	5	4	2	1	3	8	9	7
1	7	9	5	8	4	6	3	2
3	9	6	8	7	5	1	2	4
7	1	2	6	4	9	5	8	3
8	4	5	1	3	2	7	6	9

89

8	2	1	5	9	7	6	4	3
5	7	6	4	1	3	8	2	9
3	4	9	6	8	2	5	1	7
1	9	4	3	6	5	2	7	8
6	5	7	9	2	8	4	3	1
2	8	3	7	4	1	9	5	6
7	6	5	2	3	9	1	8	4
4	3	8	1	5	6	7	9	2
9	1	2	8	7	4	3	6	5

90

5	6	3	4	9	8	1	7	2
7	1	9	3	6	2	5	4	8
4	2	8	5	1	7	3	6	9
9	8	7	1	2	5	6	3	4
1	3	2	9	4	6	8	5	7
6	4	5	7	8	3	9	2	1
8	5	1	6	7	4	2	9	3
3	9	4	2	5	1	7	8	6
2	7	6	8	3	9	4	1	5

91

4	2	1	8	6	9	5	3	7
8	5	6	2	7	3	4	9	1
3	9	7	1	5	4	8	6	2
7	3	5	9	2	8	6	1	4
1	8	9	6	4	7	3	2	5
6	4	2	3	1	5	7	8	9
9	1	4	7	8	6	2	5	3
5	6	3	4	9	2	1	7	8
2	7	8	5	3	1	9	4	6

92

2	7	4	5	9	6	3	1	8
8	3	1	2	4	7	5	9	6
5	6	9	3	8	1	4	2	7
9	2	7	8	1	5	6	4	3
4	8	3	9	6	2	7	5	1
1	5	6	4	7	3	2	8	9
3	1	2	7	5	9	8	6	4
6	4	5	1	3	8	9	7	2
7	9	8	6	2	4	1	3	5

93

2	1	5	4	8	6	3	7	9
3	9	7	2	5	1	8	6	4
6	4	8	9	7	3	1	2	5
5	6	1	8	2	7	9	4	3
4	3	9	1	6	5	2	8	7
7	8	2	3	4	9	5	1	6
1	2	6	5	9	4	7	3	8
9	7	3	6	1	8	4	5	2
8	5	4	7	3	2	6	9	1

94

3	4	7	2	1	9	5	8	6
6	5	9	4	7	8	1	3	2
8	2	1	5	6	3	4	7	9
1	9	3	7	2	6	8	4	5
7	6	5	1	8	4	2	9	3
4	8	2	9	3	5	7	6	1
2	7	4	6	9	1	3	5	8
9	1	8	3	5	7	6	2	4
5	3	6	8	4	2	9	1	7

95

8	6	3	5	1	4	2	9	7
1	5	4	2	7	9	3	6	8
9	7	2	8	3	6	4	5	1
2	4	8	6	9	3	7	1	5
3	9	7	1	4	5	6	8	2
6	1	5	7	8	2	9	4	3
7	2	9	4	5	1	8	3	6
4	8	1	3	6	7	5	2	9
5	3	6	9	2	8	1	7	4

96

9	6	2	1	4	7	5	8	3
1	7	3	5	6	8	4	2	9
4	8	5	9	3	2	7	1	6
6	9	7	8	2	4	1	3	5
5	2	4	6	1	3	8	9	7
3	1	8	7	5	9	6	4	2
2	3	6	4	7	1	9	5	8
7	4	9	3	8	5	2	6	1
8	5	1	2	9	6	3	7	4

97

6	8	7	3	1	2	5	9	4
3	2	5	9	6	4	7	1	8
4	9	1	5	8	7	6	3	2
5	4	2	8	3	9	1	7	6
9	3	6	4	7	1	2	8	5
1	7	8	2	5	6	9	4	3
7	5	4	6	9	3	8	2	1
8	1	3	7	2	5	4	6	9
2	6	9	1	4	8	3	5	7

98

7	9	4	5	2	1	8	6	3
3	1	6	9	7	8	5	4	2
8	2	5	6	3	4	1	9	7
6	8	1	4	9	2	3	7	5
2	4	7	3	5	6	9	8	1
5	3	9	8	1	7	4	2	6
4	6	2	1	8	5	7	3	9
1	7	3	2	4	9	6	5	8
9	5	8	7	6	3	2	1	4

99

5	1	6	7	2	4	9	3	8
7	3	2	9	1	8	5	4	6
9	4	8	5	3	6	7	2	1
1	5	7	8	4	2	3	6	9
4	6	3	1	5	9	2	8	7
8	2	9	3	6	7	1	5	4
6	8	5	2	7	1	4	9	3
2	9	1	4	8	3	6	7	5
3	7	4	6	9	5	8	1	2

100

8	3	7	5	1	4	2	6	9
2	4	9	7	6	3	1	5	8
6	5	1	9	8	2	7	4	3
7	1	3	4	9	5	6	8	2
9	6	2	1	7	8	4	3	5
5	8	4	3	2	6	9	1	7
1	7	8	6	3	9	5	2	4
3	9	5	2	4	1	8	7	6
4	2	6	8	5	7	3	9	1

101

9	3	1	8	2	4	7	6	5
4	8	5	7	9	6	2	1	3
7	2	6	3	1	5	4	9	8
5	9	2	1	7	8	3	4	6
3	1	4	9	6	2	5	8	7
6	7	8	5	4	3	1	2	9
8	5	9	2	3	1	6	7	4
2	6	3	4	8	7	9	5	1
1	4	7	6	5	9	8	3	2

102

9	1	2	6	5	7	8	3	4
7	6	3	2	4	8	5	9	1
4	8	5	1	3	9	7	6	2
5	2	4	7	1	6	3	8	9
6	7	1	9	8	3	4	2	5
8	3	9	4	2	5	6	1	7
1	4	7	3	6	2	9	5	8
2	5	6	8	9	4	1	7	3
3	9	8	5	7	1	2	4	6

103

1	2	5	4	7	9	8	6	3
6	8	4	2	1	3	5	7	9
7	9	3	5	8	6	4	2	1
4	5	7	8	2	1	9	3	6
8	3	2	9	6	7	1	4	5
9	6	1	3	4	5	7	8	2
3	7	9	6	5	8	2	1	4
5	4	8	1	3	2	6	9	7
2	1	6	7	9	4	3	5	8

104

7	2	1	3	6	9	4	5	8
9	5	8	7	2	4	3	6	1
6	3	4	8	1	5	2	7	9
3	7	9	6	8	1	5	4	2
5	8	6	4	9	2	1	3	7
1	4	2	5	3	7	8	9	6
8	9	3	2	4	6	7	1	5
4	1	5	9	7	8	6	2	3
2	6	7	1	5	3	9	8	4

105

2	9	1	6	3	7	5	4	8
8	6	7	9	4	5	1	3	2
4	3	5	8	2	1	9	6	7
9	5	6	4	1	2	7	8	3
1	8	2	3	7	9	6	5	4
3	7	4	5	8	6	2	9	1
6	2	8	7	9	4	3	1	5
7	4	9	1	5	3	8	2	6
5	1	3	2	6	8	4	7	9

106

5	9	1	4	7	6	3	8	2
6	2	8	9	5	3	4	7	1
7	4	3	1	2	8	6	9	5
9	3	4	5	1	7	2	6	8
1	5	7	8	6	2	9	4	3
8	6	2	3	4	9	1	5	7
2	1	6	7	9	5	8	3	4
4	8	5	6	3	1	7	2	9
3	7	9	2	8	4	5	1	6

107

4	8	1	3	9	5	7	6	2
5	9	6	7	4	2	3	8	1
2	7	3	6	8	1	5	9	4
9	1	2	8	5	6	4	3	7
8	4	5	9	3	7	1	2	6
3	6	7	2	1	4	9	5	8
6	5	4	1	2	3	8	7	9
7	3	9	4	6	8	2	1	5
1	2	8	5	7	9	6	4	3

108

4	9	7	6	3	1	8	2	5
3	5	8	9	4	2	1	7	6
6	1	2	7	8	5	4	9	3
2	6	3	4	5	7	9	8	1
8	7	1	3	2	9	6	5	4
5	4	9	8	1	6	2	3	7
1	2	6	5	9	3	7	4	8
7	8	5	2	6	4	3	1	9
9	3	4	1	7	8	5	6	2

109

5	2	1	7	8	9	4	6	3
8	4	9	6	5	3	1	2	7
7	6	3	4	1	2	8	5	9
4	8	7	2	6	1	3	9	5
3	9	6	8	7	5	2	1	4
1	5	2	9	3	4	7	8	6
2	1	5	3	4	6	9	7	8
9	3	8	5	2	7	6	4	1
6	7	4	1	9	8	5	3	2

110

1	7	4	8	3	6	5	2	9
6	2	5	9	4	7	8	3	1
8	9	3	1	5	2	6	4	7
5	6	7	4	8	9	3	1	2
2	1	8	5	7	3	9	6	4
3	4	9	6	2	1	7	5	8
9	3	1	7	6	4	2	8	5
4	8	2	3	9	5	1	7	6
7	5	6	2	1	8	4	9	3

111

8	5	4	1	3	9	7	6	2
6	9	7	5	2	8	4	1	3
1	2	3	6	7	4	8	5	9
7	6	5	4	8	2	9	3	1
4	8	2	9	1	3	6	7	5
3	1	9	7	5	6	2	4	8
5	3	8	2	6	7	1	9	4
9	7	1	8	4	5	3	2	6
2	4	6	3	9	1	5	8	7

112

3	2	9	8	7	1	4	6	5
8	1	4	9	6	5	7	3	2
5	7	6	2	4	3	9	1	8
9	6	8	1	2	4	3	5	7
2	4	1	5	3	7	8	9	6
7	3	5	6	8	9	2	4	1
6	9	2	3	1	8	5	7	4
1	5	7	4	9	2	6	8	3
4	8	3	7	5	6	1	2	9

113

8	1	6	7	2	9	5	3	4
5	9	3	6	1	4	8	2	7
4	2	7	8	3	5	1	9	6
1	6	4	9	7	3	2	5	8
2	7	8	5	6	1	9	4	3
9	3	5	2	4	8	6	7	1
6	8	2	3	5	7	4	1	9
7	5	1	4	9	6	3	8	2
3	4	9	1	8	2	7	6	5

114

1	2	7	3	4	8	6	5	9
5	8	3	2	9	6	1	4	7
9	6	4	1	7	5	3	2	8
3	5	8	9	1	2	4	7	6
2	1	9	7	6	4	5	8	3
7	4	6	5	8	3	2	9	1
4	9	1	6	5	7	8	3	2
6	3	5	8	2	9	7	1	4
8	7	2	4	3	1	9	6	5

115

6	5	8	9	4	3	2	7	1
2	9	7	5	6	1	8	4	3
1	3	4	2	7	8	9	5	6
9	1	5	6	3	7	4	2	8
7	2	3	4	8	9	1	6	5
8	4	6	1	5	2	3	9	7
4	6	2	3	1	5	7	8	9
3	8	9	7	2	6	5	1	4
5	7	1	8	9	4	6	3	2

116

9	1	2	8	6	4	7	5	3
5	3	4	1	9	7	6	8	2
8	6	7	3	5	2	4	9	1
7	2	6	9	4	5	1	3	8
3	9	5	7	1	8	2	6	4
1	4	8	6	2	3	5	7	9
2	5	9	4	3	6	8	1	7
6	8	1	2	7	9	3	4	5
4	7	3	5	8	1	9	2	6

117

8	4	1	9	6	3	5	2	7
2	3	9	7	8	5	1	6	4
5	7	6	1	4	2	8	3	9
7	5	8	4	3	9	2	1	6
3	9	4	2	1	6	7	8	5
6	1	2	8	5	7	4	9	3
4	2	5	3	9	8	6	7	1
1	8	3	6	7	4	9	5	2
9	6	7	5	2	1	3	4	8

118

7	6	8	5	2	1	4	3	9
3	5	1	6	9	4	2	8	7
4	9	2	3	7	8	1	5	6
8	1	3	2	6	5	7	9	4
2	7	5	8	4	9	6	1	3
6	4	9	7	1	3	5	2	8
5	2	6	9	8	7	3	4	1
9	3	4	1	5	6	8	7	2
1	8	7	4	3	2	9	6	5

119

7	1	4	5	6	9	2	3	8
5	9	8	3	1	2	4	7	6
2	6	3	7	8	4	1	9	5
6	2	9	4	3	5	7	8	1
3	4	7	8	2	1	6	5	9
1	8	5	6	9	7	3	4	2
9	7	2	1	5	3	8	6	4
4	5	6	2	7	8	9	1	3
8	3	1	9	4	6	5	2	7

120

3	1	7	2	4	5	9	8	6
9	6	4	8	3	7	2	5	1
5	2	8	9	6	1	4	7	3
4	7	6	5	2	3	8	1	9
2	9	3	1	8	6	5	4	7
1	8	5	4	7	9	3	6	2
7	4	2	3	1	8	6	9	5
6	3	9	7	5	4	1	2	8
8	5	1	6	9	2	7	3	4

121

3	1	9	2	6	4	7	5	8
8	2	5	3	1	7	6	4	9
7	4	6	9	8	5	2	3	1
6	3	7	5	9	2	1	8	4
2	8	4	7	3	1	9	6	5
9	5	1	8	4	6	3	2	7
4	9	3	1	2	8	5	7	6
1	7	8	6	5	3	4	9	2
5	6	2	4	7	9	8	1	3

122

5	2	3	9	8	4	1	6	7
4	9	7	5	1	6	2	3	8
8	1	6	7	2	3	4	9	5
2	8	5	1	7	9	6	4	3
3	6	9	8	4	5	7	1	2
1	7	4	3	6	2	5	8	9
9	4	8	2	5	1	3	7	6
6	3	2	4	9	7	8	5	1
7	5	1	6	3	8	9	2	4

123

7	1	2	5	6	3	9	8	4
9	6	8	7	1	4	2	3	5
3	5	4	8	2	9	7	1	6
5	9	3	6	7	8	4	2	1
2	4	7	1	9	5	3	6	8
1	8	6	3	4	2	5	9	7
8	2	1	9	5	7	6	4	3
4	3	5	2	8	6	1	7	9
6	7	9	4	3	1	8	5	2

124

9	1	5	2	4	7	8	3	6
6	8	3	1	5	9	2	7	4
2	4	7	3	6	8	5	1	9
4	2	1	7	9	5	3	6	8
3	6	9	8	2	4	7	5	1
7	5	8	6	3	1	4	9	2
1	7	4	9	8	3	6	2	5
5	9	6	4	7	2	1	8	3
8	3	2	5	1	6	9	4	7

125

6	2	9	7	4	3	5	8	1
1	3	8	9	6	5	7	2	4
4	5	7	2	1	8	3	6	9
5	4	3	6	7	2	1	9	8
7	1	6	5	8	9	2	4	3
9	8	2	4	3	1	6	7	5
2	6	1	8	5	4	9	3	7
3	7	4	1	9	6	8	5	2
8	9	5	3	2	7	4	1	6

126

4	3	7	8	1	9	5	2	6
5	9	2	3	6	7	8	4	1
1	8	6	2	4	5	7	3	9
9	4	1	7	3	6	2	5	8
8	7	5	9	2	4	1	6	3
2	6	3	1	5	8	9	7	4
6	5	9	4	8	2	3	1	7
3	2	8	6	7	1	4	9	5
7	1	4	5	9	3	6	8	2

127

5	2	3	4	1	8	7	9	6
7	1	6	5	2	9	4	8	3
4	8	9	7	3	6	1	5	2
1	5	8	9	6	4	3	2	7
9	7	2	1	5	3	8	6	4
3	6	4	8	7	2	5	1	9
8	3	7	2	9	1	6	4	5
6	9	1	3	4	5	2	7	8
2	4	5	6	8	7	9	3	1

128

8	6	7	9	4	3	2	1	5
9	2	4	6	1	5	7	8	3
3	1	5	7	8	2	9	6	4
4	5	2	3	6	1	8	7	9
1	9	8	4	5	7	6	3	2
6	7	3	8	2	9	5	4	1
7	4	1	2	9	8	3	5	6
2	8	6	5	3	4	1	9	7
5	3	9	1	7	6	4	2	8

129

2	7	8	4	9	5	1	6	3
9	5	6	2	3	1	4	7	8
4	3	1	8	6	7	5	2	9
1	2	3	6	7	9	8	4	5
5	4	7	1	2	8	9	3	6
6	8	9	5	4	3	7	1	2
7	6	4	9	5	2	3	8	1
8	9	2	3	1	4	6	5	7
3	1	5	7	8	6	2	9	4

130

7	5	4	3	8	6	1	2	9
3	2	1	4	7	9	6	8	5
6	9	8	5	2	1	3	7	4
2	6	9	1	4	7	5	3	8
8	1	3	9	5	2	7	4	6
5	4	7	8	6	3	2	9	1
1	3	2	6	9	8	4	5	7
9	7	5	2	1	4	8	6	3
4	8	6	7	3	5	9	1	2

131

5	4	6	8	3	7	1	2	9
9	8	2	6	4	1	5	3	7
3	7	1	5	2	9	8	6	4
2	1	3	7	9	5	4	8	6
7	6	5	3	8	4	2	9	1
8	9	4	2	1	6	7	5	3
6	5	9	4	7	2	3	1	8
4	2	8	1	6	3	9	7	5
1	3	7	9	5	8	6	4	2

132

7	8	9	6	2	3	1	5	4
4	5	1	8	7	9	2	3	6
3	2	6	4	1	5	9	8	7
1	6	5	3	4	7	8	2	9
2	4	8	1	9	6	3	7	5
9	7	3	5	8	2	4	6	1
5	3	4	2	6	1	7	9	8
6	1	7	9	3	8	5	4	2
8	9	2	7	5	4	6	1	3

133

7	1	5	8	3	2	4	9	6
3	8	9	7	6	4	5	1	2
2	6	4	9	1	5	7	3	8
6	9	8	1	7	3	2	5	4
4	3	7	5	2	6	9	8	1
5	2	1	4	8	9	3	6	7
9	7	2	6	5	1	8	4	3
1	4	3	2	9	8	6	7	5
8	5	6	3	4	7	1	2	9

134

9	7	2	5	1	8	3	4	6
5	1	4	2	3	6	7	9	8
3	8	6	9	4	7	2	1	5
2	6	1	8	7	5	4	3	9
4	5	3	6	9	1	8	7	2
8	9	7	4	2	3	5	6	1
1	2	5	3	6	4	9	8	7
7	3	8	1	5	9	6	2	4
6	4	9	7	8	2	1	5	3

135

9	2	4	7	5	8	6	1	3
1	5	3	6	9	2	8	4	7
8	6	7	1	4	3	9	2	5
7	3	1	9	8	4	5	6	2
4	9	6	5	2	1	7	3	8
5	8	2	3	7	6	4	9	1
2	4	5	8	1	9	3	7	6
3	1	8	4	6	7	2	5	9
6	7	9	2	3	5	1	8	4

136

5	6	4	2	3	7	1	8	9
9	7	2	1	6	8	3	5	4
8	3	1	4	9	5	6	7	2
6	2	8	5	4	9	7	3	1
1	5	3	8	7	2	4	9	6
4	9	7	6	1	3	5	2	8
7	8	6	3	2	1	9	4	5
3	1	5	9	8	4	2	6	7
2	4	9	7	5	6	8	1	3

137

4	6	9	7	2	3	8	1	5
1	5	7	4	6	8	9	3	2
8	2	3	1	5	9	4	7	6
2	3	1	9	7	6	5	4	8
7	8	6	2	4	5	1	9	3
5	9	4	8	3	1	6	2	7
9	1	2	5	8	7	3	6	4
3	4	8	6	1	2	7	5	9
6	7	5	3	9	4	2	8	1

138

4	8	9	1	2	7	6	3	5
5	6	1	3	9	8	4	7	2
2	3	7	6	4	5	1	8	9
1	4	5	2	3	6	7	9	8
9	2	8	7	5	4	3	6	1
3	7	6	8	1	9	2	5	4
8	1	4	5	6	3	9	2	7
6	5	2	9	7	1	8	4	3
7	9	3	4	8	2	5	1	6

139

9	1	5	4	2	7	6	8	3
4	3	2	5	6	8	1	7	9
6	7	8	9	3	1	4	2	5
1	9	7	3	8	6	5	4	2
3	2	6	1	4	5	8	9	7
5	8	4	2	7	9	3	6	1
8	4	1	7	5	2	9	3	6
7	6	9	8	1	3	2	5	4
2	5	3	6	9	4	7	1	8

140

7	8	3	2	9	4	6	1	5
1	4	5	6	8	3	2	9	7
2	9	6	1	5	7	3	8	4
5	7	8	4	1	6	9	2	3
3	2	4	8	7	9	5	6	1
9	6	1	3	2	5	4	7	8
4	5	7	9	6	8	1	3	2
6	3	2	7	4	1	8	5	9
8	1	9	5	3	2	7	4	6

141

7	2	1	5	9	3	4	8	6
8	6	5	7	4	2	1	9	3
4	3	9	1	8	6	7	5	2
9	8	6	4	7	5	3	2	1
2	4	3	6	1	8	9	7	5
5	1	7	2	3	9	8	6	4
6	9	4	8	2	1	5	3	7
3	7	2	9	5	4	6	1	8
1	5	8	3	6	7	2	4	9

142

6	3	2	4	8	5	9	1	7
8	5	1	7	3	9	6	4	2
9	4	7	1	6	2	3	5	8
4	9	3	8	7	1	5	2	6
1	2	6	5	9	4	7	8	3
5	7	8	3	2	6	4	9	1
7	8	4	2	5	3	1	6	9
2	1	9	6	4	7	8	3	5
3	6	5	9	1	8	2	7	4

143

2	7	9	4	6	8	1	5	3
8	4	6	5	3	1	7	9	2
5	1	3	9	7	2	4	8	6
7	6	4	1	9	5	3	2	8
3	9	8	6	2	4	5	1	7
1	5	2	7	8	3	9	6	4
4	8	5	2	1	7	6	3	9
6	3	1	8	4	9	2	7	5
9	2	7	3	5	6	8	4	1

144

5	2	6	1	8	9	4	7	3
1	9	3	7	2	4	5	8	6
4	7	8	5	3	6	9	2	1
8	4	9	6	5	1	2	3	7
6	3	5	2	4	7	8	1	9
7	1	2	8	9	3	6	4	5
3	6	4	9	1	8	7	5	2
9	5	1	4	7	2	3	6	8
2	8	7	3	6	5	1	9	4

145

6	5	1	9	8	2	3	7	4
2	3	4	1	6	7	5	9	8
9	8	7	3	4	5	2	1	6
4	2	5	7	3	8	9	6	1
3	6	8	4	9	1	7	5	2
1	7	9	2	5	6	4	8	3
5	1	3	8	2	9	6	4	7
7	4	6	5	1	3	8	2	9
8	9	2	6	7	4	1	3	5

146

9	1	3	4	7	6	2	5	8
4	5	6	2	9	8	7	3	1
7	2	8	1	3	5	4	6	9
6	8	5	9	4	3	1	7	2
3	9	7	8	2	1	5	4	6
1	4	2	5	6	7	9	8	3
8	6	4	7	1	2	3	9	5
2	3	9	6	5	4	8	1	7
5	7	1	3	8	9	6	2	4

147

4	8	5	9	2	3	6	1	7
3	1	6	4	5	7	2	9	8
2	7	9	6	1	8	5	4	3
8	5	4	7	3	9	1	6	2
6	2	3	8	4	1	9	7	5
7	9	1	5	6	2	8	3	4
5	3	2	1	9	4	7	8	6
9	4	8	2	7	6	3	5	1
1	6	7	3	8	5	4	2	9

148

4	7	6	1	2	5	3	9	8
9	1	5	7	8	3	2	6	4
3	8	2	9	4	6	7	5	1
1	6	3	5	7	4	8	2	9
8	5	9	3	1	2	4	7	6
2	4	7	6	9	8	5	1	3
7	3	4	2	6	1	9	8	5
6	9	8	4	5	7	1	3	2
5	2	1	8	3	9	6	4	7

149

8	4	1	7	2	3	9	6	5
9	7	5	6	8	4	1	2	3
3	6	2	9	5	1	8	4	7
5	2	9	3	1	8	4	7	6
1	3	7	2	4	6	5	9	8
4	8	6	5	7	9	3	1	2
2	9	8	4	6	5	7	3	1
6	1	4	8	3	7	2	5	9
7	5	3	1	9	2	6	8	4

150

9	1	4	2	3	8	6	7	5
8	3	5	9	6	7	1	4	2
6	7	2	4	5	1	9	3	8
3	8	9	6	4	5	2	1	7
4	6	7	8	1	2	3	5	9
5	2	1	7	9	3	4	8	6
7	5	6	1	2	4	8	9	3
1	9	8	3	7	6	5	2	4
2	4	3	5	8	9	7	6	1

151

8	3	7	9	2	4	1	6	5
4	5	9	3	6	1	7	2	8
2	1	6	7	5	8	9	3	4
9	8	1	4	3	2	6	5	7
7	2	4	6	9	5	8	1	3
3	6	5	8	1	7	2	4	9
6	9	2	5	7	3	4	8	1
5	7	8	1	4	6	3	9	2
1	4	3	2	8	9	5	7	6

152

7	2	5	9	8	3	4	1	6
8	4	3	6	5	1	7	9	2
1	9	6	2	4	7	8	3	5
5	3	4	1	6	9	2	8	7
2	6	8	7	3	5	9	4	1
9	7	1	4	2	8	5	6	3
6	8	2	3	7	4	1	5	9
3	5	9	8	1	2	6	7	4
4	1	7	5	9	6	3	2	8

153

9	1	3	2	7	8	4	6	5
7	6	5	1	3	4	8	2	9
8	2	4	9	6	5	1	7	3
1	9	7	6	8	3	5	4	2
4	5	2	7	9	1	6	3	8
6	3	8	4	5	2	7	9	1
2	4	6	5	1	9	3	8	7
3	7	1	8	2	6	9	5	4
5	8	9	3	4	7	2	1	6

154

8	1	7	4	6	5	9	2	3
9	4	6	1	2	3	8	7	5
3	5	2	8	9	7	6	4	1
7	6	4	3	5	1	2	9	8
2	8	5	7	4	9	3	1	6
1	3	9	6	8	2	4	5	7
6	2	3	5	1	4	7	8	9
5	9	8	2	7	6	1	3	4
4	7	1	9	3	8	5	6	2

155

5	2	7	9	6	4	3	1	8
6	3	4	1	2	8	7	5	9
9	8	1	7	3	5	6	4	2
3	6	8	2	4	1	5	9	7
7	5	9	3	8	6	4	2	1
1	4	2	5	9	7	8	3	6
4	9	3	6	7	2	1	8	5
8	1	6	4	5	9	2	7	3
2	7	5	8	1	3	9	6	4

156

7	5	4	3	1	9	6	2	8
1	2	6	7	8	4	9	5	3
8	3	9	2	5	6	4	1	7
5	4	3	6	7	1	2	8	9
2	8	1	9	3	5	7	6	4
9	6	7	4	2	8	5	3	1
6	7	8	5	4	3	1	9	2
3	9	2	1	6	7	8	4	5
4	1	5	8	9	2	3	7	6

157

6	1	5	8	4	7	9	2	3
9	4	7	6	3	2	5	8	1
3	2	8	9	5	1	4	7	6
4	6	2	5	9	8	3	1	7
7	3	1	2	6	4	8	5	9
5	8	9	7	1	3	2	6	4
8	9	4	1	7	5	6	3	2
2	7	6	3	8	9	1	4	5
1	5	3	4	2	6	7	9	8

158

4	2	9	6	7	3	1	8	5
8	5	6	9	1	2	4	7	3
1	7	3	4	5	8	9	6	2
2	6	1	7	9	5	8	3	4
7	9	8	2	3	4	6	5	1
3	4	5	8	6	1	2	9	7
6	3	4	5	2	9	7	1	8
9	1	2	3	8	7	5	4	6
5	8	7	1	4	6	3	2	9

159

4	2	1	6	7	8	3	9	5
3	5	9	4	1	2	7	6	8
8	6	7	9	3	5	4	1	2
5	3	6	1	2	9	8	4	7
1	4	2	7	8	6	9	5	3
7	9	8	3	5	4	6	2	1
6	1	5	8	9	3	2	7	4
9	7	3	2	4	1	5	8	6
2	8	4	5	6	7	1	3	9

160

2	3	8	6	7	9	5	4	1
9	7	4	1	3	5	2	6	8
6	5	1	2	4	8	9	3	7
5	9	2	3	6	7	8	1	4
3	4	7	8	2	1	6	5	9
1	8	6	5	9	4	3	7	2
7	1	3	9	8	6	4	2	5
8	6	5	4	1	2	7	9	3
4	2	9	7	5	3	1	8	6

161

6	3	5	2	4	8	9	7	1
9	4	1	3	5	7	2	6	8
8	7	2	9	1	6	5	4	3
5	9	8	4	7	1	3	2	6
1	2	7	8	6	3	4	9	5
3	6	4	5	9	2	8	1	7
2	1	3	6	8	4	7	5	9
7	8	9	1	2	5	6	3	4
4	5	6	7	3	9	1	8	2

162

2	6	4	1	7	3	5	8	9
1	7	5	6	9	8	2	4	3
3	8	9	2	4	5	6	7	1
6	5	2	4	1	7	3	9	8
9	3	7	8	2	6	4	1	5
4	1	8	3	5	9	7	6	2
5	4	3	9	6	1	8	2	7
8	2	1	7	3	4	9	5	6
7	9	6	5	8	2	1	3	4

163

7	6	1	9	4	8	2	5	3
9	4	8	5	2	3	6	7	1
3	2	5	1	6	7	9	4	8
1	5	4	8	7	2	3	6	9
6	3	9	4	5	1	7	8	2
2	8	7	6	3	9	4	1	5
8	1	2	7	9	6	5	3	4
5	9	6	3	8	4	1	2	7
4	7	3	2	1	5	8	9	6

164

3	6	7	5	1	4	8	2	9
9	4	8	2	7	6	3	1	5
2	5	1	8	9	3	4	7	6
5	9	2	6	3	7	1	4	8
8	3	4	9	2	1	6	5	7
7	1	6	4	5	8	2	9	3
4	7	3	1	6	5	9	8	2
6	8	9	7	4	2	5	3	1
1	2	5	3	8	9	7	6	4

165

3	7	2	9	1	5	8	6	4
8	4	9	2	3	6	5	7	1
6	1	5	8	4	7	3	2	9
1	5	4	3	7	2	9	8	6
2	8	6	4	9	1	7	3	5
9	3	7	6	5	8	4	1	2
5	2	3	7	6	4	1	9	8
4	9	8	1	2	3	6	5	7
7	6	1	5	8	9	2	4	3

166

7	3	2	5	6	4	9	1	8
4	1	9	8	3	7	5	6	2
8	5	6	2	1	9	4	7	3
3	9	5	7	2	1	6	8	4
6	7	1	9	4	8	3	2	5
2	4	8	6	5	3	1	9	7
5	2	7	4	9	6	8	3	1
1	6	4	3	8	2	7	5	9
9	8	3	1	7	5	2	4	6

167

1	8	5	6	9	2	7	3	4
7	4	6	5	8	3	1	2	9
2	9	3	1	4	7	5	8	6
5	7	2	3	1	4	6	9	8
4	6	9	2	7	8	3	1	5
8	3	1	9	5	6	2	4	7
3	2	4	8	6	5	9	7	1
9	5	8	7	2	1	4	6	3
6	1	7	4	3	9	8	5	2

168

2	3	9	5	6	4	1	8	7
8	7	6	9	2	1	5	3	4
1	4	5	8	3	7	2	6	9
4	2	1	6	8	5	9	7	3
3	6	7	2	1	9	8	4	5
9	5	8	4	7	3	6	2	1
7	8	3	1	9	6	4	5	2
5	1	2	7	4	8	3	9	6
6	9	4	3	5	2	7	1	8

169

9	8	5	3	1	4	2	6	7
1	4	3	2	7	6	8	9	5
2	6	7	8	9	5	3	4	1
4	1	8	5	6	9	7	2	3
3	2	6	7	8	1	9	5	4
5	7	9	4	2	3	1	8	6
8	9	1	6	4	7	5	3	2
6	5	2	1	3	8	4	7	9
7	3	4	9	5	2	6	1	8

170

2	4	1	7	8	5	6	3	9
8	6	5	4	9	3	2	1	7
7	3	9	2	1	6	4	8	5
3	8	2	6	4	7	5	9	1
5	9	4	8	2	1	7	6	3
6	1	7	3	5	9	8	4	2
9	7	8	1	6	2	3	5	4
1	2	6	5	3	4	9	7	8
4	5	3	9	7	8	1	2	6

171

7	1	5	3	8	4	9	6	2
6	9	8	2	1	5	3	4	7
4	3	2	9	6	7	5	8	1
5	6	3	7	2	9	8	1	4
9	8	7	6	4	1	2	3	5
1	2	4	8	5	3	7	9	6
3	5	9	4	7	6	1	2	8
8	7	6	1	9	2	4	5	3
2	4	1	5	3	8	6	7	9

172

5	8	7	3	6	1	9	2	4
1	3	6	4	9	2	5	7	8
4	9	2	8	7	5	1	3	6
8	7	9	2	5	3	4	6	1
6	4	5	7	1	9	3	8	2
2	1	3	6	4	8	7	9	5
9	2	8	5	3	4	6	1	7
3	6	4	1	8	7	2	5	9
7	5	1	9	2	6	8	4	3

173

2	6	8	4	3	1	7	5	9
3	4	7	6	5	9	2	8	1
1	5	9	7	8	2	6	3	4
9	3	6	5	2	8	1	4	7
7	1	5	9	4	3	8	6	2
4	8	2	1	6	7	3	9	5
6	7	3	2	9	5	4	1	8
8	9	1	3	7	4	5	2	6
5	2	4	8	1	6	9	7	3

174

7	1	9	5	8	2	6	4	3
4	8	3	6	1	9	5	7	2
2	6	5	4	7	3	9	1	8
5	7	8	2	4	1	3	6	9
9	2	6	8	3	7	4	5	1
1	3	4	9	5	6	2	8	7
8	4	1	3	9	5	7	2	6
6	9	7	1	2	4	8	3	5
3	5	2	7	6	8	1	9	4

175

6	1	3	5	9	8	4	7	2
7	9	5	4	6	2	8	1	3
2	8	4	7	1	3	6	9	5
1	6	8	2	5	4	7	3	9
9	4	2	3	7	6	1	5	8
3	5	7	9	8	1	2	6	4
5	7	1	8	2	9	3	4	6
8	3	9	6	4	7	5	2	1
4	2	6	1	3	5	9	8	7

176

4	1	7	6	8	9	2	3	5
3	2	6	5	4	1	7	8	9
9	8	5	7	3	2	4	1	6
5	7	1	2	6	3	8	9	4
2	3	8	1	9	4	5	6	7
6	9	4	8	5	7	1	2	3
7	6	3	4	1	8	9	5	2
8	5	2	9	7	6	3	4	1
1	4	9	3	2	5	6	7	8

177

2	6	8	5	9	7	4	1	3
1	7	3	4	6	2	9	8	5
4	9	5	8	1	3	7	6	2
7	8	4	2	3	9	6	5	1
9	5	1	7	8	6	3	2	4
3	2	6	1	4	5	8	9	7
5	4	7	6	2	8	1	3	9
6	1	9	3	5	4	2	7	8
8	3	2	9	7	1	5	4	6

178

1	8	7	6	9	3	5	2	4
3	5	9	4	8	2	1	6	7
4	6	2	1	7	5	3	9	8
7	9	1	8	6	4	2	5	3
6	4	5	2	3	1	7	8	9
2	3	8	7	5	9	6	4	1
8	7	3	5	4	6	9	1	2
9	2	6	3	1	8	4	7	5
5	1	4	9	2	7	8	3	6

179

6	5	9	3	7	1	8	2	4
7	2	8	5	4	9	6	3	1
3	4	1	8	6	2	7	5	9
9	1	5	6	8	3	2	4	7
2	6	3	7	1	4	9	8	5
8	7	4	2	9	5	3	1	6
5	8	7	1	3	6	4	9	2
4	3	2	9	5	7	1	6	8
1	9	6	4	2	8	5	7	3

180

8	7	1	3	6	5	9	2	4
5	4	3	8	2	9	7	6	1
6	9	2	4	7	1	5	8	3
3	1	8	9	4	2	6	5	7
7	5	9	6	3	8	4	1	2
4	2	6	5	1	7	8	3	9
1	6	5	2	9	4	3	7	8
2	3	4	7	8	6	1	9	5
9	8	7	1	5	3	2	4	6

181

7	8	6	1	3	5	9	2	4
2	5	4	9	6	7	3	8	1
3	9	1	2	4	8	6	5	7
6	2	8	5	1	9	4	7	3
9	1	3	8	7	4	2	6	5
4	7	5	6	2	3	8	1	9
5	3	2	4	8	1	7	9	6
1	6	7	3	9	2	5	4	8
8	4	9	7	5	6	1	3	2

182

4	8	7	6	3	1	5	9	2
2	3	6	7	5	9	1	8	4
9	1	5	4	2	8	7	6	3
1	6	8	3	9	4	2	7	5
7	5	9	8	1	2	3	4	6
3	2	4	5	6	7	9	1	8
6	7	3	1	4	5	8	2	9
5	9	1	2	8	6	4	3	7
8	4	2	9	7	3	6	5	1

183

8	4	5	1	2	6	3	9	7
6	2	3	5	7	9	4	8	1
1	9	7	3	8	4	2	6	5
9	5	4	6	3	7	8	1	2
7	8	2	4	1	5	9	3	6
3	6	1	2	9	8	5	7	4
5	1	6	8	4	3	7	2	9
4	7	8	9	6	2	1	5	3
2	3	9	7	5	1	6	4	8

184

2	8	5	3	6	9	4	7	1
3	6	7	1	4	2	5	9	8
1	9	4	7	8	5	2	3	6
4	3	8	5	1	6	7	2	9
5	7	6	2	9	3	1	8	4
9	2	1	8	7	4	3	6	5
8	4	2	6	5	7	9	1	3
6	5	3	9	2	1	8	4	7
7	1	9	4	3	8	6	5	2

185

7	2	9	3	6	1	5	8	4
5	4	1	2	7	8	6	9	3
8	3	6	9	5	4	1	7	2
2	8	5	4	1	9	3	6	7
6	9	3	8	2	7	4	5	1
1	7	4	5	3	6	8	2	9
3	6	8	1	9	2	7	4	5
4	1	2	7	8	5	9	3	6
9	5	7	6	4	3	2	1	8

186

1	3	8	6	7	9	2	4	5
7	5	6	2	8	4	3	1	9
9	2	4	1	3	5	8	7	6
4	1	3	7	5	6	9	8	2
6	7	5	9	2	8	4	3	1
2	8	9	4	1	3	5	6	7
3	4	7	5	6	2	1	9	8
8	6	2	3	9	1	7	5	4
5	9	1	8	4	7	6	2	3

187

8	3	7	5	4	2	6	9	1
6	2	5	7	9	1	4	8	3
4	1	9	8	3	6	7	5	2
9	6	2	1	7	4	8	3	5
1	4	8	3	6	5	2	7	9
5	7	3	2	8	9	1	6	4
3	5	4	6	2	7	9	1	8
7	9	1	4	5	8	3	2	6
2	8	6	9	1	3	5	4	7

188

9	6	4	8	5	1	2	3	7
7	5	3	6	2	4	8	1	9
8	1	2	9	3	7	6	5	4
6	3	7	4	9	5	1	8	2
1	9	8	7	6	2	3	4	5
4	2	5	1	8	3	9	7	6
3	7	9	2	4	8	5	6	1
5	4	6	3	1	9	7	2	8
2	8	1	5	7	6	4	9	3

189

2	5	8	7	3	9	4	1	6
1	6	9	8	5	4	3	2	7
7	4	3	2	6	1	8	9	5
9	7	2	3	4	6	1	5	8
6	3	1	5	2	8	7	4	9
5	8	4	9	1	7	6	3	2
8	2	5	1	7	3	9	6	4
3	9	6	4	8	5	2	7	1
4	1	7	6	9	2	5	8	3

190

6	8	1	9	5	2	7	3	4
2	5	7	4	8	3	9	6	1
9	4	3	7	1	6	2	8	5
8	7	6	1	2	9	4	5	3
5	2	4	8	3	7	6	1	9
1	3	9	5	6	4	8	2	7
3	9	5	2	4	8	1	7	6
4	6	8	3	7	1	5	9	2
7	1	2	6	9	5	3	4	8

191

3	2	6	4	9	5	1	8	7
1	4	9	8	2	7	5	6	3
8	7	5	3	1	6	2	4	9
7	6	8	1	5	3	4	9	2
2	1	4	9	7	8	6	3	5
9	5	3	6	4	2	7	1	8
6	8	2	7	3	4	9	5	1
4	9	7	5	8	1	3	2	6
5	3	1	2	6	9	8	7	4

192

8	3	7	2	5	4	9	6	1
9	1	5	8	7	6	2	4	3
2	6	4	3	1	9	5	8	7
6	7	3	9	8	2	1	5	4
1	8	2	7	4	5	3	9	6
4	5	9	6	3	1	7	2	8
7	2	1	5	6	8	4	3	9
3	9	6	4	2	7	8	1	5
5	4	8	1	9	3	6	7	2

193

5	9	6	7	3	4	8	1	2
7	1	3	9	2	8	5	4	6
2	4	8	6	5	1	3	7	9
9	2	5	1	7	3	6	8	4
8	6	7	5	4	9	2	3	1
4	3	1	8	6	2	9	5	7
1	7	9	2	8	5	4	6	3
3	5	2	4	1	6	7	9	8
6	8	4	3	9	7	1	2	5

194

2	8	9	4	6	5	3	1	7
1	7	5	9	3	2	4	8	6
6	4	3	1	7	8	2	5	9
7	5	1	2	8	4	6	9	3
3	2	8	7	9	6	1	4	5
4	9	6	5	1	3	8	7	2
5	1	2	6	4	7	9	3	8
9	3	7	8	2	1	5	6	4
8	6	4	3	5	9	7	2	1

195

8	1	2	7	9	6	5	4	3
4	5	3	8	2	1	7	6	9
6	9	7	4	5	3	1	2	8
3	4	5	2	7	8	9	1	6
1	2	9	5	6	4	8	3	7
7	8	6	1	3	9	2	5	4
9	3	8	6	1	5	4	7	2
5	7	4	3	8	2	6	9	1
2	6	1	9	4	7	3	8	5

196

3	8	1	6	4	2	7	5	9
4	7	9	1	5	8	6	2	3
2	6	5	3	7	9	1	4	8
9	2	3	5	1	6	8	7	4
8	1	4	9	2	7	5	3	6
6	5	7	4	8	3	9	1	2
7	9	2	8	3	5	4	6	1
5	4	6	2	9	1	3	8	7
1	3	8	7	6	4	2	9	5

197

7	1	3	2	6	8	9	4	5
5	9	2	3	7	4	1	8	6
4	6	8	9	1	5	2	7	3
2	8	6	1	9	3	4	5	7
3	4	7	6	5	2	8	1	9
9	5	1	8	4	7	6	3	2
6	3	4	7	8	9	5	2	1
8	2	9	5	3	1	7	6	4
1	7	5	4	2	6	3	9	8

198

4	6	2	7	3	8	1	9	5
5	7	8	9	2	1	4	6	3
1	3	9	4	6	5	2	7	8
7	1	6	5	4	9	8	3	2
2	4	5	8	7	3	9	1	6
8	9	3	2	1	6	7	5	4
6	2	4	1	5	7	3	8	9
3	8	7	6	9	4	5	2	1
9	5	1	3	8	2	6	4	7

199

9	4	8	5	6	2	3	7	1
1	6	3	9	7	4	8	2	5
7	5	2	1	3	8	6	9	4
8	1	4	2	5	9	7	3	6
3	2	7	4	1	6	9	5	8
6	9	5	7	8	3	1	4	2
4	8	6	3	9	5	2	1	7
5	7	9	8	2	1	4	6	3
2	3	1	6	4	7	5	8	9

200

7	4	3	5	1	2	9	6	8
9	1	5	7	6	8	2	3	4
8	6	2	9	3	4	1	7	5
6	7	4	1	8	5	3	9	2
1	3	8	2	7	9	5	4	6
5	2	9	6	4	3	8	1	7
4	8	1	3	2	6	7	5	9
3	9	6	8	5	7	4	2	1
2	5	7	4	9	1	6	8	3

201

5	9	1	2	4	6	7	8	3
8	3	6	7	1	9	4	5	2
2	4	7	8	3	5	6	9	1
4	5	9	1	8	2	3	6	7
3	7	8	9	6	4	1	2	5
1	6	2	5	7	3	8	4	9
6	1	5	3	2	8	9	7	4
9	8	3	4	5	7	2	1	6
7	2	4	6	9	1	5	3	8

202

6	2	4	1	8	7	5	3	9
7	1	8	3	9	5	2	6	4
9	5	3	6	2	4	7	8	1
2	8	6	7	1	9	3	4	5
5	4	1	8	3	2	6	9	7
3	9	7	4	5	6	8	1	2
4	3	9	5	7	8	1	2	6
8	7	2	9	6	1	4	5	3
1	6	5	2	4	3	9	7	8

203

9	3	7	5	4	6	2	1	8
5	2	6	7	8	1	3	9	4
4	1	8	2	3	9	5	6	7
8	5	1	9	7	2	6	4	3
7	4	2	8	6	3	9	5	1
3	6	9	4	1	5	8	7	2
6	7	5	3	2	4	1	8	9
2	9	4	1	5	8	7	3	6
1	8	3	6	9	7	4	2	5

204

2	3	4	9	1	6	5	8	7
7	6	1	8	3	5	4	9	2
9	5	8	4	7	2	3	6	1
5	4	7	1	8	3	6	2	9
6	8	9	7	2	4	1	5	3
3	1	2	6	5	9	7	4	8
1	9	5	2	6	7	8	3	4
4	7	3	5	9	8	2	1	6
8	2	6	3	4	1	9	7	5

205

9	7	1	2	4	3	6	8	5
3	4	8	6	7	5	2	1	9
6	2	5	8	9	1	3	7	4
4	9	3	7	5	2	1	6	8
1	8	2	9	6	4	5	3	7
7	5	6	1	3	8	4	9	2
5	6	7	4	1	9	8	2	3
8	3	9	5	2	6	7	4	1
2	1	4	3	8	7	9	5	6

206

2	5	6	7	1	3	8	9	4
7	9	3	2	4	8	5	1	6
4	8	1	9	6	5	3	2	7
3	4	5	6	2	9	7	8	1
9	1	7	3	8	4	2	6	5
8	6	2	1	5	7	4	3	9
5	7	9	8	3	6	1	4	2
6	2	8	4	7	1	9	5	3
1	3	4	5	9	2	6	7	8

207

8	1	5	4	9	7	3	6	2
7	9	4	6	3	2	8	1	5
6	2	3	1	5	8	7	9	4
9	4	8	5	7	3	1	2	6
5	6	7	8	2	1	9	4	3
1	3	2	9	6	4	5	7	8
3	7	9	2	8	6	4	5	1
2	8	1	7	4	5	6	3	9
4	5	6	3	1	9	2	8	7

208

7	3	5	9	8	2	6	4	1
2	6	1	3	4	5	9	7	8
4	8	9	1	7	6	5	3	2
9	5	4	8	3	1	2	6	7
1	2	3	6	5	7	4	8	9
8	7	6	4	2	9	1	5	3
3	9	2	5	6	8	7	1	4
5	4	7	2	1	3	8	9	6
6	1	8	7	9	4	3	2	5

209

8	3	5	7	1	4	2	9	6
4	7	2	3	6	9	8	1	5
6	9	1	8	2	5	7	4	3
7	6	8	2	5	1	4	3	9
9	1	3	4	7	8	5	6	2
5	2	4	9	3	6	1	8	7
2	8	6	5	4	3	9	7	1
3	4	7	1	9	2	6	5	8
1	5	9	6	8	7	3	2	4

210

4	9	8	3	6	7	5	2	1
2	7	6	1	4	5	3	8	9
1	3	5	2	8	9	7	6	4
6	1	4	7	2	8	9	3	5
7	8	9	4	5	3	2	1	6
5	2	3	9	1	6	4	7	8
3	5	2	6	9	1	8	4	7
8	4	1	5	7	2	6	9	3
9	6	7	8	3	4	1	5	2

211

6	5	9	8	1	2	3	7	4
7	3	4	5	6	9	8	1	2
1	2	8	7	4	3	6	9	5
3	4	1	6	5	8	9	2	7
8	7	5	9	2	4	1	3	6
9	6	2	3	7	1	5	4	8
5	1	3	4	8	7	2	6	9
4	9	6	2	3	5	7	8	1
2	8	7	1	9	6	4	5	3

212

4	6	3	9	7	2	5	1	8
2	7	9	8	5	1	6	4	3
5	8	1	4	6	3	2	7	9
1	3	6	2	4	8	9	5	7
7	9	4	3	1	5	8	6	2
8	5	2	7	9	6	1	3	4
6	4	7	5	2	9	3	8	1
9	1	8	6	3	4	7	2	5
3	2	5	1	8	7	4	9	6

213

3	9	6	2	7	1	8	4	5
7	1	5	9	4	8	3	6	2
4	8	2	3	6	5	1	7	9
1	3	4	6	2	7	5	9	8
5	6	9	8	3	4	7	2	1
2	7	8	1	5	9	6	3	4
8	2	7	5	9	3	4	1	6
6	5	3	4	1	2	9	8	7
9	4	1	7	8	6	2	5	3

214

9	8	6	2	7	4	3	1	5
5	7	2	6	3	1	8	9	4
1	3	4	8	9	5	2	6	7
7	4	8	1	2	3	9	5	6
6	1	9	7	5	8	4	2	3
3	2	5	9	4	6	1	7	8
2	6	7	4	8	9	5	3	1
8	9	3	5	1	7	6	4	2
4	5	1	3	6	2	7	8	9

215

5	6	3	4	1	2	8	9	7
8	1	2	5	7	9	3	6	4
4	9	7	3	8	6	2	5	1
6	7	5	8	9	3	4	1	2
2	4	8	6	5	1	9	7	3
9	3	1	7	2	4	6	8	5
1	8	6	2	4	7	5	3	9
3	2	9	1	6	5	7	4	8
7	5	4	9	3	8	1	2	6

216

9	4	2	5	8	3	6	1	7
1	7	5	2	4	6	9	8	3
3	6	8	9	7	1	5	4	2
8	1	9	7	6	5	2	3	4
6	5	7	3	2	4	1	9	8
2	3	4	1	9	8	7	5	6
4	2	1	6	3	9	8	7	5
7	9	3	8	5	2	4	6	1
5	8	6	4	1	7	3	2	9

217

5	6	2	4	3	8	7	1	9
1	8	7	5	2	9	3	4	6
3	9	4	1	7	6	2	5	8
9	2	3	6	4	1	5	8	7
7	4	8	2	9	5	6	3	1
6	5	1	7	8	3	4	9	2
4	1	6	9	5	7	8	2	3
8	7	5	3	1	2	9	6	4
2	3	9	8	6	4	1	7	5

218

4	3	1	7	6	8	5	9	2
7	8	5	1	9	2	4	3	6
2	9	6	5	3	4	1	8	7
1	4	3	9	5	7	6	2	8
6	7	8	2	1	3	9	5	4
5	2	9	8	4	6	7	1	3
3	5	4	6	2	9	8	7	1
9	6	7	3	8	1	2	4	5
8	1	2	4	7	5	3	6	9

219

8	1	7	3	9	4	5	6	2
6	2	5	1	7	8	4	3	9
9	4	3	2	6	5	1	8	7
1	7	9	4	5	6	8	2	3
4	6	2	9	8	3	7	1	5
3	5	8	7	2	1	9	4	6
2	9	6	8	4	7	3	5	1
7	3	4	5	1	2	6	9	8
5	8	1	6	3	9	2	7	4

220

8	4	3	1	5	9	2	6	7
6	5	2	7	3	4	1	9	8
1	7	9	8	6	2	3	5	4
2	3	7	4	1	5	9	8	6
9	6	1	2	7	8	5	4	3
4	8	5	3	9	6	7	2	1
7	2	4	5	8	3	6	1	9
5	1	6	9	4	7	8	3	2
3	9	8	6	2	1	4	7	5

221

7	1	6	8	2	9	5	4	3
4	9	2	7	3	5	1	8	6
3	5	8	6	1	4	9	7	2
1	8	4	2	7	6	3	5	9
2	3	5	9	8	1	4	6	7
9	6	7	5	4	3	8	2	1
5	2	3	4	9	7	6	1	8
6	7	9	1	5	8	2	3	4
8	4	1	3	6	2	7	9	5

222

9	2	7	5	6	1	4	8	3
4	8	3	9	2	7	5	1	6
1	5	6	8	3	4	2	7	9
7	3	2	4	8	9	6	5	1
6	4	8	3	1	5	9	2	7
5	9	1	2	7	6	8	3	4
2	1	9	6	5	3	7	4	8
3	6	5	7	4	8	1	9	2
8	7	4	1	9	2	3	6	5

223

7	3	8	5	1	9	6	4	2
9	1	4	2	7	6	5	8	3
6	5	2	3	8	4	7	1	9
5	2	9	1	6	3	4	7	8
4	6	1	8	2	7	9	3	5
3	8	7	4	9	5	1	2	6
8	4	5	6	3	1	2	9	7
2	7	6	9	4	8	3	5	1
1	9	3	7	5	2	8	6	4

224

5	8	3	1	9	2	6	7	4
2	9	1	7	6	4	3	5	8
4	7	6	3	8	5	2	1	9
9	5	4	2	3	6	1	8	7
6	3	8	5	1	7	9	4	2
7	1	2	9	4	8	5	6	3
8	2	9	4	5	1	7	3	6
3	4	5	6	7	9	8	2	1
1	6	7	8	2	3	4	9	5

225

3	4	7	8	9	5	6	1	2
9	2	1	4	7	6	3	5	8
6	8	5	3	1	2	7	9	4
4	5	6	1	2	3	9	8	7
2	7	8	5	4	9	1	6	3
1	3	9	6	8	7	2	4	5
7	1	2	9	5	8	4	3	6
8	6	4	2	3	1	5	7	9
5	9	3	7	6	4	8	2	1

226

4	8	2	6	9	3	5	7	1
7	3	6	4	5	1	2	8	9
5	1	9	7	2	8	3	4	6
2	9	8	3	6	7	1	5	4
6	4	3	9	1	5	7	2	8
1	5	7	2	8	4	9	6	3
9	2	4	1	7	6	8	3	5
8	6	1	5	3	2	4	9	7
3	7	5	8	4	9	6	1	2

227

2	4	9	6	3	5	8	7	1
8	6	7	4	2	1	5	3	9
3	1	5	8	9	7	4	2	6
9	7	6	1	5	2	3	4	8
5	3	1	7	8	4	9	6	2
4	8	2	3	6	9	7	1	5
7	2	8	9	4	6	1	5	3
1	5	3	2	7	8	6	9	4
6	9	4	5	1	3	2	8	7

228

2	6	3	7	4	8	1	9	5
8	9	7	2	1	5	4	6	3
1	5	4	9	3	6	7	8	2
6	2	9	3	5	1	8	4	7
4	3	8	6	9	7	5	2	1
7	1	5	4	8	2	9	3	6
5	7	6	8	2	9	3	1	4
3	8	2	1	7	4	6	5	9
9	4	1	5	6	3	2	7	8

229

6	8	1	9	5	4	2	7	3
2	4	7	8	3	1	6	5	9
9	5	3	6	2	7	8	1	4
1	2	5	7	6	3	4	9	8
7	6	9	4	8	2	1	3	5
4	3	8	1	9	5	7	2	6
3	7	2	5	4	6	9	8	1
5	9	4	2	1	8	3	6	7
8	1	6	3	7	9	5	4	2

230

5	2	1	4	9	6	7	3	8
3	9	4	1	7	8	2	6	5
6	7	8	2	5	3	9	1	4
2	8	3	9	4	7	6	5	1
7	4	9	6	1	5	8	2	3
1	6	5	8	3	2	4	7	9
9	5	2	3	6	4	1	8	7
4	3	6	7	8	1	5	9	2
8	1	7	5	2	9	3	4	6

231

9	7	8	6	5	1	4	3	2
2	3	1	8	4	7	9	5	6
4	5	6	3	9	2	8	7	1
6	8	9	1	3	5	7	2	4
5	4	7	9	2	8	1	6	3
1	2	3	7	6	4	5	8	9
8	9	2	5	1	6	3	4	7
3	6	5	4	7	9	2	1	8
7	1	4	2	8	3	6	9	5

232

7	3	9	5	8	6	2	1	4
8	1	6	2	9	4	7	3	5
5	2	4	7	1	3	6	8	9
6	4	8	9	3	5	1	7	2
3	7	1	8	4	2	5	9	6
9	5	2	6	7	1	8	4	3
1	8	5	4	6	9	3	2	7
2	9	3	1	5	7	4	6	8
4	6	7	3	2	8	9	5	1

233

5	1	3	8	9	7	6	2	4
9	2	7	3	4	6	8	1	5
6	8	4	2	5	1	9	7	3
8	5	2	9	6	4	7	3	1
7	9	6	1	2	3	4	5	8
3	4	1	7	8	5	2	6	9
4	7	5	6	3	8	1	9	2
2	6	8	5	1	9	3	4	7
1	3	9	4	7	2	5	8	6

234

1	2	6	7	5	4	3	8	9
5	7	3	2	8	9	6	1	4
9	8	4	1	6	3	5	2	7
7	4	1	5	3	2	8	9	6
2	3	8	9	7	6	1	4	5
6	9	5	8	4	1	7	3	2
4	1	7	6	9	8	2	5	3
8	5	9	3	2	7	4	6	1
3	6	2	4	1	5	9	7	8

235

6	4	1	9	8	5	3	7	2
8	7	9	4	2	3	6	1	5
5	3	2	6	7	1	9	8	4
3	1	4	7	9	6	5	2	8
7	9	8	3	5	2	4	6	1
2	6	5	1	4	8	7	3	9
9	5	6	8	1	7	2	4	3
4	8	7	2	3	9	1	5	6
1	2	3	5	6	4	8	9	7

236

8	6	7	4	1	2	3	5	9
2	4	3	7	5	9	8	1	6
1	5	9	6	8	3	7	4	2
4	7	2	5	6	1	9	8	3
6	3	5	8	9	4	1	2	7
9	8	1	3	2	7	5	6	4
7	2	8	1	3	6	4	9	5
5	9	4	2	7	8	6	3	1
3	1	6	9	4	5	2	7	8

237

8	1	3	2	9	7	5	4	6
9	4	2	1	5	6	7	8	3
7	5	6	3	4	8	1	9	2
3	8	1	5	7	2	4	6	9
4	6	9	8	1	3	2	5	7
2	7	5	4	6	9	3	1	8
6	3	4	9	2	5	8	7	1
1	9	8	7	3	4	6	2	5
5	2	7	6	8	1	9	3	4

238

3	8	4	1	5	6	9	2	7
7	6	9	3	4	2	5	1	8
1	5	2	8	9	7	3	6	4
5	2	3	9	1	4	7	8	6
6	4	1	5	7	8	2	3	9
8	9	7	2	6	3	4	5	1
4	3	5	6	8	9	1	7	2
2	7	8	4	3	1	6	9	5
9	1	6	7	2	5	8	4	3

239

6	7	3	9	2	4	8	1	5
5	4	1	6	7	8	2	9	3
9	2	8	5	1	3	7	6	4
8	3	4	2	5	6	1	7	9
2	5	7	1	4	9	3	8	6
1	9	6	3	8	7	4	5	2
3	1	9	7	6	2	5	4	8
4	6	5	8	3	1	9	2	7
7	8	2	4	9	5	6	3	1

240

6	9	3	5	4	7	8	1	2
4	1	5	2	3	8	6	9	7
7	2	8	1	9	6	4	3	5
9	6	7	3	2	5	1	4	8
1	3	2	6	8	4	5	7	9
8	5	4	7	1	9	3	2	6
5	7	9	4	6	1	2	8	3
2	8	1	9	5	3	7	6	4
3	4	6	8	7	2	9	5	1

241

8	3	7	9	4	5	6	2	1
5	6	2	8	3	1	4	9	7
9	1	4	2	7	6	3	8	5
6	5	8	4	1	3	2	7	9
7	4	3	5	2	9	1	6	8
2	9	1	6	8	7	5	3	4
3	8	5	1	9	2	7	4	6
4	2	6	7	5	8	9	1	3
1	7	9	3	6	4	8	5	2

242

8	4	6	3	1	5	9	7	2
3	7	5	9	2	4	8	6	1
1	2	9	7	8	6	5	3	4
5	3	4	6	9	1	7	2	8
9	6	1	8	7	2	3	4	5
7	8	2	5	4	3	1	9	6
2	9	7	1	6	8	4	5	3
4	5	8	2	3	7	6	1	9
6	1	3	4	5	9	2	8	7

243

9	7	5	4	2	8	1	3	6
2	4	8	3	1	6	5	7	9
1	3	6	7	9	5	2	4	8
8	9	7	5	4	1	3	6	2
5	2	3	8	6	7	9	1	4
6	1	4	2	3	9	8	5	7
7	8	9	1	5	4	6	2	3
3	6	1	9	7	2	4	8	5
4	5	2	6	8	3	7	9	1

244

8	4	5	9	2	7	3	6	1
3	6	2	4	1	5	7	8	9
1	7	9	3	6	8	2	4	5
6	9	3	7	8	2	1	5	4
7	5	1	6	4	9	8	3	2
4	2	8	1	5	3	9	7	6
9	8	4	2	7	6	5	1	3
5	3	6	8	9	1	4	2	7
2	1	7	5	3	4	6	9	8

245

2	6	5	3	9	8	1	7	4
9	3	7	4	2	1	5	6	8
4	1	8	6	5	7	2	3	9
7	8	4	2	1	9	3	5	6
3	2	6	5	8	4	9	1	7
1	5	9	7	6	3	4	8	2
5	7	2	1	4	6	8	9	3
8	4	3	9	7	5	6	2	1
6	9	1	8	3	2	7	4	5

246

2	4	5	3	6	1	8	7	9
8	3	6	7	9	2	4	5	1
1	9	7	8	5	4	3	2	6
9	5	2	6	4	8	1	3	7
3	7	8	9	1	5	6	4	2
6	1	4	2	3	7	9	8	5
5	6	9	4	2	3	7	1	8
7	2	3	1	8	6	5	9	4
4	8	1	5	7	9	2	6	3

247

4	8	1	7	5	2	6	9	3
6	9	7	3	4	1	8	2	5
5	3	2	6	9	8	4	1	7
2	1	8	9	7	5	3	6	4
9	7	4	2	6	3	1	5	8
3	5	6	1	8	4	9	7	2
1	2	5	8	3	9	7	4	6
7	4	3	5	1	6	2	8	9
8	6	9	4	2	7	5	3	1

248

3	5	1	6	2	8	7	9	4
4	9	6	3	5	7	1	8	2
8	7	2	1	4	9	5	3	6
1	3	7	9	8	2	6	4	5
9	6	8	5	1	4	2	7	3
5	2	4	7	3	6	8	1	9
6	8	9	2	7	3	4	5	1
7	1	3	4	6	5	9	2	8
2	4	5	8	9	1	3	6	7

249

8	9	5	3	1	6	7	2	4
3	7	1	2	8	4	6	5	9
2	6	4	7	9	5	8	3	1
9	4	6	5	2	7	3	1	8
1	8	7	4	3	9	2	6	5
5	3	2	8	6	1	9	4	7
6	5	9	1	7	2	4	8	3
4	2	8	9	5	3	1	7	6
7	1	3	6	4	8	5	9	2

250

1	7	6	9	3	4	2	5	8
3	2	5	7	6	8	4	9	1
8	9	4	1	2	5	7	6	3
7	5	9	3	1	6	8	2	4
2	6	1	8	4	7	5	3	9
4	3	8	2	5	9	1	7	6
5	4	2	6	9	1	3	8	7
9	8	3	4	7	2	6	1	5
6	1	7	5	8	3	9	4	2

251

3	6	5	2	9	4	7	8	1
9	2	7	6	1	8	5	4	3
1	8	4	7	3	5	2	9	6
4	7	6	5	8	1	3	2	9
5	9	3	4	6	2	8	1	7
2	1	8	3	7	9	4	6	5
6	5	9	8	4	7	1	3	2
7	4	1	9	2	3	6	5	8
8	3	2	1	5	6	9	7	4

252

9	6	5	4	2	7	8	1	3
8	2	4	5	1	3	9	7	6
7	1	3	9	8	6	4	5	2
2	7	8	3	6	1	5	9	4
6	5	9	8	4	2	7	3	1
4	3	1	7	9	5	6	2	8
3	4	2	6	7	9	1	8	5
5	8	7	1	3	4	2	6	9
1	9	6	2	5	8	3	4	7

253

9	4	7	2	1	6	8	5	3
6	3	2	8	5	9	4	1	7
5	1	8	3	4	7	9	6	2
1	9	6	4	7	2	5	3	8
8	2	5	6	3	1	7	4	9
4	7	3	9	8	5	1	2	6
2	6	4	1	9	8	3	7	5
7	8	1	5	2	3	6	9	4
3	5	9	7	6	4	2	8	1

254

9	3	2	4	5	7	6	8	1
4	6	5	9	8	1	3	2	7
7	8	1	6	3	2	9	5	4
8	5	7	2	1	3	4	9	6
3	9	4	7	6	5	8	1	2
1	2	6	8	4	9	7	3	5
6	4	3	1	2	8	5	7	9
5	1	9	3	7	6	2	4	8
2	7	8	5	9	4	1	6	3

255

1	9	5	6	7	8	3	2	4
8	4	3	2	5	1	7	9	6
7	2	6	4	9	3	1	8	5
6	5	7	3	4	9	2	1	8
3	8	9	5	1	2	6	4	7
2	1	4	7	8	6	5	3	9
9	3	8	1	6	5	4	7	2
5	7	2	9	3	4	8	6	1
4	6	1	8	2	7	9	5	3

256

6	2	4	5	7	9	8	3	1
9	8	7	2	1	3	4	6	5
1	5	3	4	8	6	9	2	7
5	7	1	6	2	8	3	4	9
4	6	9	1	3	7	2	5	8
8	3	2	9	5	4	1	7	6
7	1	6	3	9	2	5	8	4
2	4	5	8	6	1	7	9	3
3	9	8	7	4	5	6	1	2

257

5	9	6	2	4	8	7	3	1
2	7	1	5	6	3	9	4	8
4	3	8	9	7	1	2	5	6
1	6	7	4	3	5	8	2	9
9	4	2	6	8	7	5	1	3
8	5	3	1	2	9	4	6	7
7	1	5	3	9	4	6	8	2
3	2	9	8	5	6	1	7	4
6	8	4	7	1	2	3	9	5

258

9	5	6	2	3	8	4	7	1
4	1	3	9	6	7	2	8	5
7	2	8	4	5	1	3	9	6
3	8	2	6	1	9	7	5	4
5	6	4	8	7	2	9	1	3
1	7	9	5	4	3	6	2	8
2	3	1	7	8	4	5	6	9
8	9	5	3	2	6	1	4	7
6	4	7	1	9	5	8	3	2

259

1	8	2	4	7	5	3	6	9
7	5	4	3	9	6	2	8	1
3	9	6	2	8	1	5	7	4
6	1	7	9	5	4	8	2	3
2	3	9	1	6	8	4	5	7
8	4	5	7	2	3	1	9	6
9	2	3	5	1	7	6	4	8
4	7	8	6	3	2	9	1	5
5	6	1	8	4	9	7	3	2

260

9	7	3	6	8	1	4	5	2
4	1	2	7	9	5	6	8	3
6	8	5	3	4	2	7	1	9
2	6	4	1	7	8	3	9	5
1	9	8	4	5	3	2	6	7
5	3	7	2	6	9	8	4	1
7	5	9	8	3	4	1	2	6
8	2	6	5	1	7	9	3	4
3	4	1	9	2	6	5	7	8

261

7	5	6	4	8	1	2	9	3
3	9	8	5	7	2	1	6	4
2	4	1	3	6	9	7	5	8
5	7	2	6	3	4	8	1	9
4	6	9	8	1	7	3	2	5
1	8	3	2	9	5	4	7	6
8	3	7	1	5	6	9	4	2
9	2	5	7	4	8	6	3	1
6	1	4	9	2	3	5	8	7

262

7	6	3	5	1	2	9	4	8
4	1	5	6	8	9	2	3	7
9	8	2	7	3	4	5	6	1
8	2	9	1	6	3	4	7	5
6	4	1	2	7	5	3	8	9
3	5	7	4	9	8	1	2	6
2	7	4	9	5	6	8	1	3
5	3	6	8	2	1	7	9	4
1	9	8	3	4	7	6	5	2

263

8	5	7	4	2	9	3	1	6
1	3	2	8	6	5	9	4	7
6	9	4	1	3	7	5	8	2
2	8	5	6	7	1	4	3	9
7	4	3	9	5	8	2	6	1
9	1	6	3	4	2	8	7	5
4	6	9	5	1	3	7	2	8
3	2	8	7	9	6	1	5	4
5	7	1	2	8	4	6	9	3

264

8	1	5	4	2	6	7	9	3
6	3	2	5	9	7	8	1	4
4	9	7	1	8	3	5	2	6
7	8	3	2	4	9	1	6	5
1	2	6	3	7	5	9	4	8
9	5	4	6	1	8	3	7	2
3	4	9	8	6	1	2	5	7
5	6	1	7	3	2	4	8	9
2	7	8	9	5	4	6	3	1

265

6	7	8	1	3	2	4	5	9
5	2	9	6	8	4	1	3	7
1	4	3	9	7	5	6	8	2
4	1	5	3	2	6	7	9	8
9	6	7	8	5	1	3	2	4
3	8	2	4	9	7	5	1	6
7	9	4	2	1	3	8	6	5
8	3	6	5	4	9	2	7	1
2	5	1	7	6	8	9	4	3

266

7	2	1	6	3	4	8	9	5
4	3	6	5	8	9	1	7	2
5	8	9	2	1	7	4	3	6
2	6	7	9	5	8	3	4	1
3	1	4	7	6	2	9	5	8
8	9	5	3	4	1	6	2	7
6	4	3	8	7	5	2	1	9
9	7	8	1	2	3	5	6	4
1	5	2	4	9	6	7	8	3

267

6	4	8	2	5	9	7	1	3
7	9	3	8	1	6	4	5	2
5	1	2	3	7	4	6	9	8
4	6	1	9	2	3	8	7	5
9	2	7	6	8	5	3	4	1
3	8	5	1	4	7	2	6	9
8	7	6	5	3	1	9	2	4
1	3	4	7	9	2	5	8	6
2	5	9	4	6	8	1	3	7

268

9	1	7	3	6	5	8	4	2
5	2	4	7	8	9	3	1	6
6	8	3	4	2	1	9	5	7
7	6	2	1	4	3	5	9	8
4	9	5	6	7	8	1	2	3
8	3	1	9	5	2	7	6	4
2	7	8	5	1	4	6	3	9
1	4	9	8	3	6	2	7	5
3	5	6	2	9	7	4	8	1

269

9	8	3	1	4	7	6	2	5
6	5	4	9	8	2	7	1	3
2	1	7	5	6	3	9	4	8
4	9	5	8	2	1	3	7	6
8	2	6	3	7	9	1	5	4
7	3	1	6	5	4	2	8	9
5	4	2	7	3	6	8	9	1
3	7	9	4	1	8	5	6	2
1	6	8	2	9	5	4	3	7

270

8	4	7	9	2	6	5	3	1
9	5	1	4	8	3	7	6	2
3	2	6	5	7	1	9	4	8
7	8	4	3	9	2	6	1	5
2	9	3	6	1	5	4	8	7
1	6	5	7	4	8	2	9	3
5	1	8	2	6	4	3	7	9
6	3	9	1	5	7	8	2	4
4	7	2	8	3	9	1	5	6

271

2	7	3	9	6	4	8	5	1
6	9	5	2	8	1	7	3	4
1	8	4	3	5	7	6	9	2
7	4	8	6	1	9	5	2	3
5	2	9	8	7	3	1	4	6
3	1	6	4	2	5	9	8	7
9	6	7	5	3	2	4	1	8
8	5	2	1	4	6	3	7	9
4	3	1	7	9	8	2	6	5

272

6	5	9	8	4	2	3	1	7
3	1	4	9	6	7	5	8	2
7	2	8	1	5	3	4	6	9
4	7	1	6	2	8	9	5	3
5	3	2	7	9	1	8	4	6
8	9	6	5	3	4	2	7	1
9	8	5	3	1	6	7	2	4
2	6	3	4	7	5	1	9	8
1	4	7	2	8	9	6	3	5

273

6	8	7	9	4	1	5	3	2
4	2	3	7	6	5	1	8	9
1	5	9	3	8	2	7	4	6
9	1	5	2	3	6	4	7	8
3	4	2	1	7	8	9	6	5
7	6	8	5	9	4	2	1	3
5	7	4	8	2	3	6	9	1
8	9	1	6	5	7	3	2	4
2	3	6	4	1	9	8	5	7

274

6	9	5	8	4	2	1	3	7
2	1	3	7	9	6	8	5	4
4	7	8	1	3	5	6	9	2
3	4	6	9	1	8	2	7	5
5	2	1	4	6	7	9	8	3
7	8	9	2	5	3	4	1	6
9	6	2	3	7	1	5	4	8
8	3	4	5	2	9	7	6	1
1	5	7	6	8	4	3	2	9

275

2	4	3	9	8	6	1	7	5
7	9	5	4	2	1	8	6	3
1	8	6	3	7	5	4	9	2
4	6	2	8	1	3	7	5	9
3	1	8	7	5	9	2	4	6
9	5	7	2	6	4	3	1	8
5	3	4	1	9	8	6	2	7
6	2	1	5	3	7	9	8	4
8	7	9	6	4	2	5	3	1

276

2	8	3	4	1	9	6	7	5
4	1	6	2	5	7	8	9	3
9	7	5	3	8	6	2	1	4
8	4	9	6	3	5	7	2	1
3	2	1	9	7	8	5	4	6
5	6	7	1	4	2	9	3	8
6	9	4	8	2	1	3	5	7
1	5	8	7	9	3	4	6	2
7	3	2	5	6	4	1	8	9

277

2	7	5	1	9	8	4	6	3
9	4	1	3	2	6	7	8	5
3	6	8	5	4	7	1	2	9
1	9	4	2	5	3	8	7	6
5	2	7	8	6	9	3	4	1
8	3	6	7	1	4	5	9	2
7	5	2	9	8	1	6	3	4
6	1	3	4	7	2	9	5	8
4	8	9	6	3	5	2	1	7

278

2	1	8	3	5	7	9	4	6
4	9	3	2	1	6	8	5	7
6	5	7	8	9	4	1	2	3
5	6	9	4	7	8	2	3	1
1	8	2	9	6	3	4	7	5
3	7	4	5	2	1	6	8	9
7	3	1	6	4	2	5	9	8
9	4	6	7	8	5	3	1	2
8	2	5	1	3	9	7	6	4

279

8	6	7	2	4	9	3	5	1
9	5	3	8	6	1	7	2	4
4	2	1	7	3	5	6	9	8
2	4	5	6	8	7	1	3	9
7	9	6	3	1	4	2	8	5
1	3	8	5	9	2	4	6	7
6	8	4	1	5	3	9	7	2
3	7	9	4	2	8	5	1	6
5	1	2	9	7	6	8	4	3

280

5	1	4	8	6	7	9	3	2
8	9	7	5	3	2	4	6	1
6	3	2	4	1	9	5	8	7
1	2	5	9	8	4	6	7	3
9	8	3	1	7	6	2	4	5
7	4	6	3	2	5	1	9	8
3	6	8	2	4	1	7	5	9
2	7	9	6	5	8	3	1	4
4	5	1	7	9	3	8	2	6

281

6	4	5	1	2	7	8	9	3
9	7	3	6	5	8	2	4	1
8	1	2	4	3	9	5	6	7
1	3	6	5	8	4	9	7	2
4	2	9	7	6	3	1	8	5
7	5	8	9	1	2	4	3	6
3	8	1	2	9	6	7	5	4
2	6	4	8	7	5	3	1	9
5	9	7	3	4	1	6	2	8

282

5	8	9	6	1	4	7	3	2
7	2	3	9	8	5	6	1	4
6	1	4	7	3	2	9	5	8
4	6	7	3	5	1	2	8	9
1	5	2	8	4	9	3	6	7
3	9	8	2	7	6	5	4	1
2	4	1	5	6	7	8	9	3
8	7	5	4	9	3	1	2	6
9	3	6	1	2	8	4	7	5

283

9	8	7	5	2	3	4	6	1
1	6	2	4	8	7	3	9	5
3	4	5	6	1	9	8	2	7
8	2	6	7	5	1	9	4	3
4	1	9	2	3	6	7	5	8
7	5	3	9	4	8	6	1	2
2	9	1	8	7	4	5	3	6
5	7	4	3	6	2	1	8	9
6	3	8	1	9	5	2	7	4

284

1	4	6	2	3	5	8	9	7
2	3	5	9	7	8	6	4	1
8	7	9	1	4	6	5	3	2
7	8	2	4	1	9	3	5	6
4	5	3	8	6	7	2	1	9
9	6	1	5	2	3	4	7	8
3	1	4	6	9	2	7	8	5
6	9	8	7	5	4	1	2	3
5	2	7	3	8	1	9	6	4

285

5	7	4	8	2	9	3	6	1
3	1	6	7	4	5	8	2	9
8	9	2	6	3	1	5	7	4
2	3	8	9	7	6	1	4	5
1	4	5	2	8	3	6	9	7
9	6	7	1	5	4	2	3	8
6	2	1	5	9	7	4	8	3
7	8	3	4	1	2	9	5	6
4	5	9	3	6	8	7	1	2

286

3	9	5	4	8	6	2	7	1
4	1	6	5	2	7	3	9	8
2	7	8	9	1	3	4	5	6
8	2	1	7	6	4	5	3	9
6	5	3	2	9	1	8	4	7
7	4	9	8	3	5	6	1	2
9	3	2	1	4	8	7	6	5
1	6	7	3	5	2	9	8	4
5	8	4	6	7	9	1	2	3

287

3	4	1	5	8	7	9	2	6
9	2	6	1	4	3	8	7	5
5	8	7	2	6	9	3	4	1
4	5	9	8	2	1	7	6	3
6	1	3	4	7	5	2	9	8
8	7	2	9	3	6	5	1	4
2	6	4	3	9	8	1	5	7
1	9	8	7	5	4	6	3	2
7	3	5	6	1	2	4	8	9

288

9	1	7	5	3	6	4	2	8
3	4	8	7	1	2	5	6	9
5	6	2	8	9	4	1	3	7
7	3	1	4	8	5	6	9	2
6	5	4	2	7	9	8	1	3
8	2	9	1	6	3	7	5	4
2	7	3	6	5	8	9	4	1
4	8	6	9	2	1	3	7	5
1	9	5	3	4	7	2	8	6

289

4	3	2	8	5	9	1	7	6
5	8	7	3	6	1	9	4	2
9	6	1	2	4	7	8	5	3
6	1	4	7	9	8	2	3	5
7	5	3	1	2	4	6	9	8
8	2	9	5	3	6	4	1	7
1	7	5	4	8	2	3	6	9
3	9	8	6	1	5	7	2	4
2	4	6	9	7	3	5	8	1

290

5	9	1	7	8	2	6	3	4
3	6	4	9	5	1	7	2	8
2	8	7	3	4	6	5	9	1
4	3	9	5	7	8	1	6	2
6	5	8	2	1	9	4	7	3
1	7	2	4	6	3	8	5	9
7	1	3	6	2	4	9	8	5
9	4	5	8	3	7	2	1	6
8	2	6	1	9	5	3	4	7

291

5	2	6	4	3	8	7	9	1
4	7	9	6	1	5	8	3	2
8	1	3	2	9	7	4	5	6
3	8	7	5	4	1	2	6	9
1	5	2	7	6	9	3	4	8
9	6	4	3	8	2	1	7	5
2	9	5	1	7	4	6	8	3
7	3	8	9	2	6	5	1	4
6	4	1	8	5	3	9	2	7

292

4	1	6	7	3	8	2	9	5
3	2	5	6	1	9	4	7	8
8	7	9	4	2	5	3	6	1
2	9	4	3	5	1	7	8	6
7	8	1	2	6	4	9	5	3
5	6	3	9	8	7	1	4	2
6	5	7	1	9	2	8	3	4
1	4	8	5	7	3	6	2	9
9	3	2	8	4	6	5	1	7

293

8	4	3	7	6	1	9	2	5
9	1	6	3	2	5	4	7	8
5	7	2	8	4	9	1	3	6
2	6	5	4	3	7	8	9	1
3	9	7	5	1	8	6	4	2
4	8	1	2	9	6	7	5	3
1	2	8	9	5	4	3	6	7
6	5	4	1	7	3	2	8	9
7	3	9	6	8	2	5	1	4

294

2	8	4	3	1	9	7	6	5
7	6	1	5	2	8	3	4	9
5	9	3	6	7	4	8	1	2
6	3	5	9	8	7	1	2	4
1	7	9	2	4	5	6	3	8
4	2	8	1	6	3	9	5	7
9	1	2	7	5	6	4	8	3
8	5	7	4	3	1	2	9	6
3	4	6	8	9	2	5	7	1

295

2	7	8	5	6	3	4	9	1
9	6	4	1	8	7	3	5	2
1	5	3	4	9	2	6	7	8
3	4	9	2	1	6	5	8	7
7	8	1	3	4	5	9	2	6
5	2	6	9	7	8	1	3	4
4	1	5	8	2	9	7	6	3
6	9	2	7	3	1	8	4	5
8	3	7	6	5	4	2	1	9

296

9	8	7	3	4	5	1	6	2
4	3	1	8	6	2	9	7	5
5	2	6	7	1	9	4	8	3
7	1	5	4	3	8	6	2	9
8	9	3	2	7	6	5	4	1
6	4	2	9	5	1	8	3	7
1	6	8	5	2	3	7	9	4
3	5	4	6	9	7	2	1	8
2	7	9	1	8	4	3	5	6

297

8	7	3	9	6	4	2	1	5
5	6	2	3	1	7	9	4	8
1	4	9	8	2	5	7	6	3
3	1	4	5	7	2	8	9	6
9	2	8	6	4	3	5	7	1
6	5	7	1	9	8	3	2	4
2	9	5	4	3	1	6	8	7
7	3	1	2	8	6	4	5	9
4	8	6	7	5	9	1	3	2

298

4	7	5	3	1	9	8	6	2
3	2	6	4	5	8	1	7	9
1	9	8	7	6	2	4	5	3
5	1	4	9	8	7	2	3	6
9	6	7	1	2	3	5	4	8
2	8	3	6	4	5	9	1	7
8	4	1	2	7	6	3	9	5
6	5	9	8	3	1	7	2	4
7	3	2	5	9	4	6	8	1

299

2	8	5	3	7	6	9	1	4
9	6	3	5	1	4	8	2	7
1	7	4	9	8	2	3	6	5
3	9	6	4	2	5	7	8	1
7	5	1	6	9	8	4	3	2
8	4	2	1	3	7	5	9	6
6	1	9	7	5	3	2	4	8
5	3	8	2	4	1	6	7	9
4	2	7	8	6	9	1	5	3

300

9	2	3	7	4	5	1	8	6
4	1	8	9	2	6	5	7	3
5	7	6	1	8	3	4	9	2
6	8	5	2	7	4	9	3	1
2	3	4	5	9	1	7	6	8
1	9	7	6	3	8	2	5	4
8	4	9	3	5	2	6	1	7
3	5	1	4	6	7	8	2	9
7	6	2	8	1	9	3	4	5

301

8	9	1	5	3	7	4	2	6
6	5	4	1	8	2	9	3	7
2	3	7	4	9	6	5	8	1
9	2	3	8	5	1	7	6	4
7	4	6	3	2	9	1	5	8
5	1	8	6	7	4	2	9	3
1	7	5	9	6	8	3	4	2
3	6	2	7	4	5	8	1	9
4	8	9	2	1	3	6	7	5

302

2	7	8	9	3	1	4	6	5
9	1	5	2	6	4	3	7	8
6	3	4	8	7	5	2	9	1
3	5	6	1	4	2	9	8	7
7	8	1	3	5	9	6	2	4
4	2	9	6	8	7	5	1	3
8	6	2	4	1	3	7	5	9
5	9	3	7	2	8	1	4	6
1	4	7	5	9	6	8	3	2

303

2	3	9	4	1	6	8	5	7
4	7	8	9	3	5	1	6	2
1	5	6	2	7	8	9	3	4
3	4	1	8	5	7	6	2	9
8	9	5	3	6	2	7	4	1
6	2	7	1	9	4	5	8	3
7	6	3	5	2	1	4	9	8
9	1	4	6	8	3	2	7	5
5	8	2	7	4	9	3	1	6

304

3	1	8	4	6	5	9	2	7
9	6	4	3	2	7	1	5	8
5	2	7	9	8	1	6	4	3
7	5	6	2	4	3	8	1	9
4	9	2	8	1	6	7	3	5
8	3	1	7	5	9	2	6	4
6	4	5	1	9	8	3	7	2
1	8	3	5	7	2	4	9	6
2	7	9	6	3	4	5	8	1

305

8	9	2	6	1	7	4	3	5
6	4	1	5	8	3	7	9	2
3	5	7	4	9	2	6	8	1
7	6	9	2	3	8	1	5	4
2	8	5	9	4	1	3	6	7
4	1	3	7	5	6	8	2	9
1	7	8	3	2	5	9	4	6
9	2	6	8	7	4	5	1	3
5	3	4	1	6	9	2	7	8

306

9	3	5	2	4	1	8	6	7
4	6	1	7	8	3	2	9	5
7	2	8	5	6	9	3	4	1
1	9	2	3	7	4	6	5	8
5	7	6	8	1	2	4	3	9
3	8	4	6	9	5	1	7	2
8	4	7	1	5	6	9	2	3
2	5	9	4	3	8	7	1	6
6	1	3	9	2	7	5	8	4

307

5	2	4	9	6	7	3	1	8
9	1	3	8	5	4	7	2	6
6	8	7	3	1	2	4	5	9
8	7	5	2	9	3	1	6	4
2	6	9	1	4	8	5	3	7
4	3	1	6	7	5	9	8	2
1	5	6	7	8	9	2	4	3
7	4	2	5	3	6	8	9	1
3	9	8	4	2	1	6	7	5

308

3	7	8	2	4	9	6	5	1
6	9	2	8	5	1	4	7	3
5	1	4	3	7	6	9	2	8
9	5	6	1	8	2	7	3	4
1	8	3	7	9	4	2	6	5
4	2	7	5	6	3	1	8	9
2	4	1	6	3	8	5	9	7
7	3	9	4	2	5	8	1	6
8	6	5	9	1	7	3	4	2

309

7	3	9	8	2	4	1	5	6
8	5	2	9	6	1	3	7	4
6	4	1	7	5	3	9	8	2
4	8	3	1	9	7	2	6	5
2	7	5	3	4	6	8	9	1
1	9	6	5	8	2	7	4	3
5	1	8	6	3	9	4	2	7
9	2	7	4	1	5	6	3	8
3	6	4	2	7	8	5	1	9

310

7	2	4	1	6	5	8	3	9
6	5	3	2	8	9	7	1	4
1	9	8	3	4	7	2	5	6
9	6	1	5	7	2	3	4	8
3	4	7	6	9	8	1	2	5
2	8	5	4	1	3	6	9	7
4	3	9	8	2	6	5	7	1
8	1	2	7	5	4	9	6	3
5	7	6	9	3	1	4	8	2

311

5	6	2	8	3	9	7	4	1
9	1	7	6	4	5	2	8	3
4	8	3	2	7	1	5	9	6
2	3	8	4	6	7	1	5	9
7	5	9	1	2	8	3	6	4
6	4	1	5	9	3	8	2	7
3	7	6	9	8	2	4	1	5
8	9	5	7	1	4	6	3	2
1	2	4	3	5	6	9	7	8

312

7	1	6	2	4	5	8	9	3
8	4	9	3	6	1	2	5	7
2	5	3	9	7	8	4	1	6
5	3	2	4	9	7	1	6	8
6	7	1	8	3	2	5	4	9
4	9	8	1	5	6	7	3	2
3	8	5	7	1	9	6	2	4
9	6	7	5	2	4	3	8	1
1	2	4	6	8	3	9	7	5

313

3	2	4	6	7	9	5	1	8
8	9	6	1	4	5	7	3	2
5	1	7	8	3	2	4	6	9
1	3	2	7	9	4	8	5	6
6	4	8	5	1	3	2	9	7
7	5	9	2	6	8	1	4	3
2	8	3	4	5	6	9	7	1
9	7	5	3	2	1	6	8	4
4	6	1	9	8	7	3	2	5

314

5	9	3	8	6	1	4	7	2
8	7	6	4	5	2	3	1	9
4	2	1	3	9	7	6	8	5
6	3	9	7	8	4	2	5	1
7	4	8	2	1	5	9	6	3
2	1	5	9	3	6	8	4	7
3	6	2	1	7	8	5	9	4
1	5	4	6	2	9	7	3	8
9	8	7	5	4	3	1	2	6

315

8	5	7	4	6	9	3	1	2
3	4	1	2	5	8	9	7	6
2	6	9	7	3	1	5	4	8
1	7	3	9	4	2	6	8	5
6	9	4	3	8	5	1	2	7
5	2	8	1	7	6	4	3	9
7	3	6	5	2	4	8	9	1
4	1	5	8	9	7	2	6	3
9	8	2	6	1	3	7	5	4

316

5	3	8	6	1	9	4	7	2
2	4	6	5	8	7	1	9	3
9	1	7	2	4	3	6	8	5
3	7	4	9	2	1	5	6	8
1	8	2	4	6	5	9	3	7
6	9	5	3	7	8	2	1	4
8	2	1	7	9	4	3	5	6
7	6	3	1	5	2	8	4	9
4	5	9	8	3	6	7	2	1

317

4	6	8	3	2	5	7	9	1
7	5	2	1	8	9	4	6	3
9	3	1	4	6	7	2	8	5
8	2	3	7	4	1	9	5	6
1	9	6	5	3	2	8	4	7
5	4	7	8	9	6	1	3	2
3	7	9	6	1	4	5	2	8
6	1	4	2	5	8	3	7	9
2	8	5	9	7	3	6	1	4

318

5	4	1	8	7	2	9	3	6
2	6	8	9	5	3	7	1	4
9	7	3	4	1	6	5	8	2
6	9	5	3	8	4	2	7	1
4	3	2	1	9	7	6	5	8
1	8	7	2	6	5	3	4	9
3	5	4	6	2	1	8	9	7
8	1	6	7	3	9	4	2	5
7	2	9	5	4	8	1	6	3

319

2	3	8	9	7	6	1	4	5
7	4	5	8	1	3	6	9	2
9	6	1	5	4	2	3	7	8
3	8	7	1	5	9	4	2	6
5	1	6	4	2	7	8	3	9
4	2	9	3	6	8	7	5	1
8	7	2	6	3	5	9	1	4
1	9	3	2	8	4	5	6	7
6	5	4	7	9	1	2	8	3

320

2	3	4	1	8	5	9	6	7
9	1	8	6	4	7	5	2	3
7	5	6	2	9	3	1	4	8
6	7	1	8	5	4	2	3	9
4	9	5	7	3	2	8	1	6
8	2	3	9	6	1	4	7	5
5	8	7	4	1	6	3	9	2
3	4	2	5	7	9	6	8	1
1	6	9	3	2	8	7	5	4

321

9	6	1	2	3	5	8	4	7
3	2	7	6	8	4	5	9	1
5	8	4	1	9	7	6	3	2
1	9	5	3	6	8	2	7	4
4	3	8	7	1	2	9	5	6
6	7	2	4	5	9	1	8	3
8	1	3	5	7	6	4	2	9
2	5	6	9	4	3	7	1	8
7	4	9	8	2	1	3	6	5

322

7	9	2	1	6	3	8	5	4
5	6	3	4	7	8	9	2	1
1	4	8	5	2	9	6	7	3
3	5	9	7	4	2	1	6	8
6	2	1	3	8	5	7	4	9
8	7	4	9	1	6	5	3	2
9	1	7	6	3	4	2	8	5
2	3	5	8	9	7	4	1	6
4	8	6	2	5	1	3	9	7

323

3	8	2	7	9	6	5	4	1
7	5	6	3	4	1	8	9	2
9	4	1	2	8	5	3	6	7
4	1	3	5	6	2	7	8	9
5	6	8	1	7	9	4	2	3
2	7	9	8	3	4	1	5	6
8	2	7	6	5	3	9	1	4
1	9	5	4	2	7	6	3	8
6	3	4	9	1	8	2	7	5

324

1	2	6	5	3	9	7	8	4
3	7	9	6	8	4	1	2	5
5	8	4	7	1	2	9	6	3
6	3	5	8	2	1	4	7	9
8	9	2	4	7	5	6	3	1
7	4	1	9	6	3	2	5	8
2	5	8	1	9	6	3	4	7
4	1	3	2	5	7	8	9	6
9	6	7	3	4	8	5	1	2

325

7	2	8	5	6	9	1	4	3
6	3	9	1	7	4	5	8	2
1	4	5	3	8	2	6	9	7
2	8	7	6	4	1	3	5	9
4	1	3	7	9	5	8	2	6
9	5	6	8	2	3	7	1	4
3	9	1	4	5	6	2	7	8
5	7	4	2	3	8	9	6	1
8	6	2	9	1	7	4	3	5

326

5	8	4	2	9	6	3	7	1
1	6	7	8	5	3	9	2	4
3	9	2	7	4	1	5	8	6
6	5	1	4	3	2	8	9	7
9	7	3	5	1	8	4	6	2
2	4	8	6	7	9	1	5	3
7	1	6	9	8	4	2	3	5
8	3	5	1	2	7	6	4	9
4	2	9	3	6	5	7	1	8

327

1	4	9	7	2	8	3	5	6
7	8	2	3	5	6	9	1	4
5	3	6	4	9	1	2	7	8
8	6	7	2	3	9	5	4	1
4	5	3	1	8	7	6	9	2
9	2	1	5	6	4	8	3	7
3	1	8	6	4	5	7	2	9
2	9	4	8	7	3	1	6	5
6	7	5	9	1	2	4	8	3

328

8	5	7	6	3	9	4	2	1
6	4	2	7	5	1	8	9	3
3	1	9	8	4	2	6	7	5
1	2	5	4	9	8	3	6	7
9	3	6	5	1	7	2	4	8
7	8	4	3	2	6	5	1	9
4	6	3	9	7	5	1	8	2
2	7	8	1	6	3	9	5	4
5	9	1	2	8	4	7	3	6

329

3	9	7	5	2	8	6	4	1
2	5	8	4	6	1	9	7	3
6	1	4	7	3	9	5	2	8
4	6	1	9	8	2	7	3	5
7	8	9	3	5	6	2	1	4
5	3	2	1	4	7	8	6	9
9	4	3	2	7	5	1	8	6
8	7	5	6	1	3	4	9	2
1	2	6	8	9	4	3	5	7

330

3	9	7	8	5	6	4	2	1
6	4	8	1	7	2	3	9	5
5	2	1	4	3	9	6	7	8
1	3	9	2	6	5	8	4	7
7	8	2	9	4	3	5	1	6
4	6	5	7	1	8	9	3	2
2	7	3	5	8	4	1	6	9
9	5	4	6	2	1	7	8	3
8	1	6	3	9	7	2	5	4

331

5	7	4	1	3	2	6	8	9
6	8	2	9	4	5	1	7	3
1	3	9	6	7	8	2	4	5
4	9	3	7	2	1	8	5	6
8	1	7	5	9	6	4	3	2
2	5	6	3	8	4	7	9	1
9	6	1	8	5	7	3	2	4
7	4	5	2	1	3	9	6	8
3	2	8	4	6	9	5	1	7

332

5	9	8	4	3	2	6	7	1
4	3	6	8	1	7	2	9	5
2	1	7	5	6	9	3	8	4
7	4	3	1	8	5	9	2	6
9	8	5	6	2	4	1	3	7
6	2	1	9	7	3	5	4	8
3	7	4	2	5	1	8	6	9
8	5	9	3	4	6	7	1	2
1	6	2	7	9	8	4	5	3

333

2	6	7	1	5	3	4	9	8
8	4	9	7	2	6	5	3	1
1	5	3	8	4	9	7	2	6
3	9	6	5	1	4	2	8	7
7	2	4	9	6	8	1	5	3
5	1	8	2	3	7	9	6	4
9	8	5	6	7	1	3	4	2
4	7	2	3	8	5	6	1	9
6	3	1	4	9	2	8	7	5

334

1	6	9	4	5	8	7	2	3
8	7	5	9	2	3	6	1	4
3	2	4	7	6	1	5	9	8
4	3	6	5	9	2	1	8	7
9	8	1	6	3	7	4	5	2
2	5	7	1	8	4	9	3	6
7	1	3	2	4	9	8	6	5
5	9	8	3	7	6	2	4	1
6	4	2	8	1	5	3	7	9

335

3	7	5	9	8	2	6	4	1
1	2	8	5	6	4	7	9	3
6	4	9	1	7	3	8	5	2
8	9	6	7	5	1	2	3	4
7	1	4	3	2	9	5	8	6
5	3	2	8	4	6	1	7	9
2	8	3	6	9	5	4	1	7
4	5	1	2	3	7	9	6	8
9	6	7	4	1	8	3	2	5

336

2	6	3	1	4	5	8	7	9
7	1	4	2	9	8	5	3	6
5	8	9	6	7	3	4	1	2
3	5	8	9	2	4	7	6	1
6	2	7	5	8	1	3	9	4
9	4	1	3	6	7	2	8	5
4	3	6	8	1	2	9	5	7
8	9	2	7	5	6	1	4	3
1	7	5	4	3	9	6	2	8

337

2	3	5	7	4	6	8	1	9
1	9	7	8	3	2	5	4	6
8	4	6	9	5	1	7	2	3
6	1	3	4	8	9	2	7	5
9	2	8	5	1	7	3	6	4
5	7	4	6	2	3	1	9	8
4	5	2	1	9	8	6	3	7
3	6	9	2	7	5	4	8	1
7	8	1	3	6	4	9	5	2

338

2	1	5	9	7	8	4	3	6
7	6	8	5	3	4	2	1	9
4	3	9	2	6	1	7	5	8
9	4	2	8	1	5	6	7	3
6	5	3	7	2	9	1	8	4
8	7	1	6	4	3	5	9	2
3	8	6	1	5	2	9	4	7
1	9	7	4	8	6	3	2	5
5	2	4	3	9	7	8	6	1

339

3	7	8	5	1	9	2	4	6
2	5	9	6	3	4	1	7	8
6	1	4	7	8	2	9	3	5
5	8	2	1	9	3	4	6	7
9	6	3	2	4	7	5	8	1
1	4	7	8	6	5	3	9	2
8	3	1	4	2	6	7	5	9
7	9	6	3	5	1	8	2	4
4	2	5	9	7	8	6	1	3

340

8	5	4	7	9	6	1	3	2
3	6	9	8	2	1	7	4	5
2	7	1	5	3	4	9	8	6
7	4	6	9	5	3	2	1	8
1	2	3	4	8	7	6	5	9
9	8	5	6	1	2	3	7	4
4	3	8	2	7	9	5	6	1
5	1	2	3	6	8	4	9	7
6	9	7	1	4	5	8	2	3

341

3	8	2	9	4	1	7	5	6
5	7	4	3	6	2	8	1	9
6	1	9	7	8	5	2	3	4
7	4	8	5	9	3	6	2	1
9	6	1	4	2	7	3	8	5
2	5	3	6	1	8	9	4	7
8	2	5	1	7	6	4	9	3
1	9	6	2	3	4	5	7	8
4	3	7	8	5	9	1	6	2

342

5	1	6	2	8	4	7	3	9
4	9	3	1	5	7	8	2	6
2	8	7	9	6	3	4	1	5
3	6	2	7	9	8	5	4	1
1	4	9	5	3	2	6	8	7
8	7	5	4	1	6	3	9	2
9	2	8	3	7	5	1	6	4
7	3	4	6	2	1	9	5	8
6	5	1	8	4	9	2	7	3

343

6	4	5	8	3	9	7	1	2
2	1	8	6	4	7	5	3	9
7	3	9	1	5	2	6	8	4
3	2	6	9	7	4	1	5	8
8	7	1	5	2	6	4	9	3
9	5	4	3	8	1	2	7	6
4	8	3	7	6	5	9	2	1
5	9	2	4	1	3	8	6	7
1	6	7	2	9	8	3	4	5

344

8	1	5	3	2	7	9	4	6
7	4	2	8	6	9	5	1	3
3	9	6	1	4	5	8	2	7
5	8	9	6	3	2	1	7	4
1	3	4	9	7	8	2	6	5
6	2	7	5	1	4	3	8	9
2	6	8	4	5	3	7	9	1
4	7	3	2	9	1	6	5	8
9	5	1	7	8	6	4	3	2

345

1	4	8	3	9	2	5	6	7
9	7	6	1	5	8	2	3	4
2	5	3	4	7	6	8	1	9
7	6	1	9	4	5	3	8	2
8	9	5	7	2	3	1	4	6
4	3	2	6	8	1	9	7	5
6	8	7	5	1	9	4	2	3
3	2	9	8	6	4	7	5	1
5	1	4	2	3	7	6	9	8

346

8	3	2	9	4	7	6	1	5
5	1	6	8	3	2	4	9	7
7	4	9	6	5	1	2	3	8
2	5	4	3	8	6	1	7	9
1	8	7	4	2	9	3	5	6
9	6	3	7	1	5	8	4	2
3	7	8	2	9	4	5	6	1
6	2	5	1	7	3	9	8	4
4	9	1	5	6	8	7	2	3

347

7	5	8	6	9	4	1	2	3
2	9	3	8	1	7	4	5	6
1	6	4	3	5	2	9	8	7
5	1	2	9	6	3	7	4	8
6	8	7	2	4	1	5	3	9
4	3	9	5	7	8	6	1	2
3	4	5	7	8	6	2	9	1
9	2	6	1	3	5	8	7	4
8	7	1	4	2	9	3	6	5

348

6	8	1	3	5	9	4	2	7
2	3	4	8	6	7	9	5	1
9	7	5	4	1	2	3	6	8
3	6	2	9	8	1	7	4	5
4	1	8	5	7	3	6	9	2
5	9	7	6	2	4	1	8	3
8	2	9	1	3	6	5	7	4
7	4	3	2	9	5	8	1	6
1	5	6	7	4	8	2	3	9

349

4	1	9	5	3	8	2	6	7
6	7	8	9	2	4	3	1	5
2	3	5	1	7	6	9	4	8
8	4	1	2	9	3	5	7	6
5	6	3	8	1	7	4	2	9
9	2	7	6	4	5	1	8	3
3	5	6	4	8	1	7	9	2
1	8	2	7	5	9	6	3	4
7	9	4	3	6	2	8	5	1

350

3	2	5	4	8	9	1	6	7
7	4	6	5	3	1	9	8	2
9	8	1	2	7	6	5	3	4
5	7	8	1	6	4	2	9	3
4	6	2	9	5	3	8	7	1
1	9	3	8	2	7	4	5	6
8	3	4	7	9	2	6	1	5
2	5	7	6	1	8	3	4	9
6	1	9	3	4	5	7	2	8

351

1	9	4	7	3	5	2	6	8
7	5	3	6	8	2	9	1	4
2	8	6	4	1	9	5	7	3
5	2	7	9	6	3	4	8	1
3	6	1	5	4	8	7	2	9
9	4	8	1	2	7	3	5	6
8	7	9	3	5	1	6	4	2
4	1	5	2	9	6	8	3	7
6	3	2	8	7	4	1	9	5

352

7	2	9	5	4	8	3	6	1
4	1	8	2	3	6	9	7	5
6	5	3	7	1	9	2	8	4
8	4	7	1	6	2	5	3	9
1	9	5	8	7	3	4	2	6
2	3	6	9	5	4	7	1	8
5	7	2	4	8	1	6	9	3
9	6	1	3	2	5	8	4	7
3	8	4	6	9	7	1	5	2

353

6	7	9	4	8	1	5	3	2
8	5	3	9	2	6	4	7	1
2	4	1	5	3	7	6	8	9
7	9	8	1	4	2	3	6	5
4	6	5	7	9	3	1	2	8
3	1	2	8	6	5	7	9	4
1	2	6	3	5	8	9	4	7
9	3	7	2	1	4	8	5	6
5	8	4	6	7	9	2	1	3

354

8	3	6	1	7	5	2	4	9
5	9	4	8	6	2	3	1	7
1	2	7	9	3	4	8	6	5
2	1	8	3	5	7	4	9	6
4	6	9	2	8	1	7	5	3
7	5	3	4	9	6	1	2	8
6	4	5	7	1	8	9	3	2
9	8	2	6	4	3	5	7	1
3	7	1	5	2	9	6	8	4

355

1	5	8	3	9	6	2	4	7
4	9	2	1	7	5	3	6	8
7	6	3	8	2	4	5	9	1
9	4	5	7	6	2	1	8	3
6	2	1	5	8	3	4	7	9
3	8	7	4	1	9	6	5	2
5	7	4	9	3	1	8	2	6
8	1	6	2	5	7	9	3	4
2	3	9	6	4	8	7	1	5

356

4	3	9	8	2	6	5	1	7
1	5	7	3	4	9	8	6	2
2	6	8	1	5	7	4	3	9
7	4	1	5	6	2	9	8	3
9	2	5	4	8	3	6	7	1
6	8	3	7	9	1	2	5	4
5	1	2	6	3	4	7	9	8
3	9	6	2	7	8	1	4	5
8	7	4	9	1	5	3	2	6

357

8	1	5	2	3	6	4	9	7
4	7	3	8	9	1	6	5	2
2	9	6	5	7	4	3	8	1
3	8	7	1	6	9	2	4	5
9	2	4	3	8	5	1	7	6
5	6	1	4	2	7	9	3	8
1	4	8	9	5	2	7	6	3
6	3	2	7	4	8	5	1	9
7	5	9	6	1	3	8	2	4

358

1	7	4	8	6	9	2	5	3
5	2	3	1	7	4	6	9	8
8	9	6	2	3	5	4	1	7
7	8	2	6	4	1	5	3	9
4	5	1	7	9	3	8	2	6
3	6	9	5	2	8	7	4	1
2	1	5	3	8	6	9	7	4
9	3	8	4	5	7	1	6	2
6	4	7	9	1	2	3	8	5

359

9	8	7	2	1	3	4	6	5
6	3	1	4	8	5	9	7	2
2	5	4	7	6	9	8	3	1
7	1	3	8	9	4	5	2	6
8	4	2	3	5	6	1	9	7
5	9	6	1	7	2	3	8	4
1	6	9	5	3	7	2	4	8
4	7	5	9	2	8	6	1	3
3	2	8	6	4	1	7	5	9

360

9	7	8	1	4	6	5	3	2
4	3	2	7	8	5	6	1	9
5	6	1	3	2	9	7	8	4
1	2	4	5	6	8	9	7	3
7	8	5	4	9	3	2	6	1
3	9	6	2	1	7	4	5	8
2	5	7	9	3	1	8	4	6
6	4	3	8	5	2	1	9	7
8	1	9	6	7	4	3	2	5

361

5	2	4	1	6	8	3	9	7
1	7	6	4	3	9	5	2	8
9	3	8	5	2	7	6	1	4
7	6	1	8	5	2	4	3	9
4	5	3	6	9	1	7	8	2
2	8	9	7	4	3	1	5	6
3	4	7	2	8	5	9	6	1
6	9	2	3	1	4	8	7	5
8	1	5	9	7	6	2	4	3

362

3	9	1	2	5	6	8	4	7
4	5	7	3	1	8	9	6	2
6	2	8	9	7	4	1	3	5
8	6	9	7	4	2	3	5	1
7	4	5	1	9	3	6	2	8
2	1	3	6	8	5	7	9	4
1	7	4	5	6	9	2	8	3
5	3	6	8	2	1	4	7	9
9	8	2	4	3	7	5	1	6

363

8	7	4	1	3	2	5	9	6
6	1	5	4	7	9	2	3	8
2	9	3	6	8	5	1	7	4
7	4	1	2	5	3	6	8	9
3	5	2	8	9	6	7	4	1
9	8	6	7	1	4	3	2	5
4	2	7	9	6	1	8	5	3
5	6	9	3	2	8	4	1	7
1	3	8	5	4	7	9	6	2

364

2	8	4	5	1	9	6	7	3
7	3	6	8	4	2	9	5	1
5	1	9	6	3	7	2	8	4
9	6	3	7	5	1	4	2	8
4	5	7	2	8	6	3	1	9
8	2	1	4	9	3	5	6	7
1	7	5	9	2	4	8	3	6
6	9	8	3	7	5	1	4	2
3	4	2	1	6	8	7	9	5

365

1	8	9	2	5	7	3	4	6
5	4	2	3	8	6	7	9	1
7	6	3	4	9	1	8	2	5
8	1	5	7	3	9	2	6	4
9	7	4	6	1	2	5	8	3
2	3	6	8	4	5	9	1	7
3	2	1	5	6	8	4	7	9
4	9	8	1	7	3	6	5	2
6	5	7	9	2	4	1	3	8

366

7	1	8	4	2	3	6	5	9
5	9	3	1	6	7	8	4	2
2	6	4	8	5	9	1	3	7
1	7	6	3	9	2	4	8	5
8	4	5	7	1	6	9	2	3
9	3	2	5	8	4	7	1	6
3	5	7	9	4	1	2	6	8
4	2	9	6	3	8	5	7	1
6	8	1	2	7	5	3	9	4

367

7	5	8	4	2	6	3	1	9
3	4	6	9	5	1	8	2	7
1	2	9	7	8	3	4	5	6
6	9	5	3	1	2	7	4	8
2	7	1	8	9	4	5	6	3
8	3	4	6	7	5	1	9	2
4	6	2	1	3	8	9	7	5
5	8	7	2	4	9	6	3	1
9	1	3	5	6	7	2	8	4

368

6	7	9	1	5	8	3	2	4
8	4	5	2	6	3	9	7	1
3	2	1	7	9	4	5	6	8
5	8	2	3	1	7	6	4	9
7	9	3	8	4	6	1	5	2
4	1	6	5	2	9	8	3	7
2	5	7	6	8	1	4	9	3
1	3	4	9	7	5	2	8	6
9	6	8	4	3	2	7	1	5

369

8	9	5	7	2	4	1	3	6
2	4	7	3	1	6	9	8	5
6	3	1	5	9	8	2	4	7
9	2	4	6	5	7	3	1	8
7	6	3	1	8	2	5	9	4
1	5	8	9	4	3	7	6	2
5	1	2	4	6	9	8	7	3
3	8	6	2	7	1	4	5	9
4	7	9	8	3	5	6	2	1

370

8	4	1	7	5	6	9	3	2
7	9	5	3	1	2	6	4	8
3	2	6	4	9	8	5	7	1
4	3	9	8	7	1	2	6	5
6	8	2	5	4	3	1	9	7
1	5	7	2	6	9	3	8	4
5	6	3	1	8	4	7	2	9
2	1	8	9	3	7	4	5	6
9	7	4	6	2	5	8	1	3

371

6	2	5	8	3	9	4	1	7
1	9	7	4	6	2	8	5	3
4	8	3	7	1	5	9	2	6
5	4	9	1	2	6	3	7	8
7	1	8	5	4	3	6	9	2
3	6	2	9	7	8	5	4	1
9	3	6	2	5	1	7	8	4
2	5	4	6	8	7	1	3	9
8	7	1	3	9	4	2	6	5

372

8	6	7	2	9	4	5	3	1
5	2	3	8	6	1	9	4	7
4	1	9	7	5	3	6	8	2
9	5	6	1	8	7	3	2	4
2	4	1	5	3	6	7	9	8
7	3	8	9	4	2	1	5	6
1	7	4	3	2	5	8	6	9
3	8	2	6	7	9	4	1	5
6	9	5	4	1	8	2	7	3

373

1	3	8	9	6	5	2	4	7
7	2	6	4	1	3	8	5	9
4	5	9	7	2	8	6	3	1
9	7	5	3	8	4	1	2	6
2	1	4	6	5	7	9	8	3
8	6	3	1	9	2	5	7	4
5	4	1	2	7	6	3	9	8
6	8	7	5	3	9	4	1	2
3	9	2	8	4	1	7	6	5

374

6	4	2	1	5	8	7	9	3
9	3	1	4	7	6	5	2	8
8	7	5	3	2	9	1	6	4
2	1	8	9	4	7	6	3	5
3	5	4	8	6	1	9	7	2
7	6	9	5	3	2	4	8	1
4	8	7	2	9	5	3	1	6
5	2	6	7	1	3	8	4	9
1	9	3	6	8	4	2	5	7

375

4	5	8	6	7	3	1	2	9
3	6	2	8	9	1	5	7	4
7	9	1	2	4	5	6	3	8
6	1	3	4	2	7	8	9	5
2	7	4	5	8	9	3	6	1
9	8	5	3	1	6	2	4	7
8	3	9	1	6	4	7	5	2
5	2	7	9	3	8	4	1	6
1	4	6	7	5	2	9	8	3

376

9	1	2	8	3	4	5	7	6
6	4	7	1	5	9	2	8	3
3	5	8	7	6	2	4	9	1
7	3	4	5	1	8	9	6	2
8	6	9	4	2	3	1	5	7
5	2	1	6	9	7	3	4	8
4	8	5	3	7	1	6	2	9
1	9	6	2	8	5	7	3	4
2	7	3	9	4	6	8	1	5

377

3	8	7	6	2	1	9	4	5
4	6	9	3	8	5	1	2	7
2	1	5	4	9	7	8	3	6
1	5	6	9	4	8	2	7	3
8	4	2	7	1	3	5	6	9
7	9	3	2	5	6	4	8	1
9	7	8	5	3	4	6	1	2
5	3	4	1	6	2	7	9	8
6	2	1	8	7	9	3	5	4

378

9	4	5	2	7	3	6	1	8
3	6	2	5	1	8	4	9	7
7	8	1	9	4	6	5	2	3
5	7	4	8	2	9	3	6	1
1	9	3	7	6	4	8	5	2
8	2	6	3	5	1	9	7	4
6	5	8	1	3	2	7	4	9
2	3	7	4	9	5	1	8	6
4	1	9	6	8	7	2	3	5

379

6	1	3	9	7	4	2	5	8
2	5	9	1	8	6	7	4	3
4	7	8	5	2	3	6	1	9
1	2	5	7	9	8	3	6	4
8	3	6	2	4	1	9	7	5
9	4	7	3	6	5	1	8	2
5	9	4	6	3	7	8	2	1
7	8	2	4	1	9	5	3	6
3	6	1	8	5	2	4	9	7

380

7	9	2	4	6	3	8	1	5
8	6	4	5	1	7	9	2	3
5	3	1	8	2	9	4	7	6
1	7	6	2	5	4	3	8	9
2	4	9	3	8	6	1	5	7
3	8	5	9	7	1	2	6	4
4	5	8	7	9	2	6	3	1
9	1	7	6	3	8	5	4	2
6	2	3	1	4	5	7	9	8

381

8	4	6	2	3	5	9	7	1
5	2	9	6	1	7	4	3	8
7	1	3	8	9	4	5	2	6
9	8	7	3	4	6	1	5	2
4	3	2	5	7	1	6	8	9
1	6	5	9	8	2	7	4	3
3	5	8	4	6	9	2	1	7
6	7	4	1	2	3	8	9	5
2	9	1	7	5	8	3	6	4

382

7	8	5	2	1	3	6	4	9
9	6	3	4	5	8	1	2	7
2	1	4	9	6	7	5	8	3
1	5	2	7	9	6	8	3	4
6	7	8	5	3	4	2	9	1
3	4	9	1	8	2	7	5	6
4	3	6	8	2	1	9	7	5
8	9	7	6	4	5	3	1	2
5	2	1	3	7	9	4	6	8

383

2	8	9	1	3	4	7	6	5
5	3	1	8	6	7	2	9	4
7	4	6	2	9	5	8	1	3
4	1	5	7	2	6	9	3	8
8	7	2	9	5	3	1	4	6
9	6	3	4	8	1	5	7	2
6	5	8	3	7	9	4	2	1
1	2	7	6	4	8	3	5	9
3	9	4	5	1	2	6	8	7

384

1	4	8	6	3	5	7	2	9
9	6	3	7	2	4	5	8	1
2	5	7	9	8	1	3	6	4
4	1	5	2	9	3	8	7	6
7	9	6	1	5	8	4	3	2
3	8	2	4	7	6	9	1	5
6	2	9	8	4	7	1	5	3
8	3	1	5	6	9	2	4	7
5	7	4	3	1	2	6	9	8

385

9	5	4	3	1	8	7	2	6
2	1	6	7	5	9	8	3	4
3	8	7	6	2	4	1	5	9
6	9	5	2	7	3	4	8	1
1	7	3	8	4	6	2	9	5
4	2	8	5	9	1	3	6	7
5	4	9	1	3	2	6	7	8
7	6	2	4	8	5	9	1	3
8	3	1	9	6	7	5	4	2

386

6	7	3	5	4	2	9	8	1
9	8	1	6	3	7	4	2	5
2	4	5	9	8	1	6	7	3
5	1	7	8	2	9	3	6	4
4	6	8	7	1	3	2	5	9
3	2	9	4	5	6	8	1	7
8	5	6	3	7	4	1	9	2
1	9	4	2	6	5	7	3	8
7	3	2	1	9	8	5	4	6

387

2	4	1	8	9	7	6	5	3
8	3	6	2	4	5	7	9	1
5	7	9	3	6	1	8	2	4
1	8	2	9	3	6	5	4	7
4	9	7	5	1	2	3	8	6
3	6	5	4	7	8	2	1	9
6	1	8	7	2	4	9	3	5
9	2	4	6	5	3	1	7	8
7	5	3	1	8	9	4	6	2

388

1	2	5	8	7	3	9	6	4
7	4	8	5	9	6	3	1	2
3	6	9	4	1	2	7	8	5
4	5	6	9	2	1	8	7	3
8	1	3	6	5	7	2	4	9
9	7	2	3	4	8	1	5	6
5	9	1	2	8	4	6	3	7
6	8	4	7	3	9	5	2	1
2	3	7	1	6	5	4	9	8

389

5	4	3	7	9	6	1	8	2
6	9	8	2	5	1	4	7	3
1	7	2	4	3	8	9	6	5
7	3	5	1	6	4	8	2	9
2	1	9	3	8	5	6	4	7
8	6	4	9	2	7	3	5	1
4	5	7	6	1	3	2	9	8
9	8	1	5	4	2	7	3	6
3	2	6	8	7	9	5	1	4

390

6	5	9	3	4	7	1	2	8
4	1	3	2	9	8	5	7	6
2	8	7	5	6	1	9	3	4
5	7	2	8	1	6	4	9	3
1	6	8	9	3	4	7	5	2
9	3	4	7	5	2	8	6	1
3	4	6	1	7	9	2	8	5
8	9	5	4	2	3	6	1	7
7	2	1	6	8	5	3	4	9

391

1	5	3	8	6	4	7	2	9
4	7	8	3	9	2	5	6	1
6	9	2	1	5	7	8	3	4
2	6	7	5	3	1	9	4	8
8	4	1	6	2	9	3	5	7
9	3	5	4	7	8	2	1	6
5	2	9	7	4	6	1	8	3
7	1	6	2	8	3	4	9	5
3	8	4	9	1	5	6	7	2

392

3	7	5	6	2	1	8	9	4
6	4	9	3	5	8	2	7	1
1	2	8	7	9	4	6	5	3
2	6	1	5	4	9	3	8	7
7	8	4	1	6	3	9	2	5
9	5	3	2	8	7	4	1	6
8	3	6	9	7	5	1	4	2
4	1	7	8	3	2	5	6	9
5	9	2	4	1	6	7	3	8

393

1	7	4	6	2	5	8	9	3
9	6	5	1	3	8	7	4	2
2	3	8	4	9	7	6	1	5
5	4	2	7	8	1	9	3	6
7	8	6	3	4	9	5	2	1
3	9	1	5	6	2	4	8	7
4	2	3	8	5	6	1	7	9
6	1	9	2	7	4	3	5	8
8	5	7	9	1	3	2	6	4

394

7	9	5	6	8	3	2	1	4
3	2	8	4	9	1	6	7	5
6	4	1	7	5	2	9	8	3
8	6	9	1	4	7	3	5	2
5	1	2	9	3	6	7	4	8
4	3	7	5	2	8	1	9	6
2	5	4	3	1	9	8	6	7
9	7	3	8	6	5	4	2	1
1	8	6	2	7	4	5	3	9

395

6	9	8	7	3	2	1	4	5
1	7	4	8	6	5	2	9	3
5	3	2	4	9	1	8	7	6
9	8	3	2	1	6	4	5	7
7	4	6	3	5	8	9	1	2
2	1	5	9	7	4	6	3	8
3	2	1	5	8	9	7	6	4
8	6	7	1	4	3	5	2	9
4	5	9	6	2	7	3	8	1

396

2	6	8	9	1	7	3	4	5
5	1	9	6	4	3	7	2	8
4	3	7	8	2	5	6	1	9
9	5	2	1	6	8	4	3	7
1	8	6	3	7	4	9	5	2
3	7	4	5	9	2	1	8	6
7	9	3	2	8	1	5	6	4
6	2	5	4	3	9	8	7	1
8	4	1	7	5	6	2	9	3

397

9	6	7	1	4	5	3	2	8
2	3	1	7	9	8	4	5	6
4	5	8	3	6	2	1	7	9
1	7	4	2	3	6	9	8	5
5	2	6	8	1	9	7	4	3
3	8	9	5	7	4	2	6	1
8	4	5	9	2	3	6	1	7
7	9	2	6	5	1	8	3	4
6	1	3	4	8	7	5	9	2

398

1	6	3	5	7	8	4	2	9
2	4	5	1	6	9	7	8	3
7	9	8	4	3	2	6	1	5
9	7	6	3	2	5	1	4	8
8	5	2	6	4	1	9	3	7
3	1	4	9	8	7	5	6	2
4	3	7	8	9	6	2	5	1
6	2	1	7	5	3	8	9	4
5	8	9	2	1	4	3	7	6

399

3	8	5	1	2	6	4	7	9
2	7	1	5	4	9	8	6	3
9	4	6	7	8	3	1	5	2
4	1	7	3	9	5	2	8	6
6	9	3	2	7	8	5	1	4
8	5	2	4	6	1	9	3	7
7	3	9	8	5	2	6	4	1
1	2	8	6	3	4	7	9	5
5	6	4	9	1	7	3	2	8

400

6	4	3	2	9	5	7	1	8
9	5	8	1	3	7	4	6	2
7	1	2	4	8	6	3	5	9
1	6	7	5	4	9	8	2	3
5	2	4	8	7	3	1	9	6
3	8	9	6	1	2	5	4	7
2	3	5	7	6	4	9	8	1
8	7	6	9	5	1	2	3	4
4	9	1	3	2	8	6	7	5

401

4	9	1	3	8	2	7	5	6
8	2	6	9	5	7	4	1	3
5	7	3	1	4	6	8	2	9
1	6	7	4	9	5	2	3	8
3	8	2	7	6	1	9	4	5
9	4	5	8	2	3	1	6	7
7	5	4	2	3	9	6	8	1
2	3	9	6	1	8	5	7	4
6	1	8	5	7	4	3	9	2

402

5	8	9	3	1	6	4	2	7
6	1	3	7	4	2	5	9	8
7	2	4	5	9	8	6	1	3
9	7	1	4	5	3	2	8	6
4	6	8	2	7	9	3	5	1
2	3	5	8	6	1	7	4	9
8	9	2	6	3	5	1	7	4
1	4	6	9	2	7	8	3	5
3	5	7	1	8	4	9	6	2

403

8	4	9	1	5	3	2	7	6
7	6	5	8	9	2	4	1	3
2	1	3	6	7	4	8	5	9
3	2	1	5	8	7	9	6	4
4	7	8	2	6	9	1	3	5
9	5	6	4	3	1	7	8	2
1	9	7	3	4	6	5	2	8
6	8	2	9	1	5	3	4	7
5	3	4	7	2	8	6	9	1

404

8	7	4	2	3	5	9	1	6
2	1	9	8	4	6	3	5	7
3	5	6	9	1	7	4	2	8
4	6	5	1	8	3	7	9	2
9	3	2	6	7	4	1	8	5
7	8	1	5	9	2	6	3	4
1	9	7	4	5	8	2	6	3
6	4	8	3	2	9	5	7	1
5	2	3	7	6	1	8	4	9

405

7	3	4	9	5	2	1	6	8
6	8	2	7	3	1	5	9	4
5	9	1	4	6	8	2	3	7
4	5	3	6	7	9	8	1	2
9	2	8	1	4	3	7	5	6
1	6	7	2	8	5	9	4	3
3	7	5	8	9	6	4	2	1
2	4	6	5	1	7	3	8	9
8	1	9	3	2	4	6	7	5

406

5	8	7	4	3	2	1	9	6
3	9	1	8	7	6	5	2	4
4	6	2	1	5	9	3	7	8
7	2	6	3	9	4	8	5	1
9	3	4	5	8	1	2	6	7
1	5	8	2	6	7	4	3	9
6	1	3	9	2	8	7	4	5
2	4	9	7	1	5	6	8	3
8	7	5	6	4	3	9	1	2

407

1	7	5	3	8	4	2	6	9
4	2	8	6	9	5	3	1	7
9	6	3	1	2	7	4	8	5
5	1	7	9	6	3	8	2	4
8	3	6	5	4	2	7	9	1
2	9	4	7	1	8	5	3	6
6	5	2	8	7	9	1	4	3
7	4	9	2	3	1	6	5	8
3	8	1	4	5	6	9	7	2

408

4	7	1	8	9	6	2	3	5
3	9	8	2	4	5	1	6	7
2	5	6	7	3	1	4	8	9
8	1	4	9	7	3	5	2	6
7	6	9	5	2	4	8	1	3
5	3	2	6	1	8	7	9	4
9	8	7	4	6	2	3	5	1
6	2	3	1	5	7	9	4	8
1	4	5	3	8	9	6	7	2

409

7	3	1	9	6	4	8	2	5
9	5	8	2	1	3	7	4	6
4	2	6	7	5	8	3	9	1
1	9	4	3	2	5	6	7	8
5	7	3	8	4	6	9	1	2
8	6	2	1	7	9	4	5	3
2	4	7	6	8	1	5	3	9
6	1	9	5	3	7	2	8	4
3	8	5	4	9	2	1	6	7

410

3	8	1	6	7	9	4	5	2
5	4	9	1	8	2	3	7	6
7	2	6	4	5	3	8	1	9
8	3	5	9	4	7	6	2	1
2	1	4	5	6	8	9	3	7
9	6	7	2	3	1	5	4	8
6	5	2	8	1	4	7	9	3
4	9	3	7	2	6	1	8	5
1	7	8	3	9	5	2	6	4

411

3	1	8	6	5	2	4	9	7
2	6	9	8	7	4	1	5	3
5	4	7	3	1	9	2	6	8
4	9	6	7	2	3	5	8	1
8	2	1	5	4	6	3	7	9
7	3	5	9	8	1	6	4	2
1	7	3	4	6	8	9	2	5
6	8	2	1	9	5	7	3	4
9	5	4	2	3	7	8	1	6

412

6	7	4	2	3	8	5	1	9
9	1	8	6	7	5	2	3	4
5	3	2	4	1	9	7	6	8
3	5	7	1	6	4	9	8	2
1	8	9	3	5	2	6	4	7
4	2	6	8	9	7	1	5	3
8	6	3	7	2	1	4	9	5
7	9	1	5	4	3	8	2	6
2	4	5	9	8	6	3	7	1

413

6	3	4	1	2	7	9	5	8
2	7	5	3	8	9	4	1	6
1	9	8	4	5	6	3	7	2
5	2	1	6	7	3	8	9	4
7	6	9	5	4	8	1	2	3
4	8	3	9	1	2	5	6	7
9	5	7	2	3	4	6	8	1
8	4	6	7	9	1	2	3	5
3	1	2	8	6	5	7	4	9

414

8	7	4	1	9	5	6	2	3
1	5	6	8	2	3	4	7	9
3	9	2	4	7	6	1	5	8
6	2	8	5	1	7	9	3	4
4	3	9	2	6	8	7	1	5
7	1	5	9	3	4	8	6	2
5	4	3	6	8	1	2	9	7
2	6	7	3	4	9	5	8	1
9	8	1	7	5	2	3	4	6

415

1	2	7	6	5	4	8	3	9
3	6	8	7	1	9	5	4	2
9	5	4	3	8	2	1	6	7
5	1	9	2	3	6	7	8	4
2	4	6	1	7	8	3	9	5
7	8	3	9	4	5	6	2	1
8	3	1	4	9	7	2	5	6
4	7	2	5	6	3	9	1	8
6	9	5	8	2	1	4	7	3

416

6	2	5	1	4	9	8	3	7
8	3	4	7	5	2	9	6	1
1	7	9	6	3	8	4	2	5
7	9	6	2	8	5	3	1	4
4	5	2	3	7	1	6	9	8
3	1	8	9	6	4	5	7	2
5	6	1	8	9	7	2	4	3
2	4	3	5	1	6	7	8	9
9	8	7	4	2	3	1	5	6

417

7	8	5	3	2	1	9	4	6
9	6	4	7	8	5	1	3	2
1	3	2	6	9	4	8	5	7
6	1	8	4	7	2	3	9	5
4	7	9	8	5	3	6	2	1
2	5	3	1	6	9	7	8	4
5	2	6	9	3	7	4	1	8
8	9	1	2	4	6	5	7	3
3	4	7	5	1	8	2	6	9

418

3	9	2	7	6	5	1	4	8
1	6	4	2	9	8	7	5	3
7	8	5	1	3	4	6	2	9
8	4	1	3	7	9	5	6	2
2	7	9	6	5	1	3	8	4
6	5	3	8	4	2	9	7	1
9	1	8	5	2	6	4	3	7
5	2	7	4	1	3	8	9	6
4	3	6	9	8	7	2	1	5

419

4	8	2	6	3	1	9	5	7
6	7	3	2	5	9	1	8	4
9	1	5	4	8	7	2	3	6
3	4	6	7	9	8	5	1	2
7	2	8	1	4	5	6	9	3
5	9	1	3	2	6	4	7	8
2	6	7	9	1	3	8	4	5
8	3	9	5	6	4	7	2	1
1	5	4	8	7	2	3	6	9

420

3	2	5	8	9	1	7	6	4
4	7	8	3	6	5	9	1	2
9	1	6	7	4	2	3	5	8
8	9	1	4	5	7	2	3	6
5	6	7	2	8	3	4	9	1
2	4	3	6	1	9	5	8	7
6	5	4	9	7	8	1	2	3
7	3	9	1	2	6	8	4	5
1	8	2	5	3	4	6	7	9

421

3	1	4	2	6	9	5	7	8
9	6	8	3	7	5	1	4	2
2	7	5	8	1	4	3	6	9
6	5	2	4	9	8	7	1	3
8	9	7	5	3	1	4	2	6
4	3	1	6	2	7	9	8	5
5	4	3	1	8	2	6	9	7
7	8	6	9	4	3	2	5	1
1	2	9	7	5	6	8	3	4

422

2	8	9	6	4	3	5	1	7
3	5	1	8	7	2	6	9	4
4	6	7	5	1	9	2	3	8
6	1	2	3	5	8	7	4	9
8	7	4	9	2	1	3	5	6
9	3	5	4	6	7	8	2	1
5	9	8	7	3	4	1	6	2
7	2	3	1	9	6	4	8	5
1	4	6	2	8	5	9	7	3

423

5	1	4	7	2	9	6	3	8
7	8	3	4	1	6	9	2	5
6	2	9	5	8	3	7	4	1
8	7	2	6	3	1	5	9	4
9	3	1	8	4	5	2	6	7
4	6	5	2	9	7	1	8	3
2	5	8	9	7	4	3	1	6
3	4	6	1	5	2	8	7	9
1	9	7	3	6	8	4	5	2

424

7	6	2	8	3	4	5	9	1
4	3	8	5	1	9	7	6	2
9	5	1	6	7	2	3	8	4
5	7	9	1	4	3	8	2	6
1	8	4	2	5	6	9	3	7
3	2	6	7	9	8	1	4	5
2	4	5	3	8	1	6	7	9
6	1	3	9	2	7	4	5	8
8	9	7	4	6	5	2	1	3

425

7	3	1	6	8	5	4	2	9
4	9	8	3	1	2	5	6	7
5	2	6	7	4	9	1	3	8
1	5	7	8	2	3	9	4	6
3	6	4	1	9	7	8	5	2
2	8	9	4	5	6	3	7	1
6	1	5	2	3	8	7	9	4
9	4	2	5	7	1	6	8	3
8	7	3	9	6	4	2	1	5

426

2	7	8	9	6	1	3	5	4
3	5	4	7	8	2	6	9	1
6	1	9	3	4	5	8	2	7
1	3	5	4	9	8	7	6	2
8	9	7	1	2	6	5	4	3
4	2	6	5	7	3	9	1	8
5	4	3	6	1	7	2	8	9
7	8	1	2	5	9	4	3	6
9	6	2	8	3	4	1	7	5

427

1	2	6	9	7	3	5	8	4
3	8	4	2	5	6	7	1	9
7	9	5	1	4	8	6	3	2
8	7	3	5	9	4	1	2	6
6	5	2	8	1	7	9	4	3
4	1	9	6	3	2	8	7	5
9	3	7	4	8	5	2	6	1
2	4	1	7	6	9	3	5	8
5	6	8	3	2	1	4	9	7

428

5	6	8	7	4	9	2	1	3
7	4	9	1	3	2	5	6	8
1	2	3	5	8	6	4	7	9
4	5	6	9	2	1	8	3	7
3	8	2	6	7	4	9	5	1
9	1	7	8	5	3	6	4	2
2	9	4	3	6	7	1	8	5
8	7	1	4	9	5	3	2	6
6	3	5	2	1	8	7	9	4

429

8	1	2	5	7	9	6	4	3
6	7	5	1	3	4	2	9	8
4	9	3	6	8	2	7	1	5
7	8	9	4	1	3	5	2	6
1	3	6	2	5	7	4	8	9
5	2	4	9	6	8	1	3	7
3	4	7	8	2	6	9	5	1
2	6	1	3	9	5	8	7	4
9	5	8	7	4	1	3	6	2

430

4	1	2	8	6	7	5	9	3
9	5	3	2	1	4	6	8	7
7	6	8	5	3	9	1	2	4
6	9	4	1	8	3	7	5	2
8	3	5	6	7	2	9	4	1
1	2	7	9	4	5	3	6	8
5	7	9	4	2	1	8	3	6
2	8	1	3	9	6	4	7	5
3	4	6	7	5	8	2	1	9

431

4	3	2	6	5	7	8	9	1
7	5	8	1	2	9	3	6	4
6	9	1	3	4	8	5	2	7
2	6	9	7	3	1	4	8	5
3	7	5	4	8	2	9	1	6
1	8	4	9	6	5	2	7	3
8	1	6	5	9	4	7	3	2
9	4	7	2	1	3	6	5	8
5	2	3	8	7	6	1	4	9

432

8	7	9	2	1	6	3	5	4
6	4	1	9	5	3	2	7	8
5	2	3	8	4	7	9	1	6
4	5	2	7	3	8	1	6	9
1	6	7	5	9	2	8	4	3
3	9	8	1	6	4	5	2	7
2	1	6	3	7	9	4	8	5
7	3	5	4	8	1	6	9	2
9	8	4	6	2	5	7	3	1

433

3	9	1	4	5	7	2	6	8
8	6	5	9	1	2	3	7	4
4	7	2	8	6	3	9	1	5
1	5	4	6	7	9	8	2	3
2	8	7	3	4	1	6	5	9
9	3	6	5	2	8	1	4	7
5	1	9	2	3	4	7	8	6
6	2	8	7	9	5	4	3	1
7	4	3	1	8	6	5	9	2

434

4	2	9	7	3	5	8	1	6
1	6	3	9	4	8	2	7	5
5	8	7	6	1	2	4	9	3
2	9	1	4	8	3	6	5	7
3	7	6	5	2	9	1	8	4
8	5	4	1	6	7	9	3	2
6	3	8	2	7	1	5	4	9
7	4	5	8	9	6	3	2	1
9	1	2	3	5	4	7	6	8

435

7	2	1	8	3	5	6	9	4
6	4	5	1	2	9	7	8	3
9	3	8	4	6	7	1	5	2
2	6	3	5	7	4	8	1	9
8	5	7	9	1	2	4	3	6
4	1	9	3	8	6	2	7	5
1	9	2	6	5	8	3	4	7
5	8	6	7	4	3	9	2	1
3	7	4	2	9	1	5	6	8

436

6	1	4	7	3	2	5	9	8
7	8	5	1	9	4	3	2	6
9	3	2	5	8	6	4	7	1
4	6	7	9	2	5	8	1	3
8	5	1	4	7	3	2	6	9
3	2	9	8	6	1	7	5	4
5	7	6	3	1	8	9	4	2
1	9	3	2	4	7	6	8	5
2	4	8	6	5	9	1	3	7

437

9	4	1	5	2	7	6	3	8
8	7	3	1	4	6	2	9	5
2	6	5	3	8	9	4	7	1
3	1	9	8	5	4	7	6	2
6	8	7	9	1	2	3	5	4
5	2	4	7	6	3	1	8	9
1	9	2	6	3	8	5	4	7
7	5	6	4	9	1	8	2	3
4	3	8	2	7	5	9	1	6

438

8	3	9	6	2	4	7	1	5
4	6	2	7	1	5	8	3	9
1	5	7	9	3	8	2	4	6
5	8	1	2	9	3	6	7	4
3	2	6	4	8	7	5	9	1
9	7	4	1	5	6	3	2	8
6	9	8	3	7	1	4	5	2
2	4	3	5	6	9	1	8	7
7	1	5	8	4	2	9	6	3

439

2	3	5	7	8	6	4	9	1
7	8	1	9	4	3	5	6	2
9	4	6	5	2	1	7	8	3
8	2	4	1	3	9	6	5	7
3	6	9	2	5	7	8	1	4
5	1	7	4	6	8	2	3	9
1	5	2	6	9	4	3	7	8
6	9	8	3	7	2	1	4	5
4	7	3	8	1	5	9	2	6

440

8	2	7	9	5	4	6	1	3
5	9	6	1	2	3	8	7	4
3	1	4	8	6	7	9	5	2
4	8	5	3	7	9	2	6	1
7	6	9	5	1	2	4	3	8
2	3	1	4	8	6	7	9	5
6	4	2	7	3	1	5	8	9
9	5	3	6	4	8	1	2	7
1	7	8	2	9	5	3	4	6

441

2	1	5	4	6	9	7	8	3
7	4	9	8	2	3	5	1	6
3	8	6	5	1	7	2	9	4
9	7	3	6	5	2	8	4	1
4	5	2	3	8	1	9	6	7
1	6	8	9	7	4	3	5	2
6	2	7	1	9	8	4	3	5
8	3	1	2	4	5	6	7	9
5	9	4	7	3	6	1	2	8

442

2	3	9	8	6	4	1	5	7
6	8	1	3	5	7	9	4	2
5	7	4	9	1	2	3	6	8
1	4	5	6	7	8	2	3	9
9	6	7	5	2	3	8	1	4
8	2	3	4	9	1	6	7	5
7	5	8	2	3	6	4	9	1
3	1	2	7	4	9	5	8	6
4	9	6	1	8	5	7	2	3

443

4	5	2	1	3	7	8	9	6
3	9	8	4	5	6	7	2	1
6	1	7	8	2	9	5	3	4
2	3	1	5	6	8	4	7	9
7	4	6	9	1	3	2	8	5
5	8	9	7	4	2	6	1	3
1	6	3	2	7	4	9	5	8
9	2	5	6	8	1	3	4	7
8	7	4	3	9	5	1	6	2

444

1	5	4	8	7	9	6	2	3
2	9	7	6	4	3	5	1	8
3	8	6	1	2	5	4	9	7
6	7	1	4	9	2	3	8	5
4	2	5	3	1	8	9	7	6
9	3	8	7	5	6	1	4	2
5	6	9	2	8	1	7	3	4
8	4	3	9	6	7	2	5	1
7	1	2	5	3	4	8	6	9

445

2	7	4	6	3	5	9	8	1
9	6	8	4	7	1	5	3	2
3	1	5	8	2	9	7	4	6
1	8	2	3	6	7	4	9	5
6	5	7	2	9	4	3	1	8
4	9	3	1	5	8	6	2	7
8	3	9	5	1	6	2	7	4
5	2	1	7	4	3	8	6	9
7	4	6	9	8	2	1	5	3

446

7	2	9	3	5	8	1	6	4
4	3	5	1	2	6	7	8	9
8	1	6	7	9	4	2	3	5
2	9	8	5	1	7	6	4	3
6	7	3	8	4	9	5	2	1
1	5	4	6	3	2	9	7	8
5	4	7	2	8	1	3	9	6
9	6	1	4	7	3	8	5	2
3	8	2	9	6	5	4	1	7

447

8	3	9	7	1	4	6	2	5
6	1	7	8	2	5	3	4	9
5	2	4	6	3	9	7	1	8
1	6	8	3	7	2	9	5	4
7	4	3	5	9	1	8	6	2
2	9	5	4	6	8	1	7	3
9	5	6	1	4	3	2	8	7
4	7	2	9	8	6	5	3	1
3	8	1	2	5	7	4	9	6

448

3	9	6	5	7	8	4	1	2
5	4	1	3	9	2	6	8	7
2	8	7	4	1	6	9	3	5
8	2	3	6	4	9	7	5	1
1	6	9	7	5	3	8	2	4
4	7	5	2	8	1	3	6	9
9	5	2	8	3	7	1	4	6
6	1	8	9	2	4	5	7	3
7	3	4	1	6	5	2	9	8

449

1	6	9	4	5	2	3	7	8
4	8	5	6	7	3	2	1	9
7	3	2	8	9	1	4	5	6
3	5	1	9	2	6	8	4	7
2	4	6	1	8	7	5	9	3
9	7	8	3	4	5	1	6	2
8	9	3	5	6	4	7	2	1
6	2	4	7	1	8	9	3	5
5	1	7	2	3	9	6	8	4

450

9	5	2	6	7	1	3	8	4
8	1	7	9	4	3	6	5	2
4	6	3	8	2	5	7	1	9
2	4	1	7	9	8	5	3	6
7	9	6	5	3	4	8	2	1
3	8	5	1	6	2	4	9	7
6	7	8	2	5	9	1	4	3
5	3	9	4	1	6	2	7	8
1	2	4	3	8	7	9	6	5

451

9	8	7	4	5	6	2	1	3
5	6	4	1	2	3	9	8	7
1	2	3	8	7	9	6	5	4
7	3	2	9	4	8	1	6	5
4	5	8	6	1	2	3	7	9
6	1	9	7	3	5	8	4	2
2	4	6	3	8	7	5	9	1
3	9	1	5	6	4	7	2	8
8	7	5	2	9	1	4	3	6

452

5	9	3	1	4	6	2	8	7
1	8	4	5	7	2	6	3	9
2	6	7	8	9	3	4	5	1
6	4	8	9	3	1	5	7	2
3	1	2	7	8	5	9	6	4
9	7	5	2	6	4	8	1	3
4	5	9	6	1	7	3	2	8
7	3	6	4	2	8	1	9	5
8	2	1	3	5	9	7	4	6

453

6	3	9	1	4	7	2	5	8
1	2	4	8	6	5	9	7	3
5	7	8	3	9	2	1	4	6
2	1	5	4	7	3	6	8	9
9	6	7	5	8	1	4	3	2
4	8	3	6	2	9	5	1	7
8	4	1	2	3	6	7	9	5
7	5	6	9	1	8	3	2	4
3	9	2	7	5	4	8	6	1

454

8	3	5	2	4	1	6	7	9
7	4	2	8	9	6	1	5	3
9	6	1	3	5	7	4	8	2
3	9	6	5	2	8	7	4	1
2	7	4	6	1	9	5	3	8
1	5	8	7	3	4	9	2	6
6	8	9	4	7	2	3	1	5
5	1	7	9	8	3	2	6	4
4	2	3	1	6	5	8	9	7

455

8	5	7	2	6	9	3	1	4
2	4	1	8	7	3	6	5	9
6	9	3	5	4	1	7	8	2
9	6	8	3	1	2	5	4	7
4	1	2	9	5	7	8	3	6
3	7	5	4	8	6	9	2	1
7	2	9	1	3	5	4	6	8
1	3	4	6	9	8	2	7	5
5	8	6	7	2	4	1	9	3

456

6	2	8	1	4	5	9	7	3
9	1	3	7	2	6	8	4	5
5	4	7	3	8	9	1	2	6
1	5	6	4	9	2	7	3	8
7	3	4	5	1	8	6	9	2
2	8	9	6	7	3	4	5	1
4	7	5	2	6	1	3	8	9
8	6	2	9	3	4	5	1	7
3	9	1	8	5	7	2	6	4

457

9	7	5	2	4	6	1	3	8
8	3	6	9	1	5	7	2	4
2	4	1	3	8	7	5	9	6
4	8	7	5	9	2	3	6	1
1	6	9	8	3	4	2	7	5
5	2	3	6	7	1	4	8	9
3	9	4	7	5	8	6	1	2
7	1	2	4	6	9	8	5	3
6	5	8	1	2	3	9	4	7

458

1	3	4	8	2	5	6	9	7
8	5	7	3	9	6	2	1	4
6	2	9	7	4	1	8	5	3
4	9	2	1	8	7	3	6	5
3	6	8	9	5	2	4	7	1
5	7	1	6	3	4	9	8	2
2	8	3	5	7	9	1	4	6
9	1	5	4	6	3	7	2	8
7	4	6	2	1	8	5	3	9

459

1	4	6	3	2	8	5	7	9
7	8	2	5	4	9	1	6	3
9	5	3	6	1	7	4	8	2
3	1	4	8	6	2	9	5	7
2	9	5	7	3	1	8	4	6
8	6	7	4	9	5	2	3	1
5	2	8	9	7	6	3	1	4
6	3	1	2	8	4	7	9	5
4	7	9	1	5	3	6	2	8

460

7	4	9	2	5	1	6	3	8
1	6	8	7	3	9	4	5	2
2	5	3	4	8	6	9	7	1
9	3	1	5	2	7	8	4	6
5	2	6	8	1	4	3	9	7
8	7	4	6	9	3	2	1	5
4	1	5	9	6	8	7	2	3
6	9	2	3	7	5	1	8	4
3	8	7	1	4	2	5	6	9

461

6	8	4	5	2	9	1	7	3
1	3	5	7	6	8	9	2	4
7	2	9	1	4	3	8	6	5
8	7	6	9	5	1	3	4	2
5	9	1	2	3	4	7	8	6
2	4	3	6	8	7	5	9	1
4	1	2	8	7	5	6	3	9
9	6	7	3	1	2	4	5	8
3	5	8	4	9	6	2	1	7

462

5	2	8	9	4	6	3	1	7
1	3	4	2	5	7	8	6	9
6	7	9	3	8	1	2	5	4
3	5	2	7	1	9	4	8	6
7	9	6	8	2	4	1	3	5
4	8	1	6	3	5	9	7	2
9	4	7	1	6	8	5	2	3
2	1	5	4	7	3	6	9	8
8	6	3	5	9	2	7	4	1

463

9	8	5	1	6	3	2	4	7
4	2	3	9	7	5	6	1	8
1	6	7	4	2	8	5	9	3
5	4	9	3	8	6	1	7	2
8	1	2	5	9	7	4	3	6
7	3	6	2	1	4	9	8	5
2	7	8	6	4	9	3	5	1
6	5	4	7	3	1	8	2	9
3	9	1	8	5	2	7	6	4

464

7	4	5	1	6	3	2	8	9
9	3	2	7	5	8	6	1	4
1	8	6	9	2	4	7	3	5
2	5	7	3	8	9	4	6	1
4	9	1	2	7	6	8	5	3
8	6	3	5	4	1	9	7	2
5	7	8	4	1	2	3	9	6
3	1	4	6	9	7	5	2	8
6	2	9	8	3	5	1	4	7

465

6	2	8	5	9	1	7	4	3
3	4	1	2	8	7	9	5	6
9	7	5	3	6	4	2	1	8
8	1	9	7	2	6	4	3	5
4	3	6	9	5	8	1	7	2
7	5	2	1	4	3	6	8	9
5	6	3	4	7	9	8	2	1
1	9	4	8	3	2	5	6	7
2	8	7	6	1	5	3	9	4

466

7	9	1	3	6	2	8	5	4
3	4	8	7	1	5	2	9	6
6	5	2	4	9	8	1	3	7
5	1	7	8	3	4	6	2	9
2	6	3	5	7	9	4	1	8
9	8	4	6	2	1	5	7	3
4	7	6	2	5	3	9	8	1
8	2	9	1	4	7	3	6	5
1	3	5	9	8	6	7	4	2

467

3	5	6	1	4	8	2	7	9
1	4	8	2	7	9	5	3	6
7	2	9	6	5	3	4	1	8
5	1	2	4	6	7	9	8	3
6	9	3	5	8	2	7	4	1
8	7	4	9	3	1	6	5	2
2	6	5	8	1	4	3	9	7
9	3	1	7	2	5	8	6	4
4	8	7	3	9	6	1	2	5

468

3	1	4	2	6	5	8	7	9
5	7	9	8	3	4	2	1	6
2	6	8	1	7	9	4	3	5
6	8	2	5	4	1	3	9	7
1	3	7	9	8	6	5	2	4
9	4	5	7	2	3	1	6	8
8	5	1	6	9	2	7	4	3
4	2	6	3	5	7	9	8	1
7	9	3	4	1	8	6	5	2

469

4	5	3	8	6	2	7	9	1
2	1	9	3	4	7	6	8	5
7	8	6	5	9	1	3	4	2
5	3	2	9	8	4	1	6	7
6	4	8	7	1	3	2	5	9
1	9	7	2	5	6	8	3	4
3	6	4	1	7	9	5	2	8
9	7	5	6	2	8	4	1	3
8	2	1	4	3	5	9	7	6

470

1	4	3	5	7	9	6	8	2
8	6	7	3	1	2	5	4	9
9	2	5	4	6	8	3	7	1
5	7	6	2	4	3	1	9	8
3	1	9	7	8	6	2	5	4
4	8	2	9	5	1	7	3	6
7	3	1	8	2	4	9	6	5
6	9	4	1	3	5	8	2	7
2	5	8	6	9	7	4	1	3

471

9	5	8	2	1	4	6	7	3
4	7	1	5	3	6	9	2	8
6	3	2	9	7	8	1	4	5
5	9	4	3	6	7	2	8	1
3	1	6	4	8	2	7	5	9
8	2	7	1	9	5	4	3	6
1	8	5	7	4	9	3	6	2
7	6	9	8	2	3	5	1	4
2	4	3	6	5	1	8	9	7

472

2	7	1	4	9	6	8	3	5
9	3	8	7	1	5	4	2	6
6	5	4	2	8	3	7	9	1
3	1	6	8	5	9	2	4	7
4	8	7	3	6	2	5	1	9
5	2	9	1	7	4	6	8	3
1	4	2	6	3	7	9	5	8
8	6	5	9	2	1	3	7	4
7	9	3	5	4	8	1	6	2

473

7	4	9	2	5	6	3	1	8
1	2	8	3	9	4	5	7	6
3	5	6	8	1	7	4	9	2
8	6	5	4	3	1	7	2	9
2	7	1	9	8	5	6	4	3
9	3	4	7	6	2	8	5	1
5	8	2	1	4	3	9	6	7
6	9	7	5	2	8	1	3	4
4	1	3	6	7	9	2	8	5

474

3	7	6	5	9	4	1	8	2
1	5	8	6	2	3	4	9	7
2	9	4	1	7	8	3	5	6
5	4	9	3	8	2	6	7	1
8	3	7	4	6	1	9	2	5
6	2	1	7	5	9	8	3	4
9	1	3	2	4	5	7	6	8
4	6	5	8	3	7	2	1	9
7	8	2	9	1	6	5	4	3

475

6	9	5	4	7	3	1	8	2
2	4	1	8	9	5	7	3	6
8	3	7	2	6	1	5	4	9
1	8	2	3	4	9	6	5	7
3	7	6	1	5	8	2	9	4
4	5	9	6	2	7	3	1	8
9	6	4	5	3	2	8	7	1
7	1	3	9	8	6	4	2	5
5	2	8	7	1	4	9	6	3

476

9	4	5	2	7	1	3	6	8
3	7	8	4	5	6	2	1	9
2	6	1	8	3	9	7	4	5
5	1	7	3	2	8	4	9	6
6	2	3	9	4	5	1	8	7
8	9	4	6	1	7	5	2	3
4	5	9	1	6	3	8	7	2
1	3	6	7	8	2	9	5	4
7	8	2	5	9	4	6	3	1

477

9	5	4	2	6	3	8	7	1
7	8	1	5	9	4	3	2	6
6	2	3	1	8	7	4	5	9
4	6	2	7	1	8	5	9	3
1	3	5	9	2	6	7	4	8
8	9	7	3	4	5	6	1	2
3	4	9	6	5	2	1	8	7
5	1	6	8	7	9	2	3	4
2	7	8	4	3	1	9	6	5

478

3	4	7	9	2	1	5	6	8
5	9	1	4	8	6	2	7	3
2	8	6	3	5	7	9	1	4
1	5	8	6	7	2	4	3	9
6	3	9	8	4	5	7	2	1
7	2	4	1	3	9	8	5	6
9	7	3	5	1	8	6	4	2
4	6	5	2	9	3	1	8	7
8	1	2	7	6	4	3	9	5

479

5	9	1	6	2	7	8	3	4
8	6	3	9	5	4	1	7	2
4	2	7	1	8	3	6	9	5
3	8	9	2	7	5	4	6	1
7	1	6	4	9	8	2	5	3
2	4	5	3	1	6	9	8	7
6	7	4	8	3	2	5	1	9
9	5	8	7	4	1	3	2	6
1	3	2	5	6	9	7	4	8

480

9	5	2	6	7	3	8	4	1
8	7	4	1	9	5	3	2	6
6	1	3	4	8	2	7	9	5
5	8	1	3	4	7	2	6	9
4	9	6	2	1	8	5	7	3
3	2	7	5	6	9	4	1	8
2	4	5	9	3	1	6	8	7
1	3	8	7	2	6	9	5	4
7	6	9	8	5	4	1	3	2

481

1	6	3	5	4	2	9	8	7
9	7	8	6	1	3	4	2	5
4	5	2	9	8	7	6	3	1
8	9	1	7	3	5	2	6	4
6	4	7	1	2	8	5	9	3
2	3	5	4	6	9	7	1	8
5	8	9	2	7	1	3	4	6
7	1	4	3	9	6	8	5	2
3	2	6	8	5	4	1	7	9

482

9	1	3	5	4	6	8	2	7
6	8	5	2	9	7	1	3	4
2	4	7	8	1	3	5	6	9
5	7	9	6	8	2	4	1	3
4	6	8	7	3	1	2	9	5
1	3	2	9	5	4	7	8	6
3	9	1	4	2	5	6	7	8
8	5	6	1	7	9	3	4	2
7	2	4	3	6	8	9	5	1

483

7	8	2	9	1	3	4	6	5
6	4	5	2	7	8	3	9	1
3	1	9	4	6	5	7	8	2
5	9	8	6	2	7	1	3	4
1	6	3	8	5	4	9	2	7
2	7	4	1	3	9	6	5	8
4	2	1	5	9	6	8	7	3
9	5	7	3	8	1	2	4	6
8	3	6	7	4	2	5	1	9

484

3	6	7	8	4	2	5	9	1
1	4	5	9	3	6	7	2	8
9	8	2	1	5	7	6	3	4
2	9	6	7	1	3	8	4	5
7	1	4	5	9	8	2	6	3
8	5	3	2	6	4	1	7	9
6	2	9	3	8	1	4	5	7
4	3	1	6	7	5	9	8	2
5	7	8	4	2	9	3	1	6

485

9	1	6	3	5	2	4	7	8
4	5	2	6	8	7	9	1	3
7	3	8	1	4	9	6	2	5
8	6	1	7	3	4	2	5	9
5	4	3	2	9	8	1	6	7
2	7	9	5	1	6	3	8	4
6	9	4	8	2	5	7	3	1
3	8	7	4	6	1	5	9	2
1	2	5	9	7	3	8	4	6

486

9	3	4	7	8	2	5	1	6
2	6	7	5	1	4	3	8	9
8	1	5	6	9	3	4	7	2
5	2	8	3	7	1	6	9	4
3	7	6	8	4	9	1	2	5
1	4	9	2	6	5	8	3	7
4	9	3	1	5	7	2	6	8
6	5	2	9	3	8	7	4	1
7	8	1	4	2	6	9	5	3

487

3	2	6	7	9	5	4	8	1
8	5	4	3	1	6	9	7	2
7	1	9	2	8	4	3	5	6
5	9	2	4	3	8	6	1	7
6	7	3	5	2	1	8	4	9
4	8	1	6	7	9	2	3	5
9	6	5	1	4	3	7	2	8
1	3	7	8	6	2	5	9	4
2	4	8	9	5	7	1	6	3

488

7	4	9	2	6	3	1	5	8
8	1	3	9	7	5	2	6	4
6	2	5	4	8	1	7	9	3
4	3	2	7	9	6	8	1	5
9	6	7	1	5	8	3	4	2
1	5	8	3	4	2	6	7	9
5	7	1	8	2	9	4	3	6
2	9	4	6	3	7	5	8	1
3	8	6	5	1	4	9	2	7

489

1	9	3	2	6	5	4	8	7
4	8	6	7	9	3	2	1	5
7	5	2	8	4	1	6	3	9
6	4	8	5	3	7	1	9	2
2	1	7	9	8	4	3	5	6
9	3	5	1	2	6	8	7	4
5	7	4	6	1	8	9	2	3
8	6	9	3	5	2	7	4	1
3	2	1	4	7	9	5	6	8

490

9	3	6	8	4	7	2	5	1
5	4	7	1	9	2	6	8	3
1	8	2	5	3	6	4	9	7
7	1	8	6	5	4	9	3	2
2	5	9	3	7	1	8	4	6
4	6	3	2	8	9	1	7	5
3	9	1	4	2	5	7	6	8
6	7	5	9	1	8	3	2	4
8	2	4	7	6	3	5	1	9

491

9	1	8	2	3	4	5	6	7
2	6	7	9	1	5	3	8	4
3	5	4	7	8	6	1	2	9
6	3	2	4	7	1	9	5	8
4	9	1	5	6	8	7	3	2
8	7	5	3	2	9	6	4	1
7	8	6	1	5	2	4	9	3
5	4	3	8	9	7	2	1	6
1	2	9	6	4	3	8	7	5

492

7	5	3	4	8	1	6	2	9
6	1	4	5	2	9	3	8	7
8	2	9	3	6	7	4	1	5
1	9	5	6	4	8	7	3	2
2	7	8	9	5	3	1	4	6
3	4	6	1	7	2	5	9	8
5	6	2	8	1	4	9	7	3
4	3	7	2	9	5	8	6	1
9	8	1	7	3	6	2	5	4

493

1	2	6	9	8	4	3	5	7
7	9	3	1	5	6	4	2	8
5	8	4	2	3	7	9	6	1
9	5	7	6	4	3	8	1	2
4	1	8	7	2	5	6	9	3
3	6	2	8	9	1	7	4	5
8	3	1	5	6	9	2	7	4
6	4	5	3	7	2	1	8	9
2	7	9	4	1	8	5	3	6

494

9	3	1	8	6	4	2	7	5
2	7	5	9	3	1	6	8	4
8	4	6	7	5	2	9	3	1
4	9	7	1	2	6	3	5	8
6	8	3	4	9	5	1	2	7
5	1	2	3	7	8	4	9	6
7	6	9	5	4	3	8	1	2
1	5	4	2	8	9	7	6	3
3	2	8	6	1	7	5	4	9

495

2	6	8	4	3	5	1	9	7
4	3	5	9	7	1	2	8	6
7	9	1	6	2	8	3	5	4
8	5	9	3	1	7	4	6	2
6	2	7	5	4	9	8	3	1
3	1	4	8	6	2	9	7	5
9	8	2	1	5	6	7	4	3
5	7	3	2	8	4	6	1	9
1	4	6	7	9	3	5	2	8

496

6	2	3	1	7	8	4	5	9
7	8	5	9	4	2	1	3	6
1	9	4	3	5	6	7	2	8
3	7	8	4	2	9	6	1	5
9	4	2	5	6	1	8	7	3
5	6	1	8	3	7	2	9	4
8	5	6	7	1	3	9	4	2
4	1	9	2	8	5	3	6	7
2	3	7	6	9	4	5	8	1

497

5	1	8	3	6	7	2	9	4
4	7	9	2	1	5	3	8	6
6	2	3	4	8	9	1	5	7
8	4	6	5	2	3	9	7	1
1	5	7	8	9	6	4	3	2
9	3	2	1	7	4	5	6	8
2	9	1	7	5	8	6	4	3
3	8	5	6	4	1	7	2	9
7	6	4	9	3	2	8	1	5

498

2	7	9	8	4	3	6	5	1
1	5	6	9	7	2	4	3	8
4	3	8	5	1	6	2	9	7
6	1	2	4	3	5	8	7	9
5	9	3	6	8	7	1	2	4
8	4	7	1	2	9	5	6	3
7	2	1	3	5	8	9	4	6
3	6	4	2	9	1	7	8	5
9	8	5	7	6	4	3	1	2

499

4	5	9	8	7	3	1	6	2
2	6	8	9	1	5	7	3	4
7	3	1	4	2	6	9	8	5
9	1	5	7	8	2	6	4	3
6	2	7	5	3	4	8	9	1
3	8	4	1	6	9	5	2	7
1	9	6	3	4	7	2	5	8
8	4	2	6	5	1	3	7	9
5	7	3	2	9	8	4	1	6

500

7	2	8	5	3	4	1	9	6
1	5	9	7	8	6	2	4	3
6	3	4	9	2	1	7	8	5
5	9	3	4	6	2	8	1	7
8	4	7	1	5	9	6	3	2
2	6	1	3	7	8	4	5	9
3	7	2	8	4	5	9	6	1
9	8	6	2	1	3	5	7	4
4	1	5	6	9	7	3	2	8

501

4	7	6	1	9	3	8	2	5
9	3	5	4	8	2	7	6	1
2	8	1	6	5	7	3	4	9
3	9	4	5	6	8	1	7	2
8	1	7	9	2	4	6	5	3
6	5	2	3	7	1	4	9	8
7	6	3	2	1	9	5	8	4
1	2	8	7	4	5	9	3	6
5	4	9	8	3	6	2	1	7

502

8	1	6	2	9	5	3	4	7
2	5	7	8	4	3	9	6	1
4	9	3	7	6	1	5	2	8
1	3	4	5	2	7	6	8	9
7	6	8	3	1	9	2	5	4
9	2	5	6	8	4	7	1	3
3	7	2	1	5	8	4	9	6
6	8	9	4	7	2	1	3	5
5	4	1	9	3	6	8	7	2

503

6	9	3	5	2	1	7	4	8
8	2	4	3	6	7	9	5	1
1	5	7	4	9	8	3	6	2
9	7	1	6	5	2	4	8	3
2	8	5	7	4	3	6	1	9
3	4	6	1	8	9	5	2	7
4	1	9	2	7	6	8	3	5
5	3	8	9	1	4	2	7	6
7	6	2	8	3	5	1	9	4

504

5	4	7	2	9	8	6	1	3
9	1	8	7	3	6	4	5	2
3	6	2	4	1	5	8	9	7
1	2	4	3	6	9	7	8	5
7	5	3	1	8	2	9	6	4
6	8	9	5	4	7	2	3	1
2	3	6	9	7	1	5	4	8
4	9	5	8	2	3	1	7	6
8	7	1	6	5	4	3	2	9

505

2	1	6	8	9	3	4	7	5
4	5	8	7	2	1	6	3	9
7	9	3	4	5	6	8	1	2
9	3	1	6	7	4	5	2	8
5	4	7	1	8	2	3	9	6
8	6	2	9	3	5	1	4	7
1	2	4	5	6	9	7	8	3
3	8	5	2	1	7	9	6	4
6	7	9	3	4	8	2	5	1

506

8	4	1	9	6	3	2	7	5
3	9	6	2	5	7	4	8	1
5	2	7	8	1	4	3	6	9
1	7	2	3	4	5	8	9	6
4	3	5	6	8	9	1	2	7
9	6	8	7	2	1	5	4	3
2	1	3	4	9	6	7	5	8
7	8	9	5	3	2	6	1	4
6	5	4	1	7	8	9	3	2

507

7	4	6	3	2	8	5	1	9
8	2	9	1	4	5	7	3	6
1	3	5	9	6	7	2	4	8
4	9	2	6	7	3	8	5	1
6	5	1	8	9	2	4	7	3
3	7	8	5	1	4	9	6	2
9	8	4	7	3	6	1	2	5
5	6	7	2	8	1	3	9	4
2	1	3	4	5	9	6	8	7

508

9	5	7	6	2	1	3	4	8
4	2	8	3	7	5	1	6	9
1	6	3	9	4	8	5	7	2
5	1	2	4	6	9	7	8	3
8	7	6	1	3	2	4	9	5
3	4	9	5	8	7	6	2	1
2	3	1	7	9	4	8	5	6
7	9	5	8	1	6	2	3	4
6	8	4	2	5	3	9	1	7

509

3	1	7	2	9	8	5	4	6
6	5	8	1	7	4	3	2	9
9	2	4	5	3	6	7	8	1
1	9	3	7	6	2	4	5	8
7	6	2	8	4	5	9	1	3
4	8	5	9	1	3	6	7	2
5	7	1	6	2	9	8	3	4
2	3	9	4	8	7	1	6	5
8	4	6	3	5	1	2	9	7

510

6	1	2	3	7	4	5	9	8
3	7	9	1	5	8	6	2	4
5	4	8	2	6	9	3	1	7
2	9	5	8	4	6	7	3	1
7	6	1	9	2	3	8	4	5
4	8	3	5	1	7	2	6	9
9	3	6	7	8	1	4	5	2
1	5	7	4	3	2	9	8	6
8	2	4	6	9	5	1	7	3

511

2	7	5	3	8	6	1	4	9
6	3	1	2	9	4	7	8	5
8	9	4	5	1	7	6	2	3
7	8	6	9	2	3	5	1	4
4	1	3	7	6	5	2	9	8
9	5	2	1	4	8	3	7	6
5	2	7	8	3	9	4	6	1
1	4	8	6	5	2	9	3	7
3	6	9	4	7	1	8	5	2

512

7	6	9	2	5	4	3	8	1
5	8	2	7	3	1	4	6	9
3	1	4	6	9	8	7	2	5
4	5	6	3	8	7	9	1	2
2	9	7	4	1	5	8	3	6
8	3	1	9	2	6	5	7	4
6	2	8	5	7	9	1	4	3
9	7	3	1	4	2	6	5	8
1	4	5	8	6	3	2	9	7

513

2	4	9	6	8	7	1	3	5
1	7	5	4	9	3	6	8	2
8	6	3	5	2	1	4	9	7
5	8	1	3	4	2	7	6	9
7	9	6	1	5	8	2	4	3
4	3	2	9	7	6	8	5	1
6	5	8	7	1	9	3	2	4
9	2	7	8	3	4	5	1	6
3	1	4	2	6	5	9	7	8

514

6	3	8	9	1	7	5	4	2
1	7	4	8	2	5	6	9	3
5	2	9	4	3	6	7	1	8
7	5	2	3	6	9	1	8	4
4	8	1	7	5	2	9	3	6
3	9	6	1	8	4	2	5	7
2	1	3	5	7	8	4	6	9
9	6	5	2	4	3	8	7	1
8	4	7	6	9	1	3	2	5

515

1	9	5	2	8	7	3	6	4
6	3	4	1	9	5	8	2	7
8	2	7	3	4	6	5	1	9
9	8	2	6	7	4	1	5	3
7	5	3	9	1	2	6	4	8
4	1	6	5	3	8	9	7	2
2	6	9	4	5	3	7	8	1
3	4	8	7	6	1	2	9	5
5	7	1	8	2	9	4	3	6

516

4	7	6	5	1	3	9	2	8
1	3	9	2	4	8	5	6	7
5	2	8	7	9	6	1	4	3
6	5	2	3	8	7	4	9	1
9	4	3	6	5	1	8	7	2
7	8	1	9	2	4	3	5	6
3	1	7	4	6	5	2	8	9
8	9	5	1	7	2	6	3	4
2	6	4	8	3	9	7	1	5

517

8	7	2	4	6	5	1	9	3
5	6	1	8	3	9	4	7	2
3	9	4	7	1	2	8	5	6
6	8	3	9	5	4	7	2	1
4	1	9	6	2	7	5	3	8
2	5	7	1	8	3	9	6	4
7	4	6	3	9	1	2	8	5
1	3	5	2	7	8	6	4	9
9	2	8	5	4	6	3	1	7

518

8	2	5	4	9	3	7	6	1
7	1	4	2	8	6	5	3	9
9	6	3	7	5	1	4	8	2
4	5	6	9	2	8	1	7	3
3	8	9	5	1	7	2	4	6
1	7	2	6	3	4	9	5	8
2	4	8	3	7	9	6	1	5
6	9	1	8	4	5	3	2	7
5	3	7	1	6	2	8	9	4

519

8	6	9	2	5	1	3	4	7
5	2	4	7	3	8	1	9	6
1	3	7	4	6	9	2	5	8
3	8	6	9	7	2	4	1	5
4	1	5	6	8	3	7	2	9
9	7	2	5	1	4	6	8	3
6	5	1	8	2	7	9	3	4
2	9	8	3	4	6	5	7	1
7	4	3	1	9	5	8	6	2

520

4	6	1	3	7	5	9	2	8
5	7	8	9	2	6	1	4	3
3	9	2	4	1	8	6	7	5
1	8	7	2	6	9	3	5	4
2	3	6	5	4	1	7	8	9
9	4	5	7	8	3	2	6	1
7	1	4	8	9	2	5	3	6
6	2	3	1	5	4	8	9	7
8	5	9	6	3	7	4	1	2

521

2	6	5	8	3	9	7	1	4
4	8	3	6	1	7	2	5	9
9	7	1	5	4	2	3	6	8
7	3	4	1	9	5	6	8	2
1	2	9	4	6	8	5	3	7
8	5	6	2	7	3	4	9	1
5	1	2	3	8	4	9	7	6
6	4	7	9	5	1	8	2	3
3	9	8	7	2	6	1	4	5

522

3	9	7	8	1	6	2	5	4
2	8	5	9	4	3	7	6	1
1	6	4	5	7	2	3	8	9
5	7	3	4	8	9	1	2	6
9	1	6	2	3	7	8	4	5
4	2	8	1	6	5	9	7	3
8	4	9	7	5	1	6	3	2
7	3	2	6	9	4	5	1	8
6	5	1	3	2	8	4	9	7

523

8	7	3	6	1	5	9	2	4
2	4	5	9	8	3	6	1	7
9	6	1	2	4	7	8	3	5
1	9	7	8	6	4	2	5	3
4	2	8	5	3	1	7	9	6
5	3	6	7	9	2	1	4	8
7	8	2	3	5	9	4	6	1
3	1	9	4	7	6	5	8	2
6	5	4	1	2	8	3	7	9

524

2	7	5	1	9	8	3	6	4
6	9	8	5	3	4	7	1	2
4	3	1	7	2	6	9	5	8
7	8	3	9	1	2	6	4	5
9	1	2	4	6	5	8	7	3
5	4	6	3	8	7	1	2	9
8	6	7	2	5	9	4	3	1
1	2	4	8	7	3	5	9	6
3	5	9	6	4	1	2	8	7

525

6	8	9	4	1	7	5	2	3
4	3	2	6	9	5	8	1	7
5	7	1	2	8	3	6	9	4
2	9	6	1	7	4	3	8	5
8	5	3	9	6	2	4	7	1
1	4	7	5	3	8	9	6	2
3	6	5	7	2	9	1	4	8
9	2	8	3	4	1	7	5	6
7	1	4	8	5	6	2	3	9

526

8	1	9	5	4	6	2	7	3
3	6	4	8	2	7	1	9	5
5	7	2	9	1	3	6	8	4
1	4	6	7	3	9	8	5	2
7	9	5	1	8	2	4	3	6
2	8	3	4	6	5	9	1	7
6	5	8	3	9	4	7	2	1
4	3	1	2	7	8	5	6	9
9	2	7	6	5	1	3	4	8

527

2	3	7	6	4	9	8	1	5
9	6	1	8	2	5	3	4	7
5	4	8	3	7	1	9	2	6
8	9	3	7	1	4	6	5	2
7	5	4	9	6	2	1	3	8
1	2	6	5	8	3	4	7	9
4	8	5	1	9	7	2	6	3
6	7	2	4	3	8	5	9	1
3	1	9	2	5	6	7	8	4

528

4	1	6	5	7	3	9	8	2
9	3	5	1	2	8	6	7	4
8	2	7	6	9	4	5	3	1
6	7	2	4	3	5	8	1	9
5	9	1	7	8	2	3	4	6
3	8	4	9	1	6	7	2	5
2	4	9	8	5	7	1	6	3
7	5	3	2	6	1	4	9	8
1	6	8	3	4	9	2	5	7

529

5	1	3	8	9	7	6	4	2
2	8	7	3	4	6	1	9	5
9	6	4	2	5	1	3	8	7
1	2	8	6	7	3	9	5	4
3	4	6	9	2	5	8	7	1
7	5	9	1	8	4	2	3	6
8	3	5	7	1	2	4	6	9
4	9	1	5	6	8	7	2	3
6	7	2	4	3	9	5	1	8

530

5	9	3	4	7	6	8	2	1
8	1	6	2	5	9	7	4	3
7	4	2	1	3	8	6	5	9
3	7	8	9	6	2	5	1	4
9	2	1	8	4	5	3	6	7
6	5	4	7	1	3	9	8	2
4	8	5	3	9	1	2	7	6
2	3	7	6	8	4	1	9	5
1	6	9	5	2	7	4	3	8

531

6	4	2	7	3	5	9	1	8
8	5	1	2	6	9	7	4	3
3	9	7	1	8	4	2	6	5
1	8	6	4	2	7	3	5	9
9	2	3	6	5	1	4	8	7
4	7	5	3	9	8	1	2	6
5	6	4	9	1	3	8	7	2
7	3	8	5	4	2	6	9	1
2	1	9	8	7	6	5	3	4

532

4	3	8	9	1	5	2	7	6
9	5	1	6	7	2	8	3	4
6	7	2	8	4	3	5	1	9
3	6	4	2	5	9	1	8	7
2	1	9	4	8	7	3	6	5
5	8	7	1	3	6	9	4	2
8	2	3	5	6	4	7	9	1
7	4	5	3	9	1	6	2	8
1	9	6	7	2	8	4	5	3

533

7	4	3	9	2	5	1	6	8
8	5	6	3	7	1	9	4	2
1	2	9	8	4	6	3	5	7
4	1	7	5	8	3	2	9	6
9	3	2	4	6	7	8	1	5
5	6	8	2	1	9	4	7	3
6	9	4	7	3	2	5	8	1
2	8	1	6	5	4	7	3	9
3	7	5	1	9	8	6	2	4

534

3	6	5	7	4	8	2	9	1
1	2	8	3	6	9	4	5	7
9	7	4	1	5	2	6	8	3
7	1	6	9	2	3	5	4	8
2	8	3	5	7	4	1	6	9
5	4	9	6	8	1	3	7	2
8	9	1	4	3	6	7	2	5
4	3	7	2	9	5	8	1	6
6	5	2	8	1	7	9	3	4

535

9	2	1	7	4	8	5	6	3
4	6	8	9	3	5	7	2	1
5	3	7	2	1	6	4	9	8
1	4	6	8	5	9	2	3	7
8	9	5	3	2	7	1	4	6
3	7	2	1	6	4	8	5	9
6	1	9	4	7	2	3	8	5
2	8	3	5	9	1	6	7	4
7	5	4	6	8	3	9	1	2

536

2	1	4	5	6	3	7	8	9
3	9	5	4	7	8	1	2	6
7	8	6	1	9	2	3	5	4
8	6	1	2	4	5	9	3	7
4	3	7	6	8	9	2	1	5
5	2	9	3	1	7	6	4	8
1	7	2	9	5	4	8	6	3
9	4	3	8	2	6	5	7	1
6	5	8	7	3	1	4	9	2

537

4	7	9	3	2	1	8	5	6
3	2	1	6	5	8	9	4	7
8	6	5	9	4	7	1	2	3
1	8	7	2	6	3	5	9	4
5	4	3	7	1	9	6	8	2
2	9	6	5	8	4	7	3	1
7	1	2	8	3	5	4	6	9
9	3	8	4	7	6	2	1	5
6	5	4	1	9	2	3	7	8

538

4	6	9	5	3	8	2	1	7
5	1	2	9	4	7	3	8	6
8	3	7	6	1	2	4	9	5
7	4	6	8	5	9	1	2	3
3	9	1	7	2	4	5	6	8
2	5	8	3	6	1	9	7	4
9	7	5	2	8	3	6	4	1
6	2	4	1	7	5	8	3	9
1	8	3	4	9	6	7	5	2

539

4	9	7	6	5	1	2	3	8
3	2	8	4	7	9	1	6	5
6	5	1	3	8	2	4	7	9
7	4	3	5	2	6	9	8	1
5	1	2	8	9	3	6	4	7
9	8	6	1	4	7	5	2	3
2	3	4	7	1	5	8	9	6
1	6	9	2	3	8	7	5	4
8	7	5	9	6	4	3	1	2

540

8	2	4	3	7	1	5	6	9
6	3	5	9	4	2	1	8	7
1	7	9	6	8	5	3	2	4
4	6	7	8	3	9	2	1	5
3	9	2	1	5	7	8	4	6
5	1	8	2	6	4	7	9	3
9	4	1	7	2	3	6	5	8
7	5	6	4	1	8	9	3	2
2	8	3	5	9	6	4	7	1

541

6	3	9	8	4	2	1	7	5
8	4	7	9	1	5	3	6	2
1	2	5	3	7	6	4	8	9
9	1	3	6	8	7	2	5	4
5	7	6	4	2	9	8	3	1
4	8	2	1	5	3	7	9	6
7	9	1	2	6	8	5	4	3
3	5	4	7	9	1	6	2	8
2	6	8	5	3	4	9	1	7

542

3	5	4	7	1	8	6	9	2
8	2	7	4	9	6	5	1	3
1	6	9	3	5	2	4	8	7
9	7	3	1	6	5	2	4	8
4	1	2	8	7	3	9	6	5
5	8	6	9	2	4	7	3	1
2	9	5	6	3	1	8	7	4
6	4	1	5	8	7	3	2	9
7	3	8	2	4	9	1	5	6

543

7	1	3	4	6	5	2	8	9
9	5	6	2	3	8	4	1	7
2	4	8	1	9	7	3	5	6
6	7	4	5	8	3	1	9	2
8	2	5	6	1	9	7	4	3
1	3	9	7	2	4	8	6	5
5	8	7	9	4	2	6	3	1
3	6	2	8	5	1	9	7	4
4	9	1	3	7	6	5	2	8

544

4	6	8	7	1	9	5	2	3
9	1	7	3	5	2	8	6	4
2	5	3	4	8	6	1	7	9
7	3	4	5	9	1	6	8	2
8	9	1	6	2	4	7	3	5
5	2	6	8	7	3	9	4	1
6	4	9	1	3	8	2	5	7
3	7	2	9	6	5	4	1	8
1	8	5	2	4	7	3	9	6

545

1	4	2	5	7	6	3	8	9
7	3	6	4	8	9	5	2	1
9	8	5	3	2	1	7	4	6
2	9	7	1	5	4	6	3	8
6	1	4	8	9	3	2	7	5
8	5	3	2	6	7	9	1	4
4	2	1	9	3	5	8	6	7
3	6	9	7	1	8	4	5	2
5	7	8	6	4	2	1	9	3

546

1	8	7	5	9	6	3	2	4
4	6	2	3	1	7	5	9	8
5	3	9	8	2	4	1	7	6
8	9	5	6	4	2	7	3	1
7	2	4	1	5	3	6	8	9
3	1	6	7	8	9	2	4	5
9	5	3	4	7	1	8	6	2
2	7	1	9	6	8	4	5	3
6	4	8	2	3	5	9	1	7

547

5	7	1	9	3	6	4	2	8
4	2	3	5	8	1	6	7	9
6	8	9	7	2	4	3	5	1
9	4	6	8	1	7	2	3	5
3	5	7	6	9	2	1	8	4
2	1	8	3	4	5	7	9	6
8	3	2	4	6	9	5	1	7
7	9	4	1	5	3	8	6	2
1	6	5	2	7	8	9	4	3

548

3	7	9	2	8	4	5	6	1
2	1	5	3	7	6	8	4	9
8	6	4	9	1	5	2	7	3
6	3	8	5	4	7	9	1	2
1	5	7	6	2	9	4	3	8
9	4	2	8	3	1	7	5	6
7	8	1	4	9	3	6	2	5
5	9	3	7	6	2	1	8	4
4	2	6	1	5	8	3	9	7

549

8	5	9	2	4	1	6	7	3
4	2	6	5	7	3	8	1	9
3	1	7	8	9	6	4	5	2
7	6	2	3	5	8	9	4	1
9	8	1	4	2	7	3	6	5
5	4	3	1	6	9	7	2	8
6	3	5	7	8	2	1	9	4
1	7	4	9	3	5	2	8	6
2	9	8	6	1	4	5	3	7

550

2	9	8	1	3	4	6	5	7
7	4	6	5	9	8	2	1	3
1	3	5	6	7	2	4	8	9
9	6	3	8	1	7	5	4	2
8	1	7	2	4	5	3	9	6
4	5	2	3	6	9	1	7	8
3	2	9	7	5	1	8	6	4
5	8	4	9	2	6	7	3	1
6	7	1	4	8	3	9	2	5

551

8	2	4	7	6	1	5	3	9
5	6	7	3	2	9	1	4	8
3	1	9	4	8	5	7	6	2
2	8	5	9	4	6	3	7	1
1	9	3	5	7	2	6	8	4
7	4	6	8	1	3	9	2	5
6	5	8	1	3	4	2	9	7
9	7	2	6	5	8	4	1	3
4	3	1	2	9	7	8	5	6

552

4	1	8	3	7	6	2	9	5
3	2	6	5	4	9	7	8	1
9	7	5	2	8	1	4	3	6
8	3	2	6	9	7	5	1	4
6	9	7	4	1	5	3	2	8
1	5	4	8	2	3	9	6	7
5	4	1	9	3	8	6	7	2
2	8	3	7	6	4	1	5	9
7	6	9	1	5	2	8	4	3

553

6	3	5	4	2	1	8	9	7
4	1	7	9	6	8	2	3	5
9	2	8	7	5	3	1	6	4
1	8	3	2	7	4	6	5	9
7	9	2	5	3	6	4	1	8
5	6	4	8	1	9	3	7	2
3	4	9	6	8	5	7	2	1
8	7	6	1	9	2	5	4	3
2	5	1	3	4	7	9	8	6

554

6	9	7	5	1	2	3	4	8
5	8	2	9	4	3	6	1	7
4	1	3	6	7	8	9	2	5
1	3	5	8	9	6	4	7	2
9	7	6	4	2	5	1	8	3
2	4	8	1	3	7	5	6	9
8	5	4	2	6	9	7	3	1
7	2	1	3	5	4	8	9	6
3	6	9	7	8	1	2	5	4

555

5	8	6	9	3	1	2	4	7
2	4	3	5	8	7	9	6	1
9	1	7	2	6	4	5	3	8
1	2	5	6	4	8	3	7	9
6	9	8	3	7	2	4	1	5
7	3	4	1	9	5	6	8	2
8	6	1	4	5	9	7	2	3
3	5	2	7	1	6	8	9	4
4	7	9	8	2	3	1	5	6

556

3	6	1	2	8	9	5	4	7
8	5	9	7	4	6	3	1	2
7	4	2	3	1	5	9	6	8
2	8	4	5	3	1	7	9	6
1	3	6	8	9	7	2	5	4
9	7	5	4	6	2	1	8	3
6	1	3	9	2	8	4	7	5
4	9	7	6	5	3	8	2	1
5	2	8	1	7	4	6	3	9

557

4	1	8	6	9	5	2	7	3
3	9	2	4	1	7	5	8	6
7	6	5	3	2	8	4	9	1
1	4	3	9	6	2	7	5	8
5	8	9	1	7	4	6	3	2
2	7	6	8	5	3	1	4	9
6	5	7	2	3	9	8	1	4
8	3	1	7	4	6	9	2	5
9	2	4	5	8	1	3	6	7

558

3	1	5	4	2	8	9	7	6
2	8	9	7	5	6	1	4	3
6	4	7	1	9	3	8	5	2
9	3	1	8	4	2	5	6	7
4	2	6	5	7	1	3	9	8
7	5	8	3	6	9	4	2	1
5	6	3	9	8	7	2	1	4
8	7	4	2	1	5	6	3	9
1	9	2	6	3	4	7	8	5

559

3	8	1	6	9	2	4	5	7
5	9	6	1	7	4	8	2	3
7	2	4	3	8	5	1	9	6
9	3	8	5	2	1	7	6	4
2	4	7	9	6	3	5	1	8
6	1	5	7	4	8	9	3	2
8	7	3	2	5	9	6	4	1
4	5	2	8	1	6	3	7	9
1	6	9	4	3	7	2	8	5

560

3	9	7	6	4	2	5	8	1
8	2	4	3	1	5	9	6	7
5	1	6	7	9	8	2	4	3
4	8	2	1	7	9	3	5	6
9	6	5	2	3	4	7	1	8
7	3	1	8	5	6	4	9	2
6	7	9	4	8	3	1	2	5
1	4	8	5	2	7	6	3	9
2	5	3	9	6	1	8	7	4

561

7	9	2	6	5	4	8	3	1
4	5	3	8	9	1	7	2	6
8	6	1	2	7	3	5	9	4
2	4	7	9	8	5	6	1	3
1	8	5	3	6	2	9	4	7
9	3	6	1	4	7	2	5	8
6	7	4	5	3	9	1	8	2
5	2	8	4	1	6	3	7	9
3	1	9	7	2	8	4	6	5

562

9	8	6	4	5	7	2	1	3
5	4	1	8	3	2	6	7	9
2	7	3	6	1	9	8	5	4
3	9	8	5	7	1	4	6	2
7	1	2	3	6	4	9	8	5
6	5	4	9	2	8	7	3	1
8	6	5	2	4	3	1	9	7
4	3	7	1	9	6	5	2	8
1	2	9	7	8	5	3	4	6

563

5	3	8	1	7	9	2	6	4
1	9	4	5	2	6	8	3	7
7	6	2	4	8	3	9	1	5
9	1	3	8	4	5	6	7	2
2	5	7	3	6	1	4	8	9
4	8	6	2	9	7	1	5	3
6	4	5	9	3	8	7	2	1
8	2	1	7	5	4	3	9	6
3	7	9	6	1	2	5	4	8

564

2	6	7	3	5	1	8	9	4
1	8	9	4	7	6	5	3	2
5	4	3	2	8	9	6	1	7
8	5	4	9	6	2	1	7	3
9	3	1	7	4	8	2	5	6
6	7	2	5	1	3	9	4	8
3	2	6	1	9	7	4	8	5
7	9	5	8	2	4	3	6	1
4	1	8	6	3	5	7	2	9

565

6	4	7	9	8	3	5	2	1
2	1	3	6	5	4	7	9	8
8	5	9	7	2	1	4	6	3
5	2	6	8	3	7	1	4	9
7	8	4	5	1	9	6	3	2
9	3	1	2	4	6	8	7	5
1	7	8	3	6	2	9	5	4
4	6	2	1	9	5	3	8	7
3	9	5	4	7	8	2	1	6

566

7	4	9	5	2	8	6	1	3
3	5	6	1	7	4	2	8	9
1	8	2	6	3	9	5	4	7
2	6	8	9	4	7	1	3	5
4	9	7	3	1	5	8	6	2
5	3	1	2	8	6	9	7	4
8	1	5	4	9	3	7	2	6
9	2	3	7	6	1	4	5	8
6	7	4	8	5	2	3	9	1

567

4	2	5	8	7	9	6	1	3
8	3	1	6	5	2	9	4	7
6	9	7	1	3	4	8	5	2
9	4	6	2	8	7	1	3	5
3	5	2	4	6	1	7	9	8
1	7	8	3	9	5	2	6	4
5	6	3	7	1	8	4	2	9
2	8	9	5	4	6	3	7	1
7	1	4	9	2	3	5	8	6

568

2	7	8	9	6	4	1	3	5
1	9	6	3	8	5	4	7	2
3	5	4	7	1	2	6	8	9
9	8	5	4	3	1	7	2	6
6	3	2	5	7	9	8	1	4
7	4	1	8	2	6	9	5	3
8	6	3	2	4	7	5	9	1
4	2	9	1	5	8	3	6	7
5	1	7	6	9	3	2	4	8

569

2	9	3	5	1	4	8	6	7
7	5	6	9	3	8	1	2	4
8	4	1	6	7	2	5	9	3
3	8	4	1	6	7	9	5	2
5	6	7	2	9	3	4	8	1
1	2	9	4	8	5	7	3	6
6	1	2	8	4	9	3	7	5
9	3	5	7	2	1	6	4	8
4	7	8	3	5	6	2	1	9

570

9	2	4	8	6	3	1	7	5
3	7	6	1	5	9	2	4	8
5	8	1	7	4	2	3	9	6
7	9	8	2	3	6	5	1	4
1	3	5	9	8	4	6	2	7
4	6	2	5	1	7	9	8	3
6	4	9	3	7	1	8	5	2
8	1	3	4	2	5	7	6	9
2	5	7	6	9	8	4	3	1

571

1	4	9	3	5	7	6	8	2
7	3	6	1	2	8	4	5	9
2	5	8	6	4	9	3	7	1
3	8	2	4	1	6	7	9	5
4	1	5	7	9	2	8	6	3
9	6	7	8	3	5	1	2	4
6	9	3	5	8	1	2	4	7
5	7	4	2	6	3	9	1	8
8	2	1	9	7	4	5	3	6

572

5	2	7	3	9	8	4	1	6
8	3	1	7	6	4	5	9	2
4	9	6	5	1	2	3	7	8
3	4	5	9	8	6	7	2	1
2	1	9	4	7	3	6	8	5
7	6	8	1	2	5	9	4	3
6	5	2	8	4	7	1	3	9
1	7	3	2	5	9	8	6	4
9	8	4	6	3	1	2	5	7

573

3	8	6	9	7	1	4	2	5
4	7	1	5	8	2	6	3	9
2	9	5	6	4	3	7	8	1
6	3	2	7	5	9	8	1	4
5	4	8	2	1	6	3	9	7
9	1	7	8	3	4	5	6	2
1	6	3	4	2	7	9	5	8
7	5	9	1	6	8	2	4	3
8	2	4	3	9	5	1	7	6

574

2	3	7	8	9	6	1	5	4
5	4	8	7	1	3	2	6	9
9	6	1	2	4	5	7	3	8
7	2	4	6	3	9	5	8	1
3	1	5	4	2	8	6	9	7
8	9	6	5	7	1	3	4	2
1	7	3	9	5	4	8	2	6
4	8	2	3	6	7	9	1	5
6	5	9	1	8	2	4	7	3

575

9	8	7	5	1	6	4	2	3
6	2	4	3	9	7	1	5	8
1	3	5	2	8	4	7	9	6
4	9	3	6	2	5	8	1	7
5	1	2	7	3	8	6	4	9
7	6	8	1	4	9	2	3	5
2	5	1	8	6	3	9	7	4
3	4	6	9	7	1	5	8	2
8	7	9	4	5	2	3	6	1

576

7	1	4	3	2	9	8	5	6
6	9	5	1	8	7	4	2	3
8	2	3	4	5	6	1	9	7
1	8	2	7	9	4	6	3	5
9	3	6	5	1	8	7	4	2
5	4	7	6	3	2	9	8	1
4	5	8	2	6	1	3	7	9
3	6	9	8	7	5	2	1	4
2	7	1	9	4	3	5	6	8

577

5	8	9	2	7	3	4	6	1
7	2	1	8	4	6	3	9	5
4	3	6	5	9	1	7	8	2
8	6	3	1	5	4	9	2	7
2	4	5	9	6	7	1	3	8
1	9	7	3	2	8	5	4	6
3	7	2	4	8	5	6	1	9
9	5	4	6	1	2	8	7	3
6	1	8	7	3	9	2	5	4

578

2	8	6	9	3	5	1	4	7
4	1	9	8	7	6	2	3	5
3	7	5	1	2	4	8	9	6
7	6	1	2	9	8	3	5	4
8	3	4	7	5	1	9	6	2
5	9	2	6	4	3	7	1	8
6	5	8	3	1	2	4	7	9
1	2	7	4	6	9	5	8	3
9	4	3	5	8	7	6	2	1

579

6	7	9	5	1	3	2	4	8
2	1	5	7	4	8	9	6	3
4	3	8	2	6	9	1	5	7
1	5	6	9	8	7	4	3	2
9	8	2	3	5	4	6	7	1
7	4	3	6	2	1	8	9	5
3	9	4	1	7	2	5	8	6
5	2	7	8	9	6	3	1	4
8	6	1	4	3	5	7	2	9

580

3	7	5	6	9	8	2	1	4
6	4	2	1	7	3	9	8	5
1	8	9	4	5	2	6	3	7
2	9	1	5	8	6	4	7	3
8	5	3	9	4	7	1	2	6
4	6	7	2	3	1	8	5	9
9	3	4	8	2	5	7	6	1
5	2	6	7	1	9	3	4	8
7	1	8	3	6	4	5	9	2

581

4	1	5	9	2	3	8	7	6
7	6	8	4	1	5	3	9	2
9	3	2	8	6	7	1	4	5
2	8	9	7	4	6	5	3	1
3	5	4	1	8	2	7	6	9
1	7	6	5	3	9	4	2	8
6	9	7	3	5	8	2	1	4
8	2	1	6	7	4	9	5	3
5	4	3	2	9	1	6	8	7

582

8	4	2	6	7	9	1	5	3
6	7	5	4	1	3	8	2	9
9	1	3	5	8	2	6	7	4
1	3	8	2	4	5	9	6	7
7	6	9	1	3	8	2	4	5
2	5	4	7	9	6	3	8	1
4	9	7	8	6	1	5	3	2
3	2	6	9	5	4	7	1	8
5	8	1	3	2	7	4	9	6

583

4	2	6	8	3	1	9	7	5
3	9	8	2	5	7	4	6	1
5	7	1	6	9	4	8	2	3
6	1	7	3	4	9	2	5	8
2	3	4	1	8	5	7	9	6
9	8	5	7	2	6	3	1	4
1	5	2	4	7	3	6	8	9
7	6	3	9	1	8	5	4	2
8	4	9	5	6	2	1	3	7

584

1	3	4	7	5	8	6	9	2
2	7	8	6	1	9	3	5	4
5	9	6	3	2	4	7	1	8
9	2	7	5	8	3	1	4	6
6	5	3	2	4	1	8	7	9
4	8	1	9	7	6	5	2	3
7	4	5	8	3	2	9	6	1
8	6	2	1	9	7	4	3	5
3	1	9	4	6	5	2	8	7

585

2	8	5	9	3	1	4	6	7
6	7	9	8	5	4	1	3	2
3	1	4	6	2	7	9	8	5
9	2	1	3	6	5	8	7	4
8	3	6	7	4	2	5	1	9
5	4	7	1	9	8	3	2	6
4	6	8	5	7	3	2	9	1
1	9	2	4	8	6	7	5	3
7	5	3	2	1	9	6	4	8

586

9	8	2	3	1	5	4	6	7
3	5	6	9	7	4	8	1	2
4	1	7	8	2	6	3	5	9
5	4	1	2	8	7	6	9	3
7	6	3	5	4	9	1	2	8
2	9	8	1	6	3	5	7	4
1	3	9	7	5	8	2	4	6
6	7	5	4	3	2	9	8	1
8	2	4	6	9	1	7	3	5

587

9	6	2	4	8	7	3	1	5
7	1	5	6	2	3	8	9	4
8	3	4	1	5	9	7	6	2
5	7	6	3	9	8	4	2	1
1	2	3	7	4	5	6	8	9
4	9	8	2	1	6	5	3	7
6	8	9	5	7	1	2	4	3
3	4	7	9	6	2	1	5	8
2	5	1	8	3	4	9	7	6

588

3	5	1	7	4	8	6	2	9
9	4	7	2	5	6	3	1	8
8	6	2	9	1	3	7	4	5
4	3	5	6	9	2	1	8	7
2	7	6	1	8	5	9	3	4
1	9	8	4	3	7	5	6	2
5	1	4	8	6	9	2	7	3
7	8	9	3	2	1	4	5	6
6	2	3	5	7	4	8	9	1

589

5	3	7	4	2	9	8	1	6
6	1	2	3	5	8	4	9	7
8	9	4	1	7	6	5	2	3
4	5	3	9	8	2	7	6	1
7	6	8	5	3	1	9	4	2
9	2	1	7	6	4	3	8	5
2	8	5	6	9	3	1	7	4
3	4	6	8	1	7	2	5	9
1	7	9	2	4	5	6	3	8

590

8	1	5	3	4	7	6	2	9
3	6	4	8	2	9	7	1	5
7	2	9	6	5	1	4	8	3
9	7	2	4	1	6	5	3	8
1	4	3	5	7	8	2	9	6
5	8	6	2	9	3	1	4	7
6	3	1	7	8	2	9	5	4
4	9	8	1	6	5	3	7	2
2	5	7	9	3	4	8	6	1

591

6	7	9	3	1	4	5	2	8
8	4	3	6	2	5	9	7	1
1	5	2	9	8	7	3	6	4
5	1	7	8	4	3	2	9	6
4	3	8	2	6	9	1	5	7
2	9	6	7	5	1	8	4	3
7	6	1	5	9	8	4	3	2
3	8	5	4	7	2	6	1	9
9	2	4	1	3	6	7	8	5

592

3	2	1	4	6	7	8	9	5
4	6	9	2	8	5	1	7	3
8	7	5	9	1	3	6	2	4
9	4	3	1	2	8	5	6	7
2	1	8	5	7	6	4	3	9
7	5	6	3	4	9	2	8	1
1	3	4	6	9	2	7	5	8
5	8	2	7	3	1	9	4	6
6	9	7	8	5	4	3	1	2

593

8	2	4	7	1	6	9	5	3
5	7	1	4	9	3	2	8	6
9	6	3	8	2	5	4	7	1
2	1	7	3	4	8	6	9	5
3	9	5	2	6	7	1	4	8
6	4	8	9	5	1	7	3	2
7	3	9	6	8	2	5	1	4
1	8	2	5	7	4	3	6	9
4	5	6	1	3	9	8	2	7

594

9	8	1	7	2	5	3	4	6
3	2	5	9	6	4	8	1	7
7	4	6	8	1	3	9	5	2
2	5	9	6	4	1	7	8	3
4	6	7	2	3	8	5	9	1
1	3	8	5	9	7	2	6	4
6	1	2	3	5	9	4	7	8
5	7	4	1	8	2	6	3	9
8	9	3	4	7	6	1	2	5

595

7	4	9	2	8	5	1	6	3
1	8	2	7	6	3	5	4	9
3	5	6	1	4	9	2	8	7
6	9	1	4	5	7	8	3	2
5	7	8	6	3	2	4	9	1
4	2	3	9	1	8	7	5	6
2	6	5	8	9	1	3	7	4
8	1	4	3	7	6	9	2	5
9	3	7	5	2	4	6	1	8

596

7	1	2	4	8	6	3	5	9
5	6	9	1	2	3	8	7	4
8	3	4	9	7	5	1	6	2
1	5	3	8	9	4	7	2	6
4	2	8	5	6	7	9	3	1
6	9	7	3	1	2	5	4	8
2	7	1	6	5	8	4	9	3
3	8	6	7	4	9	2	1	5
9	4	5	2	3	1	6	8	7

597

7	6	9	1	3	8	4	2	5
3	2	8	6	4	5	7	9	1
5	4	1	7	2	9	6	8	3
2	8	3	5	1	4	9	7	6
1	7	4	9	8	6	3	5	2
6	9	5	2	7	3	8	1	4
8	1	2	4	6	7	5	3	9
4	5	7	3	9	2	1	6	8
9	3	6	8	5	1	2	4	7

598

9	7	4	8	6	1	2	3	5
5	3	1	7	4	2	8	6	9
2	6	8	3	9	5	1	7	4
1	4	5	2	7	3	6	9	8
3	8	6	1	5	9	7	4	2
7	2	9	6	8	4	3	5	1
4	1	2	5	3	6	9	8	7
6	5	7	9	2	8	4	1	3
8	9	3	4	1	7	5	2	6

599

1	4	8	5	3	2	6	7	9
2	6	3	8	7	9	5	4	1
7	9	5	4	6	1	2	3	8
5	3	6	9	1	8	4	2	7
4	8	2	7	5	6	1	9	3
9	1	7	3	2	4	8	5	6
3	5	1	2	8	7	9	6	4
8	2	4	6	9	3	7	1	5
6	7	9	1	4	5	3	8	2

600

8	2	4	5	7	3	1	6	9
7	9	5	8	1	6	4	2	3
6	3	1	9	4	2	7	8	5
9	6	2	3	8	7	5	1	4
5	7	8	1	6	4	3	9	2
4	1	3	2	9	5	8	7	6
2	5	9	7	3	1	6	4	8
3	4	7	6	2	8	9	5	1
1	8	6	4	5	9	2	3	7

601

8	4	1	9	6	5	2	3	7
9	7	2	1	4	3	8	6	5
6	5	3	2	8	7	4	9	1
1	2	4	3	9	6	7	5	8
3	8	9	7	5	2	1	4	6
5	6	7	8	1	4	9	2	3
2	9	6	5	7	1	3	8	4
7	3	5	4	2	8	6	1	9
4	1	8	6	3	9	5	7	2

602

1	3	4	8	7	6	9	5	2
2	9	5	4	3	1	8	6	7
7	8	6	5	2	9	4	3	1
5	2	3	1	9	7	6	4	8
4	6	8	3	5	2	1	7	9
9	7	1	6	8	4	3	2	5
8	5	2	9	4	3	7	1	6
3	1	9	7	6	5	2	8	4
6	4	7	2	1	8	5	9	3

603

1	7	8	6	9	2	4	5	3
5	3	6	4	1	8	2	9	7
4	9	2	7	5	3	6	1	8
3	5	7	2	6	1	9	8	4
9	8	1	5	3	4	7	2	6
6	2	4	8	7	9	5	3	1
8	4	3	9	2	6	1	7	5
2	1	5	3	4	7	8	6	9
7	6	9	1	8	5	3	4	2

604

9	4	3	5	6	2	8	1	7
8	5	6	4	1	7	9	2	3
2	7	1	9	8	3	5	4	6
3	2	7	1	9	5	6	8	4
5	1	8	2	4	6	3	7	9
4	6	9	7	3	8	2	5	1
7	3	5	6	2	1	4	9	8
1	8	4	3	5	9	7	6	2
6	9	2	8	7	4	1	3	5

605

4	1	8	3	9	2	6	7	5
7	9	3	8	5	6	2	4	1
2	5	6	1	4	7	8	9	3
6	3	9	2	8	5	7	1	4
8	2	7	4	3	1	9	5	6
5	4	1	6	7	9	3	2	8
3	6	5	9	2	4	1	8	7
1	7	2	5	6	8	4	3	9
9	8	4	7	1	3	5	6	2

606

2	8	7	1	3	9	4	6	5
3	9	5	6	8	4	1	2	7
4	1	6	5	2	7	9	8	3
7	2	1	3	4	6	8	5	9
9	6	8	7	5	1	2	3	4
5	4	3	8	9	2	7	1	6
1	5	2	4	7	3	6	9	8
6	3	4	9	1	8	5	7	2
8	7	9	2	6	5	3	4	1

607

4	5	9	2	6	1	7	8	3
2	1	8	9	3	7	5	4	6
7	6	3	4	5	8	2	1	9
9	7	1	8	4	2	6	3	5
8	2	5	6	9	3	1	7	4
6	3	4	7	1	5	9	2	8
3	8	7	5	2	9	4	6	1
1	9	6	3	7	4	8	5	2
5	4	2	1	8	6	3	9	7

608

8	6	4	2	9	1	7	5	3
3	7	2	8	4	5	1	6	9
5	1	9	7	6	3	2	4	8
1	9	7	6	5	4	8	3	2
4	5	3	9	8	2	6	7	1
6	2	8	1	3	7	4	9	5
2	3	1	5	7	6	9	8	4
9	4	6	3	2	8	5	1	7
7	8	5	4	1	9	3	2	6

609

7	5	8	9	6	2	3	1	4
9	4	6	1	3	8	2	5	7
3	1	2	5	7	4	9	8	6
8	6	4	7	9	5	1	2	3
1	3	7	2	8	6	4	9	5
2	9	5	4	1	3	6	7	8
6	8	1	3	2	7	5	4	9
4	7	9	6	5	1	8	3	2
5	2	3	8	4	9	7	6	1

610

9	7	2	5	4	1	3	6	8
3	6	8	7	9	2	1	5	4
4	5	1	3	6	8	7	2	9
1	8	3	2	5	6	4	9	7
7	9	5	8	1	4	2	3	6
2	4	6	9	7	3	5	8	1
8	3	9	1	2	7	6	4	5
5	1	4	6	3	9	8	7	2
6	2	7	4	8	5	9	1	3

611

8	9	3	5	1	4	6	7	2
2	4	6	9	7	3	1	8	5
1	5	7	2	8	6	3	4	9
3	7	1	8	2	9	4	5	6
4	8	9	6	5	1	7	2	3
5	6	2	4	3	7	8	9	1
6	3	8	7	9	5	2	1	4
7	1	5	3	4	2	9	6	8
9	2	4	1	6	8	5	3	7

612

1	2	8	7	5	3	9	4	6
9	3	4	2	1	6	5	8	7
7	5	6	8	9	4	2	3	1
8	1	2	9	3	5	7	6	4
5	7	9	4	6	8	3	1	2
6	4	3	1	7	2	8	9	5
4	9	1	3	2	7	6	5	8
3	6	7	5	8	1	4	2	9
2	8	5	6	4	9	1	7	3

613

9	1	5	3	8	6	7	4	2
4	7	8	2	5	9	1	3	6
3	6	2	7	4	1	8	5	9
5	9	3	6	1	4	2	8	7
7	2	4	9	3	8	6	1	5
6	8	1	5	2	7	3	9	4
1	4	9	8	7	2	5	6	3
8	3	7	4	6	5	9	2	1
2	5	6	1	9	3	4	7	8

614

5	7	6	1	2	3	9	4	8
3	1	2	9	4	8	6	7	5
8	4	9	7	5	6	3	1	2
4	2	8	6	1	9	7	5	3
9	3	1	4	7	5	2	8	6
7	6	5	3	8	2	1	9	4
1	5	4	2	6	7	8	3	9
2	9	7	8	3	4	5	6	1
6	8	3	5	9	1	4	2	7

615

1	3	4	2	6	9	8	7	5
2	5	9	1	7	8	4	3	6
8	7	6	3	4	5	9	1	2
5	1	2	9	8	7	6	4	3
3	6	7	4	5	1	2	9	8
9	4	8	6	2	3	1	5	7
6	9	5	8	3	4	7	2	1
4	8	3	7	1	2	5	6	9
7	2	1	5	9	6	3	8	4

616

4	6	3	7	2	1	5	8	9
2	8	1	3	5	9	4	6	7
5	7	9	4	8	6	2	3	1
9	2	4	8	7	3	6	1	5
6	1	8	2	9	5	7	4	3
3	5	7	6	1	4	8	9	2
8	3	2	9	4	7	1	5	6
1	4	6	5	3	2	9	7	8
7	9	5	1	6	8	3	2	4

617

6	1	3	9	5	7	2	4	8
2	9	7	4	1	8	6	5	3
4	5	8	2	6	3	7	1	9
8	7	1	5	9	6	3	2	4
9	3	6	8	2	4	5	7	1
5	4	2	7	3	1	8	9	6
7	6	4	1	8	2	9	3	5
1	8	5	3	7	9	4	6	2
3	2	9	6	4	5	1	8	7

618

7	2	1	3	9	6	4	8	5
4	3	5	8	2	1	6	9	7
9	6	8	7	5	4	2	1	3
8	4	9	2	3	5	1	7	6
3	7	6	1	8	9	5	2	4
1	5	2	4	6	7	9	3	8
5	9	3	6	7	2	8	4	1
2	8	4	5	1	3	7	6	9
6	1	7	9	4	8	3	5	2

619

7	6	8	2	5	1	3	9	4
1	3	2	4	7	9	6	8	5
9	4	5	8	6	3	2	7	1
4	2	1	7	8	5	9	3	6
8	9	3	6	1	4	5	2	7
5	7	6	9	3	2	1	4	8
2	1	9	5	4	8	7	6	3
3	8	7	1	9	6	4	5	2
6	5	4	3	2	7	8	1	9

620

6	4	2	5	7	8	9	1	3
5	7	9	1	3	2	6	8	4
8	1	3	4	6	9	5	2	7
4	5	8	2	9	3	7	6	1
7	3	1	6	8	5	2	4	9
9	2	6	7	4	1	3	5	8
3	9	5	8	2	4	1	7	6
2	8	7	9	1	6	4	3	5
1	6	4	3	5	7	8	9	2

621

9	6	3	4	2	8	5	1	7
1	2	4	5	3	7	8	6	9
5	7	8	1	6	9	2	3	4
4	5	7	2	1	3	6	9	8
6	8	1	9	7	4	3	2	5
3	9	2	6	8	5	4	7	1
8	4	6	7	9	2	1	5	3
7	1	5	3	4	6	9	8	2
2	3	9	8	5	1	7	4	6

622

8	1	9	4	5	2	3	6	7
2	4	3	8	7	6	5	1	9
7	6	5	1	9	3	8	4	2
1	8	6	3	2	9	7	5	4
5	7	4	6	1	8	9	2	3
3	9	2	5	4	7	6	8	1
4	5	7	9	6	1	2	3	8
6	2	8	7	3	4	1	9	5
9	3	1	2	8	5	4	7	6

623

4	2	7	3	6	5	9	8	1
6	3	8	2	9	1	7	4	5
9	1	5	4	7	8	6	3	2
8	6	9	7	5	3	2	1	4
3	4	2	1	8	9	5	7	6
7	5	1	6	4	2	3	9	8
5	9	4	8	2	7	1	6	3
1	7	6	5	3	4	8	2	9
2	8	3	9	1	6	4	5	7

624

1	2	3	9	6	4	7	5	8
5	9	6	7	2	8	1	4	3
4	7	8	1	5	3	9	2	6
6	4	5	2	3	1	8	9	7
3	8	2	6	9	7	5	1	4
9	1	7	8	4	5	6	3	2
7	3	1	4	8	9	2	6	5
8	6	4	5	1	2	3	7	9
2	5	9	3	7	6	4	8	1

625

5	3	6	8	2	9	7	1	4
4	8	1	3	5	7	9	2	6
2	7	9	6	1	4	3	5	8
3	5	7	2	9	6	4	8	1
1	4	2	5	8	3	6	9	7
9	6	8	7	4	1	5	3	2
7	2	4	9	3	8	1	6	5
8	1	3	4	6	5	2	7	9
6	9	5	1	7	2	8	4	3

626

6	5	9	7	2	4	3	1	8
3	4	7	8	9	1	5	2	6
8	2	1	5	6	3	9	7	4
5	3	8	6	7	2	1	4	9
9	7	2	1	4	5	8	6	3
1	6	4	3	8	9	7	5	2
2	1	6	9	3	7	4	8	5
7	8	3	4	5	6	2	9	1
4	9	5	2	1	8	6	3	7

627

1	7	6	4	5	2	3	8	9
2	8	5	7	9	3	6	4	1
4	9	3	6	8	1	7	2	5
5	2	1	9	6	4	8	7	3
3	4	9	8	1	7	2	5	6
7	6	8	3	2	5	1	9	4
6	3	2	5	7	9	4	1	8
8	5	7	1	4	6	9	3	2
9	1	4	2	3	8	5	6	7

628

5	1	6	3	7	4	2	8	9
2	4	7	9	6	8	5	3	1
3	9	8	5	1	2	4	6	7
7	3	9	2	8	5	6	1	4
4	6	1	7	9	3	8	2	5
8	2	5	1	4	6	7	9	3
6	5	3	4	2	9	1	7	8
9	7	2	8	5	1	3	4	6
1	8	4	6	3	7	9	5	2

629

7	2	6	1	3	5	8	9	4
8	1	4	6	2	9	7	5	3
3	9	5	4	7	8	2	1	6
6	5	7	8	1	2	3	4	9
2	8	3	5	9	4	1	6	7
1	4	9	3	6	7	5	2	8
5	6	1	9	8	3	4	7	2
9	7	8	2	4	1	6	3	5
4	3	2	7	5	6	9	8	1

630

3	8	1	6	5	7	9	2	4
7	9	2	8	3	4	6	5	1
4	5	6	1	2	9	3	7	8
2	6	9	7	8	1	5	4	3
5	1	3	4	6	2	8	9	7
8	7	4	3	9	5	1	6	2
9	2	7	5	1	8	4	3	6
6	4	8	9	7	3	2	1	5
1	3	5	2	4	6	7	8	9

631

1	9	3	8	4	5	6	2	7
6	2	8	9	1	7	4	5	3
7	4	5	3	6	2	8	9	1
3	7	9	2	8	6	5	1	4
5	6	4	7	9	1	2	3	8
8	1	2	5	3	4	7	6	9
9	5	7	4	2	3	1	8	6
2	8	1	6	7	9	3	4	5
4	3	6	1	5	8	9	7	2

632

9	2	1	8	3	5	6	7	4
3	7	8	4	2	6	9	5	1
5	4	6	1	7	9	3	2	8
2	3	7	9	6	8	4	1	5
6	9	4	7	5	1	2	8	3
8	1	5	2	4	3	7	9	6
4	8	2	3	1	7	5	6	9
7	6	9	5	8	4	1	3	2
1	5	3	6	9	2	8	4	7

633

7	6	4	1	9	8	5	3	2
3	9	2	6	4	5	1	8	7
5	8	1	2	3	7	6	9	4
4	1	5	3	2	6	8	7	9
6	2	9	8	7	4	3	1	5
8	7	3	9	5	1	4	2	6
1	5	7	4	8	2	9	6	3
9	4	8	7	6	3	2	5	1
2	3	6	5	1	9	7	4	8

634

4	3	7	6	5	8	1	9	2
9	1	5	7	4	2	8	3	6
8	2	6	3	1	9	5	4	7
1	5	2	9	8	6	4	7	3
7	8	9	2	3	4	6	1	5
3	6	4	1	7	5	2	8	9
2	7	3	4	6	1	9	5	8
5	9	1	8	2	3	7	6	4
6	4	8	5	9	7	3	2	1

635

8	7	4	1	3	9	5	6	2
2	9	1	5	6	8	7	3	4
3	6	5	4	2	7	1	9	8
9	1	7	2	8	4	3	5	6
4	5	3	9	1	6	8	2	7
6	2	8	7	5	3	4	1	9
7	4	2	3	9	5	6	8	1
5	8	9	6	7	1	2	4	3
1	3	6	8	4	2	9	7	5

636

8	5	4	7	9	2	6	1	3
6	3	2	4	8	1	5	7	9
1	9	7	6	3	5	2	4	8
3	8	1	2	4	9	7	5	6
4	7	9	5	1	6	3	8	2
5	2	6	8	7	3	4	9	1
9	4	3	1	2	7	8	6	5
2	6	8	9	5	4	1	3	7
7	1	5	3	6	8	9	2	4

637

9	1	8	6	3	5	4	2	7
3	6	5	7	4	2	9	1	8
2	4	7	1	8	9	6	5	3
1	5	4	8	6	7	3	9	2
8	9	2	5	1	3	7	4	6
7	3	6	2	9	4	1	8	5
5	7	9	4	2	6	8	3	1
6	8	3	9	5	1	2	7	4
4	2	1	3	7	8	5	6	9

638

7	2	9	8	4	3	1	5	6
4	5	1	6	7	2	9	3	8
6	3	8	5	9	1	7	2	4
8	1	2	3	5	6	4	7	9
5	6	7	9	1	4	2	8	3
9	4	3	2	8	7	5	6	1
3	9	4	7	6	5	8	1	2
1	7	6	4	2	8	3	9	5
2	8	5	1	3	9	6	4	7

639

6	8	7	9	4	5	1	2	3
3	9	5	1	6	2	4	8	7
4	1	2	8	3	7	5	6	9
7	4	3	5	1	6	2	9	8
5	6	9	2	8	3	7	4	1
8	2	1	4	7	9	6	3	5
9	7	8	6	5	4	3	1	2
1	3	6	7	2	8	9	5	4
2	5	4	3	9	1	8	7	6

640

9	5	7	4	6	2	1	3	8
1	6	2	3	7	8	5	9	4
3	8	4	5	9	1	7	6	2
5	3	9	6	2	7	8	4	1
7	4	6	1	8	3	2	5	9
8	2	1	9	4	5	3	7	6
4	1	8	7	5	6	9	2	3
6	7	3	2	1	9	4	8	5
2	9	5	8	3	4	6	1	7

641

8	5	3	2	4	1	7	9	6
9	2	7	3	6	5	1	4	8
4	6	1	9	8	7	5	3	2
5	3	9	1	7	6	8	2	4
6	7	4	5	2	8	9	1	3
2	1	8	4	9	3	6	7	5
3	8	2	6	1	9	4	5	7
1	4	6	7	5	2	3	8	9
7	9	5	8	3	4	2	6	1

642

7	2	4	9	5	8	6	3	1
1	6	8	4	7	3	2	9	5
9	3	5	1	6	2	4	8	7
8	5	6	7	4	1	9	2	3
3	9	1	6	2	5	7	4	8
2	4	7	8	3	9	1	5	6
4	1	2	5	8	7	3	6	9
6	8	9	3	1	4	5	7	2
5	7	3	2	9	6	8	1	4

643

8	9	7	4	6	1	5	3	2
1	5	4	3	9	2	7	8	6
3	2	6	8	7	5	1	9	4
2	3	9	1	5	7	4	6	8
4	1	5	2	8	6	9	7	3
7	6	8	9	4	3	2	5	1
9	8	2	5	3	4	6	1	7
6	4	3	7	1	9	8	2	5
5	7	1	6	2	8	3	4	9

644

9	5	4	8	2	1	6	3	7
1	2	3	5	6	7	4	8	9
7	6	8	4	3	9	5	2	1
8	4	5	2	1	3	9	7	6
3	7	9	6	4	5	2	1	8
6	1	2	9	7	8	3	4	5
5	3	7	1	9	2	8	6	4
2	9	6	7	8	4	1	5	3
4	8	1	3	5	6	7	9	2

645

6	3	4	2	5	7	9	1	8
8	5	7	6	9	1	3	2	4
2	1	9	8	3	4	5	7	6
5	8	1	4	6	2	7	9	3
9	2	6	1	7	3	4	8	5
4	7	3	9	8	5	2	6	1
1	9	2	3	4	8	6	5	7
7	4	8	5	2	6	1	3	9
3	6	5	7	1	9	8	4	2

646

7	8	9	6	2	4	1	3	5
2	3	5	8	1	7	4	6	9
1	4	6	9	3	5	2	8	7
5	9	8	1	7	2	6	4	3
4	7	3	5	8	6	9	2	1
6	2	1	3	4	9	5	7	8
9	1	2	7	6	8	3	5	4
8	5	4	2	9	3	7	1	6
3	6	7	4	5	1	8	9	2

647

9	2	1	7	6	3	5	4	8
3	5	6	1	4	8	2	7	9
4	7	8	9	2	5	3	1	6
1	4	3	6	5	2	9	8	7
6	9	7	3	8	1	4	5	2
2	8	5	4	7	9	1	6	3
7	1	2	8	9	4	6	3	5
5	6	4	2	3	7	8	9	1
8	3	9	5	1	6	7	2	4

648

8	4	2	5	1	6	9	3	7
1	6	3	7	8	9	4	5	2
5	9	7	4	3	2	1	6	8
9	1	5	6	7	8	2	4	3
7	2	4	3	9	5	6	8	1
3	8	6	1	2	4	5	7	9
6	7	9	8	5	1	3	2	4
2	5	8	9	4	3	7	1	6
4	3	1	2	6	7	8	9	5

649

9	4	8	5	3	1	7	6	2
5	1	3	6	7	2	4	8	9
6	7	2	9	4	8	1	3	5
2	6	7	8	9	5	3	4	1
3	9	5	4	1	6	8	2	7
1	8	4	3	2	7	9	5	6
8	2	9	1	5	3	6	7	4
7	3	1	2	6	4	5	9	8
4	5	6	7	8	9	2	1	3

650

4	9	7	6	3	2	5	1	8
3	6	5	1	8	7	2	9	4
1	8	2	5	4	9	6	3	7
5	3	6	9	7	1	8	4	2
9	1	4	2	6	8	7	5	3
2	7	8	4	5	3	1	6	9
6	4	3	8	2	5	9	7	1
8	5	9	7	1	4	3	2	6
7	2	1	3	9	6	4	8	5

651

9	3	7	1	8	6	4	2	5
6	1	4	9	2	5	3	7	8
8	5	2	7	3	4	9	1	6
7	9	5	8	4	3	2	6	1
1	8	3	6	7	2	5	4	9
4	2	6	5	9	1	7	8	3
5	4	8	2	6	9	1	3	7
3	6	9	4	1	7	8	5	2
2	7	1	3	5	8	6	9	4

652

2	9	4	1	8	6	7	3	5
1	5	7	4	9	3	6	2	8
3	8	6	2	5	7	4	9	1
9	3	5	8	2	4	1	6	7
6	1	8	9	7	5	3	4	2
7	4	2	3	6	1	8	5	9
5	7	9	6	3	8	2	1	4
4	2	3	7	1	9	5	8	6
8	6	1	5	4	2	9	7	3

653

9	3	5	6	2	1	4	8	7
4	1	2	7	3	8	6	9	5
8	7	6	9	4	5	3	2	1
5	4	3	2	9	7	1	6	8
6	2	9	8	1	4	5	7	3
7	8	1	5	6	3	2	4	9
3	6	7	4	5	9	8	1	2
2	5	8	1	7	6	9	3	4
1	9	4	3	8	2	7	5	6

654

1	3	7	6	8	2	4	5	9
4	9	5	7	1	3	2	8	6
2	6	8	5	4	9	1	7	3
9	2	1	3	5	6	7	4	8
8	5	3	2	7	4	9	6	1
6	7	4	8	9	1	5	3	2
5	4	2	1	6	8	3	9	7
7	1	6	9	3	5	8	2	4
3	8	9	4	2	7	6	1	5

655

9	4	8	3	2	6	5	7	1
5	2	3	9	7	1	6	4	8
1	6	7	5	8	4	9	2	3
7	3	5	1	9	2	4	8	6
8	9	2	4	6	7	3	1	5
4	1	6	8	3	5	7	9	2
3	7	9	6	1	8	2	5	4
2	5	1	7	4	3	8	6	9
6	8	4	2	5	9	1	3	7

656

1	9	2	8	6	4	5	7	3
7	4	5	2	1	3	8	9	6
3	6	8	9	7	5	1	4	2
8	2	4	7	9	6	3	5	1
5	3	7	1	4	2	9	6	8
9	1	6	3	5	8	4	2	7
6	8	9	4	2	1	7	3	5
4	5	1	6	3	7	2	8	9
2	7	3	5	8	9	6	1	4

657

1	5	4	3	6	7	8	9	2
7	6	9	4	2	8	3	1	5
2	3	8	9	1	5	7	6	4
5	4	1	7	9	3	6	2	8
6	7	2	1	8	4	9	5	3
8	9	3	6	5	2	4	7	1
3	2	7	5	4	9	1	8	6
9	8	6	2	3	1	5	4	7
4	1	5	8	7	6	2	3	9

658

1	8	2	4	6	3	7	5	9
3	9	4	5	8	7	6	2	1
5	7	6	9	1	2	3	4	8
2	6	7	1	3	9	4	8	5
8	5	9	2	7	4	1	3	6
4	3	1	8	5	6	9	7	2
9	4	8	3	2	1	5	6	7
7	2	3	6	9	5	8	1	4
6	1	5	7	4	8	2	9	3

659

4	3	2	5	1	6	7	8	9
9	6	8	7	3	2	4	5	1
5	7	1	4	9	8	3	6	2
7	4	6	8	2	1	5	9	3
2	8	3	6	5	9	1	7	4
1	9	5	3	7	4	8	2	6
6	2	4	1	8	5	9	3	7
3	5	9	2	4	7	6	1	8
8	1	7	9	6	3	2	4	5

660

7	4	6	2	1	8	3	9	5
2	3	8	4	5	9	1	7	6
9	1	5	3	7	6	8	2	4
4	6	2	9	3	1	7	5	8
8	5	7	6	4	2	9	1	3
1	9	3	7	8	5	6	4	2
3	8	9	1	2	4	5	6	7
6	7	4	5	9	3	2	8	1
5	2	1	8	6	7	4	3	9

661

2	6	9	1	5	3	7	4	8
8	3	1	6	7	4	5	2	9
4	5	7	8	2	9	3	6	1
9	1	8	5	6	7	2	3	4
5	7	4	3	1	2	8	9	6
6	2	3	9	4	8	1	7	5
3	9	5	2	8	6	4	1	7
7	8	2	4	9	1	6	5	3
1	4	6	7	3	5	9	8	2

662

1	4	9	8	3	2	7	6	5
6	5	8	9	1	7	2	3	4
3	2	7	4	6	5	8	1	9
9	1	2	7	4	6	3	5	8
7	8	4	2	5	3	6	9	1
5	3	6	1	9	8	4	2	7
4	7	1	3	2	9	5	8	6
2	9	5	6	8	4	1	7	3
8	6	3	5	7	1	9	4	2

663

5	8	4	7	1	9	3	6	2
7	9	2	5	6	3	4	8	1
6	3	1	4	8	2	9	7	5
3	4	8	9	7	1	5	2	6
1	5	6	2	3	8	7	9	4
9	2	7	6	5	4	8	1	3
2	1	3	8	9	5	6	4	7
8	7	5	1	4	6	2	3	9
4	6	9	3	2	7	1	5	8

664

1	3	9	6	8	2	5	7	4
4	2	7	5	3	9	6	8	1
5	8	6	4	7	1	2	3	9
9	4	5	8	6	7	3	1	2
8	6	1	2	9	3	4	5	7
2	7	3	1	5	4	9	6	8
6	1	2	7	4	5	8	9	3
7	9	8	3	2	6	1	4	5
3	5	4	9	1	8	7	2	6

665

6	2	1	9	7	5	4	8	3
4	9	7	2	3	8	5	1	6
8	3	5	1	6	4	2	9	7
7	8	6	5	1	3	9	2	4
5	4	9	6	8	2	7	3	1
2	1	3	7	4	9	6	5	8
3	6	2	4	9	1	8	7	5
9	7	8	3	5	6	1	4	2
1	5	4	8	2	7	3	6	9

666

1	4	2	9	6	5	7	3	8
9	8	5	4	7	3	6	1	2
3	6	7	1	2	8	9	4	5
4	9	1	3	8	2	5	6	7
6	5	8	7	4	9	1	2	3
7	2	3	5	1	6	8	9	4
8	7	9	6	3	4	2	5	1
5	1	4	2	9	7	3	8	6
2	3	6	8	5	1	4	7	9

667

5	9	2	8	1	4	7	3	6
6	7	1	2	3	9	5	8	4
4	3	8	6	5	7	9	1	2
8	2	9	1	6	3	4	5	7
3	4	6	7	8	5	1	2	9
7	1	5	9	4	2	8	6	3
1	5	3	4	7	6	2	9	8
9	8	7	3	2	1	6	4	5
2	6	4	5	9	8	3	7	1

668

4	1	9	6	3	5	2	8	7
7	6	5	1	2	8	3	4	9
2	8	3	7	4	9	5	6	1
6	4	2	5	9	1	8	7	3
9	5	8	2	7	3	4	1	6
3	7	1	4	8	6	9	5	2
8	9	4	3	6	7	1	2	5
5	2	7	9	1	4	6	3	8
1	3	6	8	5	2	7	9	4

669

6	4	7	5	1	8	9	2	3
9	8	1	4	2	3	5	7	6
3	2	5	7	6	9	4	1	8
4	1	3	2	9	5	8	6	7
8	6	9	1	4	7	2	3	5
5	7	2	8	3	6	1	9	4
1	9	6	3	5	4	7	8	2
7	3	4	9	8	2	6	5	1
2	5	8	6	7	1	3	4	9

670

5	9	3	4	8	1	2	6	7
8	6	1	9	2	7	3	5	4
7	2	4	6	5	3	8	9	1
1	8	7	2	9	4	5	3	6
3	4	9	7	6	5	1	8	2
2	5	6	3	1	8	7	4	9
9	1	8	5	4	2	6	7	3
6	7	2	8	3	9	4	1	5
4	3	5	1	7	6	9	2	8

671

3	9	4	5	8	6	1	2	7
6	7	2	3	4	1	9	5	8
8	1	5	2	7	9	4	3	6
1	8	7	6	5	2	3	9	4
2	5	3	7	9	4	8	6	1
4	6	9	8	1	3	5	7	2
5	2	1	4	3	7	6	8	9
7	4	8	9	6	5	2	1	3
9	3	6	1	2	8	7	4	5

672

4	6	2	7	9	5	8	1	3
8	9	7	2	3	1	5	4	6
5	1	3	6	8	4	2	9	7
1	4	6	9	2	8	7	3	5
2	8	9	3	5	7	4	6	1
3	7	5	1	4	6	9	2	8
6	3	8	4	7	9	1	5	2
7	2	4	5	1	3	6	8	9
9	5	1	8	6	2	3	7	4

673

2	9	7	4	1	8	6	5	3
1	4	8	6	5	3	2	9	7
6	3	5	7	2	9	8	1	4
4	6	9	3	8	1	5	7	2
5	8	2	9	4	7	1	3	6
3	7	1	2	6	5	9	4	8
9	1	6	8	3	4	7	2	5
8	5	3	1	7	2	4	6	9
7	2	4	5	9	6	3	8	1

674

1	5	8	6	3	7	2	4	9
6	4	3	9	2	5	8	1	7
2	7	9	4	8	1	5	6	3
7	3	1	8	4	9	6	5	2
5	9	6	3	1	2	7	8	4
8	2	4	5	7	6	3	9	1
4	1	7	2	5	8	9	3	6
3	6	5	7	9	4	1	2	8
9	8	2	1	6	3	4	7	5

675

8	2	6	1	3	4	9	5	7
1	7	9	8	6	5	4	2	3
4	3	5	2	9	7	1	8	6
6	8	7	9	1	3	5	4	2
5	9	2	7	4	6	8	3	1
3	4	1	5	8	2	6	7	9
7	6	3	4	5	9	2	1	8
2	5	8	6	7	1	3	9	4
9	1	4	3	2	8	7	6	5

676

9	5	3	8	4	6	7	1	2
7	1	8	2	5	9	3	4	6
6	2	4	1	3	7	9	5	8
8	9	7	4	6	3	5	2	1
2	6	5	9	1	8	4	3	7
3	4	1	7	2	5	6	8	9
1	8	9	5	7	4	2	6	3
4	3	2	6	9	1	8	7	5
5	7	6	3	8	2	1	9	4

677

3	5	8	7	1	6	2	4	9
7	2	1	4	9	5	6	3	8
4	9	6	2	8	3	1	7	5
1	6	4	8	7	9	5	2	3
9	3	7	5	6	2	4	8	1
5	8	2	3	4	1	7	9	6
2	7	3	6	5	8	9	1	4
6	4	9	1	3	7	8	5	2
8	1	5	9	2	4	3	6	7

678

1	2	4	6	7	5	3	8	9
8	9	5	2	4	3	1	7	6
3	7	6	1	9	8	5	2	4
9	1	3	5	2	7	4	6	8
7	5	8	9	6	4	2	3	1
6	4	2	8	3	1	9	5	7
4	6	1	3	8	2	7	9	5
5	3	9	7	1	6	8	4	2
2	8	7	4	5	9	6	1	3

679

5	4	7	1	8	3	2	6	9
8	6	2	9	4	7	5	3	1
1	3	9	5	2	6	8	7	4
9	5	8	3	6	2	4	1	7
6	1	4	8	7	5	9	2	3
2	7	3	4	1	9	6	5	8
3	2	6	7	9	4	1	8	5
7	9	1	2	5	8	3	4	6
4	8	5	6	3	1	7	9	2

680

1	8	7	6	5	9	4	2	3
4	6	3	7	1	2	8	9	5
9	5	2	3	8	4	7	6	1
5	9	8	4	7	3	2	1	6
6	3	1	2	9	8	5	7	4
2	7	4	1	6	5	3	8	9
3	4	6	8	2	1	9	5	7
7	2	5	9	4	6	1	3	8
8	1	9	5	3	7	6	4	2

681

4	2	9	5	8	7	3	6	1
5	3	8	4	1	6	7	2	9
7	6	1	3	9	2	5	8	4
8	5	7	9	4	3	6	1	2
1	9	2	7	6	5	4	3	8
6	4	3	8	2	1	9	7	5
9	7	6	1	5	8	2	4	3
3	1	4	2	7	9	8	5	6
2	8	5	6	3	4	1	9	7

682

4	1	2	7	5	3	9	6	8
7	5	9	1	6	8	3	4	2
3	8	6	9	4	2	5	7	1
9	4	7	3	8	6	2	1	5
5	6	8	2	7	1	4	9	3
2	3	1	5	9	4	6	8	7
8	9	3	6	2	7	1	5	4
6	2	4	8	1	5	7	3	9
1	7	5	4	3	9	8	2	6

683

2	1	4	6	7	8	9	5	3
9	6	8	2	5	3	1	7	4
5	7	3	4	1	9	2	6	8
3	5	1	7	8	4	6	9	2
6	9	7	1	3	2	8	4	5
8	4	2	9	6	5	3	1	7
1	2	5	3	4	6	7	8	9
4	3	6	8	9	7	5	2	1
7	8	9	5	2	1	4	3	6

684

5	1	2	9	7	8	3	4	6
8	3	7	1	4	6	5	9	2
4	9	6	3	5	2	7	1	8
2	6	3	7	1	4	9	8	5
9	7	8	5	6	3	1	2	4
1	5	4	2	8	9	6	7	3
7	4	9	6	2	5	8	3	1
6	8	1	4	3	7	2	5	9
3	2	5	8	9	1	4	6	7

685

2	9	4	1	3	6	7	5	8
3	8	7	9	5	4	2	6	1
6	1	5	2	8	7	4	3	9
8	2	3	6	7	1	9	4	5
1	4	9	5	2	3	8	7	6
7	5	6	4	9	8	1	2	3
4	7	8	3	6	9	5	1	2
9	6	2	7	1	5	3	8	4
5	3	1	8	4	2	6	9	7

686

3	2	9	4	6	5	8	1	7
5	6	4	7	8	1	2	9	3
8	1	7	9	3	2	6	4	5
7	9	3	2	4	6	1	5	8
2	8	5	3	1	9	4	7	6
6	4	1	8	5	7	9	3	2
4	7	2	5	9	8	3	6	1
1	3	8	6	7	4	5	2	9
9	5	6	1	2	3	7	8	4

687

4	2	7	1	5	6	9	3	8
3	8	6	7	2	9	5	1	4
5	9	1	3	8	4	7	2	6
7	6	4	9	3	1	2	8	5
1	5	9	2	4	8	3	6	7
8	3	2	6	7	5	1	4	9
2	7	8	5	6	3	4	9	1
9	4	5	8	1	2	6	7	3
6	1	3	4	9	7	8	5	2

688

3	5	4	6	8	1	2	7	9
1	2	8	9	3	7	4	5	6
6	7	9	2	4	5	8	3	1
4	8	3	5	2	6	9	1	7
5	1	7	3	9	8	6	2	4
9	6	2	1	7	4	5	8	3
7	4	6	8	5	3	1	9	2
2	3	5	4	1	9	7	6	8
8	9	1	7	6	2	3	4	5

689

7	2	8	5	3	4	1	9	6
1	5	6	8	9	2	7	4	3
9	4	3	6	1	7	2	8	5
8	9	1	4	5	3	6	7	2
4	6	2	9	7	1	5	3	8
3	7	5	2	8	6	9	1	4
5	3	4	1	6	9	8	2	7
6	1	7	3	2	8	4	5	9
2	8	9	7	4	5	3	6	1

690

1	8	4	7	9	6	2	3	5
5	3	7	4	2	8	9	6	1
2	6	9	5	3	1	8	7	4
4	9	3	1	5	7	6	2	8
8	5	6	2	4	9	7	1	3
7	1	2	6	8	3	4	5	9
3	4	1	9	7	2	5	8	6
9	2	8	3	6	5	1	4	7
6	7	5	8	1	4	3	9	2

691

1	7	3	5	6	4	9	8	2
4	8	9	1	7	2	3	5	6
5	2	6	3	8	9	1	7	4
7	9	2	6	4	3	8	1	5
8	6	5	2	1	7	4	3	9
3	4	1	9	5	8	6	2	7
9	3	4	8	2	5	7	6	1
2	1	8	7	9	6	5	4	3
6	5	7	4	3	1	2	9	8

692

2	4	5	6	1	8	7	3	9
1	6	9	5	3	7	4	2	8
3	8	7	4	9	2	5	1	6
8	9	4	1	6	5	2	7	3
6	1	2	8	7	3	9	4	5
5	7	3	2	4	9	8	6	1
4	2	6	9	5	1	3	8	7
9	3	1	7	8	4	6	5	2
7	5	8	3	2	6	1	9	4

693

1	2	7	9	5	3	6	4	8
5	8	9	1	6	4	7	3	2
4	3	6	7	2	8	5	1	9
9	4	1	3	8	5	2	6	7
2	6	3	4	7	9	8	5	1
8	7	5	6	1	2	4	9	3
6	5	2	8	9	1	3	7	4
7	1	4	2	3	6	9	8	5
3	9	8	5	4	7	1	2	6

694

2	5	4	6	8	7	1	9	3
9	1	3	5	2	4	6	8	7
7	8	6	9	3	1	2	5	4
5	2	1	8	7	3	9	4	6
8	6	9	4	5	2	7	3	1
3	4	7	1	9	6	8	2	5
6	3	2	7	4	8	5	1	9
4	7	5	2	1	9	3	6	8
1	9	8	3	6	5	4	7	2

695

9	6	5	1	8	7	2	4	3
4	7	1	6	2	3	5	9	8
3	2	8	5	9	4	1	6	7
7	1	4	9	5	8	6	3	2
5	9	2	4	3	6	8	7	1
6	8	3	7	1	2	9	5	4
2	3	7	8	6	5	4	1	9
8	5	9	3	4	1	7	2	6
1	4	6	2	7	9	3	8	5

696

1	8	2	6	5	7	3	4	9
9	6	4	2	3	8	5	7	1
3	5	7	1	4	9	2	6	8
2	9	6	4	7	5	1	8	3
7	4	8	9	1	3	6	5	2
5	1	3	8	2	6	4	9	7
4	7	5	3	9	1	8	2	6
8	2	1	7	6	4	9	3	5
6	3	9	5	8	2	7	1	4

697

3	6	7	8	9	4	1	2	5
8	1	2	7	6	5	9	3	4
5	9	4	2	1	3	6	8	7
1	3	5	9	8	7	2	4	6
6	2	8	5	4	1	3	7	9
4	7	9	6	3	2	8	5	1
7	4	1	3	2	6	5	9	8
9	5	3	1	7	8	4	6	2
2	8	6	4	5	9	7	1	3

698

3	4	6	7	8	2	9	5	1
8	2	9	3	1	5	7	4	6
7	5	1	4	9	6	8	3	2
9	6	5	8	2	1	4	7	3
2	7	4	5	3	9	6	1	8
1	8	3	6	4	7	2	9	5
6	3	7	9	5	8	1	2	4
5	9	2	1	6	4	3	8	7
4	1	8	2	7	3	5	6	9

699

2	7	3	4	1	8	9	5	6
4	6	8	5	9	2	7	1	3
5	1	9	3	6	7	8	2	4
8	2	1	7	4	3	6	9	5
7	4	6	2	5	9	3	8	1
9	3	5	1	8	6	2	4	7
1	8	7	9	3	4	5	6	2
3	9	4	6	2	5	1	7	8
6	5	2	8	7	1	4	3	9

700

3	1	8	6	9	7	2	5	4
7	9	2	3	5	4	1	6	8
6	5	4	1	8	2	9	7	3
1	3	5	4	2	9	7	8	6
2	6	9	7	3	8	5	4	1
4	8	7	5	1	6	3	9	2
5	2	6	9	4	1	8	3	7
8	4	3	2	7	5	6	1	9
9	7	1	8	6	3	4	2	5

701

9	8	1	7	6	5	3	4	2
2	5	3	1	9	4	8	7	6
6	4	7	8	3	2	5	9	1
7	6	8	9	1	3	2	5	4
5	3	9	2	4	6	7	1	8
4	1	2	5	7	8	6	3	9
1	9	5	6	8	7	4	2	3
8	7	4	3	2	9	1	6	5
3	2	6	4	5	1	9	8	7

702

8	6	1	7	9	4	5	2	3
3	2	5	6	1	8	4	7	9
4	9	7	3	2	5	6	8	1
5	3	9	8	4	2	7	1	6
1	4	6	9	3	7	2	5	8
7	8	2	1	5	6	3	9	4
9	1	4	2	7	3	8	6	5
2	5	8	4	6	9	1	3	7
6	7	3	5	8	1	9	4	2

703

7	3	4	1	6	8	5	9	2
5	6	2	4	7	9	3	8	1
1	8	9	2	3	5	7	4	6
3	7	6	8	4	1	9	2	5
4	9	5	6	2	3	1	7	8
8	2	1	9	5	7	6	3	4
6	1	7	3	8	2	4	5	9
9	5	8	7	1	4	2	6	3
2	4	3	5	9	6	8	1	7

704

7	1	4	3	8	2	9	6	5
5	6	2	1	4	9	8	7	3
8	3	9	7	6	5	4	2	1
3	2	1	6	9	8	5	4	7
4	5	8	2	3	7	6	1	9
9	7	6	4	5	1	3	8	2
2	4	5	8	1	3	7	9	6
1	8	3	9	7	6	2	5	4
6	9	7	5	2	4	1	3	8

705

8	5	3	7	4	9	1	6	2
2	1	6	5	8	3	9	7	4
7	9	4	1	2	6	8	3	5
3	7	1	9	5	4	2	8	6
9	2	8	6	1	7	5	4	3
4	6	5	8	3	2	7	1	9
1	3	9	4	7	5	6	2	8
5	8	2	3	6	1	4	9	7
6	4	7	2	9	8	3	5	1

706

1	5	3	8	9	4	6	2	7
8	6	9	7	1	2	5	4	3
2	4	7	6	5	3	8	1	9
4	8	5	2	6	9	3	7	1
9	7	1	4	3	8	2	5	6
3	2	6	5	7	1	9	8	4
5	1	4	9	2	6	7	3	8
6	3	2	1	8	7	4	9	5
7	9	8	3	4	5	1	6	2

707

6	4	5	3	7	8	1	2	9
1	8	9	5	6	2	4	7	3
3	2	7	4	9	1	6	8	5
4	3	1	7	5	9	8	6	2
8	5	6	2	1	4	9	3	7
7	9	2	6	8	3	5	4	1
2	1	4	8	3	5	7	9	6
5	6	8	9	2	7	3	1	4
9	7	3	1	4	6	2	5	8

708

2	4	1	6	7	8	5	9	3
8	3	7	5	1	9	4	6	2
5	9	6	2	4	3	1	7	8
1	7	9	4	3	5	2	8	6
6	8	5	7	9	2	3	1	4
3	2	4	1	8	6	7	5	9
7	6	8	3	5	4	9	2	1
4	1	2	9	6	7	8	3	5
9	5	3	8	2	1	6	4	7

709

6	4	9	5	7	2	1	3	8
3	1	8	6	4	9	5	2	7
2	7	5	8	1	3	4	9	6
9	2	4	1	6	5	8	7	3
8	3	1	9	2	7	6	4	5
5	6	7	4	3	8	2	1	9
4	9	2	3	8	6	7	5	1
1	8	3	7	5	4	9	6	2
7	5	6	2	9	1	3	8	4

710

4	8	3	6	7	1	2	9	5
7	2	6	3	9	5	4	1	8
9	1	5	2	8	4	6	3	7
2	3	1	7	5	9	8	6	4
6	4	8	1	3	2	5	7	9
5	7	9	4	6	8	1	2	3
3	6	4	8	2	7	9	5	1
1	9	2	5	4	3	7	8	6
8	5	7	9	1	6	3	4	2

711

4	9	2	6	5	1	7	8	3
6	8	5	9	7	3	2	1	4
1	3	7	8	4	2	6	9	5
3	1	6	2	9	8	5	4	7
9	5	8	7	3	4	1	6	2
7	2	4	5	1	6	9	3	8
8	4	9	1	2	7	3	5	6
2	6	1	3	8	5	4	7	9
5	7	3	4	6	9	8	2	1

712

5	1	7	9	8	2	4	3	6
2	8	9	6	3	4	1	7	5
6	3	4	5	7	1	9	8	2
9	6	2	7	1	5	8	4	3
1	7	5	8	4	3	6	2	9
3	4	8	2	6	9	7	5	1
7	2	3	1	9	8	5	6	4
8	5	1	4	2	6	3	9	7
4	9	6	3	5	7	2	1	8

713

9	7	1	5	6	2	3	4	8
8	4	5	1	7	3	9	2	6
2	6	3	9	8	4	1	5	7
3	5	2	8	1	6	4	7	9
6	1	9	7	4	5	2	8	3
7	8	4	2	3	9	6	1	5
4	9	7	3	2	8	5	6	1
5	2	8	6	9	1	7	3	4
1	3	6	4	5	7	8	9	2

714

7	9	3	4	1	8	6	5	2
5	8	2	7	9	6	1	3	4
6	1	4	5	3	2	9	8	7
2	4	8	3	7	9	5	6	1
3	5	9	2	6	1	4	7	8
1	6	7	8	5	4	2	9	3
8	7	1	6	2	5	3	4	9
4	2	6	9	8	3	7	1	5
9	3	5	1	4	7	8	2	6

715

4	6	7	3	5	9	8	1	2
1	9	3	8	4	2	6	7	5
5	8	2	1	7	6	9	3	4
2	3	4	9	6	1	7	5	8
6	7	9	5	2	8	3	4	1
8	1	5	7	3	4	2	6	9
3	4	6	2	9	5	1	8	7
9	5	8	6	1	7	4	2	3
7	2	1	4	8	3	5	9	6

716

1	7	2	6	3	4	8	5	9
5	9	8	2	1	7	4	3	6
6	4	3	5	8	9	7	2	1
2	6	9	4	5	1	3	8	7
8	3	5	7	6	2	1	9	4
4	1	7	3	9	8	5	6	2
7	2	6	8	4	3	9	1	5
3	5	1	9	7	6	2	4	8
9	8	4	1	2	5	6	7	3

717

4	6	3	9	1	8	5	7	2
7	1	2	5	4	3	8	9	6
8	5	9	6	2	7	1	4	3
6	9	1	7	3	2	4	5	8
2	4	8	1	6	5	9	3	7
5	3	7	4	8	9	6	2	1
9	7	6	3	5	1	2	8	4
3	8	4	2	9	6	7	1	5
1	2	5	8	7	4	3	6	9

718

5	8	4	1	7	6	9	2	3
3	2	1	4	5	9	6	7	8
9	7	6	3	8	2	1	5	4
1	4	8	7	2	5	3	9	6
7	6	3	8	9	1	2	4	5
2	9	5	6	3	4	7	8	1
8	3	9	5	1	7	4	6	2
6	5	7	2	4	3	8	1	9
4	1	2	9	6	8	5	3	7

719

7	3	2	4	1	6	5	8	9
9	6	1	8	7	5	3	2	4
8	5	4	9	3	2	1	6	7
3	8	5	7	6	9	2	4	1
2	4	7	1	5	8	9	3	6
1	9	6	3	2	4	8	7	5
5	7	8	2	4	1	6	9	3
4	1	9	6	8	3	7	5	2
6	2	3	5	9	7	4	1	8

720

9	4	3	6	7	5	8	1	2
1	2	6	4	9	8	7	5	3
5	7	8	2	3	1	9	4	6
7	5	4	1	2	9	3	6	8
8	1	9	5	6	3	4	2	7
3	6	2	8	4	7	1	9	5
2	9	5	3	8	4	6	7	1
4	8	1	7	5	6	2	3	9
6	3	7	9	1	2	5	8	4

721

7	8	9	1	6	3	2	5	4
1	5	6	2	7	4	8	9	3
3	2	4	8	5	9	7	1	6
4	9	5	7	2	6	1	3	8
2	1	7	4	3	8	9	6	5
6	3	8	5	9	1	4	2	7
9	7	3	6	8	2	5	4	1
8	4	2	3	1	5	6	7	9
5	6	1	9	4	7	3	8	2

722

5	1	2	9	3	4	6	7	8
4	8	9	5	7	6	2	1	3
3	7	6	2	8	1	5	9	4
6	3	5	4	2	9	1	8	7
2	9	1	8	6	7	4	3	5
8	4	7	1	5	3	9	6	2
7	5	4	6	1	8	3	2	9
9	6	3	7	4	2	8	5	1
1	2	8	3	9	5	7	4	6

723

9	7	1	3	2	6	8	4	5
6	4	3	5	9	8	1	7	2
5	8	2	1	4	7	6	9	3
8	6	5	7	1	9	3	2	4
7	3	4	8	5	2	9	6	1
1	2	9	6	3	4	7	5	8
2	5	8	9	7	1	4	3	6
3	1	7	4	6	5	2	8	9
4	9	6	2	8	3	5	1	7

724

1	5	2	3	6	8	9	7	4
3	7	9	4	1	5	6	2	8
8	6	4	7	9	2	5	1	3
7	9	1	5	8	6	4	3	2
5	2	6	1	3	4	7	8	9
4	8	3	2	7	9	1	5	6
9	4	5	8	2	1	3	6	7
2	1	7	6	4	3	8	9	5
6	3	8	9	5	7	2	4	1

725

5	9	7	1	6	4	3	2	8
8	1	4	5	2	3	7	9	6
6	2	3	9	7	8	4	5	1
2	8	1	3	4	6	9	7	5
4	5	6	8	9	7	1	3	2
7	3	9	2	1	5	6	8	4
3	6	8	4	5	9	2	1	7
1	7	5	6	3	2	8	4	9
9	4	2	7	8	1	5	6	3

726

6	8	3	7	1	2	5	4	9
9	4	1	3	8	5	7	2	6
2	5	7	6	4	9	3	8	1
5	2	4	1	9	6	8	3	7
8	1	9	2	3	7	6	5	4
7	3	6	4	5	8	9	1	2
3	6	2	8	7	1	4	9	5
4	7	5	9	2	3	1	6	8
1	9	8	5	6	4	2	7	3

727

2	1	5	8	3	9	4	6	7
9	8	3	4	6	7	5	1	2
4	6	7	1	2	5	9	3	8
6	5	8	7	9	1	3	2	4
1	3	4	6	8	2	7	9	5
7	2	9	3	5	4	1	8	6
3	7	6	9	4	8	2	5	1
5	9	1	2	7	6	8	4	3
8	4	2	5	1	3	6	7	9

728

6	7	8	9	1	3	5	4	2
5	1	4	6	8	2	9	3	7
9	3	2	5	7	4	6	8	1
8	4	3	2	5	7	1	6	9
2	6	9	3	4	1	8	7	5
7	5	1	8	9	6	4	2	3
1	2	5	4	3	8	7	9	6
4	9	6	7	2	5	3	1	8
3	8	7	1	6	9	2	5	4

729

6	1	5	2	7	3	4	8	9
4	8	9	6	1	5	3	7	2
2	3	7	9	4	8	6	1	5
9	4	6	8	3	7	5	2	1
1	5	3	4	9	2	8	6	7
7	2	8	1	5	6	9	4	3
5	9	4	7	8	1	2	3	6
8	6	1	3	2	9	7	5	4
3	7	2	5	6	4	1	9	8

730

5	2	1	8	9	7	4	3	6
6	9	4	3	5	1	2	8	7
3	8	7	6	2	4	5	1	9
7	4	6	1	3	8	9	2	5
8	1	9	2	6	5	7	4	3
2	5	3	7	4	9	8	6	1
1	6	8	9	7	2	3	5	4
9	3	5	4	8	6	1	7	2
4	7	2	5	1	3	6	9	8

731

6	7	4	8	1	2	9	5	3
5	9	3	6	4	7	2	1	8
8	1	2	9	3	5	7	6	4
4	2	7	1	5	3	6	8	9
1	5	8	4	9	6	3	2	7
3	6	9	2	7	8	5	4	1
7	8	6	3	2	1	4	9	5
9	3	1	5	6	4	8	7	2
2	4	5	7	8	9	1	3	6

732

8	5	3	4	9	2	7	1	6
4	6	1	5	3	7	9	2	8
7	9	2	6	8	1	5	4	3
3	8	9	7	4	5	2	6	1
6	1	7	8	2	3	4	5	9
5	2	4	9	1	6	8	3	7
1	3	8	2	5	9	6	7	4
9	7	5	1	6	4	3	8	2
2	4	6	3	7	8	1	9	5

733

6	2	7	1	3	8	9	5	4
1	5	9	2	6	4	7	3	8
4	3	8	7	9	5	2	6	1
5	9	2	3	8	6	4	1	7
3	7	6	4	1	9	5	8	2
8	4	1	5	7	2	6	9	3
7	6	3	9	2	1	8	4	5
9	1	5	8	4	7	3	2	6
2	8	4	6	5	3	1	7	9

734

4	2	8	9	5	3	7	6	1
3	6	9	1	7	2	4	8	5
7	5	1	6	8	4	2	3	9
1	3	2	7	6	5	8	9	4
5	8	4	2	9	1	6	7	3
6	9	7	3	4	8	1	5	2
8	1	6	4	3	9	5	2	7
9	4	5	8	2	7	3	1	6
2	7	3	5	1	6	9	4	8

735

6	9	5	4	3	2	7	8	1
4	3	2	1	7	8	5	6	9
8	7	1	5	9	6	3	4	2
2	8	3	9	4	5	1	7	6
7	5	4	6	1	3	9	2	8
1	6	9	8	2	7	4	3	5
5	4	7	2	8	1	6	9	3
3	1	8	7	6	9	2	5	4
9	2	6	3	5	4	8	1	7

736

4	3	8	7	6	2	1	9	5
9	2	6	5	3	1	8	7	4
5	7	1	9	8	4	3	2	6
6	5	4	8	2	9	7	3	1
2	8	3	6	1	7	5	4	9
1	9	7	4	5	3	6	8	2
8	1	2	3	9	5	4	6	7
7	6	5	2	4	8	9	1	3
3	4	9	1	7	6	2	5	8

737

3	7	9	2	6	8	1	4	5
4	2	5	7	9	1	3	6	8
6	8	1	3	5	4	7	9	2
8	3	7	4	2	5	9	1	6
1	5	6	8	7	9	2	3	4
9	4	2	6	1	3	5	8	7
7	1	3	5	8	6	4	2	9
2	6	4	9	3	7	8	5	1
5	9	8	1	4	2	6	7	3

738

9	3	1	8	4	7	6	2	5
8	6	5	1	2	3	7	4	9
2	7	4	5	9	6	3	8	1
1	5	3	9	8	2	4	7	6
6	8	2	7	1	4	9	5	3
7	4	9	6	3	5	2	1	8
5	2	7	3	6	1	8	9	4
4	9	6	2	5	8	1	3	7
3	1	8	4	7	9	5	6	2

739

7	3	6	9	5	2	8	4	1
2	5	8	3	4	1	9	7	6
9	1	4	7	6	8	5	3	2
4	9	5	1	7	3	6	2	8
8	6	7	2	9	4	1	5	3
3	2	1	5	8	6	7	9	4
5	4	2	8	1	7	3	6	9
1	7	3	6	2	9	4	8	5
6	8	9	4	3	5	2	1	7

740

2	6	1	7	9	4	5	3	8
5	8	4	2	6	3	9	1	7
3	7	9	1	8	5	6	4	2
7	1	8	4	2	6	3	5	9
6	3	2	5	7	9	1	8	4
4	9	5	8	3	1	2	7	6
9	5	7	6	1	8	4	2	3
1	2	3	9	4	7	8	6	5
8	4	6	3	5	2	7	9	1

741

8	9	1	4	5	6	7	2	3
7	5	2	9	3	1	6	4	8
6	3	4	2	7	8	1	9	5
2	7	9	3	6	5	8	1	4
5	6	8	1	4	9	2	3	7
1	4	3	7	8	2	5	6	9
9	1	7	8	2	3	4	5	6
4	2	5	6	9	7	3	8	1
3	8	6	5	1	4	9	7	2

742

5	2	7	8	1	4	9	6	3
9	4	1	7	6	3	2	8	5
3	6	8	9	2	5	1	4	7
4	8	2	1	3	7	6	5	9
1	9	3	5	4	6	8	7	2
6	7	5	2	8	9	3	1	4
7	3	9	6	5	1	4	2	8
2	1	4	3	7	8	5	9	6
8	5	6	4	9	2	7	3	1

743

4	3	2	8	7	1	5	6	9
5	8	1	4	9	6	7	3	2
9	6	7	2	5	3	8	4	1
6	7	5	3	1	8	2	9	4
3	1	8	9	2	4	6	7	5
2	4	9	7	6	5	3	1	8
1	2	4	5	3	7	9	8	6
7	9	6	1	8	2	4	5	3
8	5	3	6	4	9	1	2	7

744

7	5	8	2	1	9	3	6	4
9	6	1	5	3	4	8	2	7
3	2	4	7	6	8	1	9	5
6	1	9	4	7	2	5	3	8
5	4	2	9	8	3	6	7	1
8	7	3	6	5	1	2	4	9
4	8	7	1	2	6	9	5	3
1	9	6	3	4	5	7	8	2
2	3	5	8	9	7	4	1	6

745

9	8	1	5	2	4	3	6	7
2	7	5	1	3	6	8	9	4
3	6	4	7	8	9	1	2	5
1	3	9	6	7	2	4	5	8
8	5	2	4	9	3	7	1	6
7	4	6	8	5	1	9	3	2
4	9	8	2	1	5	6	7	3
6	2	3	9	4	7	5	8	1
5	1	7	3	6	8	2	4	9

746

1	5	4	7	3	6	9	8	2
8	6	3	5	2	9	1	4	7
7	2	9	4	8	1	6	5	3
4	3	1	6	5	2	7	9	8
5	9	6	1	7	8	2	3	4
2	8	7	9	4	3	5	1	6
9	4	2	3	6	5	8	7	1
3	1	8	2	9	7	4	6	5
6	7	5	8	1	4	3	2	9

747

8	1	4	9	3	7	6	5	2
5	6	3	8	2	4	7	1	9
9	7	2	1	5	6	8	3	4
4	3	5	7	9	1	2	8	6
6	9	8	3	4	2	1	7	5
1	2	7	6	8	5	9	4	3
3	8	6	4	1	9	5	2	7
2	4	9	5	7	8	3	6	1
7	5	1	2	6	3	4	9	8

748

7	2	9	1	8	3	4	5	6
1	6	5	9	4	2	3	8	7
4	8	3	7	5	6	2	9	1
6	7	2	8	1	4	9	3	5
5	1	4	2	3	9	7	6	8
9	3	8	5	6	7	1	4	2
8	4	1	3	2	5	6	7	9
2	9	6	4	7	8	5	1	3
3	5	7	6	9	1	8	2	4

749

7	3	6	8	1	9	5	4	2
9	8	2	6	4	5	3	7	1
4	1	5	7	3	2	9	6	8
8	4	3	1	6	7	2	9	5
5	9	7	3	2	8	6	1	4
2	6	1	5	9	4	8	3	7
1	7	9	2	8	6	4	5	3
6	5	8	4	7	3	1	2	9
3	2	4	9	5	1	7	8	6

750

9	8	6	4	7	1	2	3	5
2	1	5	6	3	8	4	9	7
7	4	3	2	5	9	1	8	6
6	2	9	1	8	7	5	4	3
4	5	1	3	6	2	8	7	9
3	7	8	9	4	5	6	1	2
1	3	2	5	9	4	7	6	8
8	9	4	7	2	6	3	5	1
5	6	7	8	1	3	9	2	4

751

4	8	7	5	6	2	3	1	9
5	3	1	7	8	9	4	6	2
9	6	2	4	3	1	8	7	5
8	5	4	6	7	3	9	2	1
1	7	9	2	5	4	6	8	3
3	2	6	9	1	8	5	4	7
6	1	5	8	9	7	2	3	4
7	4	8	3	2	5	1	9	6
2	9	3	1	4	6	7	5	8

752

4	1	3	7	8	2	5	9	6
6	8	2	3	5	9	4	7	1
7	9	5	6	1	4	3	2	8
8	7	6	4	2	5	9	1	3
9	2	1	8	3	6	7	4	5
3	5	4	9	7	1	8	6	2
2	4	8	5	6	7	1	3	9
5	6	7	1	9	3	2	8	4
1	3	9	2	4	8	6	5	7

753

4	6	9	3	5	7	1	2	8
2	5	1	6	4	8	3	7	9
7	3	8	9	2	1	6	4	5
3	7	5	4	9	2	8	1	6
6	9	4	1	8	5	2	3	7
8	1	2	7	3	6	9	5	4
5	8	3	2	6	4	7	9	1
1	2	6	5	7	9	4	8	3
9	4	7	8	1	3	5	6	2

754

6	1	7	4	2	9	5	8	3
4	2	5	3	1	8	9	7	6
3	9	8	7	5	6	4	1	2
9	5	1	6	3	2	8	4	7
7	8	3	9	4	1	2	6	5
2	4	6	8	7	5	3	9	1
8	3	4	5	6	7	1	2	9
5	7	2	1	9	4	6	3	8
1	6	9	2	8	3	7	5	4

755

6	1	3	9	4	8	2	5	7
7	5	8	2	6	3	4	1	9
4	2	9	5	7	1	6	3	8
9	4	7	6	8	5	3	2	1
8	3	5	4	1	2	9	7	6
1	6	2	3	9	7	5	8	4
5	7	4	1	3	9	8	6	2
3	8	6	7	2	4	1	9	5
2	9	1	8	5	6	7	4	3

756

7	2	9	8	3	1	5	4	6
8	4	3	9	6	5	1	2	7
5	1	6	2	7	4	9	3	8
3	5	4	6	1	8	2	7	9
2	8	1	4	9	7	6	5	3
6	9	7	5	2	3	4	8	1
4	7	5	1	8	9	3	6	2
1	3	2	7	4	6	8	9	5
9	6	8	3	5	2	7	1	4

757

9	4	3	8	5	6	7	2	1
5	6	8	2	1	7	4	3	9
7	1	2	9	4	3	8	6	5
4	7	5	1	8	2	6	9	3
1	8	6	4	3	9	2	5	7
3	2	9	6	7	5	1	8	4
8	3	7	5	6	4	9	1	2
6	9	4	3	2	1	5	7	8
2	5	1	7	9	8	3	4	6

758

2	3	8	5	1	9	6	4	7
4	1	9	7	6	8	2	5	3
7	5	6	2	3	4	9	1	8
9	4	1	6	8	3	7	2	5
5	6	2	4	7	1	3	8	9
8	7	3	9	2	5	1	6	4
1	9	4	3	5	2	8	7	6
3	2	7	8	4	6	5	9	1
6	8	5	1	9	7	4	3	2

759

2	5	1	9	4	8	6	7	3
7	8	3	6	1	2	9	5	4
6	9	4	5	7	3	1	8	2
9	3	8	7	6	4	5	2	1
4	7	5	3	2	1	8	6	9
1	2	6	8	9	5	4	3	7
8	4	9	2	3	6	7	1	5
5	1	2	4	8	7	3	9	6
3	6	7	1	5	9	2	4	8

760

1	5	8	4	3	9	2	6	7
4	3	7	8	6	2	1	9	5
9	6	2	5	7	1	8	3	4
3	1	6	7	4	8	5	2	9
7	2	5	6	9	3	4	8	1
8	9	4	1	2	5	3	7	6
5	8	9	2	1	7	6	4	3
2	4	3	9	5	6	7	1	8
6	7	1	3	8	4	9	5	2

761

2	6	4	7	9	8	1	5	3
7	3	9	6	5	1	4	8	2
5	1	8	2	3	4	6	9	7
9	8	5	3	6	2	7	4	1
3	7	1	5	4	9	8	2	6
6	4	2	1	8	7	9	3	5
4	2	3	8	7	6	5	1	9
1	9	7	4	2	5	3	6	8
8	5	6	9	1	3	2	7	4

762

8	7	6	1	3	9	2	5	4
9	1	4	5	7	2	6	8	3
5	3	2	6	4	8	9	7	1
7	8	3	2	9	4	5	1	6
2	9	5	8	1	6	4	3	7
4	6	1	3	5	7	8	9	2
6	4	7	9	8	1	3	2	5
1	5	8	4	2	3	7	6	9
3	2	9	7	6	5	1	4	8

763

9	2	3	4	1	5	8	7	6
4	8	1	7	2	6	9	3	5
5	7	6	8	3	9	4	2	1
1	4	2	9	7	8	5	6	3
6	3	9	2	5	4	7	1	8
8	5	7	1	6	3	2	4	9
7	1	5	3	8	2	6	9	4
2	6	4	5	9	1	3	8	7
3	9	8	6	4	7	1	5	2

764

3	4	1	6	8	7	2	9	5
2	5	8	4	1	9	6	3	7
9	6	7	2	5	3	1	4	8
5	2	9	1	4	8	7	6	3
1	7	4	5	3	6	8	2	9
6	8	3	7	9	2	4	5	1
8	1	6	3	2	5	9	7	4
7	9	5	8	6	4	3	1	2
4	3	2	9	7	1	5	8	6

765

4	8	7	1	6	5	3	2	9
5	9	3	7	8	2	6	1	4
6	1	2	3	9	4	7	8	5
1	2	4	8	7	6	5	9	3
8	3	9	5	4	1	2	6	7
7	5	6	2	3	9	8	4	1
3	4	1	6	2	7	9	5	8
9	6	8	4	5	3	1	7	2
2	7	5	9	1	8	4	3	6

766

1	9	5	4	8	3	2	6	7
8	4	3	6	7	2	9	1	5
2	6	7	5	9	1	4	8	3
6	5	4	2	1	9	7	3	8
9	7	2	8	3	5	1	4	6
3	1	8	7	6	4	5	9	2
4	8	6	1	5	7	3	2	9
5	2	9	3	4	6	8	7	1
7	3	1	9	2	8	6	5	4

767

3	1	4	2	8	6	5	7	9
7	2	5	4	9	1	3	6	8
6	8	9	5	3	7	1	4	2
9	7	1	8	2	3	4	5	6
5	4	3	7	6	9	8	2	1
8	6	2	1	5	4	9	3	7
2	3	6	9	4	8	7	1	5
1	5	8	3	7	2	6	9	4
4	9	7	6	1	5	2	8	3

768

8	3	9	5	1	7	6	4	2
4	1	7	6	2	8	9	3	5
6	5	2	3	9	4	7	8	1
5	9	1	7	8	6	3	2	4
3	4	6	2	5	9	1	7	8
2	7	8	4	3	1	5	6	9
7	6	5	9	4	2	8	1	3
1	2	3	8	7	5	4	9	6
9	8	4	1	6	3	2	5	7

769

1	7	5	3	2	9	4	8	6
8	6	9	1	4	5	7	3	2
4	2	3	6	7	8	9	5	1
5	1	2	8	3	7	6	4	9
9	8	7	4	6	1	5	2	3
6	3	4	5	9	2	1	7	8
2	9	8	7	1	4	3	6	5
7	5	6	9	8	3	2	1	4
3	4	1	2	5	6	8	9	7

770

9	7	1	6	8	5	2	4	3
6	8	2	9	3	4	1	7	5
5	4	3	2	1	7	8	9	6
7	6	5	1	4	9	3	8	2
8	3	4	7	2	6	9	5	1
1	2	9	3	5	8	7	6	4
3	9	8	4	6	1	5	2	7
2	5	6	8	7	3	4	1	9
4	1	7	5	9	2	6	3	8

771

2	8	7	4	3	5	1	6	9
3	6	5	9	1	2	4	7	8
9	1	4	7	8	6	3	5	2
5	9	2	3	6	8	7	1	4
7	3	6	2	4	1	9	8	5
1	4	8	5	9	7	2	3	6
8	5	3	1	2	9	6	4	7
6	2	1	8	7	4	5	9	3
4	7	9	6	5	3	8	2	1

772

5	1	4	3	9	6	7	2	8
9	2	3	5	7	8	6	1	4
7	6	8	1	4	2	3	5	9
4	5	9	6	8	7	1	3	2
2	7	6	4	1	3	8	9	5
8	3	1	9	2	5	4	6	7
6	9	2	8	3	4	5	7	1
3	4	7	2	5	1	9	8	6
1	8	5	7	6	9	2	4	3

773

3	7	4	1	6	5	2	9	8
2	6	1	8	4	9	3	7	5
5	8	9	2	7	3	1	4	6
6	1	8	9	5	7	4	3	2
7	3	2	4	1	8	5	6	9
9	4	5	3	2	6	7	8	1
1	5	3	6	9	4	8	2	7
4	2	6	7	8	1	9	5	3
8	9	7	5	3	2	6	1	4

774

9	5	8	1	3	2	7	6	4
2	4	6	9	7	8	1	3	5
7	3	1	4	5	6	2	9	8
1	2	3	7	4	9	8	5	6
6	8	7	5	2	3	9	4	1
4	9	5	6	8	1	3	7	2
5	6	9	8	1	7	4	2	3
3	1	4	2	9	5	6	8	7
8	7	2	3	6	4	5	1	9

775

6	4	5	3	7	9	2	8	1
9	2	1	6	8	4	5	3	7
8	7	3	2	1	5	9	6	4
2	9	8	5	6	7	4	1	3
1	5	4	8	9	3	6	7	2
3	6	7	4	2	1	8	5	9
5	8	9	7	3	2	1	4	6
4	3	2	1	5	6	7	9	8
7	1	6	9	4	8	3	2	5

776

2	7	3	1	6	8	4	5	9
6	5	9	4	7	2	3	8	1
4	1	8	9	5	3	6	2	7
7	4	6	8	3	1	5	9	2
9	3	2	7	4	5	8	1	6
1	8	5	2	9	6	7	4	3
8	9	7	6	1	4	2	3	5
3	2	1	5	8	7	9	6	4
5	6	4	3	2	9	1	7	8

777

7	4	5	6	2	9	8	1	3
3	8	2	4	7	1	9	6	5
6	9	1	3	8	5	2	7	4
4	1	8	9	6	2	3	5	7
9	2	3	7	5	4	1	8	6
5	6	7	1	3	8	4	2	9
2	3	4	5	1	7	6	9	8
1	7	9	8	4	6	5	3	2
8	5	6	2	9	3	7	4	1

778

3	8	1	5	9	4	6	2	7
4	9	5	2	6	7	1	3	8
6	7	2	8	1	3	5	4	9
9	6	7	3	4	1	2	8	5
2	3	8	7	5	9	4	1	6
1	5	4	6	2	8	7	9	3
7	4	9	1	8	6	3	5	2
5	1	3	9	7	2	8	6	4
8	2	6	4	3	5	9	7	1

779

2	8	7	9	3	5	4	1	6
4	1	9	2	6	8	7	5	3
3	6	5	1	4	7	2	9	8
7	2	8	5	9	4	6	3	1
6	5	3	8	1	2	9	4	7
1	9	4	6	7	3	8	2	5
5	3	2	4	8	6	1	7	9
9	7	6	3	2	1	5	8	4
8	4	1	7	5	9	3	6	2

780

2	8	6	1	7	3	4	5	9
3	5	7	8	4	9	6	2	1
4	1	9	2	5	6	8	7	3
9	7	8	4	1	2	5	3	6
1	3	4	5	6	7	2	9	8
6	2	5	9	3	8	7	1	4
8	4	2	7	9	1	3	6	5
5	6	1	3	2	4	9	8	7
7	9	3	6	8	5	1	4	2

781

6	2	9	4	3	7	8	5	1
5	4	8	1	2	9	7	6	3
3	1	7	5	6	8	4	2	9
2	5	4	7	1	3	6	9	8
1	9	3	2	8	6	5	4	7
8	7	6	9	5	4	1	3	2
4	3	2	6	7	1	9	8	5
7	6	5	8	9	2	3	1	4
9	8	1	3	4	5	2	7	6

782

6	9	7	8	2	1	3	4	5
4	5	2	7	6	3	9	1	8
8	3	1	5	9	4	7	2	6
1	4	6	3	7	5	2	8	9
5	2	3	4	8	9	6	7	1
9	7	8	2	1	6	4	5	3
3	6	4	1	5	7	8	9	2
2	1	9	6	4	8	5	3	7
7	8	5	9	3	2	1	6	4

783

6	8	3	5	1	7	2	4	9
4	9	1	3	8	2	5	6	7
5	2	7	6	9	4	8	1	3
1	3	8	4	2	6	9	7	5
9	7	5	8	3	1	4	2	6
2	4	6	9	7	5	3	8	1
7	6	9	2	5	8	1	3	4
3	1	2	7	4	9	6	5	8
8	5	4	1	6	3	7	9	2

784

6	7	2	8	9	4	1	5	3
9	8	4	5	3	1	7	6	2
5	3	1	2	6	7	8	9	4
7	5	9	3	2	6	4	8	1
2	1	3	9	4	8	5	7	6
8	4	6	1	7	5	3	2	9
4	6	8	7	1	2	9	3	5
3	2	7	4	5	9	6	1	8
1	9	5	6	8	3	2	4	7

785

1	3	4	6	5	8	9	7	2
7	5	6	3	2	9	8	4	1
2	9	8	7	4	1	3	5	6
3	1	5	4	6	7	2	9	8
8	6	7	2	9	5	1	3	4
9	4	2	8	1	3	5	6	7
4	7	9	1	3	2	6	8	5
5	8	1	9	7	6	4	2	3
6	2	3	5	8	4	7	1	9

786

9	7	8	6	5	4	3	1	2
5	2	4	8	3	1	7	6	9
1	6	3	9	7	2	5	4	8
8	9	7	5	4	6	2	3	1
2	5	6	3	1	9	8	7	4
3	4	1	2	8	7	6	9	5
6	8	2	4	9	3	1	5	7
7	3	9	1	2	5	4	8	6
4	1	5	7	6	8	9	2	3

787

3	8	5	6	4	7	9	1	2
4	9	7	3	1	2	6	8	5
6	1	2	8	5	9	3	7	4
1	6	3	9	8	4	2	5	7
8	5	9	7	2	3	1	4	6
2	7	4	5	6	1	8	3	9
9	3	1	2	7	5	4	6	8
5	4	8	1	9	6	7	2	3
7	2	6	4	3	8	5	9	1

788

2	6	3	9	7	5	1	4	8
9	8	5	1	4	6	3	2	7
7	4	1	8	2	3	9	5	6
1	7	8	4	6	2	5	9	3
6	2	4	5	3	9	7	8	1
3	5	9	7	1	8	4	6	2
4	3	2	6	5	7	8	1	9
5	9	6	3	8	1	2	7	4
8	1	7	2	9	4	6	3	5

789

5	2	3	7	6	4	9	8	1
1	6	8	9	3	2	5	4	7
4	7	9	1	8	5	6	2	3
7	9	2	3	4	1	8	5	6
6	5	1	2	7	8	4	3	9
8	3	4	5	9	6	7	1	2
9	1	7	8	5	3	2	6	4
2	4	5	6	1	9	3	7	8
3	8	6	4	2	7	1	9	5

790

3	1	5	6	8	2	9	4	7
2	4	9	7	5	1	6	3	8
6	7	8	3	9	4	1	5	2
4	5	6	9	2	7	3	8	1
7	8	2	5	1	3	4	6	9
9	3	1	4	6	8	2	7	5
8	2	3	1	4	5	7	9	6
5	6	7	2	3	9	8	1	4
1	9	4	8	7	6	5	2	3

791

5	8	9	4	7	3	6	1	2
3	6	2	9	5	1	4	7	8
1	4	7	6	8	2	3	9	5
8	7	4	5	9	6	2	3	1
6	5	3	2	1	4	9	8	7
9	2	1	7	3	8	5	6	4
4	1	8	3	2	9	7	5	6
2	3	5	1	6	7	8	4	9
7	9	6	8	4	5	1	2	3

792

7	8	3	5	4	2	1	6	9
5	9	1	3	8	6	4	2	7
6	2	4	1	9	7	8	5	3
4	6	8	2	5	9	7	3	1
1	5	7	4	6	3	2	9	8
9	3	2	8	7	1	5	4	6
2	7	6	9	1	5	3	8	4
8	1	5	6	3	4	9	7	2
3	4	9	7	2	8	6	1	5

793

8	7	3	1	9	5	2	4	6
9	6	1	8	4	2	5	3	7
2	5	4	7	3	6	8	9	1
5	4	2	3	7	9	1	6	8
6	1	7	2	8	4	3	5	9
3	8	9	6	5	1	7	2	4
7	9	8	5	6	3	4	1	2
1	3	6	4	2	8	9	7	5
4	2	5	9	1	7	6	8	3

794

2	9	3	6	8	5	7	4	1
7	4	6	2	9	1	8	3	5
5	1	8	3	4	7	6	2	9
1	2	5	9	7	6	3	8	4
4	3	9	8	5	2	1	7	6
6	8	7	4	1	3	9	5	2
9	6	2	7	3	4	5	1	8
8	7	1	5	2	9	4	6	3
3	5	4	1	6	8	2	9	7

795

1	4	6	2	9	8	3	7	5
5	7	2	1	6	3	8	9	4
3	8	9	7	5	4	1	6	2
4	5	1	6	2	7	9	8	3
6	2	7	8	3	9	5	4	1
8	9	3	4	1	5	6	2	7
7	6	4	3	8	1	2	5	9
9	1	8	5	7	2	4	3	6
2	3	5	9	4	6	7	1	8

796

3	7	2	8	5	1	9	4	6
5	1	8	4	6	9	3	2	7
9	6	4	2	3	7	8	1	5
2	3	6	7	4	5	1	9	8
1	8	7	6	9	3	2	5	4
4	5	9	1	8	2	6	7	3
8	2	1	5	7	6	4	3	9
6	9	5	3	1	4	7	8	2
7	4	3	9	2	8	5	6	1

797

2	4	5	7	1	3	6	8	9
7	1	3	8	6	9	4	2	5
8	6	9	5	2	4	1	3	7
1	8	4	9	7	2	5	6	3
9	7	2	3	5	6	8	4	1
3	5	6	4	8	1	9	7	2
5	3	8	6	9	7	2	1	4
4	9	1	2	3	8	7	5	6
6	2	7	1	4	5	3	9	8

798

7	9	1	5	6	2	3	4	8
4	6	5	7	8	3	9	2	1
2	8	3	1	4	9	5	7	6
9	2	6	3	1	4	8	5	7
3	5	7	2	9	8	1	6	4
1	4	8	6	7	5	2	9	3
5	7	2	4	3	1	6	8	9
8	1	4	9	2	6	7	3	5
6	3	9	8	5	7	4	1	2

799

9	2	1	3	6	7	5	8	4
8	6	3	1	5	4	9	7	2
5	4	7	9	2	8	1	6	3
3	5	6	7	4	1	2	9	8
7	1	8	2	3	9	4	5	6
2	9	4	5	8	6	3	1	7
4	7	9	8	1	3	6	2	5
6	8	2	4	9	5	7	3	1
1	3	5	6	7	2	8	4	9

800

4	9	8	3	2	1	5	7	6
5	3	6	7	8	9	4	2	1
1	7	2	4	5	6	3	9	8
6	5	1	8	7	4	2	3	9
9	8	7	2	6	3	1	4	5
2	4	3	1	9	5	6	8	7
3	2	9	6	1	7	8	5	4
8	1	5	9	4	2	7	6	3
7	6	4	5	3	8	9	1	2

ABOUT THE AUTHORS

Donald Christensen

PETER GORDON (left) is the Editorial Director of Sterling Publishing's Puzzlewright Press imprint, overseeing the puzzle and game books. His crosswords have appeared in *The New York Times*, *The Wall Street Journal*, *USA Today*, the *Los Angeles Times*, *Newsday*, and numerous puzzle magazines, including *Games*, where he was an editor for seven years. He writes a weekly current events crossword for *The Week* and edits the weekly Post Puzzler in *The Washington Post*. From 2002 to 2008, he was the crossword editor for *The New York Sun*. Gordon's books include *Hall of Fame Crosswords*, *Gold Medal Crosswords*, *Yahtzee Scratch & Play*, *Sit & Solve Nice & Easy Crosswords*, *Match Wits With Mensa: Test Your Trivia Smarts*, and *Verbiage for the Verbose*. The 50+ books written and edited by Gordon have combined sales of more than a million copies.

FRANK LONGO is a freelance puzzlemaker living in Hoboken, New Jersey. He writes, edits, and fact-checks puzzles, specializing in sudoku, having published more than 90 sudoku books. His wide array of titles encompasses both standard and variety sudoku puzzles, and include: four *Official Book of Wordoku* books, *10×10 Sudoku*, *Oy Vey! Sudoku*, four *Mensa Absolutely Nasty Sudoku* books, *Beyond Black Belt Sudoku*, *The World's Longest Sudoku Puzzle*, *Sports-doku*, *Movie-doku*, *Trivial Pursuit Sudoku*, *Word Search Sudoku*, *Magnetic Sudoku*, *The Big Book of Wordoku Puzzles*, *The Sudoku Code* (with Francis Heaney), *Crosswordoku* (with Patrick Blindauer), *Sudokugrams* (with Alan Stillson), and *Boggle Sudoku* (with Stephen J. Herschkorn). He is known for being able to produce puzzles that are diabolically difficult yet fair, requiring the solver to use advanced techniques not found in typical newspaper and magazine sudoku puzzles. Longo's books have sold more than four million copies.

In addition to this book, Gordon and Longo have combined on *Scrabble-doku* and *Stupendous Scrabble Sudoku*.